STAR WARS

OMNIBUS

A LONG TIME AGO.....

VOLUME 3

DARK HORSE BOOKS®

cover illustration Tom Palmer
publisher Mike Richardson
series editors Danny Fingeroth, Louise Jones, Al Milgrom, Jim Salicrup, and Jim Shooter
collection editor Randy Stradley
assistant editor Freddye Lins
collection designer Heather Doornink

special thanks to Jann Moorhead, David Anderman, Troy Alders, Leland Chee, Sue Rostoni, and Carol Roeder at Lucas Licensing

Star Wars® Omnibus: A Long Time Ago. . . . Volume Three

This volume collects Marvel *Star Wars* issues #50–#67 and *Star Wars King Size Annual* #2.

Published by Dark Horse Books
A division of Dark Horse Comics, Inc.
10956 SE Main Street
Milwaukie, OR 97222

darkhorse.com | starwars.com

To find a comics shop in your area, call the Comic Shop Locator Service toll-free at 1-888-266-4226

publisher Mike Richardson • executive vice president Neil Hankerson • chief financial officer Tom Weddle • vice president of publishing Randy Stradley • vice president of business development Michael Martens • vice president of business affairs Anita Nelson • vice president of marketing Micha Hershman • vice president of product development David Scroggy • vice president of information technology Dale LaFountain • director of purchasing Darlene Vogel • general counsel Ken Lizzi • editorial director Davey Estrada • senior managing editor Scott Allie • senior books editor Chris Warner • executive editor Diana Schutz • director of design and production Cary Grazzini • art director Lia Ribacchi • director of scheduling Cara Niece

Library of Congress Cataloging-in-Publication Data

Star Wars omnibus. A long time ago / writers, Archie Goodwin ... [et al.] ; artists, Howard Chaykin ... [et al.] ; colorists, Janice Cohen ... [et al.]. -- 1st ed.
    v. cm.
ISBN 978-1-59582-486-8 (v. 1)
1. Comic books, strips, etc. I. Goodwin, Archie. II. Dark Horse Comics. III. Title: Long time ago.
PN6728.S73S7336 2010
741.5'973--dc22
                    2010000142

Printed at 1010 Printing International, Ltd., Guangdong Province, China

First edition: February 2011
ISBN 978-1-59582-639-8

10 9 8 7 6 5 4 3 2 1

CONTENTS

75¢ | 50 AUG 02817

A SUPER-
SIZED
STAR
WARS
SAGA!
GIANT
50th
COLLECTORS
ISSUE!

STAR WARS™

Long ago in a galaxy far, far away. . .there exists a state of cosmic *civil war*. A brave alliance of *underground freedom fighters* has challenged the tyranny and oppression of the awesome *Galactic Empire*. This is their story!

LucasFilm PRESENTS: **STAR WARS** ™ *THE GREATEST* SPACE FANTASY *OF ALL!*

ARCHIE GOODWIN
WRITER

AL WILLIAMSON, TOM PALMER & WALT SIMONSON
ARTISTS

ED STUART
LETTERER

DON WARFIELD
COLORIST

LOUISE JONES
EDITOR

JIM SHOOTER
EDITOR-IN-CHIEF

The CRIMSON FOREVER!

THE GALAXY IS VAST, BUT GETTING AROUND IT USED TO BE SIMPLE. YOU PICKED YOUR DESTINATION, SET YOUR NAVI-COMPUTER, AND LET THE HYPERDRIVE TAKE IT FROM THERE.

BUT THAT WAS **BEFORE** THE EMPEROR DECLARED MARTIAL LAW. NOW, MORE ROUNDABOUT ROUTES FROM OBSCURE SYSTEM TO OBSCURE SYSTEM ARE NECESSARY TO AVOID "IMPERIAL ENTANGLEMENTS." AND EVEN THEN...

VAROWRRRK!

ALL RIGHT, ALL RIGHT, CHEWBACCA! I *KNOW* HAN WOULD BE BETTER AT THIS!

THOSE YEARS I SPENT AS ADMINISTRATOR AT CLOUD CITY HAVE LEFT ME A LITTLE *RUSTY.*

BUT THE WAY WE KEEP DROPPING INTO SPOTS WHERE THE EMPIRE HAS ESTABLISHED *NEW BASES*--

--I'M GETTING BACK INTO PRACTICE *FASTER* THAN I LIKE!

IT KIND OF SEEMS THE WHOLE GALAXY DOESN'T *WANT* US TO REACH TATOOINE AND RESCUE HAN FROM JABBA THE HUT.

NARAWWWK!

MY UNDERSTANDING OF *WOOKIEE* IS NEARLY AS STALE AS MY STYLE WITH A LASER CANNON --

--BUT IF THAT WAS A SUBTLE REMINDER THAN HAN WOULDN'T *BE* IN THIS FIX EXCEPT FOR HIS OLD PAL *LANDO CALRISSIAN*--

--NO *NEED*, CHEWIE. NOBODY WANTS TO UNDO BETRAYING HIM INTO THE HANDS OF JABBA'S BOUNTY HUNTER, *BOBA FETT*, MORE THAN ME!

I'M NOT ABOUT TO FORGET MY *PROMISE* TO LEIA ABOUT BRINGING HAN *BACK*--

--ONLY I'M HAVING SERIOUS *DOUBTS* ABOUT KEEPING *ALIVE* LONG ENOUGH TO DO IT!

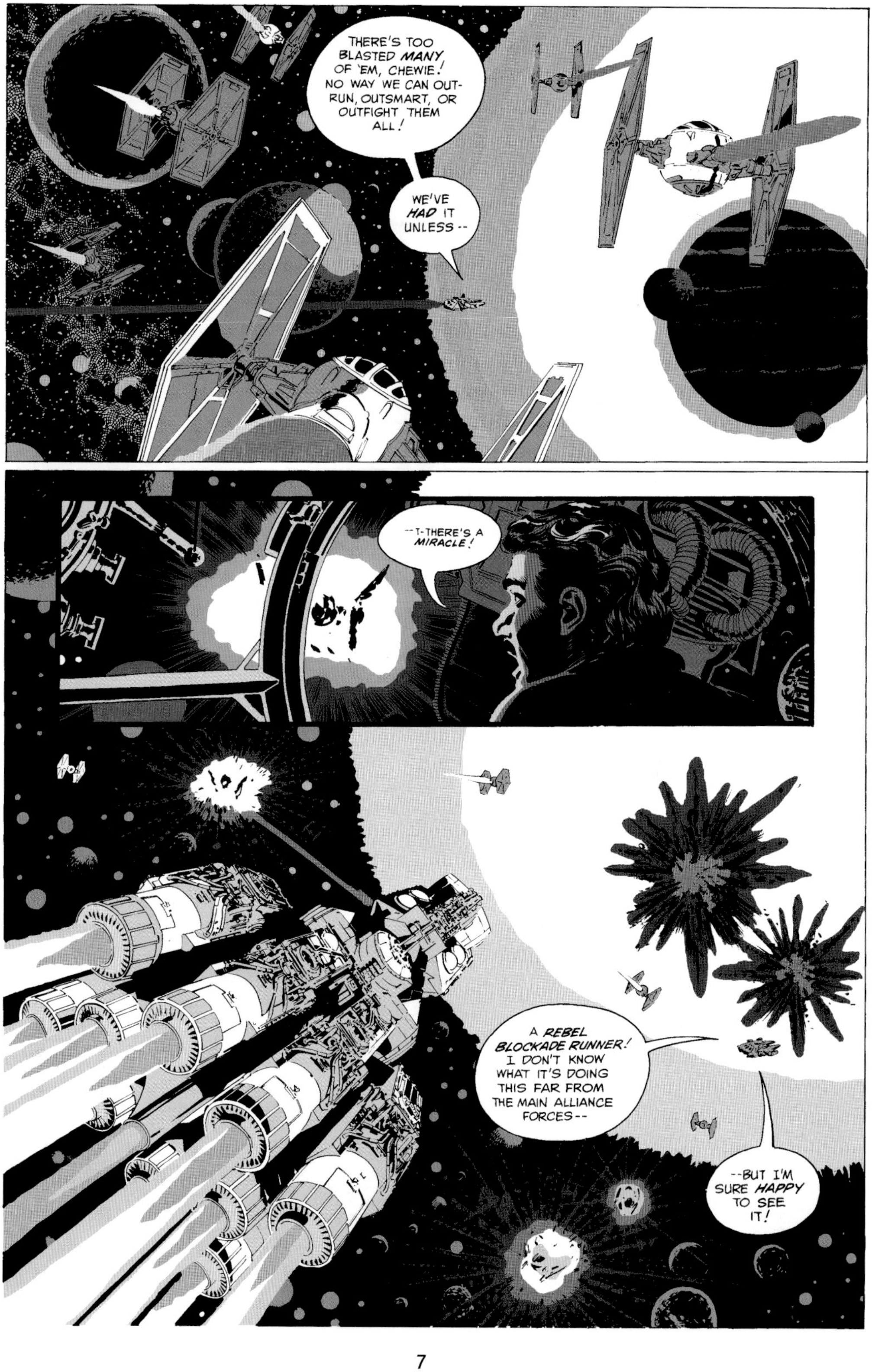
THERE'S TOO BLASTED MANY OF 'EM, CHEWIE! NO WAY WE CAN OUT-RUN, OUTSMART, OR OUTFIGHT THEM ALL!
WE'VE HAD IT UNLESS--
--T-THERE'S A MIRACLE!
A REBEL BLOCKADE RUNNER! I DON'T KNOW WHAT IT'S DOING THIS FAR FROM THE MAIN ALLIANCE FORCES--
--BUT I'M SURE HAPPY TO SEE IT!

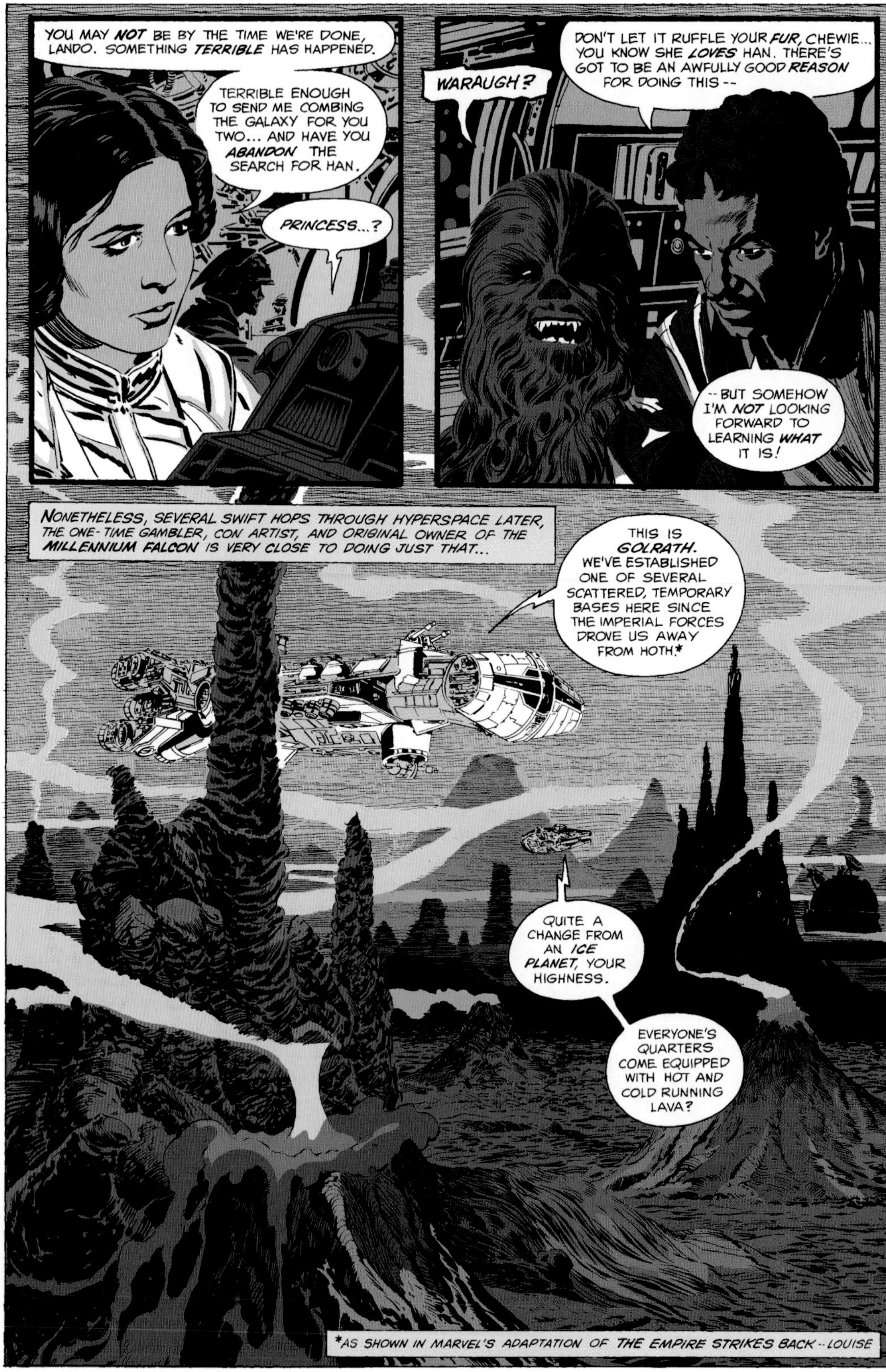
YOU MAY NOT BE BY THE TIME WE'RE DONE, LANDO. SOMETHING TERRIBLE HAS HAPPENED.
TERRIBLE ENOUGH TO SEND ME COMBING THE GALAXY FOR YOU TWO... AND HAVE YOU ABANDON THE SEARCH FOR HAN.
PRINCESS...?
DON'T LET IT RUFFLE YOUR FUR, CHEWIE... YOU KNOW SHE LOVES HAN. THERE'S GOT TO BE AN AWFULLY GOOD REASON FOR DOING THIS --
WARAUGH?
-- BUT SOMEHOW I'M NOT LOOKING FORWARD TO LEARNING WHAT IT IS!
NONETHELESS, SEVERAL SWIFT HOPS THROUGH HYPERSPACE LATER, THE ONE-TIME GAMBLER, CON ARTIST, AND ORIGINAL OWNER OF THE MILLENNIUM FALCON IS VERY CLOSE TO DOING JUST THAT...
THIS IS GOLRATH. WE'VE ESTABLISHED ONE OF SEVERAL SCATTERED, TEMPORARY BASES HERE SINCE THE IMPERIAL FORCES DROVE US AWAY FROM HOTH.*
QUITE A CHANGE FROM AN ICE PLANET, YOUR HIGHNESS.
EVERYONE'S QUARTERS COME EQUIPPED WITH HOT AND COLD RUNNING LAVA?
*AS SHOWN IN MARVEL'S ADAPTATION OF THE EMPIRE STRIKES BACK -- LOUISE

VERY NEARLY, LANDO. WE'VE TAKEN OVER THIS PLAYED OUT *MAGMA* SMELTING PLANT...

IT SITS WITHIN THE CRATER OF ONE OF THE PLANET'S LARGEST VOLCANOES... A CITY-SIZE STRUCTURE ANCHORED IN A SEA OF MOLTEN LAVA, TARNISHED, CORRODED FROM YEARS OF DISUSE...

...BUT INSIDE, ALIVE WITH DESPERATE NEW ACTIVITY.

WHY THE BREATH MASKS? ACCORDING TO THE *FALCON'S* INSTRUMENTS... EVEN THE OUTSIDE ATMOSPHERE IS BREATHABLE.

JUST A PRECAUTION... FOR ANYONE ENTERING THE *MEDICAL WING.*

SHE'S *BACK*, ARTOO... PRINCESS LEIA IS BACK! AND SHE'S *FOUND* THEM... CHEWBACCA AND MASTER LANDO! THANK THE ORIGINAL MAKER... THERE MAY BE *HOPE* YET!

THREEPIO, HAS THERE BEEN ANY *CHANGE?*

SURGEON DROID *TOO-ONEBEE* SAYS MASTER LUKE'S DETERIORATION HAS BEEN *SLOWED*, YOUR MAJESTY... BUT NO KNOWN MEDICAL EFFORTS SEEM TO TRULY *STOP* IT.

WHAT'S *HAPPENED* TO THE KID? HIS *EYES*... THEY'RE COMPLETELY *RED!*

YES, THAT'S HOW IT BEGINS... *THE CRIMSON FOREVER!*

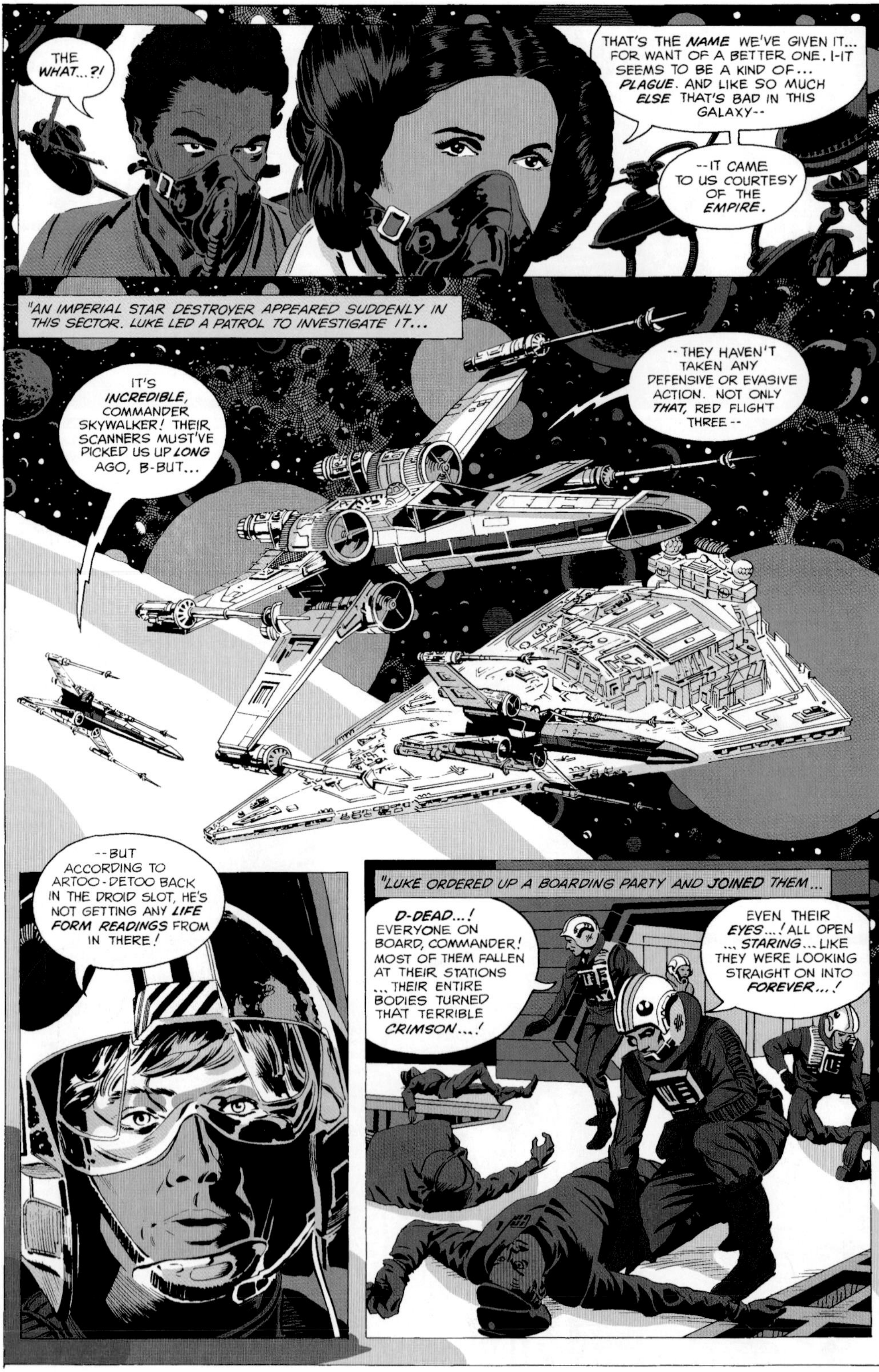
THE WHAT...?!
THAT'S THE NAME WE'VE GIVEN IT... FOR WANT OF A BETTER ONE. I-IT SEEMS TO BE A KIND OF... PLAGUE. AND LIKE SO MUCH ELSE THAT'S BAD IN THIS GALAXY--
--IT CAME TO US COURTESY OF THE EMPIRE.
"AN IMPERIAL STAR DESTROYER APPEARED SUDDENLY IN THIS SECTOR. LUKE LED A PATROL TO INVESTIGATE IT...
IT'S INCREDIBLE, COMMANDER SKYWALKER! THEIR SCANNERS MUST'VE PICKED US UP LONG AGO, B-BUT...
--THEY HAVEN'T TAKEN ANY DEFENSIVE OR EVASIVE ACTION. NOT ONLY THAT, RED FLIGHT THREE--
--BUT ACCORDING TO ARTOO-DETOO BACK IN THE DROID SLOT, HE'S NOT GETTING ANY LIFE FORM READINGS FROM IN THERE!
"LUKE ORDERED UP A BOARDING PARTY AND JOINED THEM...
D-DEAD...! EVERYONE ON BOARD, COMMANDER! MOST OF THEM FALLEN AT THEIR STATIONS ...THEIR ENTIRE BODIES TURNED THAT TERRIBLE CRIMSON...!
EVEN THEIR EYES...! ALL OPEN ...STARING... LIKE THEY WERE LOOKING STRAIGHT ON INTO FOREVER...!

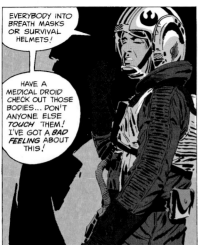

EVERYBODY INTO BREATH MASKS OR SURVIVAL HELMETS!

HAVE A MEDICAL DROID CHECK OUT THOSE BODIES... DON'T ANYONE ELSE *TOUCH* THEM! I'VE GOT A *BAD FEELING* ABOUT THIS!

"THE MEDICAL VERDICT WAS THAT IT WAS THE WORK OF A VIRUS... TOTALLY *ALIEN*, UNLIKE ANYTHING EVER ENCOUNTERED IN THIS GALAXY...

SIR...! IN ONE OF THE *LABS* ... WE FOUND... FOUND...

"TOTALLY ALIEN... AND TOTALLY INFECTUOUS.

HE PICKED UP THAT *JEWEL* IN A SHIPBOARD LABORATORY?

TUMBLED OUT OF A CARBONITE CANNISTER, COMMANDER SKYWALKER... LOOKED LIKE THEY HAD A ROUGH REENTRY FROM HYPERSPACE AND THE CANNISTER'S *SEALS* BROKE.

B-BUT... A *ROCK* COULDN'T TRANSMIT A VIRUS...! RIGHT, SIR...RIGHT? AND ANYWAY...

WE PUT ON OUR MASKS THE INSTANT WE HEARD YOUR ORDERS ON THE COMLINK...! WE *CAN'T* HAVE CONTRACTED THE SAME THING THAT GOT THOSE IMPERIALS...! W-WE JUST... *CAN'T*...!

"BUT OF COURSE, THEY BOTH HAD.

"LUKE ORDERED AN IMMEDIATE EVACUATION AND CONTACTED US TO ESTABLISH TOTAL ISOLATION FACILITIES FOR EVERY MEMBER OF THE BOARDING PARTY..."

SHOULDN'T WE *VAPORIZE* THAT LUMBERING PLAGUE SHIP, COMMANDER...?

IT MAY STILL HOLD SOME *ANSWERS*. AND WE'RE GOING TO BE PRETTY DESPERATE FOR THOSE ...PARTICULARY IF IT TURNS OUT THE *REST* OF US ARE INFECTED!

11

THEY *WERE*, LANDO... AND NOTHING WE DID COULD *SAVE* THEM. ONLY *LUKE* HASN'T TOTALLY SUCCUMBED.

PERHAPS HIS WAY WITH THE *FORCE* HAS ENABLED HIM TO *FIGHT* IT BETTER--

--BUT IT SEEMS ONLY A MATTER OF TIME UNTIL THE CRIMSON FOREVER KILLS *HIM* AS WELL!

LEIA, THAT *JEWEL* LEFT ABOARD THE IMPERIAL SHIP--

IT'S DEFINITELY THE *SOURCE* OF THE CONTAMINATION, LANDO... A ROBOT INSPECTION TEAM WE SENT UP *PROVED* THAT. BUT ITS MAKE-UP IS SO TOTALLY *ALIEN*... IT'S BEYOND THEIR ABILITY TO SCAN!

SUPPOSE YOU JUST BLOW IT AND THAT STAR DESTROYER INTO ATOMS?

WE DON'T KNOW *WHAT* WE'RE DEALING WITH... OR HOW IT WILL REACT UNDER ANY KIND OF FORCE.

ANY ATTEMPT TO *DESTROY* THE JEWEL--OR EVEN THE BODIES OF ITS VICTIMS --MIGHT CAUSE THE VIRUS TO *MUTATE* INTO SOMETHING EVEN WORSE!

LUKE'S INSTINCTS WERE TO KEEP IT *CONTAINED*. PERHAPS THE FORCE GUIDED HIM, PERHAPS IT DIDN'T... BUT SO FAR, IT SEEMS THE BEST COURSE.

TAKE IT FROM AN OLD GAMBLER, PRINCESS... YOU NEED A *BETTER HAND* TO STAND PAT. YOU CAN'T BE CERTAIN THE EMPIRE ISN'T IMPORTING *MORE* OF THOSE LITTLE GEMS.

LANDO, THAT'S WHY I WENT TO SUCH GREAT LENGTHS TO FIND YOU AND--MOST ESPECIALLY --*CHEWBACCA*.

WOWRRRK?

HAN ONCE TOLD ME OF SOMETHING THAT HAPPENED TO YOU AND HIM... A MISADVENTURE OF SORTS WHICH TOOK YOU *BEYOND* THE KNOWN GALAXY.

IT INVOLVED *TREASURE*... TWO HUGE *RED JEWELS*...!

ROARWKK!

ER... I BELIEVE THAT *UPSET* HIM, YOUR MAJESTY.

APPARENTLY CAPTAIN SOLO HAD PROMISED NEVER TO *MENTION* THAT PARTICULAR EPISODE.

PLEASE, CHEWIE, YOU *MUST* REALIZE HOW MUCH IS AT STAKE. IF THERE'S *ANY* CONNECTION BETWEEN THE RED GEMS HAN MENTIONED AND THIS ONE CAUSING THE CRIMSON FOREVER ... WE *HAVE* TO KNOW!

TELL US THE *WHOLE STORY*... PLEASE.

GNURRRGH...

THERE! I KNEW HE WAS BASICALLY A GOOD SPORT...EVEN IF HE DOES INSIST ON ALWAYS *WINNING* AT HOLOGRAPHIC CHESS!

BUT AS THE GROUP MOVES TOWARD A QUIET SPOT WHERE SEE THREEPIO CAN *TRANSLATE* THE WOOKIEE'S TALE, THERE IS STRANGE *ACTIVITY* IN THE MEDICAL WARD THEY HAVE LEFT. ACTIVITY THAT TAKES PLACE WITHIN THE VIRUS-TORTURED *MIND* OF LUKE SKYWALKER...

THERE IS *MORE* HERE THAN MIST, YOUNG *JEDI*...

MIST....! EVERYWHERE I TURN... *RED MIST!* CAN'T *ESCAPE* IT...! B-BUT I'VE *GOT* TO OR ELSE --

13

N-NO....! I CAN'T FIGHT THE MAN WHO MAY BE MY OWN FATHER...

DEFEND YOURSELF-- OR JOIN ME!

BUT I WON'T GIVE IN TO WHAT YOU REPRESENT! I WON'T EMBRACE THE DARK SIDE OF THE FORCE!

LUKE.....! GO BACK! YOU'RE CHOOSING THE WRONG PATH.

B-BEN...? YODA....?

TO OBI-WAN LISTEN! AFTER ALL MY TRAINING...STILL JUDGE YOU BY APPEARANCES ONLY?

HOW CAN I BELIEVE EITHER OF YOU? YOU NEVER WARNED ME... NEVER EVEN HINTED... ABOUT DARTH VADER'S TRUE IDENTITY!

WE TAUGHT YOU TO TRUST YOUR FEELINGS, LUKE. LET THEM LEAD YOU TO WHAT IS TRUE AND WHAT IS NOT--

..PARTICULARY IN THE MATTER NOW AT HAND.

CONFUSION FILLS THE FEVER-DREAMING MIND OF THE YOUNG STUDENT OF THE FORCE...

...THEN **INSTINCT** TAKES OVER. INSTINCT THAT HAS LED HIM TO **TRUST** THE CALM VOICE OF OBI-WAN KENOBI SO OFTEN IN THE PAST.

AND SUDDENLY, LUKE PERCEIVES THAT HE FACES FAR **MORE** THAN THE DARK LORD OF THE SITH.

STRIKE! DESTROY ME BEFORE I DESTROY YOU!

INSTEAD, LUKE **SMILES**... AND LETS HIS LIGHTSABER FALL.

NO.

THEN HE STEPS FORWARD... INTO THE **KILLING STROKE** OF DARTH VADER...

...AS HIS DREAM ENDS WITH AN EXPLOSION OF CRIMSON WHICH OVERWHELMS ALL ELSE.

THE GALLERY IS STILL EXCEPT FOR THE RELENTLESS PACING OF THE GIANT WOOKIEE AND AN OCCASIONAL WHINE OF SERVO-MOTORS FROM THE TRANSLATOR DROID VALIANTLY TRYING TO KEEP UP WITH HIM.

EVERYONE ELSE REMAINS TENSE, UNMOVING, AS FROM CHEWBACCA'S LOW GROWLS AND RUMBLINGS...

...SEE THREEPIO PIECES TOGETHER AN INCREDIBLE STORY.

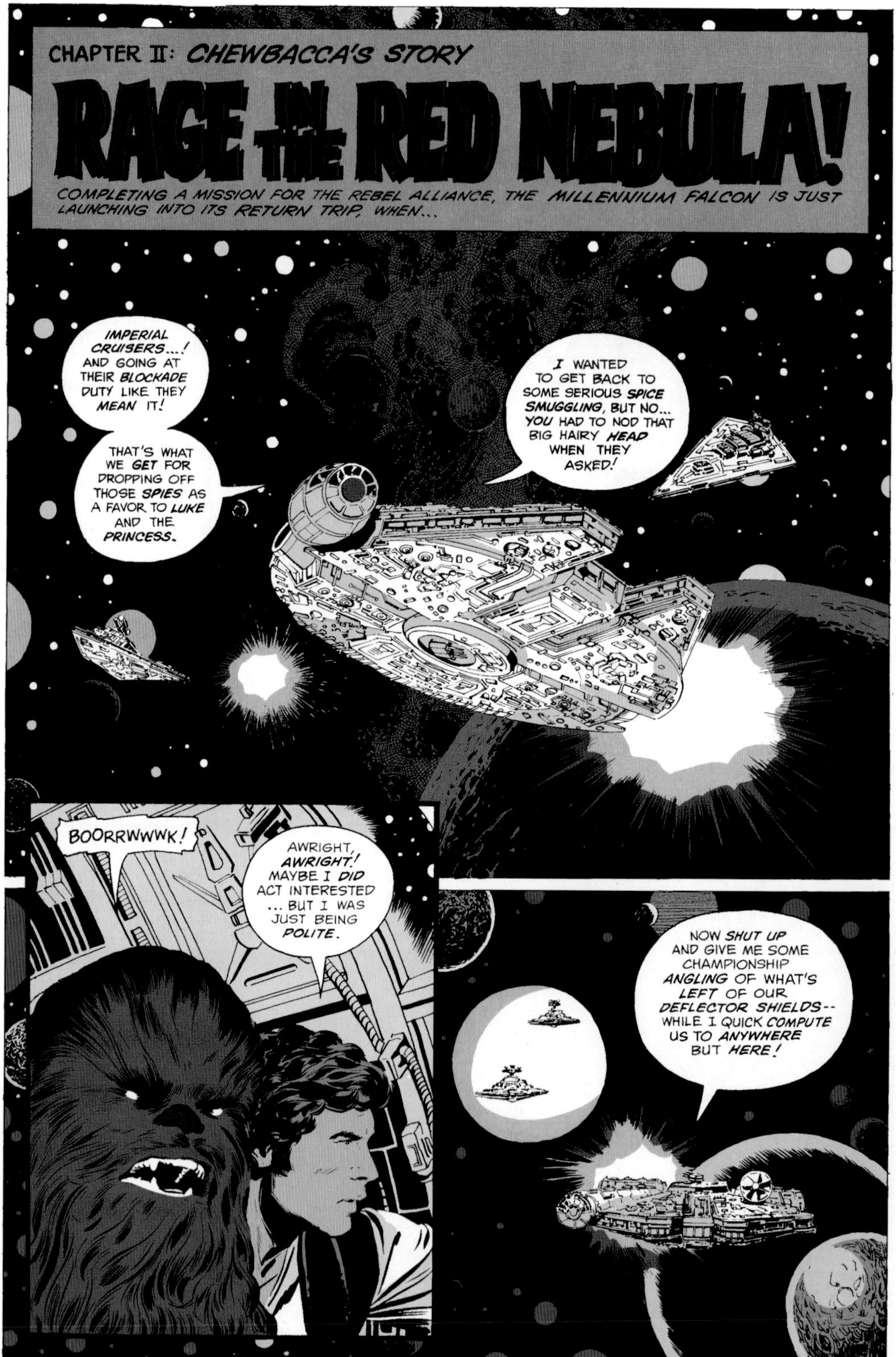
CHAPTER II: CHEWBACCA'S STORY
RAGE IN THE RED NEBULA!
COMPLETING A MISSION FOR THE REBEL ALLIANCE, THE MILLENNIUM FALCON IS JUST LAUNCHING INTO ITS RETURN TRIP, WHEN...
IMPERIAL CRUISERS...! AND GOING AT THEIR BLOCKADE DUTY LIKE THEY MEAN IT!
THAT'S WHAT WE GET FOR DROPPING OFF THOSE SPIES AS A FAVOR TO LUKE AND THE PRINCESS.
I WANTED TO GET BACK TO SOME SERIOUS SPICE SMUGGLING, BUT NO... YOU HAD TO NOD THAT BIG HAIRY HEAD WHEN THEY ASKED!
BOORRWWWK!
AWRIGHT, AWRIGHT! MAYBE I DID ACT INTERESTED ... BUT I WAS JUST BEING POLITE.
NOW SHUT UP AND GIVE ME SOME CHAMPIONSHIP ANGLING OF WHAT'S LEFT OF OUR DEFLECTOR SHIELDS-- WHILE I QUICK COMPUTE US TO ANYWHERE BUT HERE!

A DANGEROUSLY SWIFT WARP AND SOME HARD TRAVELING LATER... THE CORELLIAN VESSEL IS APPROACHING THE WORLD CALLED TERMINUS.

NOT BAD FOR SHORT NOTICE, HUH, CHEWIE? SINCE THIS IS ONE OF THE CENTERS FOR CROSS-GALACTIC SHIPPING --

-- WE CAN LOSE OURSELVES EASILY AMONG ALL THIS TRAFFIC.

LOOK AT THOSE MONSTERS! SOME OF THEIR VOYAGES TAKE *YEARS*... NO PLACE FOR A COUPLE OF FOOTLOOSE STAR HOPPERS LIKE *US*, RIGHT?

ALL SET, BIG BUDDY! WITH THE FALCON SAFELY STORED AWAY UNDER PHONEY *CREDENTIALS*... WE'LL COOL OUR HEELS AND GIVE THE EMPIRE TIME TO *FORGET* US.

AS I RECALL, THIS PORT OFFERS SOME OF THE MOST DELIGHTFULLY *WICKED* HEEL-COOLING SPOTS IN THE GALAXY!

AROOOL!

NOT *NOW*, CHEWIE... I'M TRYING TO THINK OF THE NAME OF THAT *CANTINA* WHERE THOSE TWO *SWAMP MAIDENS* DANCED.

IT WAS DOWN *ONE* OF THESE ARCADES WHERE THE TOURISTS NEVER VENTURE. DON'T *BUG* ME UNTIL--

BEFORE HAN OR HIS *WOOKIEE* FIRST MATE CAN SAY *MORE*... THE SHADOWS MOVE AND THE AIR IS FILLED WITH *BLASTER FIRE!*

FROAK!

WTAM!

SH-PON!

18

DARKNESS. AND SUDDENLY, TOO SUDDENLY... IT *ENDS!*

HEY! W-WHAT TH--!?

WUURRRGHH!

THAT'S *TYPICAL*... BLAME THE POOR *DROID!* I'M ONLY FOLLOWING *PROGRAMMED PROCEDURE*... BUT GO *AHEAD*, GET ANGRY AT *ME.*

I DIDN'T *STUN BLAST* YOU... I DIDN'T PUT THOSE *ENERGY SHACKLES* ON YOU... BUT WHO GETS *ROARED* AT? WHO GETS *ABUSE* FOR MERELY DOING HIS *JOB?*

OKAY, *OKAY*, SILVERTREADS...! WE'RE *SORRY* WE WOKE UP GROUCHY THINKING YOU'VE BEEN *KILLED* DOES THAT TO YOU SOMETIMES!

HOW ABOUT LETTING US *IN* ON WHAT'S *HAPPENING?*

THIS IS THE INTERGALACTIC BULK-FREIGHTER, *NOVA PRINCE.* YOU AND EVERYONE *ELSE* DOWN HERE HAVE BEEN *IMPRESSED* INTO SERVICE --

I DON'T HAVE TIME TO *CHAT*... THERE ARE A *LOT* OF PRISONERS TO WAKE UP. BUT AS LONG AS YOU'VE MORE OR LESS ASKED *NICELY*...

--SINCE NO SENTIENT IN THEIR RIGHT *MIND* WOULD INTENTIONALLY SIGN ON FOR A CRUISE TO THE *RED NEBULA.*

GNARRF!

THE *RED NEBULA?!* THAT LIES *BEYOND* THE GALAXY... OUT IN THE *UNKNOWN!*

YOU'RE *DOING* IT AGAIN... YOU'RE RAISING YOUR *VOICE.* I'M ONLY A MOBILE HOLD-TENDER... *NOT* THE SHIP'S COMPUTER!

BESIDES... THERE'S NO *POINT* WORRYING. WE'RE *ALREADY* ON OUR WAY!

SUDDENLY, CHIMES SOUND. AND HIGH IN THE DARKNESS OF THE VAST PRISON HOLD... A HOLOGRAPHIC IMAGE APPEARS!

GRNORRRK?

YOUR GUESS IS GOOD AS *MINE*, PAL... BUT WHATEVER'S UP, I DOUBT WE'RE GONNA *LIKE* IT!

I AM *KLYSK*... SPOKESMAN FOR THE GROUP WHICH OWNS THIS VESSEL. BY NOW YOU KNOW OUR DESTINATION. IF YOU ARE COOPERATIVE, WORK HARD... WE GUARANTEE *REWARD UNPARALLELED!*

SHOULD THIS NOT BE INDUCEMENT ENOUGH TO MAKE YOU FORGET THE *MANNER* IN WHICH YOU WERE RECRUITED--

--BE ADVISED THAT EVEN AFTER YOU ARE FREED, ONE SHACKLE BAND WILL REMAIN IN PLACE. IT CARRIES A FATAL *ION CHARGE* THAT WE CAN TRIGGER REMOTELY AT THE FIRST *HINT* OF DISOBEDIENCE.

SEE, CHEWIE, I *TOLD* YOU WE WOULDN'T LIKE I--

NAARLLF!

AAAAGHH!

WAROWRRRRK!

EASY, CHEWIE, I'M ALL RIGHT ... I THINK.

THAT WAS A *DEMONSTRATION*... WE HELD THE CHARGE TO MINIMUM. THERE WILL BE NO *FURTHER* SUCH CONSIDERATION.

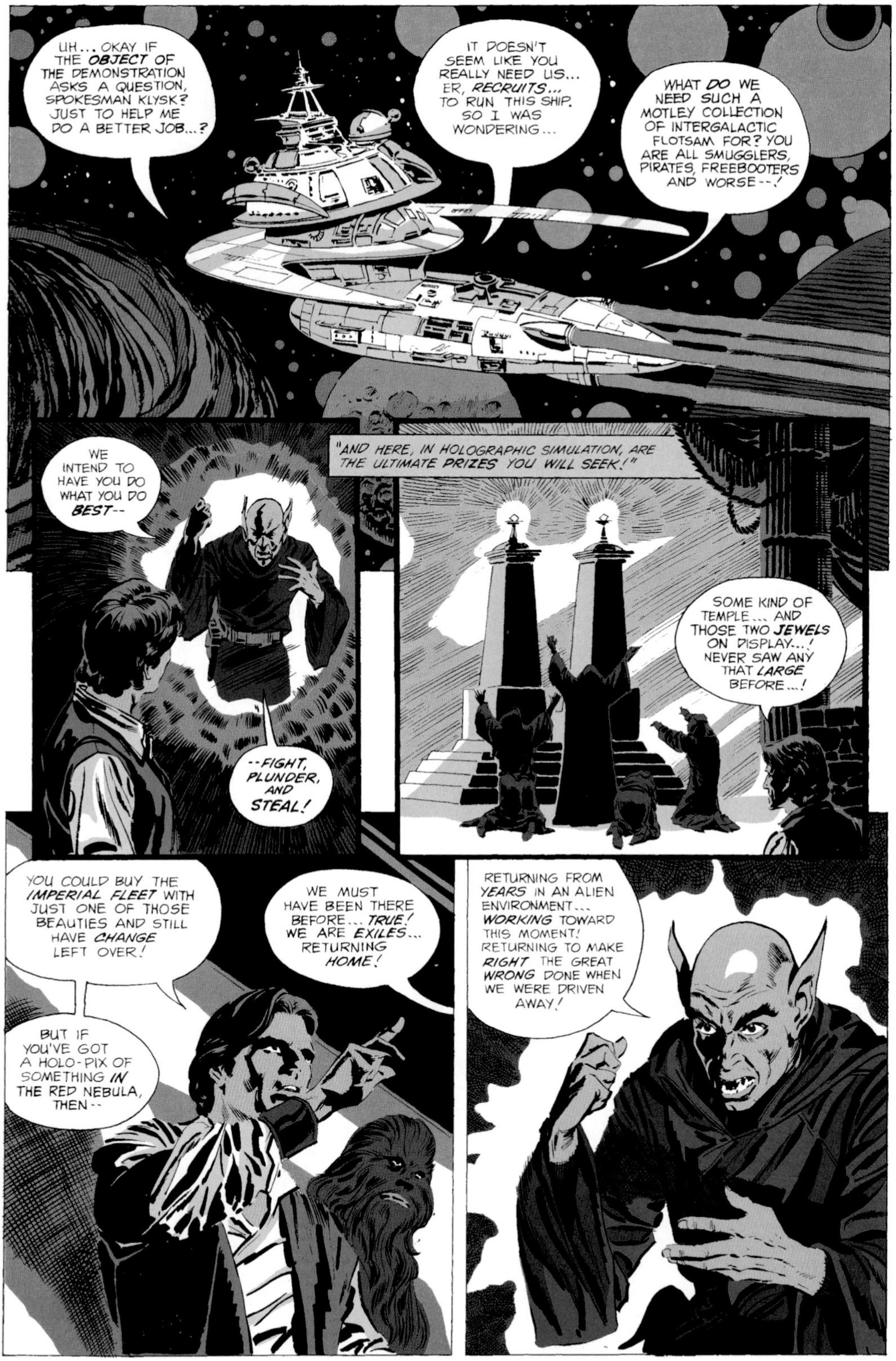
UH... OKAY IF THE OBJECT OF THE DEMONSTRATION ASKS A QUESTION, SPOKESMAN KLYSK? JUST TO HELP ME DO A BETTER JOB...?
IT DOESN'T SEEM LIKE YOU REALLY NEED US... ER, RECRUITS... TO RUN THIS SHIP. SO I WAS WONDERING...
WHAT DO WE NEED SUCH A MOTLEY COLLECTION OF INTERGALACTIC FLOTSAM FOR? YOU ARE ALL SMUGGLERS, PIRATES, FREEBOOTERS AND WORSE--!
WE INTEND TO HAVE YOU DO WHAT YOU DO BEST--
--FIGHT, PLUNDER, AND STEAL!
"AND HERE, IN HOLOGRAPHIC SIMULATION, ARE THE ULTIMATE PRIZES YOU WILL SEEK!"
SOME KIND OF TEMPLE... AND THOSE TWO JEWELS ON DISPLAY...! NEVER SAW ANY THAT LARGE BEFORE...!
YOU COULD BUY THE IMPERIAL FLEET WITH JUST ONE OF THOSE BEAUTIES AND STILL HAVE CHANGE LEFT OVER!
BUT IF YOU'VE GOT A HOLO-PIX OF SOMETHING IN THE RED NEBULA, THEN--
WE MUST HAVE BEEN THERE BEFORE... TRUE! WE ARE EXILES... RETURNING HOME!
RETURNING FROM YEARS IN AN ALIEN ENVIRONMENT... WORKING TOWARD THIS MOMENT! RETURNING TO MAKE RIGHT THE GREAT WRONG DONE WHEN WE WERE DRIVEN AWAY!

AND WITH A LENGTHY LEAP THROUGH HYPERSPACE... THE RETURN KLYSK SPEAKS OF IS ACCOMPLISHED. BUT...

THE PLACE IS *ALIVE* WITH COMETS AND METEORS...!

FRAGMENTS OF LONG EXPLODED STARS AND PLANETS ...THEY FORM THE *DUST* OF THE RED NEBULA.

WELL, IF ONE OF THOSE "DUSTSPECKS" *HITS* US, YOU CAN SAY GOODBYE TO THE *NOVA PRINCE*, MR. SPOKESMAN... AND TO *LIVING!*

YOU HAVE A *POINT*, SOLO. THE SHIP WE WERE EXILED IN WAS SMALLER, MORE MANEUVERABLE...

OUR COMPUTER SETTINGS SHOULD HAVE ALLOWED FOR THAT.

A *COMPUTER* CAN'T KICK THIS LUMBERING HULK THROUGH A COSMIC STORM, KLYSK! YOU NEED A *HOT PILOT* ...LIKE *ME!*

VERY WELL, CORELLIAN... *JOIN* US ON THE BRIDGE. BUT BE *WARNED...!* ANY *TRICKS* AND--

BELIEVE ME, KLYSK!... WITH WHAT'S GOIN' ON OUTSIDE... YOU DON'T *NEED* TO MAKE THREATS!

NOW *HANG ON...* AND HOPE FOR THE *BEST!*

EACH LONG MOMENT THAT FOLLOWS SEEMS CERTAIN TO BE THE *LAST* TO EVERY HAND ABOARD THE MASSIVE BULK FREIGHTER...

STILL, HAN SOLO STAYS AT THE SLUGGISH CONTROLS, FIGHTING, CURSING, COAXING, UNTIL...

WE'RE COMIN' *OUT* OF IT! THERE'S A *SUN* AHEAD... WITH A PLANET STILL INTACT!

THE *HEART* OF THE RED NEBULA, SMUGGLER. OUR DESTINATION ... AND OUR *TARGET*.

ANCESTRAL LEGEND HAS IT THAT THIS NEBULA WAS ONCE AN ARM OF *YOUR* GALAXY... UNTIL COSMIC UPHEAVAL *SUNDERED* IT. NOW IT DRIFTS FURTHER AND FURTHER INTO THE VOID... ONLY THIS STAR AND THIS PLANET SURVIVING AGAINST ALL ODDS.

WRONG, SOLO. LIFE IS GRIM *OBLIGATION*... STRIVING UNRELENTINGLY TO FULFILL OUR *DESTINY*.

YEAH. WELL, LIFE'S FUNNY LIKE THAT, KLYSK.

IF YOU SAY SO. I'M NOT GONNA ARGUE *RELIGION* WITH A GUY WHO CAN ION-BLAST ME INTO *NOTHING*. BESIDES...

"...COMPUTER'S CUTTING BACK IN FOR OUR *LANDING APPROACH*. I GUESS THE NEXT STEP IS ALL THAT PLUNDERING AND STEALING YOU TALKED ABOUT!"

KLYSK AND COMPANY'S HOME-WORLD HAS ALL THE CHARM OF A CLASS-D *MOON*, CHEWIE...!

I'D SAY *SOME* OF THOSE METEORS WE SLIPPED THROUGH OCCASIONALLY FIND THEIR WAY *HERE*.

23

A RISE LOOMS *BEFORE* THE ADVANCING FORCE FROM THE *NOVA PRINCE*, AND AT ITS CREST... A SIGHT INCREDIBLE AND MYSTIFYING.

THERE... *OUR* OBJECTIVE!

VOWRRRT!

I CAN'T BELIEVE IT *EITHER*, PAL! A WHOLE *VALLEY*... UNTOUCHED BY THE METEOR BOMBARDMENT THAT'S OBVIOUSLY *PASTED* THE REST OF THE PLANET!

EITHER IT'S A FREAK OF THE *TERRAIN*... OR THE PLACE IS *CHARMED!*

TAKE ANY *PLUNDER* YOU WISH DURING THE ATTACK... IT IS *YOURS* TO KEEP.

ALL *EXCEPT* THE TWO GREAT GEMS WHICH LIE IN THE *TEMPLE*... THOSE YOU WILL BRING TO *ME* OR MY *COMPANIONS* ON THE SHIP.

AND AT ALL COSTS... THE JEWELS MUST BE KEPT *TOGETHER*. DO NOT *SEPARATE* THEM ... ON PAIN OF *INSTANT IONIZATION!*

NOW... *ATTACK! ATTACK!*

GIVEN A CHOICE BETWEEN IMMEDIATE DEATH AND POSSIBLE PLUNDER, THE RELUCTANT MERCENARIES ENTHUSIASTICALLY *CHARGE*...

...ONLY TO FIND THE VALLEY IS NOT WITHOUT *DEFENSES!*

COME *ON!* IT'S ONLY A COUPLE OF *LASER CANNONS!* SPLIT UP AND *OUTFLANK* 'EM!

MOVE, YOU STARHOPPERS ...*MOVE!*

GRONNNK?!

SINCE WHEN DID I BECOME SO *BRAVE?* SINCE I DECIDED THAT THE ONLY WAY TO *TRUST* KLYSK AND COMPANY TO GET US OFF THIS ROCK... IS TO HAVE THOSE TWO KING-SIZE GEMS TO *BARGAIN* WITH!

WHILE THE *REST* OF OUR MOTLEY COMPANIONS ARE HITTING THE LOCALS FOR *PERSONAL GAIN*... WE'RE GOIN' STRAIGHT TO THE *TEMPLE!*

NRAGHH WROWWK!

NO, I *DON'T* THINK THESE ION-CHARGE MANACLES WILL AFFECT OUR *BARGAINING* ABILITY.

WHILE KLYSK WAS DAZZLED BY MY *PILOTING* THROUGH THOSE COMETS... I *SHORT-CIRCUITED* HIS PUNISHMENT SYSTEM!

AND MOMENTS LATER, THE CORELLIAN AND HIS WOOKIEE FIRST MATE SLIP INTO THE GREAT DOMED TEMPLE'S VAST, DARK INTERIOR...

YOWRRRRR...!

WILL YOU STOP SNIFFLING AT *SHADOWS!* NOTHIN' TO BE *NERVOUS* ABOUT. *THERE'S* WHAT WE'RE AFTER... AND NOT EVEN A *GUARD* IN SIGHT!

THAT'S NOT QUITE *TRUE*, OFF-WORLDER!

WHO IN BLAZES ARE *YOU?!* AND WHERE'D YOU LEARN TO SPEAK--

--GALACTIC STANDARD? YOU ARE NOT THE *FIRST* VISITORS TO THE RED NEBULA. I FEAR YOU WILL NOT BE THE *LAST.*

WE TEMPLE PRIESTS HAVE SEEN THE *GREAT LIFE JEWELS* TEMPT MANY.

LEGEND SAYS THE JEWELS FELL TO THIS PLANET DURING THE AWESOME *CATACLYSM* WHICH SEVERED OUR CLUSTER OF THE GALAXY FROM THE MAIN BODY AND *CREATED* THE RED NEBULA.

IT IS OUR BELIEF THAT THE GEMS' *AURA* PROTECTS US FROM THE DESTRUCTIVE FATE WHICH SEEMED OUR *DESTINY* FROM THE TIME OF THE CATACLYSM.

WELL, YOU OUGHT TO BACK UP YOUR BELIEF WITH A *BLASTER*, BALDY... 'CAUSE CHEWIE AN' ME ARE ABOUT TO *RELIEVE* YOU OF THOSE TWO LITTLE BEAUTIES!

IT'S NECESSARY TO *OUR* SURVIVAL... AND ANYWAY, THERE'S PROBABLY REALLY SOME *NATURAL PHENOMENON* ABOUT THIS VALLEY THAT PROTECTS IT!

NO NEED TO SALVE HIS *FEELINGS* OR YOUR *CONSCIENCE*, CORELLIAN. NEITHER YOU *NOR* THE WOOKIEE ARE TAKING THOSE JEWELS BACK TO *KLYSK*--

--*WE ARE!* THROW THE STONES IN THE BAG, ZUD, WHILE WE *FINISH* OUR RIVALS AND THE PRIEST!

BE *WARNED*, OFF-WORLDERS. THERE IS A *REASON* WE DO NOT HAVE TO GO *ARMED*--

--FOR THERE IS *ANOTHER* INHABITANT OF OUR VALLEY WHO HOLDS THE JEWELS SACRED... AND ACTS AS THEIR *GUARDIAN!*

IT STEPS FROM DENSE SHADOW BEYOND THE TWIN GEMS' SHRINE. IT IS SHAGGY, FRIGHTENING, HUGE...

...BUT MOSTLY, IT IS *ENRAGED!* AND ITS WRATH IS *IMMEDIATE* UPON THE TRIO ADVANCING ON THE GLITTERING STONES IT IS SWORN TO *PROTECT!*

MIND-NUMBING SHOCK MAKES THE MERCENARIES HESITATE BEFORE FIRING...

...AND HAVING HESITATED, THEY ARE *LOST!*

WRONNNK!

RUN FOR IT...? ARE YOU *KIDDIN',* CHEWIE?

WHILE THAT THING'S TOSSING THOSE GUYS AROUND... *WE* CAN GRAB THE JEWELS!

BUT THE TOWERING GUARDIAN IS NOT OCCUPIED *LONG!* AND AS THE *MILLENNIUM FALCON'S* CAPTAIN AND FIRST MATE ACT...

...GREAT, GLEAMING EYES FALL ON THEM; A STRANGE, LOW GROWL ECHOES THROUGH THE CHAMBER...

...AND A HUGE *PAW* LASHES OUT ONCE MORE!

WOWWRRK!

CHEWIE!

I'M THE ONE WHO HAD HIS HANDS ON THE *JEWELS...* WHY DID IT GO FOR MY *PARTNER* INSTEAD OF ME?!

SOMETHING WE OF THE TEMPLE NEVER FORESAW!

THE GUARDIAN IS *FEMALE...* THE *LAST* OF HER SPECIES... LOWER YOUR WEAPON... IT IS NOT NECESSARY.

OBVIOUSLY, SHE SEES IN YOUR FRIEND... A *CUB!*

VORRAARK?!

EMBARRASSING...? IT'S *GREAT!* JUST CUDDLE UP AND KEEP HER *HAPPY* PAL... I'LL DELIVER THESE AND NEGOTIATE OUR WAY *OUT* OF THIS MESS!

BEWARE, OFF-WORLDER! WE PRIESTS PREFER TO *AVOID* VIOLENCE... KLYSK AND HIS FACTION ARE GUIDED *ONLY* BY WHAT THEY BELIEVE IS THEIR ULTIMATE *DESTINY!*

HAN SHRUGS AND STRIDES FROM THE TEMPLE, MIND CHURNING POSSIBLE COURSES OPEN TO HIM. THEN, DECIDING... HE *ACTS.* AND SOON...,

SOLO! THE OTHERS REPORT YOU WERE *FIRST* TO THE TEMPLE... I TRUST YOU DID NOT *DISAPPOINT* ME.

AFTER ALL WE'VE *BEEN* THROUGH TOGETHER...? PERISH THE THOUGHT, KLYSK.

BUT BEFORE YOU GET THE GOODIES... I'VE GOT A *FEW* DEMANDS.

28

NO, CORELLIAN. WE'VE DISCOVERED YOUR *TREACHERY* WITH THE ION-CHARGED MANACLES. IT IS *TOO LATE* TO CORRECT THAT--

--BUT THERE WILL BE *NO* BARGAINS. HAND OVER THE *GEMS*--

--YOUR FELLOW MERCENARIES WILL BE *HAPPY* TO VAPORIZE YOU TO RETAIN *THEIR* SHARE IN THE *REWARD UNPARALLELED* I PROMISED.

YOU STILL *NEED* ME, KLYSK... WHO *ELSE* IS GONNA PILOT THE *NOVA PRINCE* THROUGH THOSE COSMIC STORMS WE ENCOUNTERED *COMING* HERE?

WE WILL TRAVEL BY A *DIFFERENT* COURSE... ONE ALREADY *PRE-SET* INTO THE SHIP'S COMPUTER TO AUTOMATICALLY TAKE EFFECT THE *INSTANT* WE LIFT OFF.

I COULD *KILL* YOU, SMUGGLER... BUT ABANDONING YOU HERE AT THE *HEART* OF THE RED NEBULA SERVES JUST AS WELL!

SOMETHIN'S *COMING*, KLYSK...! T-THAT *GUARDIAN* FROM THE TEMPLE...! LET'S GET OUT OF THIS PLACE... *FAST!*

AND WITH A THUNDER OF FULL DRIVE ENGINES, THE MASSIVE INTER-GALACTIC FREIGHTER TAKES TO THE SKIES...

I TRIED TO *WARN* YOU, HAN SOLO... NOW YOU'VE *DOOMED* US ALL!

WITHOUT THE PROTECTION OF THE *SACRED JEWELS*, OUR VALLEY AND THIS WHOLE PLANET WILL SOON BE REDUCED TO COSMIC RUBBLE LIKE THE *REST* OF THE RED NEBULA!

KEEP THE LADY'S *MOTHERLY INSTINCTS* FLOWING, CHEWIE...THE PRIEST SOUNDS PUT OFF ENOUGH TO *SIC* 'ER ON ME.

AND THAT MIGHT FATALLY *IMPAIR* MY ABILITY TO *BARGAIN* WITH HIM!

YOU'RE *MAD*, OFF-WORLDER! LET ME *SHOW* YOU WHERE YOUR "BARGAINING" WITH *KLYSK* AND HIS FANATICAL FRIENDS HAS LED! *COME!*

THE SMUGGLER AND HIS WOOKIEE COMPANION ARE BROUGHT TO AN UNDERGROUND *SHELTER* IN THE VALLEY...

TRACKING EQUIPMENT!

WE ARE NOT *TOTALLY* LACKING IN *TECHNOLOGY*...

...AS YOU AND THE OTHER MERCENARIES *LEARNED* WHEN YOU FIRST ATTACKED.

AND WHEN HAN LOOKS CLOSELY AT THE *FINEBAND SCOPE*, HE SEES...

THE *NOVA PRINCE!* B-BUT...IT'S NOT HEADING *OUT* OF THE NEBULA! IT'S--

IT'S PLUNGING AT MAXIMUM SUB-LIGHT SPEED ON A COMPUTER-SET *COLLISION COURSE* WITH OUR SUN!

"*THERE...!* THE *END* IS UPON US! KLYSK'S GROUP HAS AT LAST ACCOMPLISHED THE VERY THING WE *EXILED* THEM TO PREVENT.

THEY FANATICALLY BELIEVED IT WAS OUR FATE TO *PERISH* WHEN THE RED NEBULA WAS SUNDERED FROM THE REST OF THE GALAXY SO LONG AGO. JUST AS WE CAME TO BELIEVE THE PRESENCE OF THE TWIN GEMS *PROTECTED* US FROM THE CATACLYSM...

"...KLYSK AND HIS KIND REGARDED THEM AS BLASPHEMOUS ABOMINATIONS TO BE *DESTROYED* SO OUR RACE WOULD NO LONGER LIVE IN *DEFIANCE* OF COSMIC DESTINY!

"*TODAY...THEY HAVE SUCCEEDED!*"

THE *REWARD UNPARALLELED* KLYSK KEPT TALKING ABOUT...! AND ALL THOSE MERCENARIES WHO THREW IN WITH HIM GOT TO *SHARE* IT!

AND WE *ALL* WILL, CORELLIAN! WITH THE JEWELS FOREVER LOST, THE NEBULA'S DEVASTATING RAIN OF *COMETS* AND *METEORS* WILL POUND US INTO ETERNITY!

IN FACT... I DON'T UNDERSTAND WHY IT HAS *NOT* ALREADY *BEGUN.*

WELL, I'M A CYNICAL GUY... I THINK YOUR PEOPLE *AND* KLYSK'S WENT WAY *OVERBOARD* ABOUT THOSE STONES' POWER.

BUT IF YOU'RE IN THE MOOD TO *BARGAIN...* I'VE A *CONFESSION* TO MAKE!

FOLLOWING THAT CONFESSION--AND SOME SERIOUS NEGOTIATION--HAN LEADS THE TEMPLE PRIEST TO A *GROVE* NEAR THE VALLEY'S EDGE.

YOU ARE A *DEVIOUS* MAN, CAPTAIN SOLO...

DEALIN' WITH FOLKS LIKE KLYSK, YOU *GOTTA* BE. THAT'S WHY I *HID* THE JEWELS IN HERE--

--AND SUBSTITUTED A COUPLE OF *ROCKS!* NOT MY FAULT HE WAS IN TOO BIG A HURRY TO *CHECK* OR--

UH-OH! LOOKS LIKE NOT *ALL* THE MERCENARIES WENT WITH *KLYSK!* BUT W-WHAT--?

STAY *BACK!* OBVIOUSLY THE FOOL OBSERVED YOU FROM COVER... THEN TRIED TO MAKE OFF WITH THE GEMS *ONE* AT A TIME!

FORTUNATELY HE DIDN'T GET *FAR*.... I CAN *UNDO* THE DAMAGE!

KLYSK *SAID* SOMETHING ABOUT NOT *SEPARATING* THE JEWELS... IS *THAT* WHAT DID THE GUY IN?

IGNORANCE BROUGHT HIM DOWN. COUNT YOURSELF FORTUNATE, CAPTAIN... IT COULD EASILY HAVE BEEN *YOU!*

SWIFTLY, THE PRIEST REUNITES THE RADIANT GEM WITH ITS MATE...

...AND SOON, THE JEWELS OCCUPY THEIR ORIGINAL PLACE AT THE TEMPLE.

YOU HAVE KEPT *YOUR* PART OF THE BARGAIN, CORELLIAN... NOW WE MUST KEEP *OURS.*

THOUGH I SUSPECT *ONE* OF US DOES SO WITH SOME *RELUCTANCE!*

BE *NICE,* CHEWIE... MAMA'S JUST SAYIN' *GOOD-BYE!*

AAWWWWRRRLLLL!

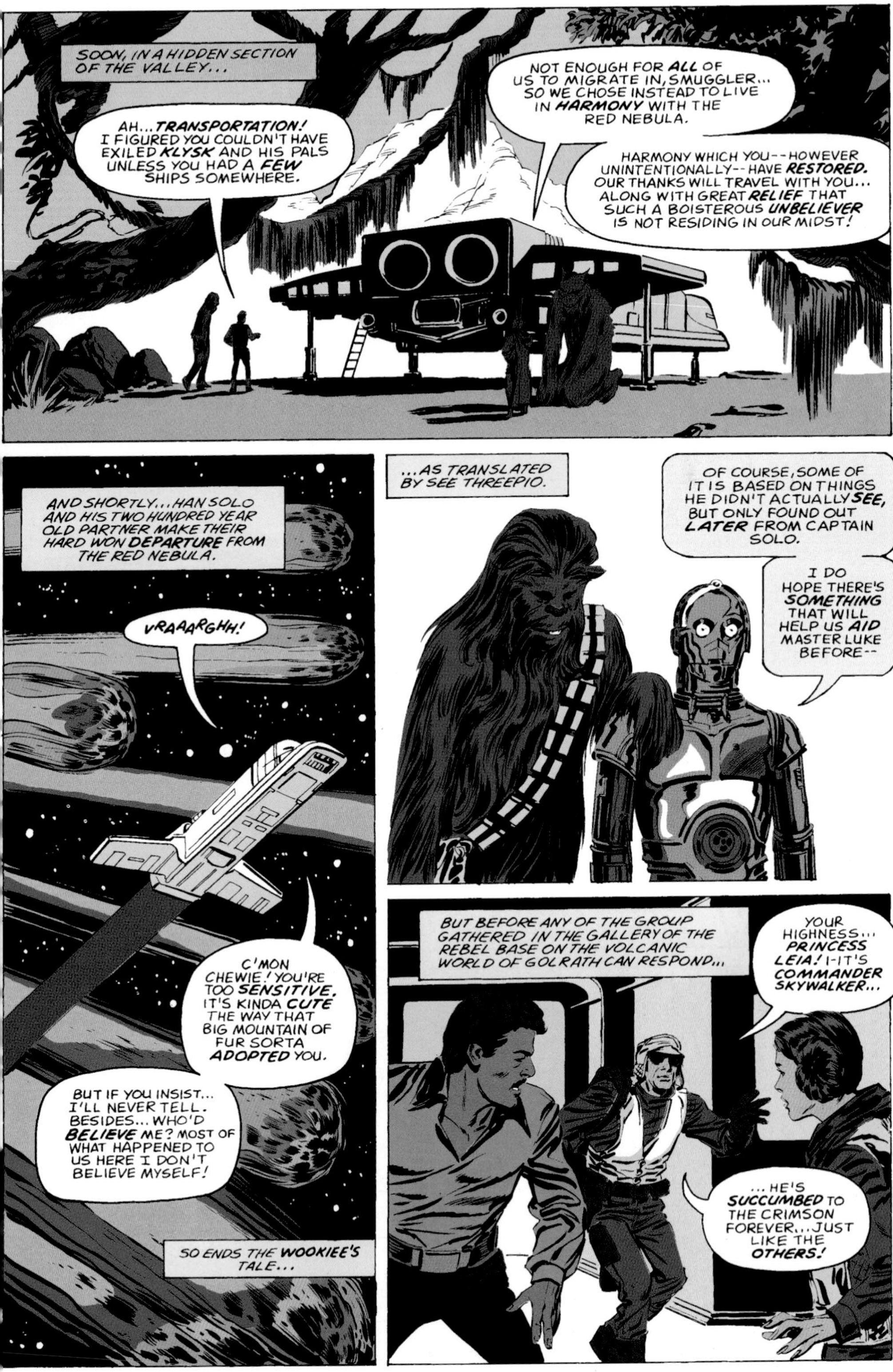
SOON, IN A HIDDEN SECTION OF THE VALLEY...
AH...TRANSPORTATION! I FIGURED YOU COULDN'T HAVE EXILED KLYSK AND HIS PALS UNLESS YOU HAD A FEW SHIPS SOMEWHERE.
NOT ENOUGH FOR ALL OF US TO MIGRATE IN, SMUGGLER... SO WE CHOSE INSTEAD TO LIVE IN HARMONY WITH THE RED NEBULA.
HARMONY WHICH YOU--HOWEVER UNINTENTIONALLY--HAVE RESTORED. OUR THANKS WILL TRAVEL WITH YOU... ALONG WITH GREAT RELIEF THAT SUCH A BOISTEROUS UNBELIEVER IS NOT RESIDING IN OUR MIDST!
AND SHORTLY... HAN SOLO AND HIS TWO HUNDRED YEAR OLD PARTNER MAKE THEIR HARD WON DEPARTURE FROM THE RED NEBULA.
VRAAARGHH!
C'MON CHEWIE! YOU'RE TOO SENSITIVE. IT'S KINDA CUTE THE WAY THAT BIG MOUNTAIN OF FUR SORTA ADOPTED YOU.
BUT IF YOU INSIST... I'LL NEVER TELL. BESIDES... WHO'D BELIEVE ME? MOST OF WHAT HAPPENED TO US HERE I DON'T BELIEVE MYSELF!
SO ENDS THE WOOKIEE'S TALE...
...AS TRANSLATED BY SEE THREEPIO.
OF COURSE, SOME OF IT IS BASED ON THINGS HE DIDN'T ACTUALLY SEE, BUT ONLY FOUND OUT LATER FROM CAPTAIN SOLO.
I DO HOPE THERE'S SOMETHING THAT WILL HELP US AID MASTER LUKE BEFORE--
BUT BEFORE ANY OF THE GROUP GATHERED IN THE GALLERY OF THE REBEL BASE ON THE VOLCANIC WORLD OF GOLRATH CAN RESPOND...
YOUR HIGHNESS... PRINCESS LEIA! I-IT'S COMMANDER SKYWALKER...
...HE'S SUCCUMBED TO THE CRIMSON FOREVER... JUST LIKE THE OTHERS!

AGAINST THE
SCARLET NIGHT!

CHAPTER III

THE *VOID*. BLACK. STAR-LESS. EMPTY. EXCEPT FOR AN ANGRY MASS OF SWIRLING SCARLET... *THE RED NEBULA*, DESTINATION OF THE *MILLENNIUM FALCON*.

IT HAS BEEN A *LONG* JOURNEY... MADE IN FRANTIC DESPERATION.

AND THOSE *WITHIN* THE BATTERED SPICE FREIGHTER STILL HAVE *FAR* TO GO.

WE'VE COME OUT OF HYPERDRIVE *TOO SOON*, LANDO. IF *HAN* HAD PROGRAMMED THE JUMP--

THAT'S THE FIRST THING THAT *OCCURED* TO *ME*, TOO, PRINCESS--

--BUT THIS IS THE *COMPUTER'S* DOING.

34

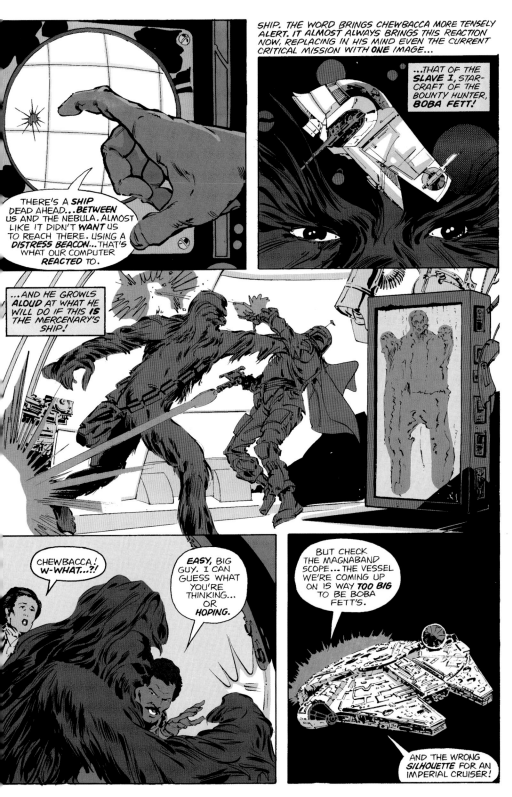

SHIP. THE WORD BRINGS CHEWBACCA MORE TENSELY ALERT. IT ALMOST ALWAYS BRINGS THIS REACTION NOW, REPLACING IN HIS MIND EVEN THE CURRENT CRITICAL MISSION WITH *ONE* IMAGE...

...THAT OF THE *SLAVE I,* STAR-CRAFT OF THE BOUNTY HUNTER, *BOBA FETT!*

THERE'S A *SHIP* DEAD AHEAD...*BETWEEN* US AND THE NEBULA. ALMOST LIKE IT DIDN'T *WANT* US TO REACH THERE. USING A *DISTRESS BEACON...*THAT'S WHAT OUR COMPUTER *REACTED* TO.

...AND HE GROWLS *ALOUD* AT WHAT HE WILL DO IF THIS *IS* THE MERCENARY'S SHIP!

CHEWBACCA! W-WHAT...?!

EASY, BIG GUY. I CAN GUESS WHAT YOU'RE THINKING... OR *HOPING.*

BUT CHECK THE MAGNABAND SCOPE... THE VESSEL WE'RE COMING UP ON IS WAY *TOO BIG* TO BE BOBA FETT'S.

AND THE WRONG *SILHOUETTE* FOR AN IMPERIAL CRUISER!

IT'S A HOUSE OF TAGGE *MINING EXPLORER!*

AT ONE TIME OR ANOTHER THAT ENTIRE *FAMILY* HAS GIVEN US TROUBLE. IF ONE OF THEIR SHIPS IS HERE, ALONG THE *BEST APPROACH* TO THE RED NEBULA--

--IT CAN'T BE BY *ACCIDENT!*

JUDGING BY THE DAMAGE, *SOMEONE* DIDN'T LIKE HER BEING HERE, PRINCESS. LIFE FORM READINGS AREN'T TOO PRECISE...BUT SHE SEEMS TO BE A *DERELICT* NOW.

THE CRIMSON FOREVER COULD SWEEP THE GALAXY LIKE THE FALL OF *NIGHT*, LANDO.

IN OUR SEARCH FOR A *SOLUTION*, WE CAN'T BYPASS *ANYTHING.*

UH-HUH. PERFECTLY LOGICAL...AND A LOT *RISKIER* THAN I PREFER.

NONETHELESS, THE *MILLENNIUM FALCON* IS SOON ANCHORING ITSELF TO AN *EMERGENCY AIRLOCK* NEAR THE BRIDGE OF THE LARGER CRAFT...

...AND LEIA AND LANDO *ENTER* TO FIND...

ALL THE FIGHTING DIDN'T HAPPEN OUTSIDE. BUT IT LOOKS LIKE THE REAL **WINNER** WAS--

--THE *CRIMSON FOREVER!*

IF **IT'S** HERE, LANDO...WHAT WE'RE **LOOKING** FOR MIGHT BE, TOO!

GUESS THAT MEANS WE FORGE **ON**...AND PRAY HAN AND CHEWIE SPOTCHECKED THESE SUITS RECENTLY FOR **LEAKS.**

I THOUGHT YOU **LIKED** GAMBLING.

DEPENDS ON THE **ODDS,** YOUR HIGHNESS.

AT LEAST THERE'S NO ONE TO GET IN OUR WAY.

IT'S STILL PRETTY **CREEPY** CHECKING ALL THESE BODIES FOR A **SECOND** JEWEL...LIKE IN CHEWBACCA'S STORY.

I LIKE DOING **SOMETHING--**

--RATHER THAN DWELLING ON **LUKE** BEING GONE OR--

THIS SECTION'S **SEALED OFF,** LANDO...FROM THE **OTHER SIDE!**

BUT NOT FOR LONG...!

IG-88 HAS YOU **COVERED!** FOLLOW HIM WITHOUT RESISTING--

--OR **DIE!**

37

THE ARMED DROID FORCES THE PAIR THROUGH A SERIES OF AIRLOCKS AND SEALED CHAMBERS-- CAREFULLY RELEASING THE POSSIBLY VIRUS-TAINTED ATMOSPHERE FROM EACH ONE BEFORE PROCEDING ON TO THE NEXT--UNTIL, FINALLY THEY FACE...

DOMINA TAGGE! I MIGHT HAVE **KNOWN!**

I'M PLEASED YOU **REMEMBER,** LEIA ORGANA. **ALMOST** AS PLEASED--

--AS I WAS TO OVERHEAR THAT **LUKE SKYWALKER** HAS FALLEN PREY TO WHAT **I'VE** UNLEASHED!

BOTH HE AND DARTH VADER **SHARE** RESPONSIBILITY FOR THE DEATH OF MY **BROTHER,** BARON ORMAN TAGGE!

AS YOU'LL **RECALL,** I SWORE NEVER TO FORGET... OR **FORGIVE** THAT!*

*STAR WARS #37--LOUISE.

A GREAT **LOSS** DESERVES A GREATER **REVENGE.** THE GREATEST **I** COULD IMAGINE WAS TO DESTROY THE **CAUSES** EACH OF THEM SERVES! SO, ARMED WITH MY FAMILY WEALTH AND NAME--

--I SET OUT TO DISCOVER A POWER THAT COULD **CRUSH** THE EMPIRE **AND** THE REBEL ALLIANCE!

"AND WHEN SPIES BROUGHT ME RUMORS OF TWO STRANGE, DEADLY **GEMS** IN THE RED NEBULA...I RUSHED TO INVESTIGATE.

"...THIS ELITE GROUP OF **BOUNTY HUNTERS** I'D HIRED CAPTURED THE JEWELS AND THE PRIEST TENDING THEM.

"AS OUR SHIP LAID WASTE TO THE PRIMITIVE CIVILIZATION THERE, DRIVING OFF SOME GIANT CREATURE...

"AFTER CONSIDERABLE 'PERSUASION'...

"...THE PRIEST WAS FORCED TO **SHARE** HIS KNOWLEDGE OF THE GEMS' DEADLY POWERS. BUT AS I TOOK STEPS TO **UTILIZE** THOSE POWERS...

"WITH OUR **DRIVE ENGINES** DESTROYED, I AGREED TO **SURRENDER** OUR FIND. BUT AS THE EMPIRE'S BOARDING PARTY RECEIVED **ONE** JEWEL IN ITS CARBONITE CANNISTER...

"WE FOUND AN **IMPERIAL CRUISER** WAITING JUST OUTSIDE THE NEBULA!

"**DARTH VADER** HAD LEARNED OF MY JOURNEY AND DISPATCHED A WARSHIP TO DISCOVER THE **SECRET** BEHIND IT.

"...MY BOUNTY HUNTERS PROVOKED A **FIREFIGHT!**

"THE BOARDERS WERE FORCED TO RETREAT WITH ONLY **HALF** THE PRIZES... AS I INTENDED.

"WHAT I **DIDN'T** INTEND WAS THAT A DYING **PRIEST,** MOMENTARILY UNGUARDED DURING THE FIGHT, WOULD REACH AND UNLEASH THE **SECOND** JEWEL!

"THE IMPERIAL'S CANNISTER HAD BEEN **RIGGED** SO ITS SEALS WOULD **BURST** UNDER THE PRESSURES OF **HYPERDRIVE...**"

...AND HAVING GIVEN THEM THE LOCATION OF YOUR NEW **GOLRATH BASE** -- LEARNED FROM SPIES -- AS PART OF OUR EARLIER BARGAINING, IT SEEMED MY **REVENGE** WAS WELL IN MOTION.

CUTE, LADY.

ONLY THE LAST ACT OF THAT PRIEST KIND'A MADE IT ALL **BACKFIRE,** EH?

THE BOUNTY HUNTERS AND I MANAGED TO **SECURE** THIS SECTION OF THE SHIP BEFORE THE DOOM CAUSED BY THE TWIN GEMS BEING **SEPARATED** COULD INFECT US.

YOU JUST COULDN'T **GO** ANYWHERE.

UNTIL **NOW.** BOSSK...ZUCKASS ...TAKE THEIR **SPACE SUITS!** WE'LL NEED THEM TO REACH THEIR **SHIP.**

RIGHT...

...AND I'VE BEEN **HOPING** FOR THE CHANCE TO **GIVE** MINE TO YOU.

SOME-THIN' **FUNNY** ABOUT THAT?

IF YOU APPRECIATE A BIT OF **IRONY.**

MY SUIT **MALFUNCTIONED** ON THE WAY IN, BOUNTY HUNTER! YOU'RE GETTING IT...**AND THE CRIMSON FOREVER!**

N-NO...!

THE MERCENARIES HAVE **SEEN** THE EFFECTS OF THE CRIMSON FOREVER. IT IS ENOUGH TO MAKE EVEN **THEM** FRANTICALLY, INSTINCTIVELY DRAW BACK...

...BUT **NOT** DOMINA TAGGE!

IT'S A **BLUFF,** YOU FOOLS! THEY'RE OPENING THE AIRLOCK!

27.5

AND BY THE TIME IG-88, WHOSE MECHANIZED FORM IS UN-AFFECTED BY THE THREAT OF DISEASE, HAS A **CLEAR SHOT...**

...THE PAIR ARE DIVING **THROUGH** THAT AIRLOCK!

THAT'S THE TROUBLE WITH **BLUFFING** AS A GAMBLING TECHNIQUE--

--SOME UNIMAGINATIVE **SPOILER** ALWAYS WANTS TO **CALL** YOU! HIT THE **DOOR SEALS,** LEIA... JAM 'EM!

40

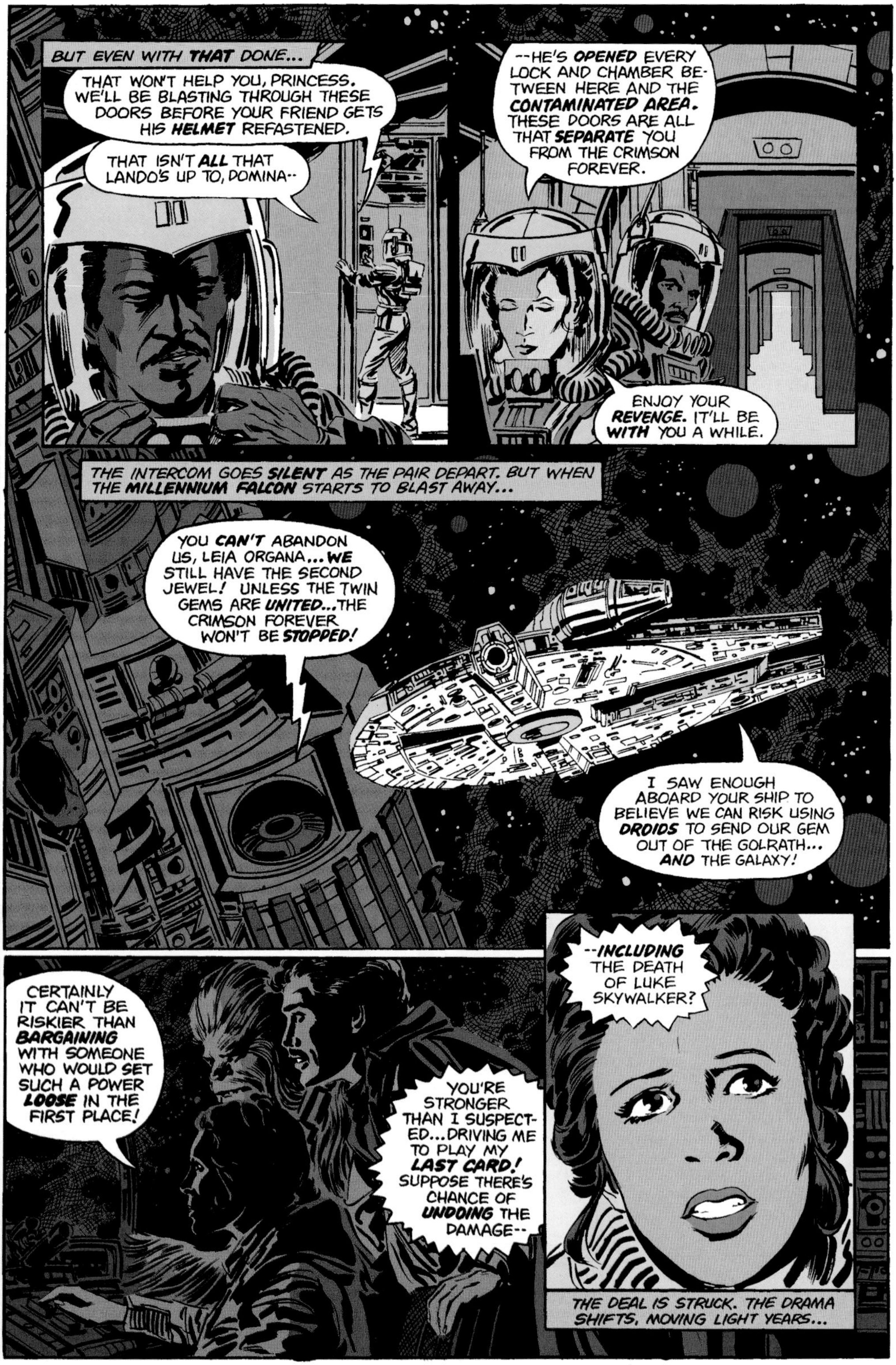
BUT EVEN WITH THAT DONE...
THAT WON'T HELP YOU, PRINCESS. WE'LL BE BLASTING THROUGH THESE DOORS BEFORE YOUR FRIEND GETS HIS HELMET REFASTENED.
THAT ISN'T ALL THAT LANDO'S UP TO, DOMINA--
--HE'S OPENED EVERY LOCK AND CHAMBER BETWEEN HERE AND THE CONTAMINATED AREA. THESE DOORS ARE ALL THAT SEPARATE YOU FROM THE CRIMSON FOREVER.
ENJOY YOUR REVENGE. IT'LL BE WITH YOU A WHILE.
THE INTERCOM GOES SILENT AS THE PAIR DEPART. BUT WHEN THE MILLENNIUM FALCON STARTS TO BLAST AWAY...
YOU CAN'T ABANDON US, LEIA ORGANA... WE STILL HAVE THE SECOND JEWEL! UNLESS THE TWIN GEMS ARE UNITED... THE CRIMSON FOREVER WON'T BE STOPPED!
I SAW ENOUGH ABOARD YOUR SHIP TO BELIEVE WE CAN RISK USING DROIDS TO SEND OUR GEM OUT OF THE GOLRATH... AND THE GALAXY!
CERTAINLY IT CAN'T BE RISKIER THAN BARGAINING WITH SOMEONE WHO WOULD SET SUCH A POWER LOOSE IN THE FIRST PLACE!
YOU'RE STRONGER THAN I SUSPECTED... DRIVING ME TO PLAY MY LAST CARD! SUPPOSE THERE'S CHANCE OF UNDOING THE DAMAGE--
--INCLUDING THE DEATH OF LUKE SKYWALKER?
THE DEAL IS STRUCK. THE DRAMA SHIFTS, MOVING LIGHT YEARS...

...FROM ONE DERELICT DRIFTING OUT BEYOND THE GALAXY TO *ANOTHER* STILL WITHIN IT.

ACCORDING TO THE PRIEST, THE GEMS ARE *LIVING ENTITIES*...LIFE FORMS FROM ANOTHER PART OF THE COSMOS SWEPT HERE BY THE CATACLYSM THAT CREATED THE RED NEBULA.

THEY'RE *MATES* OF SORTS. AS LONG AS THEY ARE *TOGETHER*, THEY RADIATE A SENSE OF *WELL BEING*, A POSITIVE *PHYSICAL AURA*--

--AN AURA THAT CAN AFFECT THEIR *SURROUNDINGS*. SEPARATED, THEIR WELL BEING TURNS TO *ANGUISH* AND THE AURA TURNS *NEGATIVE*, RADIATING STRONGER ...GROWING...

AND THAT PHYSICAL EFFECT BECOMES WHAT'S CALLED THE CRIMSON FOREVER?! BUT IF IT'S STRONG ENOUGH TO *KILL*...?

IT *ISN'T!* BUT THE POWER SO SLOWS THE VICTIM'S *LIFE FUNCTIONS*...IT BECOMES LIKE *SUSPENDED ANIMATION*, BEYOND THE ABILITY OF *OUR* INSTRUMENTS TO DETECT!

AS LONG AS THE JEWELS *STAY* SEPARATED, THAT STATE INTENSIFIES. BUT NOW THAT *IG-88* HAS *RE-UNITED* THEM--

--THE NEGATIVE AURA WILL *RECEDE*. AND ANY VICTIMS TOUCHED BY IT SHOULD *REVIVE!*

FORGIVE US IF WE TAKE A *WAIT-AND-SEE* ATTITUDE, DOMINA.

AND LONG, LONG MOMENTS SLOWLY CLICK BY. UNTIL...

SEE? IT'S *TRUE!* IF IT WEREN'T ...I'D HAVE FALLEN BY NOW.

FOR AN INSTANT, HOPE RISES AMONG THE GATHERED REBELS. THEN...

YOUR HIGHNESS, THIS FALLEN IMPERIAL IS *NOT* REVIVING. THE LADY'S THEORY IS *AC-CURATE*. BUT THE SHOCK AND STRAIN OF *SEEMING* TO CON-TRACT A DEADLY VIRUS--

--AND TRYING TO *FIGHT* IT, HAS HAD A *FATAL EFFECT*.

TOO-ONEBEE! THAT MEANS EVEN *LUKE*--

SUDDENLY...

SEE-THREEPIO COMMUNICATING FROM THE BASE MEDICAL WING, YOUR HIGHNESS. HE'S *ALIVE*! MASTER LUKE *ALIVE*!

THEN IT WASN'T *WEIRD*, FLYBOY...IT WAS *WONDERFUL*.

MAYBE IT WAS THE *FORCE*... MAYBE JUST SUBCONSCIOUS *INSTINCT*, LEIA...

...BUT THIS WEIRD *DREAM* SORTA HELPED ME FIGURE HOW TO *REACT*.

SOMETIME LATER, *TWO* VESSELS THUNDER AWAY FROM THE VOLCANIC WORLD OF GOLRATH.

ONE IS AN *ESCAPE SHIP* PROMISED TO DOMINA TAGGE AND THE BOUNTY HUNTERS SERVING HER.

THE OTHER IS AN *IMPERIAL CRUISER*, PRE-PROGRAMMED TO PLUNGE INTO HYPERDRIVE TOWARD THE GREAT *VOID* BEYOND THE GALACTIC RIM, NOTHING RIDING WITHIN ITS VAST BULK--EXCEPT TWO GLEAMING *GEMS*.

THERE THEY *GO*... HOPEFULLY WHERE THEY WON'T BE USED AS THEY WERE *HERE*.

IF ONLY I HADN'T BEEN BOUND TO *FREE* THAT TAGGE WOMAN AFTER THE *MISERY* SHE CAUSED.

A SMALL CONFESSION. BEFORE THEY LEFT, I CASUALLY LET SLIP TO HER BOUNTY-HUNTING COMPANIONS THAT BECAUSE HER SCHEME IN-VOLVED OFFENSES AGAINST THE *EMPIRE*--

--THE IMPERIALS MIGHT OFFER A *SUBSTANTIAL REWARD* FOR THE LADY. SURPRISINGLY... THEY SEEMED QUITE *INTERESTED*.

NEXT: *REBIRTH* of *EVIL!*

43

50¢ **51**
SEPT
02817

STAR WARS

RESURRECTION OF EVIL!

Long ago in a galaxy far, far away. . . .there exists a state of cosmic *civil war*. A brave alliance of *underground freedom fighters* has challenged the tyranny and oppression of the awesome *Galactic Empire*. This is their story!

 PRESENTS: **STAR WARS** THE *GREATEST* SPACE *FANTASY* OF ALL!

DAVID MICHELINIE	WALTER SIMONSON	THOMAS PALMER	JOHN MORELLI	DON WARFIELD	LOUISE JONES	JAMES SHOOTER
WRITER	PENCILER	INKER	LETTERER	COLORIST	EDITOR	ED-IN-CHIEF

THE WAR DRAGS ON! EACH DAY, EMPEROR PALPATINE DRAWS HIS BLOODSTAINED HAND EVER TIGHTER AROUND THE THROAT OF A ONCE FREE GALAXY.

AND CAPTAIN MARABA TEV, LOYAL OFFICER OF THE REBEL ALLIANCE, HAD KNOWN THAT WELL WHEN HE ACCEPTED A HIGH RISK SPY MISSION IN THE PATRIIM SYSTEM... HAD KNOWN IT EVEN BETTER WHEN FORCED TO FLEE THE SECTOR WITH A DOZEN IMPERIAL WARSHIPS IN HOT PURSUIT.

BUT HIS MOST VIVID AWARENESS HAD COME JUST SECONDS AGO, WHEN HE HAD POINTED HIS CRIPPLED AND BATTLE-BEATEN FIGHTER STRAIGHT FOR THE REBELLION'S TEMPORARY CRUISER BASE... A MERE FOUR-AND-A-HALF HEARTBEATS BEFORE HE DIED!

CAPTAIN TEV'S OVERSHOT THE DOCKING BAY!

GET THOSE MAGNETIC GRAPPLES WORKING--*NOW!*

CHOOF

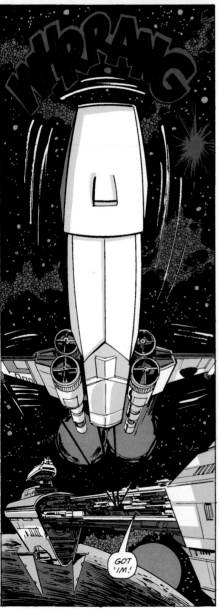

WHRRANG

GOT 'IM!

STILL NO COMMUNICATION FROM THE X-WING, BOSUN?

NO, SIR.

THEN WE HAVE TO ASSUME THAT TEV HAS BLACKED OUT--WITH HIS ENGINES SET ON FULL THRUST! AND THAT LEAVES US LITTLE CHOICE. GUNNER! LOCK ON LASERS, AND--

--FIRE!

ZRAM

ZRAM

DEAD ON, SIR! WINGS AND ENGINES CUT CLEAN! ATMOSPHERIC INTEGRITY OF THE FUSELAGE MAINTAINED!

GOOD SHOOTING, GUNNER! NOW LET'S GET THAT HULK REELED INSIDE!

GENTLY, MAN!

QUICKLY, AND CAREFULLY, THE WINGLESS FIGHTER IS DRAWN INTO A VACUUM-SHIELDED DOCKING BAY --

--WHERE SOON...

HOW IS HE?

DEAD. INTERNAL INJURIES, I THINK. AND HE'S STILL CLUTCHING A MESSAGE CANNISTER --I JUST HOPE IT WAS WORTH THIS.

SEE THAT HE RECEIVES A HERO'S FUNERAL, JACE, I'LL GET THIS CANNISTER TO THE GENERAL.

"THE GENERAL": MORE FORMALLY KNOWN AS GENERAL RIEEKAN, SUPREME COMMANDER OF THE REBEL FLEET--AND AT THIS MOMENT, A VERY TROUBLED MAN.

IF THE INFORMATION CAPTAIN TEV SECURED PROVES ACCURATE, GENTLEMEN--

AS SENIOR OFFICERS, YOU'VE ALL READ THE TRANSCRIPTS. SO YOU'LL UNDERSTAND WHY I'VE ORDERED A TRIO OF EMERGENCY RECALL TRANSMISSIONS TO BE SENT AT ONCE.

BECAUSE THE WARRIORS THOSE SIGNALS ARE DIRECTED TO COULD QUITE POSSIBLY BE OUR ONLY HOPE!

--THE REBELLION MAY WELL BE DOOMED!

WHILE SEVERAL SUN SYSTEMS AWAY, AT THE EVENTUAL DESTINATION OF ONE OF THOSE TRANSMISSIONS--

--PRINCESS LEIA ORGANA AND HER DROID COMPANION C-3PO, HAVE JUST SET FOOT ON A LUSH, UNCHARTED PLANET...

MY, BUT THIS IS A PLEASANT LITTLE WORLD, YOUR HIGHNESS.

HOW FORTUNATE THAT WE SHOULD BE THE FIRST TO COME ACROSS SUCH A SUITABLE LOCATION.

LET'S JUST HOPE IT IS SUITABLE. EVER SINCE THE EMPIRE DESTROYED OUR OUTPOST ON HOTH ✱ THE REBELLION'S BEEN SEARCHING FOR A NEW PERMANENT BASE.

AND WE NEED IT DESPERATELY!

✱ IN STAR-WARS 40-41.

47

THIS PLANET DOES LOOK PROMISING, THOUGH. IT HAS LOTS OF SHELTER FOR CONCEALMENT, LOTS OF PLANT LIFE FOR PROVISIONS, AND LOTS OF--

GUNDARKS!

NO, I DON'T SEE GUNDARKS LISTED HERE...

NOT HERE, HIGHNESS-- *THERE!* ATTACKING! AND ONCE THOSE CREATURES' TONGUES LATCH ON TO SOMETHING, THEY NEVER LET GO!

THEN STAND BACK! I'LL--

--NO, I *WON'T,* THEIR HIDES ARE TOO THICK!

THREEPIO! HURRY! CLIMB ON TOP OF ONE OF THOSE PLANTS AND START YELLING LIKE CRAZY!

I BEG YOUR PARDON?!

DO IT!

OH, VERY WELL, IF YOU INSIST!

BUT THIS IS MOST UNDIGNIFIED!

YOO-HOO! GUNDARKS! OVER HERE!

IT'S WORKING! THEY'RE HEADED STRAIGHT AT ME!

OH, DEAR.

BUT, AS RASPING TONGUES LASH OUT--

--A HAND BLASTER WHINES--

--AND A SURPRISED AND GRATEFUL DROID DROPS SUDDENLY FROM TARGET ZERO!

SLASH

UNLESS THOSE MONSTERS DECIDE TO HAVE EACH OTHER FOR LUNCH, STRAIGHTENING OUT THAT TANGLE SHOULD KEEP THEM BUSY FOR QUITE AWHILE!

MIGHT I SUGGEST, PRINCESS, THAT WE EXCULDE THIS PLANET FROM THE LIST OF POTENTIAL BASES?

THREEPIO, YOUR PERCEPTION OF THE OBVIOUS IS TRULY AMAZING.

WHY, THANK YOU.

AND SOON, AS THE SMALL PROBE SHIP BREAKS FROM PLANETARY GRAVITY...

YOUR HIGHNESS, THERE SEEMS TO BE A MESSAGE COMING IN ON THE EMERGENCY FREQUENCY. WE'RE TO RETURN TO THE FLEET AT ONCE!

ALL RIGHT THREEPIO, LET'S HEAD HOME--AND JUST HOPE THE OTHERS HAVE BEEN LUCKIER THAN WE HAVE.

BUT HALF-A-PARSEC AWAY, ONE OF THOSE "OTHERS"--REBEL COMMANDER LUKE SKYWALKER--IS HAVING LUCK OF A DIFFERENT SORT...

I KNOW, ARTOO.

THIS OVERGROWN MUDBALL SMELLS WORSE THAN A WET BANTHA! BUT IT JUST MAY BE REPULSIVE ENOUGH TO HAVE ESCAPED IMPERIAL ATTENTION. AND THAT'S EXACTLY WHAT WE NEED FOR A BASE.

THERE'S ONLY ONE HITCH.

"ON THAT LAST FLY-BY, OUR SCANNERS DETECTED SOMETHING METALLIC UNDER THE SURFACE COATING. PROBABLY JUST SOME SPACE DEBRIS--

"--BUT WE STILL NEED TO CHECK IT OUT."

HMM, ACCORDING TO THE SCANNER READINGS, THIS IS IT. DOESN'T LOOK LIKE MUCH.

BUT I GUESS I'D BETTER SCRAPE SOME OF THIS MUCK OFF AND--

--UH-OH. THAT'S NO DEBRIS --IT'S A COMMUNICATIONS BEACON! AND IT'S STILL FUNCTIONING!

I'VE GOT A BAD FEELING ABOUT THIS...

50

FAKOOM

WH-WHAT...OH GREAT! TALK ABOUT GOING FROM BAD TO WORSE!

"THAT'S A SCOUT WALKER, CUTTING ME OFF FROM MY SHIP! THE EMPIRE MUST BE USING THIS PLANETOID AS A MONITOR STATION, WITH ITS MAIN HEADQUARTERS UNDERGROUND TO AVOID SENSOR SCANS! I'VE GOT TO--"

BUT SUDDENLY, FROM ANOTHER DIRECTION...

FRRATCH

AT-AT'S! FULL-SIZED WALKERS! THAT SCOUT MUST HAVE ALERTED THE MAIN BASE-- AND NOW THEY'RE COMING AFTER ME IN FORCE!

ARTOO! ACTIVATE THE X-WING'S SHIELDS! I'LL BE RIGHT THERE!

JUST AS SOON AS I FIGURE OUT HOW!

WHILE WITHIN THE LEAD AT-AT...

SCOUT WALKER THIS IS MAJOR KUHRU. LORD VADER HAS EXPRESSED A DESIRE TO HAVE A LIVE SUBJECT FOR INTERROGATION.

THEREFORE, YOU ARE TO TO IGNORE THE REBEL --

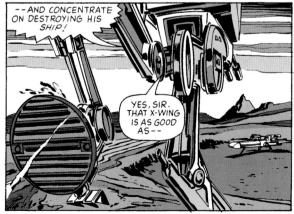

--AND CONCENTRATE ON DESTROYING HIS SHIP!

YES, SIR. THAT X-WING IS AS GOOD AS--

--AH, BETTER AMEND THAT, SIR. THERE COULD BE A SLIGHT DELAY.

IT SEEMS THAT THE FIGHTER'S DEFENSE SHIELDS HAVE BEEN ACTIVATED!

BUT EVEN ENERGY PLATING CAN'T HOLD UP FOREVER! IT'S JUST A MATTER OF--

WHUMP

--HUH?! SOMEONE'S USING PROTON GRENADES ON THE COMMUNICATIONS BEACON!

PTOOM

THAT TRANSMITTER IS VITAL TO OUR OPERATIONS, TROOPER! CANCEL PREVIOUS ORDER--AND PROTECT THAT BEACON AT ALL COSTS!

YES, SIR!

BUT THEN, FROM THE THICK SLIME BENEATH THE SCURRYING WALKER, A FIGURE RISES...

...A FIGURE WHO WIELDS AN ANCIENT WEAPON--

--CALLED A LIGHTSABER--

--WITH A DECIDEDLY DEADLY EFFECT!

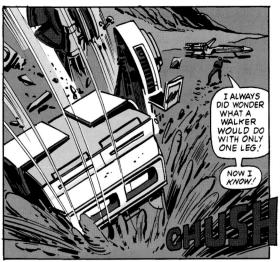

I ALWAYS DID WONDER WHAT A WALKER WOULD DO WITH ONLY ONE LEG!

NOW I KNOW!

CHUSH

BRRT DA-DEET

WE GOT A MESSAGE FROM GENERAL RIEEKAN CALLING US BACK TO THE FLEET?

THEN FIRE UP THE CONVERTERS AND HANG ON, ARTOO, 'CAUSE THAT'S ONE ORDER--

--I'M GOING TO BREAK ALL RECORDS CARRYING OUT!

I DON'T THINK LORD VADER IS GOING TO *LIKE* THIS, SIR.

CORPORAL, IF YOU VALUE WHAT'S LEFT OF YOUR CAREER, JUST...

...DRIVE.

MEANWHILE, AT THE THIRD SET OF GENERAL RIEEKAN'S *COORDINATES*, THE MILLENIUM FALCON--*PILOTED BY LANDO CALRISSIAN AND HIS WOOKIE FIRST MATE, CHEWBACCA*-- IS HAVING PROBLEMS OF ITS OWN...

GRROAK

WHAT DO YOU MEAN, "POUR ON THE SPEED," CHEWIE? I'M PUSHIN' THIS BUCKET O' BOLTS AS FAST AS I CAN!

I KNOW THAT GUNRUNNER WE'RE AFTER CAN TELL US WHERE BOBA FETT TOOK HAN *--AND I WANT SOLO BACK ALIVE JUST AS MUCH AS YOU!

* CAPTURED IN ISSUE #43--Louise

53

THAT'S WHY I'M FIRIN' OUR REMOTE LASERS *AROUND* SHEM-LERN'S SHIP, AND NOT *AT* IT!

I JUST HOPE THE SLUG APPRECIATES IT!

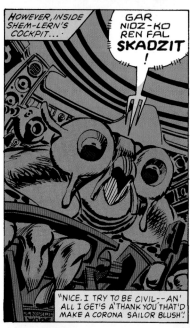

HOWEVER, INSIDE SHEM-LERN'S COCKPIT...

GAR NIDZ-KO REN FAL **SKADZIT**!

"NICE. I TRY TO BE CIVIL--AN' ALL I GET'S A 'THANK YOU' THAT'D MAKE A CORONA SAILOR BLUSH".

BETTER HIT THE WIDE DISPERSE BLASTERS, CHEWIE! IF HE GETS INTO THOSE ASTEROIDS, WE'LL LOSE HIM!

VRROWK

YEAH, I KNOW HAN'S TAKEN THE FALCON THROUGH ASTEROID BELTS BEFORE. BUT AS MUCH AS I HATE TO ADMIT IT--

WRF!

--I'M NOT *QUITE* THE PILOT HAN *WAS.*

SORRY-- "*IS.*"

BUT WE STILL NEED TO--WAIT A MINUTE! MESSAGE COMIN' IN OVER THE EMERGENCY BAND!

CALRISSIAN, THIS IS GENERAL RIEEKAN. YOUR SEARCH MISSION IS TO BE TERMINATED IMMEDIATELY!

WE'VE UNCOVERED A THREAT TO THE REBELLION THAT COULD COST *MILLIONS* OF LIVES! AND YOU BOTH ARE TO REJOIN THE FLEET AT ONCE!

I GUESS WE DON'T HAVE ANY ALTERNATIVE, CHEWIE-- WE'LL HAVE TO PICK UP SHEM-LERN'S TRAIL LATER. RESET COURSE FOR--

BLAST!

--HEY! WHAT'RE YOU DOIN'?! LEAVE THOSE CONTROLS ALONE!

SNNRARR!

UH... PLEASE.

C'MON, CHEWIE, WE *HAVE* TO TURN BACK!

IT'S WHAT HAN WOULD'VE WANTED!

VRARK

OKAY, MAYBE IT ISN'T!

BUT OUR LITTLE "DETOUR"--

--HAS GIVEN SHEM-LERN TIME TO ESCAPE INTO THE ASTEROID FIELD!

I'M SORRY, CHEWBACCA. REALLY.

ONCE MORE IN CONTROL, THE *MILLENNIUM FALCON* TURNS AND ACCELERATES--

--LEAVING BEHIND THE MOURNFUL WAIL OF A WOOKIEE DENIED.

AND SOMETIME LATER, IN A BRIEFING ROOM ABOARD THE MAIN REBEL CRUISER...

THAT'S CORRECT, PRINCESS --

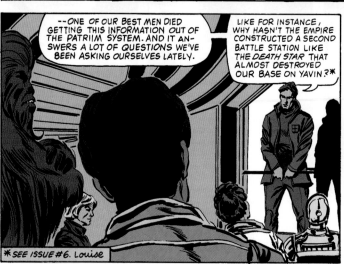

--ONE OF OUR BEST MEN DIED GETTING THIS INFORMATION OUT OF THE PATRIIM SYSTEM. AND IT ANSWERS A LOT OF QUESTIONS WE'VE BEEN ASKING OURSELVES LATELY.

LIKE FOR INSTANCE, WHY HASN'T THE EMPIRE CONSTRUCTED A SECOND BATTLE STATION LIKE THE *DEATH STAR* THAT ALMOST DESTROYED OUR BASE ON YAVIN?*

* SEE ISSUE #6. Louise

NOW WE *KNOW* WHY: THEY'VE BEEN SECRETLY CHANNELING RESOURCES INTO THE CONSTRUCTION OF A WEAPON THAT COULD BE FAR *WORSE!*

WORSE THAN A DEATH STAR?

I'M AFRAID SO, COMMANDER. THEY'VE TAKEN THE DEATH STAR'S MAIN OFFENSIVE BATTERY, THE IONIC CANNON --

--AND HAVE BUILT AROUND IT A SET OF ENGINES AND DEFENSIVE SHIELD GENERATORS UNMATCHED BY ANYTHING WE'VE EVER ENCOUNTERED!

THIS WEAPON HAS BEEN CHRISTENED "THE TARKIN" AND SHOULD IT EVER BECOME OPERATIONAL--

-- WE MAY AS WELL PLACE OUR OWN HANDS IN THE EMPIRE'S SHACKLES!

GRAND MOFF TARKIN

IN THE BRIEFING ROOM, THERE IS SILENCE.

56

...A STILLNESS MATCHED BY THE VACUUM OF SPACE AS, QUITE SOME DISTANCE AWAY, AN IMPERIAL BATTLEFLEET APPROACHES THE PATRIIM SYSTEM...

THAT FLEET IS LED BY THE GIGANTIC STAR DESTROYER, EXECUTOR, PERSONAL WARSHIP OF--

--DARTH VADER, LORD OF THE SITH!

MAJOR KUHRU, DO YOU MEAN TO TELL ME THAT YOU HAD A REBEL OFFICER WITHIN YOUR GRASP... AND YOU LET HIM SLIP AWAY?

B-BUT, MY LORD--

--WE WERE TRICKED! AND WE HAD TO PROTECT OUR COMMUNICATIONS BEACON -- IT WAS A MATTER OF PRIORITIES!

SURELY YOU UNDERST--

YOU SEEM DIS-TRAUGHT, MAJOR. PERHAPS A LONG WALK AND SOME FRESH AIR WOULD HELP CLEAR YOUR MIND.

A WALK? B-BUT, MY LORD, I DON'T SEE WHAT--

MAJOR!

≷GHLK≷

YES...WALK...

...FRESH...

...WALK...

...AIR...

...YES...

...AIR...

...MMM...

...YES...

...WALK...

...NICE...

LORD VADER! OUR INSTRUMENTS IN-DICATE THAT AN EXTERIOR AIR-LOCK HAS JUST OPENED AND CLOSED -- OF ITS OWN VOLITION!

HOW CURIOUS. A FAULTY MECHANISM, NO DOUBT.

OH. Y-YES, SIR.

OF COURSE.

57

WHILE ABOARD THE REBEL CRUISER, A HASTILY-CALLED STRATEGY MEETING DRAWS TO A CLOSE...

SO THAT'S IT. THE PROBLEM IS SIMPLE--THE SOLUTION ISN'T! SINCE THE "TARKIN" WAS BUILT WITHOUT THE SINGLE FLAW THAT ALLOWED US TO STOP THE DEATH STAR, A DIRECT ATTACK WOULD BE SUICIDE!

OUR ONLY CHANCE FOR SUCCESS IS TO GET A SMALL GROUP OF COMMANDOS INSIDE THE "TARKIN"--

--AND DESTROY IT FROM WITHIN!

UH-HUH. I THINK I UNDERSTAND WHY YOU CALLED US BACK NOW. WHAT BETTER COMMAN-DOS THAN THE ONLY REBELS TO HAVE BEEN ABOARD THE ORIGINAL DEATH STAR-- AND SURVIVED?

THAT'S RIGHT, COMMANDER. YOU, PRINCESS LEIA, CHEW-BACCA AND YOUR DROIDS WILL SERVE AS THE ASSAULT SQUAD. THAT IS, IF YOU "VOLUNTEER".

I GUESS WE DO.

WE DO?! OH WHY DID I EVER LEAVE THE DIPLO-MATIC SERVICE?

ALL THIS ADVENTURE!

AND, AS THE ASSEMBLY DISMISSES...

HEY! WHAT ABOUT ME? WHAT AM I SUPPOSED TO DO?

WHY DON'T YOU TRY LOOKING OUT FOR YOURSELF, LANDO? YOU SEEM TO DO IT SO WELL!

HUH!?!

EASY, CALRISSIAN. YOU MAY HAVE HAD NO CHOICE WHEN YOU TURNED SOLO OVER TO THE EMPIRE--

--BUT HAN HAD A LOT OF FRIENDS HERE.

AND I'M AFRAID FRIENDS DON'T FORGET EASILY!

MAYBE NOT, GENERAL.

BUT NEITHER DO I!

PREPARATIONS ARE MADE AND, AFTER A TENSE FLIGHT, THE MILLENNIUM FALCON BREAKS FROM HYPERSPACE NEAR THE OUTER RIM OF THE PATRIIM PLANETARY SYSTEM--

--WHERE SOON, LISTED AS A "SPICE FREIGHTER IN NEED OF REPAIRS", IT DOCKS ON THE SMALL GARRISON PLANET OF HOCKALEG--

-- A SPACEPORT FROM WHICH, ACCORDING TO THE REBELS' CAPTURED INFORMATION, CONSTRUCTION CREWS ARE SHUTTLED IN DAILY TO THE "TARKIN'S" ORBITING DRYDOCK.

AND THERE, THE VENTURE BEGINS!

MY, WHAT AN UNSAVORY PLACE!

I NOTICED.

AND I'VE NOTICED SOMETHING ELSE-- ALL OF THE LOCALS ARE WEARING STAN-DARDIZED UNIFORMS!

IF WE'RE GOING TO INFILTRATE THE "TARKIN'S" WORK FORCE, IT LOOKS LIKE WE'LL BE NEEDING SOME NEW OUTFITS!

AND THE QUICKEST WAY TO DO THAT, PRINCESS, IS FOR YOU TO USE YOUR FEMININE WILES.

MY WHAT?!?

LUKE EXPLAINS--CARE-FULLY--AND SOON, AT THE MOUTH OF A SIDE PATH ALLEYWAY...

SO I SAID TO THIS GUY IN THE CANTINA--

--"EITHER GET YOUR WING OUTTA MY FACE, OR I'LL"--

HI THERE, FLY-BOY. NEW IN TOWN?

--HUH?

WELL, WELL, WELL! MY NAME'S *BRUNOK*, CUTIE, AN' I GOT A FEW MINUTES 'FORE I HAFTA REPORT TO THE SHUTTLE PAD--

--SO, WHATSAY WE GO SOMEPLACE, AND GET REAL *TIRED* REAL FAST?

UH--MAYBE THIS WASN'T SUCH A GOOD IDEA AFTER AL--

AW, C'MON SWEETIE, GIVE US A KISS.

LET--

--ME--

--GO!

WOK

HEY-- W-WHAT'S GOIN' ON? I'M GETTIN' OUTTA HE--

CHEWIE!

≥--RRRRKK!≤

NOW HURRY AND GET THOSE UNIFORMS OFF! I'LL KEEP WATCH.

AND, MOMENTS LATER...

GRRWK

DON'T WORRY CHEWIE, NOBODY EXPECTS A WOOKIEE TO WEAR A UNIFORM.

DO THEY?

I DON'T KNOW. BUT I GUESS WE'LL FIND OUT WHEN WE REACH--

"--THE SHUTTLE LAUNCH!"

STEP LIVELY, THERE. WE HAVEN'T GOT ALL-- HOLD IT!

THERE'S NOTHING ON THIS MANIFEST ABOUT TWO MORE WORKERS--LET ALONE TWO DROIDS AND A WOOKIEE!

ARE YOU CERTAIN, OFFICER? COULDN'T YOU CHECK AGAIN? THERE MAY HAVE BEEN A MISTAKE.

THE EMPIRE DOESN'T MAKE MISTAKES, GRUBBER!

PLEASE?

OH, VERY WELL, IF IT WILL-- JUST A MOMENT. THERE IS ANOTHER LISTING HERE-- FOR TWO WORKERS, TWO DROIDS, AND A WOOKIEE! BUT WHY DIDN'T I--?

≡AHEM≡ ALL RIGHT. PASS.

THANK YOU.

VRRRP DIT

I KNOW, ARTOO. MASTER LUKE HAS LEARNED TO USE THE FORCE RATHER WELL, HASN'T HE?

WITH A ROAR OF ROCKETS AND THE WHISPER OF DISPLACED AIR, THE IMPERIAL SHUTTLE SOARS SKYWARD, MOVING OUT TO A PREDETERMINED ORBIT, TO THE DRYDOCK CONSTRUCTION SITE OF--

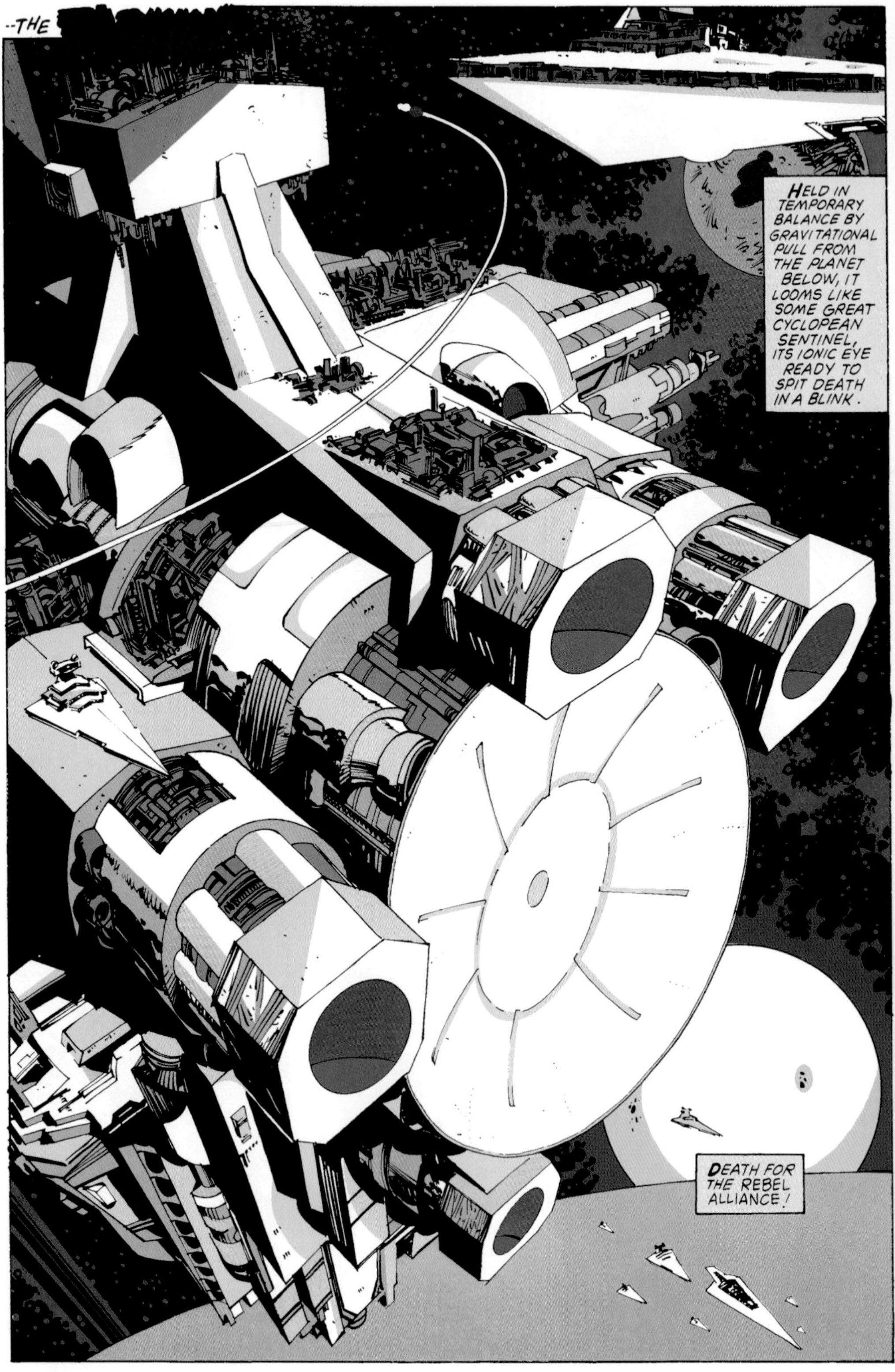
--THE
HELD IN TEMPORARY BALANCE BY GRAVITATIONAL PULL FROM THE PLANET BELOW, IT LOOMS LIKE SOME GREAT CYCLOPEAN SENTINEL, ITS IONIC EYE READY TO SPIT DEATH IN A BLINK.
DEATH FOR THE REBEL ALLIANCE!

AND SOON, AS A RECENTLY-DISPATCHED SHUTTLECRAFT APPROACHES, SEVERAL MEMBERS OF THAT SELF-SAME ALLIANCE BECOME AWARE OF THE TARKIN'S AWESOME SIZE--AS WELL AS ITS UNSETTLING RE-SEMBLANCE TO THE DE-SERVEDLY INFAMOUS DEATH STAR.

FOR LEIA ORGANA, IT SERVES AS A CHILL REMINDER OF THE DESTRUCTION OF HER HOME PLANET, ALDERAAN--ALONG WITH THAT PLANET'S ENTIRE POPULATION!

FOR LUKE SKYWALKER, IT STIRS VISIONS OF THE CORPOREAL DISSOLUTION OF HIS FRIEND AND MENTOR, OBI-WAN KENOBI.

WHILE FOR OTHERS, THE IMMENSE BATTLE STATION ENGENDERS SUCH DIVERSE EMOTIONS AS THE THRILL OF IMMINENT COMBAT--

--AND THE FEAR OF EVENTUAL PARTS DISPERSAL.

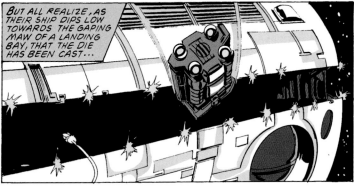

BUT ALL REALIZE, AS THEIR SHIP DIPS LOW TOWARDS THE GAPING MAW OF A LANDING BAY, THAT THE DIE HAS BEEN CAST...

...AND THERE'S NO TURNING BACK NOW!

DOCKING COMPLETE. BEGIN REPLACEMENT SHIFT DISEMBARKING PROCEDURE.

ALL RIGHT, MOVE ALONG. WE'RE BEHIND SCHEDULE, AND YOU'RE ALL TO REPORT TO YOUR ASSIGNED DUTY POSTS AT ONCE!

WHILE ABOVE...

LORD VADER, I'M NOT SURE THAT I HEARD YOU CORRECTLY. DID YOU SAY--

--TO REMOVE ALL SECURITY PERSONNEL FROM THE AREA OF THE MAIN POWER REACTORS?

I DID.

JUST ACT LIKE YOU KNOW WHAT YOU'RE DOING--NO ONE WILL SUSPECT A THING!

FOR I SENSE A PRESENCE, A PRESENCE I'VE SCOURED THE GALAXY TO FIND...

A PRESENCE THAT NOW COMES TO *ME!*

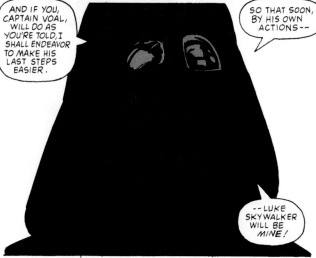

AND IF YOU, CAPTAIN VOAL, WILL DO AS YOU'RE TOLD, I SHALL ENDEAVOR TO MAKE HIS LAST STEPS EASIER.

SO THAT SOON, BY HIS OWN ACTIONS--

--LUKE SKYWALKER WILL BE *MINE!*

THE CAPTAIN COMPLIES, SEEING THAT HIS MASTER'S ORDERS ARE CARRIED OUT TO THE LETTER. AFTER WHICH HE MOVES TO A LITTLE-USED SERVICE LIFT--

--AND DROPS A DOZEN LEVELS--

--TO A MAINTENANCE AREA POPULATED ONLY BY DROIDS, BY SPARE COMPONENTS --

--AND BY DESPERATE MEN WISHING TO AVOID UNDUE NOTICE!

GOOD. WE'RE ALL HERE. HAVE A SEAT, CAPTAIN VOAL.

I WAS JUST RESTATING OUR POSITION: WE HAVE OF LATE SEEN TOO MANY OF OUR FELLOW OFFICERS FALL TO VADER'S SORCEROUS WAYS --

-- IT APPEARS THAT ANY HUMAN MISTAKE MAY WELL LEAD TO AN INHUMAN END AT THE SITH LORD'S HAND.!

THEREFORE, A PLAN HAS BEEN FORMULATED AND APPROVED, AND WE ARE ALL IN AGREE-MENT...

...THAT BEFORE THIS DAY IS OVER--

-- DARTH VADER MUST DIE!

NEXT ISSUE: TO TAKE THE TARKIN!

65

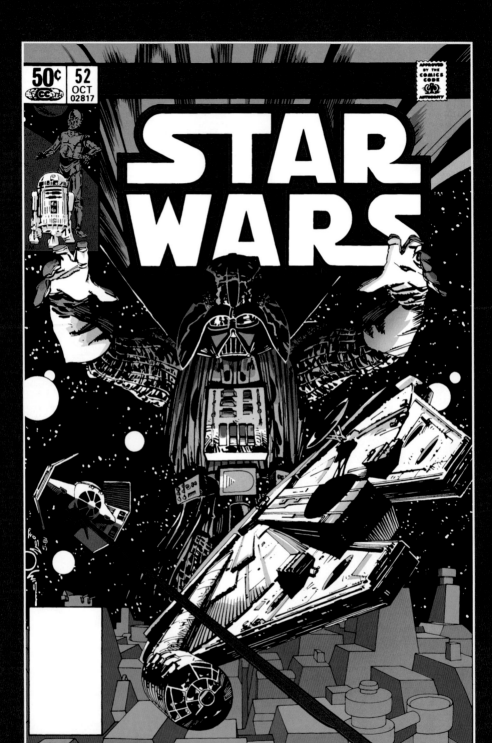

50¢ 52 OCT 02817

STAR WARS

Long ago in a galaxy far, far away. . .there exists a state of cosmic *civil war*. A brave alliance of *underground freedom fighters* has challenged the tyranny and oppression of the awesome *Galactic Empire*. This is their story!

LucasFilm PRESENTS: STAR WARS

THE GREATEST SPACE FANTASY OF ALL!

DAVID MICHELINIE WRITER	WALTER SIMONSON PENCILER	TOM PALMER INKER	JOHN MORELLI LETTERER	DON WARFIELD COLORIST	LOUISE JONES EDITOR	JIM SHOOTER THE FORCE

WITNESS THE BUILDING OF A WORLD.

THIS, THEN, IS THE TARKIN--

-- DIRECT DESCENDANT OF THE DEATH STAR, THE EMPIRE'S MOST FRIGHTFUL WEAPON.

HOVERING IN ITS DRYDOCK ORBIT ABOVE THE GARRISON PLANET CALLED HOCKALEG, IT NEARS COMPLETION. AND WHEN FULLY FUNCTIONAL--

-- IT COULD EASILY SPELL DOOM FOR THE REBEL ALLIANCE!

THUS, THE REBELLION HAS SENT FIVE OF ITS BEST-- DISGUISED AS PART OF A REPLACEMENT WORK CREW-- TO TRY TO DESTROY THE TARKIN FROM WITHIN.

BUT NOW, HAVING WITNESSED THE AWESOME SIZE AND STRENGTH OF THIS BATTLE STATION FIRST HAND, THE REBELS CAN'T HELP BUT WONDER IF THEY WERE MORE FOOLHARDY THAN FEARLESS IN ACCEPTING THEIR MISSION --

OUTSIDE, ESCORTING DESTROYERS LOOK LIK
INSECTS COMPARED TO THEIR CHARGE,
THEIR NORMALLY FORMIDABLE FIREPOWE,
LIKE STINGS COMPARED TO THE TARKIN'S
HUGE PLANET-SHATTERING IONIC CANNON

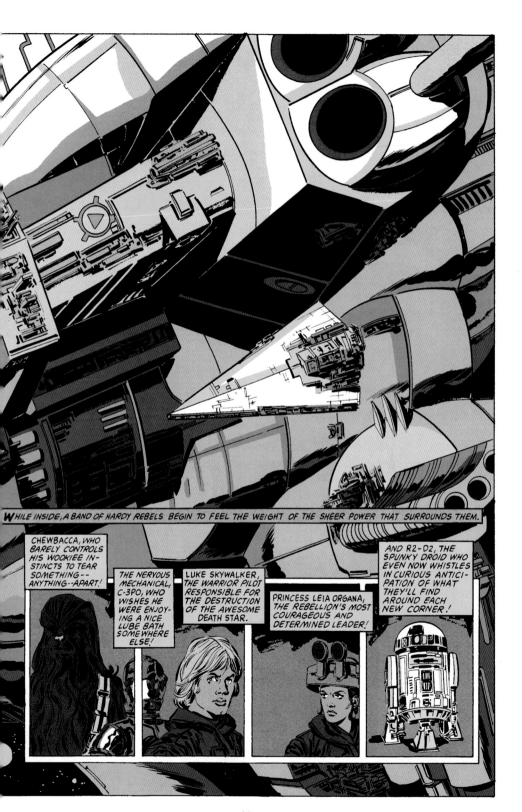

WHILE INSIDE, A BAND OF HARDY REBELS BEGIN TO FEEL THE WEIGHT OF THE SHEER POWER THAT SURROUNDS THEM.

CHEWBACCA, WHO BARELY CONTROLS HIS WOOKIEE INSTINCTS TO TEAR SOMETHING-- ANYTHING--APART!

THE NERVOUS MECHANICAL, C-3PO, WHO WISHES HE WERE ENJOYING A NICE LUBE BATH SOMEWHERE ELSE!

LUKE SKYWALKER, THE WARRIOR PILOT RESPONSIBLE FOR THE DESTRUCTION OF THE AWESOME DEATH STAR.

PRINCESS LEIA ORGANA, THE REBELLION'S MOST COURAGEOUS AND DETERMINED LEADER!

AND R2-D2, THE SPUNKY DROID WHO EVEN NOW WHISTLES IN CURIOUS ANTICIPATION OF WHAT THEY'LL FIND AROUND EACH NEW CORNER!

OR IN THIS CASE, WHAT WILL FIND THEM!

OH, UH, IMPERIAL STORMTROOPERS! W-WHAT A NICE SURPRISE!

HALT!

ACCESS TO THIS SECTION IS LIMITED.

I'LL HAVE TO SEE YOUR PAPERS.

WELL, UM, I--I SEEM TO HAVE LEFT THEM IN MY OTHER FLIGHT SUIT! BUT, IF YOU'LL JUST TRUST US THIS TIME--

HOLD IT! I'M PICKING UP AN ENERGY READING. LOOKS LIKE A PROTON GRENADE!

I THINK YOU'D BETTER RAISE YOUR HANDS, GRUBBER!

NOW!

WAIT A MINUTE!

I THINK I HAVE OUR PAPERS! YES--

--HERE THEY ARE!

LEIA--!

FRADATCH

BLAST! I'D HOPED TO GET FARTHER WITHOUT A SCENE. BUT NOW... WELL, YOU ALL KNOW YOUR JOBS, SO TAKE OFF! WE'LL MEET AT THE ESCAPE PODS WHEN WE'RE DONE!

IF WE'RE STILL ALIVE!

LUKE, SOMETIMES YOU ALMOST MAKE ME MISS HAN SOLO'S BONEHEADED OPTIMISM!

THE REBELS DISPERSE. AND MOMENTS LATER, ON THE TARKIN'S BRIDGE, A REPORT REACHES THAT BATTLE STATION'S COMMANDER-IN-CHIEF--

--DARTH VADER, LORD OF THE SITH!

THAT'S CORRECT, MY LORD--

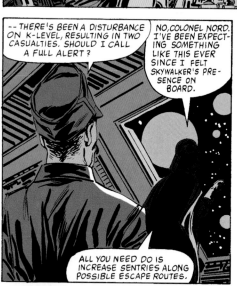

--THERE'S BEEN A DISTURBANCE ON K-LEVEL, RESULTING IN TWO CASUALTIES. SHOULD I CALL A FULL ALERT?

NO, COLONEL NORD. I'VE BEEN EXPECTING SOMETHING LIKE THIS EVER SINCE I FELT SKYWALKER'S PRESENCE ON BOARD.

ALL YOU NEED DO IS INCREASE SENTRIES ALONG POSSIBLE ESCAPE ROUTES.

AND YOUR EARLIER DIRECTIVE, SIR, TO HAVE ALL PERSONNEL REMOVED FROM THE VICINITY OF THE MAIN POWER REACTOR-- IS THAT STILL IN EFFECT?

INDEED, COLONEL. I SHALL SEE TO THE SECURITY OF THAT SECTOR--

--PERSONALLY!

A NEEDLELIKE CHILL LACES THROUGH COLONEL NORD'S CHEST AS HE TURNS FROM THE BRIDGE... AN ICY GRASP THAT TIGHTENS AS A LIFT CARRIES HIM MULTIPLE LEVELS DOWNWARD--

--TO A LITTLE-USED MAINTENANCE AREA, WHERE A BAND OF DESPERATE IMPERIAL OFFICERS NERVOUSLY WAIT...

GENERAL BIEL, I THINK THE TIME HAS COME. WE MUST ACT SOON!

COLONEL, I COULDN'T AGREE WITH YOU MORE!

PERHAPS, AND PERHAPS NOT. I'M AFRAID WE DON'T HAVE THE LUXURY OF CHOICE. WITH VADER'S THOUGHTS FOCUSED ON HIS OBSESSION WITH THAT REBEL WARRIOR--

--THIS COULD BE OUR ONLY CHANCE!

TOO MANY OF OUR FELLOW OFFICERS HAVE DIED AT THE DARK LORD'S WHIM, ALL FOR MAKING MISTAKES THAT ANYONE *HUMAN* COULD'VE UNDERSTOOD. AND ANY OF US MIGHT BE NEXT--

--UNLESS WE STOP *VADER* FIRST!

YES, GENERAL, BUT ARE WE READY FOR--

WHILE MILES BELOW ON HOCKALEG, AT A SPACEPORT WHERE QUESTIONS ARE MOST FREQUENTLY ANSWERED BY THE JANGLE OF COINS OR THE CRACK OF A BLASTER--

-- THE MILLENNIUM FALCON HAS RESTED SILENTLY EVER SINCE DEPOSITING ITS PASSENGERS, NONE OF WHOM HAD EVER SUSPECTED--

--THAT THERE HAD BEEN A *SIXTH!*

OUCH!

I'VE GOT CRAMPS IN PLACES I DIDN'T EVEN KNOW I HAD MUSCLES! THESE SMUGGLING BINS ARE TIGHT! BUT AT LEAST I'LL BE ABLE TO SHOW THE OTHERS--

--THAT *LANDO CALRISSIAN* ISN'T THE SELF-SERVING GUNDARK THEY THINK HE IS!

THEY LEFT ME OUT OF THIS MISSION BECAUSE THEY THOUGHT I COULDN'T BE TRUSTED.

BUT STOWING AWAY SO THAT I COULD BE THEIR ACE-IN-THE-HOLE SHOULD PROVE THAT-- HUH? VOICES! FROM OUTSIDE!

THIS SHIP MATCHES THE DESCRIPTION OF THE REBEL RUNNER, MEN. WE'D BETTER CHECK IT OUT!

UH-OH!

WHILE ON THE TARKIN, IN A POWER TRENCH THAT HOUSES THE EXTERIOR TRACTOR BEAM GENERATOR...

VADOOT BRRT-A-DEET DA--

YEAH, BUT WHY GUARD THIS TRENCH?

I DUNNO-- SOMETIMES I THINK NORDIE'S GOT HIS HEAD IN A BLACK HO--

HEY, WHAT'S THAT DROID DOIN' IN HERE?

BEATS ME. I'LL GET RID OF 'IM.

--BLOOP?

GO ON, SHORTY, MOVE IT-- EH? AND JUST WHO ARE YOU?

WHY, I'M C-3PO, SIR. THIS R2 UNIT IS WITH ME. WE'VE BEEN INSTRUCTED TO CARRY OUT REPAIRS ON THE TRACTOR BEAM GENERATOR.

THAT GENERATOR IS NEW-- IT DOESN'T NEED REPAIRS!

OH, BUT I ASSURE YOU, IT DOES! YOU'LL BE MAKING A GRAVE MISTAKE IF YOU DON'T--

THE ONLY GRAVE YOU GOTTA WORRY ABOUT IS THE SCRAPHEAP, 'BOT! NOW GET OUTTA HERE BEFORE I--

CHEWIE--NO!

73

WRRARK!

Ξ HHHNGK? Ξ

WHAT THE--? IT'S A WOOKIEE! ATTACKING BERL!

BLAST 'IM!

THAT DID IT, YOU SCRUFFY LUMP! NOW WE'LL NEVER GET CLOSE ENOUGH TO THAT GENER- ATOR--

"--TO--

YAHAAAA!

"--DESTROY IT...?"

PARAPOOM

WELL, I SUPPOSE YOUR METHODS DID WORK-- THOUGH THEY WERE CERTAINLY LACKING IN FINESSE!

FRHF

SILENCE. LEIA ORGANA HAS KNOWN IT WELL, IN THE VASTNESS OF SPACE.

BUT HERE, IN THE ESCAPE POD BAY OF A BRAND NEW WORLD, THE SILENCE SEEMS UNNATURAL. ALMOST AS THOUGH IT HAD BEEN--

--PLANNED! HOLD IT RIGHT THERE!

GUARDS! MUST HAVE BEEN HIDING!

DROP THAT BLASTER!

WELL, I GUESS I SHOULD...

... BUT YOU NEVER SAID NOT TO GRAB YOURS!

HUH?!

SHE MOVES SWIFTLY, PULLING THE BLASTERS FORWARD AS THE GUARDS' TRIGGER FINGERS TIGHTEN--

-- MUCH TO THE PAINFUL SURPRISE OF THEIR OPPOSITE FELLOWS!

FRAM

FRATOW

THE OTHER TWO ARE STILL SHAKEN, BUT THEY'RE ALREADY TRYING TO TARGET ME!

GOT TO GET THEM--

FDAM FKAM FRAM

--FIRST!

SOUNDS LIKE REINFORCEMENTS COMING DOWN THE FAR CORRIDOR! AND THAT MEANS WE CAN SCRATCH OUR PRIMARY ESCAPE ROUTE!

EMERGENCY

LUKE, I JUST HOPE YOUR LUCK'S BETTER THAN MINE!

BUT LUKE SKYWALKER IS CURRENTLY MORE CONCERNED WITH CIRCUMSTANCE THAN WITH FORTUNE. FOR THE CORRIDORS HE WALKS ARE STRANGELY DESERTED--

--AND HE WONDERS WHY HE HASN'T MET WITH ANY OF THE RESISTANCE HE'D EXPECTED.

THE REASON FOR THAT ABSENCE LURKS DOWN THE NEXT PASSAGEWAY, BREATHING HOLLOWLY, AT THE ENTRANCE TO THE MAIN POWER REACTOR!

GOOD. IT IS AS I ANTICIPATED. THE REBELS HAVE CHOSEN *HIM* FOR THIS PART OF THEIR MISSION. AND HE APPROACHES--

--ALONE!

WHILE ON THE BRIDGE...

BLAST! VADER'S FINALLY IN FRONT OF THE AIR-LOCK-- BUT NOW SOMEONE *ELSE* HAS ENTERED THAT SECTOR. I'M SORRY, WHOEVER YOU ARE--

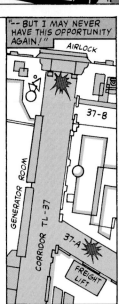

"-- BUT I MAY NEVER HAVE THIS OPPORTUNITY AGAIN!"

AIRLOCK

37-B

GENERATOR ROOM

CORRIDOR TL-37

37-A

FREIGHT LIFT

THE REACTOR ROOM SHOULD BE JUST AROUND--WAIT! SOMETHING...SOME-THING'S THERE! NO-- SOMEONE! THE IMPRESSION'S VAGUE, ALMOST LIKE IT'S BEING HIDDEN...

...BUT IT'S DEFINITELY DANGEROUS!

HE HAS LEARNED MUCH. TO SENSE MY PRESENCE AT THIS DISTANCE, BUT HIS KNOW-LEDGE OF THE FORCE WILL AVAIL HIM LITTLE.

LUKE SKYWALKER WILL JOIN ME, AND THE EMPIRE ...OR HE WILL--

SIMULTANEOUSLY... DIE, YOU SOURCEROUS SLUG--!

DIE!

76

BEHIND VADER, AIRLOCK DOORS SWING OPEN--

SO GREAT ARE THE ERUPTING WINDS THAT THEY LITER-ALLY RIP THE PROTON GRENADE FROM YOUNG SKYWALKER'S GRASP--

--AS THE ATMOSPHERE IN THE CORRIDOR SHRIEKS BLINDLY PAST, TRYING FUTILELY TO FILL THE UNFILLABLE VOID OF SPACE!

--AND SMACK IT AGAINST A NIGHT-DARK HELMET BEFORE PULLING IT IRREVOCABLY INTO THE DEADLY COLD BEYOND...

...ON A ONE-WAY JOURNEY THE STARTLED SITH LORD ALMOST JOINS!

WHILE IN THE CORRIDOR, LUKE SKYWALKER IS SAVED FROM A SIMILAR FATE ONLY BY THE STRENGTH OF HIS BIONIC HAND--

HE RELIES ON THAT HAND NOW, PULLING HIMSELF INTO AN OPEN FREIGHT LIFT--

--BRACING HIM-SELF THERE AS THE DOORS SLIDE SMOOTHLY SHUT, BRINGING SALVATION.

WHILE AT THE AIRLOCK, DARTH VADER ALSO BRACES, EASING HIS INNER RAGE, AND CALLING ON THE DARK SIDE OF THE FORCE TO DO--

--THE ONE THAT REPLACES THE NA-TURAL APPENDAGE LOST ON CLOUD CITY.

-- THE IMPOSSIBLE! SLOWLY RELEASING HIS TENUOUS HANDHOLDS, THE FALLEN JEDI... STANDS!

HE SWAYS, SLIGHTLY.

AND THEN, ARCHING FORWARD, HE BEGINS TO WALK AGAINST THE UNOPPOSABLE WINDS...

... FOOT

... BY INCONCEIVABLE FOOT...

... UNTIL AT LAST HE REACHES THE SANCTUARY OF THE ACCESS CORRIDOR... AND ACTIVATES THE MANUAL CONTROLS TO SEAL THE LETHAL DOORWAY SHUT!

IN THE LONG SILENCE THAT FOLLOWS, HE SPEAKS --

I SHALL DEAL WITH YOU LATER, COLONEL NORD!

--AS ON THE BRIDGE--

--A DEAD MAN GULPS!

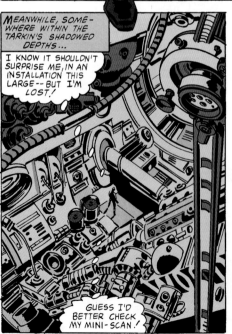

MEANWHILE, SOMEWHERE WITHIN THE TARKIN'S SHADOWED DEPTHS...

I KNOW IT SHOULDN'T SURPRISE ME, IN AN INSTALLATION THIS LARGE--BUT I'M LOST!

GUESS I'D BETTER CHECK MY MINI-SCAN!

THE SMALL, HANDHELD DEVICE FLASHES INFORMATION ACROSS ITS TINY SCREEN, TECHNICAL DATA WON BY A VALIANT REBEL WARRIOR, AT THE COST OF HIS LIFE.

QUICKLY, PRINCESS LEIA PINPOINTS HER LOCATION...

... AND SHUDDERS INVOLUNTARILY!

THIS MACHINERY! IT'S THE ACTIVATING MECHANISM FOR THE IONIC CANNON! THE SAME WEAPON USED TO DESTROY--

-- MY HOME WORLD!

THE SHUDDER PASSES -- MOSTLY -- AND SOON...

THAT'S OUR COMLINK, CHEWBACCA. PERHAPS YOU'D BEST HAND IT TO ME -- MY DICTION IS A BIT CLEARER THAN YOURS.

PIP PIP

YES, PRINCESS, WE WERE SUCCESSFUL! AND YOU?

I'M AFRAID NOT, THREEPIO.

BUT I DO HAVE AN ALTERNATE PLAN. EVERY-ONE REGROUP AT THE AFT DOCKING BAY AS SOON AS POSSIBLE.

VERY WELL, YOUR HIGHNESS. WE'LL BE THERE... AH...

... SHORTLY.

AND, ONE UNCONSCIOUS STORM-TROOPER LATER...

QUIET, CHEWIE! YOU WANT TO GET US ALL BLASTED INTO BANTHA FOOD?

I BELIEVE, PRINCESS, THAT HE WAS ASKING WHERE MASTER LUKE WAS.

I WISH I KNEW! I'VE BEEN CALLING HIM ON THE COMLINK EVER SINCE I TALKED WITH YOU.

LUKE, THIS IS LEIA. CAN YOU HEAR ME?

I HEAR YOU! I'VE BEEN HEARING YOU!

79

I'VE JUST BEEN TOO *BUSY* TO ANSWER! I'M PINNED DOWN IN SECTION TH-11--

--WITH HALF THE TARKIN'S GUARD SQUAD COMING AT ME THROUGH TH-10!

HANG ON! WE'LL BE THERE AS SOON AS--

BRR-DEET-DUT

ARTOO-DETOO, JUST *WHERE* ARE YOU GOING?!

PA-DOOP VRT-DRT

WHAT?!

YOU'RE INFORMING THE CENTRAL COMPUTER THAT THERE'S A *FIRE* IN SECTION TH-10?!

WHY, WHATEVER GOOD WILL *THAT* DO?

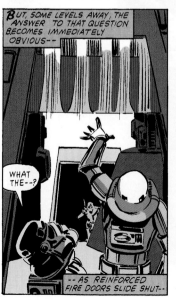

*B*UT, SOME LEVELS AWAY, THE ANSWER TO THAT QUESTION BECOMES *IMMEDIATELY OBVIOUS--*

WHAT THE--?

--AS *REINFORCED FIRE DOORS* SLIDE SHUT--

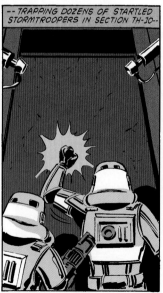

--TRAPPING DOZENS OF STARTLED STORMTROOPERS IN SECTION TH-10--

--AND *IN A SUDDEN DOWNPOUR OF FLAME-RETARDANT FOAM!*

≥GLPH!≤

WHILE AT THAT MOMENT, ON HOCKALEG...

GOOD MORNING, GENTLEMEN!

AND WHAT CAN I DO FOR THE EMPIRE'S FINEST TODAY?

YOU CAN STAND ASIDE, PILOT, AND PREPARE TO BE SEARCHED! YOUR SHIP RESEMBLES ONE WE'RE LOOKING FOR!

HEH HEH MOM ALWAYS DID SAY SMUGGLING DIDN'T PAY! OKAY, GENTS, YOU GOT ME--GUESS I'D BETTER TURN OVER MY CONTRABAND.

CONTRABAND?

THAT'S RIGHT. TWO KILOS OF GANNARIAN NARCO-SPICE.

YOU'D BETTER GET IT TO HEADQUARTERS FAST. THAT MUCH "SNIFF" COULD MAKE A MAN RICH FOR LIFE...

...IF YOU KNOW WHAT I MEAN.

I SEE. ACTUALLY--

--YOUR SHIP DOESN'T LOOK AT ALL LIKE THE ONE WE'RE AFTER. SORRY TO HAVE BOTHERED YOU, CITIZEN.

I'D BETTER MOVE!

WHEN THAT NERFER FINDS HE'S HOLDING A BAG OF SLIME YEAST FROM THE FALCON'S PROVISIONS, HE'S GONNA BE MAD!

AND BACK ON THE TARKIN, INFORMATION IS EXCHANGED...

I'M SORRY, LEIA, I COULDN'T HOLD ON TO THE GRENADE LONG ENOUGH TO--

WE CAN TALK ABOUT THAT LATER! RIGHT NOW--

--WE HAVE TO GET PAST THOSE IMPERIALS AND FIND A FUELED TRANSPORT! ANY IDEAS?

WELL, AS A MATTER OF FACT--

LUKE EXPLAINS, SOFTLY. AND SOON, HE CHANGES TO A SOMEWHAT--

-- LOUDER VOICE...

LOOK OUT! REBEL INFILTRATORS HAVE THROWN A THERMO-CHARGE!

PONK

HOLY JAF! THAT THING'S GONNA BLOW! GET OUTTA MY WAY!

I-I'M GETTIN'! I'M GETTIN'!

WONDERFUL! IT WORKED!

FOR NOW! BUT WE'D BETTER BE FAR AWAY WHEN THEY DISCOVER THAT "THERMO-CHARGE"--

--IS JUST TWO COMLINKS TIED TOGETHER!

SECONDS LATER, CONVERTERS FIRE! THRUSTERS ROAR!

AND A COMMANDEERED TRANSPORT ROCKETS INTO THE EBON INFINITY OF SPACE!

WHILE BEHIND...

HEY! THIS "THERMO-CHARGE" IS JUST TWO COMLINKS TIED TOGETHER!

I HATE WHEN THIS HAPPENS TO ME.

AND THE ONLY ONE WHO HATES IT EVEN MORE IS-- DARTH VADER!

DISPATCH T.I.E. FIGHTERS! IMMEDIATLY!

TWO SHOULD SUFFICE.

"THAT TRANSPORT HAS MINIMAL ARMAMENT AND SHIELDING, SO THERE SHOULD BE LITTLE PROBLEM IN CRIPPLING AND RE-TRIEVING THE VEHICLE INTACT."

THEY'RE AFTER US-- AND WE'RE OUTGUNNED!

NOT TO WORRY, PRINCESS! EVEN IN A CARGO-HEAVY TRANSPORT--

-- WE CAN STILL OUTFLY THEM!

WATCH THIS!

UH, I GUESS THE IMPERIAL ACADEMY'S TURNING OUT BETTER PILOTS THESE DAYS!

GROWK!

I KNOW CHEWIE! WE'RE SITTING DUCKS BUT WHAT CAN I--

FRATCHOW

P-BOOM

WHA--?

THE FALCON! BUT HOW?!

LANDO CALRISSIAN, FOLKS, AT YOUR SERVICE! JUST HOLD STEADY AN' I'LL BRING YOU ABOARD!

SO, AN UNEXPECTED PLAYER HAS ENTERED THE GAME. THEN PERHAPS IT IS TIME--

-- FOR THAT GAME TO END! ADMIRAL, HAVE MY PERSONAL FIGHTER PREPARED FOR LAUNCH!

IMMEDIATELY!

YES, MY LORD!

AND, A SURPRISINGLY SHORT TIME LATER, A TOMBSTONE-GREY FIGHTER STREAKS FROM THE TARKIN'S LAUNCH BAY, ITS TARGET--

--THE MILLENNIUM FALCON!

THAT'S VADER HIMSELF! NOW'S OUR CHANCE TO STOP HIM FOR GOOD!

OR MAYBE THE OTHER WAY AROUND! VADER'S SHIP HAS MORE SPEED AND FIREPOWER THAN STANDARD IMPERIAL ISSUE!

OUR BEST BET IS TO STAY OUT OF HIS WAY UNTIL WE CAN BUILD TO LIGHT SPEED!

HOWEVER, EVEN THAT STRATEGY FACES A DUBIOUS FUTURE, AS--

WE'VE BEEN HIT! HEAVY DAMAGE TO THE REAR SHIELDS!

IT'S NO GOOD! EVEN USING THIS DRYDOCK DEBRIS FOR COVER, VADER'S SURE TO GET A CLEAR SHOT AT OUR REACTOR BANK SOON!

MAYBE--AND MAYBE NOT! TAKE US AROUND THAT DRIFTING MACHINERY, LANDO!

THAT SHOULD PUT US OUT OF VADER'S SIGHT AND SENSORS FOR A COUPLE OF SECONDS!

AND THAT'S ALL I NEED TO JETTISON THE FALCON'S WATER SUPPLY!

AS THE OTHER REBELS SHAKE THEIR HEADS IN PUZZLEMENT, GALLONS OF WATER DROP FROM THE FALCON'S STORAGE TANKS--

--INSTANTLY FREEZING AND SWELLING IN THE VACUUM OF SPACE TO FORM A ROCK-HARD WALL OF--

ICE! DIRECTLY IN MY PATH! AND I AM TOO CLOSE, GOING TOO FAST TO AVOID A COLLISION.

WELL DONE, YOUNG SKYWALKER!

PAKRASH

COLONEL NORD! LORD VADER'S SHIP HAS BEEN DISABLED! BUT OUR SENSORS INDICATE THAT HE'S STILL ALIVE!

THEN IT'S UP TO US TO CARRY OUT HIS FINAL ORDERS.

AND IN THE PROCESS, PERHAPS CARRY OUT MY ORIGINAL PLAN!

PRIME THE IONIC CANNON! WE'LL BLOW THOSE REBELS CLEAR OUT OF THE GALAXY!

AND IF A CERTAIN SITH LORD GETS IN THE WAY, WELL... SUCH ARE THE FORTUNES OF WAR!

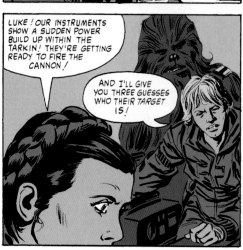

LUKE! OUR INSTRUMENTS SHOW A SUDDEN POWER BUILD UP WITHIN THE TARKIN! THEY'RE GETTING READY TO FIRE THE CANNON!

AND I'LL GIVE YOU THREE GUESSES WHO THEIR TARGET IS!

HELPLESSLY, THE STAR WARRIORS WATCH THEIR SCREENS AS, A TOO-SHORT DISTANCE AWAY, PRIMARY IGNITION IS COMPLETED.

A "FIRE" BUTTON IS PUSHED.

AND, IN AN AWSOME BLAZE OF ENERGY UNLEASHED, THE TARKIN-- THE EMPIRE'S MOST DEVASTATING WEAPON SINCE THE DEATH STAR--

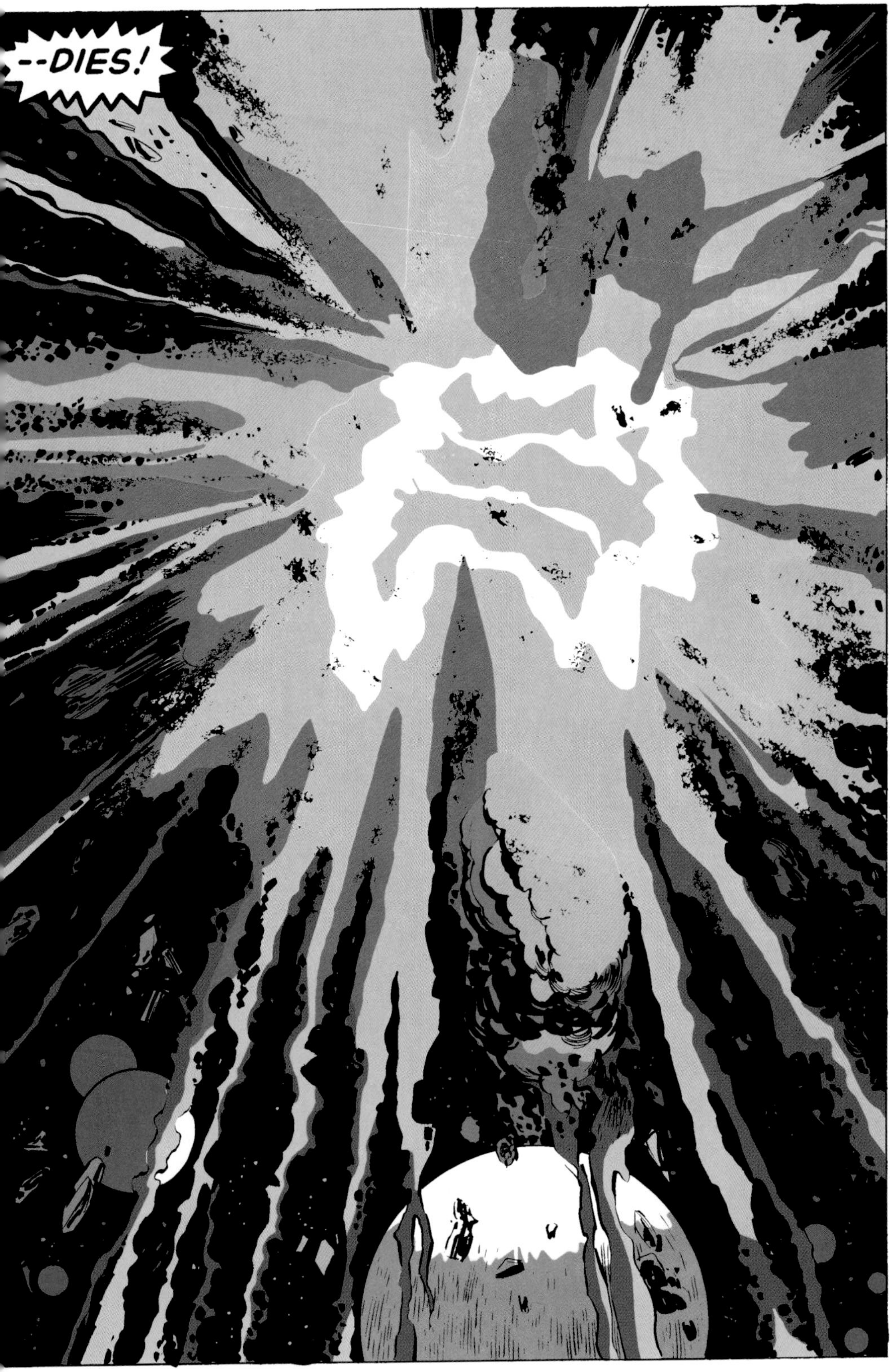
--DIES!

IT... IT EXPLODED! I-IT JUST *BLEW UP!*

ACTUALLY, IT SEEMED MORE TO HAVE SELF-DESTRUCTED.

YEAH, BUT HOW? WHAT COULD HAVE DONE IT?

NOT "WHAT," LUKE--

-- "WHO." WHEN I WAS ON THE TARKIN'S MECHANICAL LEVEL, I FOUND MYSELF IN THE SAME ROOM AS THE WORKS FOR THE IONIC CANNON.

I REALIZED THAT WE COULD *NEVER* ALLOW THE EMPIRE TO USE IT-- SO I BOUGHT US A LITTLE INSURANCE.

I REMEMBERED THE SCHEMATICS ARTOO BROUGHT US OF THE ORIGINAL DEATH STAR, AND SO, I WAS ABLE TO SWITCH A COUPLE OF WIRES TO *REVERSE* THE POLARITY MODES OF THE CANNON'S FIRE CONTROLS.

SO THAT WHEN IT WAS ACTIVATED, THE CANNON, IN ESSENCE--

-- *SHOT ITSELF!*

BUT WHAT IF WE HADN'T GOTTEN AWAY? WHAT IF THEY'D FIRED THE CANNON WHILE YOU WERE STILL ON BOARD?

WELL, LANDO--

-- THEN I WOULDN'T BE ABLE TO THANK YOU FOR DISOBEY-ING ORDERS AND PULLING OUR FAT OUT OF THE FIRE, WOULD I

PRINCESS, IT WAS MY PLEASURE!

THE REBELS SMILE RETURNING TO THEIR CONTROLS, HEADING THE MILLENNIUM FALCON OUTWARD TO THE STARS... AND TO ADVENTURE!

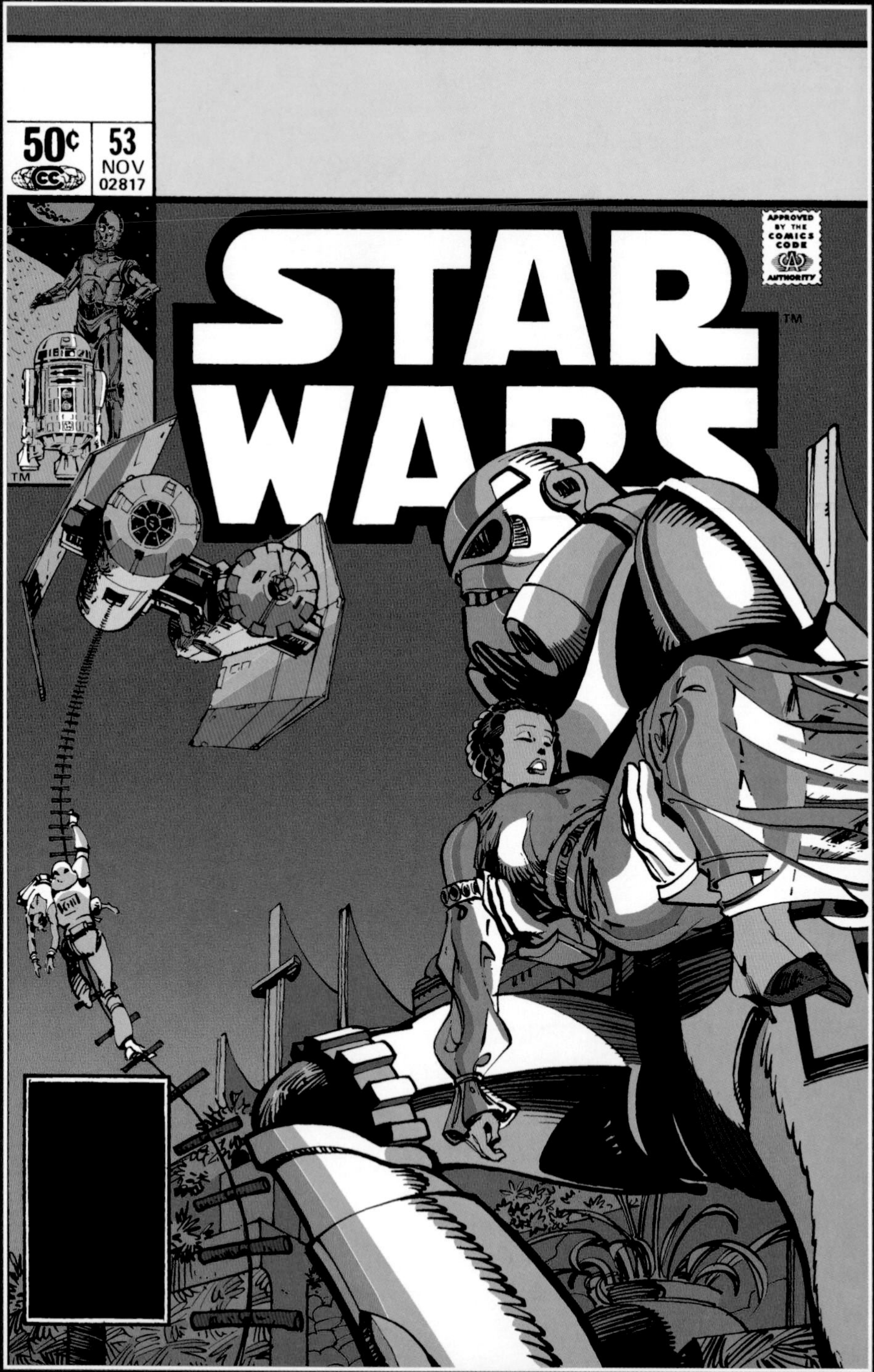

50¢
53
NOV
02817
APPROVED BY THE COMICS CODE AUTHORITY
STAR WARS
TM

Long ago in a galaxy far, far away. . .there exists a state of cosmic *civil war*. A brave alliance of *underground freedom fighters* has challenged the tyranny and oppression of the awesome *Galactic Empire*. This is their story!

LucasFilm PRESENTS: **STAR WARS** THE GREATEST SPACE FANTASY OF ALL!

| C. CLAREMONT WRITER | INFANTINO AND SIMONSON PENCILERS | KUPPERBERG AND PALMER INKERS | LEFERMAN, LETTERS G. WEIN, COLORS | LOUISE JONES, EDITOR JIM SHOOTER, EDITOR-IN-CHIEF |

THE LAST GIFT FROM ALDERAAN!

PROLOGUE! ONCE UPON A TIME, THERE WAS A WORLD NAMED ALDERAAN, HAILED BY MANY AS THE "BRIGHT CENTER OF THE UNIVERSE," FAMED THROUGHOUT THE EMPIRE FOR ITS MUSIC, ITS ART, ITS LITERATURE. IT WAS A WORLD OF JOY, OF UNSURPASSED BEAUTY, OF PEACE.

ALDERAAN: PRE-HOLOCAUST

IT NO LONGER EXISTS.

ALDERAAN SECTOR: TODAY

THIS WOMAN IS A CHILD OF THAT WORLD: LEIA ORGANA, PRINCESS OF ALDERAAN-- IMPERIAL SENATOR TURNED LEADER OF THE REBEL ALLIANCE. WHEN ALDERAAN WAS DESTROYED BY THE EMPEROR'S DEATH STAR * SHE LOST FAMILY, FRIENDS -- ALL SHE EVER KNEW AND LOVED.

SINCE THEN, SHE HAS BORNE HER LOSS WITH STOIC FORTITUDE -- BUT, EVERY SO OFTEN, HER MEMORIES OF THAT FATEFUL, TERRIBLE DAY REAR UP AND ONCE MORE BEGIN TO HAMMER AT THE WALL LEIA HAS BUILT TO PROTECT HERSELF FROM HER GRIEF.

ALONE ON THE COMMAND DECK OF A REBEL BLOCKADE RUNNER, LEIA ORGANA WALKS WITH GHOSTS.

*STAR WARS #3--L.J.

91

OH, FATHER--DID YOU KNOW WHAT WAS COMING WHEN YOUR SCANNERS SIGHTED THE DEATH STAR?

A COMMAND, A TOUCH OF A BUTTON-- AND ALDERAAN WAS *NO MORE.* IT WAS NIGHT IN OUR PALACE--WERE YOU AWAKE OR ASLEEP, WITH MOTHER ...OR *ALONE?*

WHEN THE END CAME DID YOU KNOW IT WAS *MY FAULT?*

YOU SENT ME TO FIND *OBI-WAN KENOBI*-- THE LAST OF THE JEDI KNIGHTS, AND YOUR FORMER GENERAL IN THE CLONE WARS--TO PERSUADE HIM TO JOIN THE REBEL ALLIANCE.

INSTEAD, I WAS CAPTURED BY *DARTH VADER.*

HE TOOK ME TO THE *DEATH STAR,* TO THE IMPERIAL SECTOR GOVERNOR-- GRAND MOFF TARKIN. THEY WANTED INFORMATION ABOUT THE REBELLION. TO GET IT, THEY TRIED EVERY HELLISH MEANS AT THEIR DIS- POSAL. I TOLD THEM *NOTHING.*

YOU TRUSTED ME, FATHER. I WOULD NOT BETRAY THAT TRUST.

"EVEN...HAD I KNOWN WHAT WAS TO HAPPEN, I WOULD HAVE KEPT SILENT, THE REBELLION WAS MORE IMPORTANT THAN YOUR LIVES. THAT ...REALIZATION HURTS... FAR MORE THAN ANY WOUND.

YOU WOULD PREFER WE SELECT *ANOTHER* TARGET, A MILITARY TARGET? THEN, *NAME THE SYSTEM!*

FOR THE LAST TIME-- *WHERE IS THE REBEL BASE?*

DANTOOINE. THEY'RE ON DANTOOINE.

THERE, YOU *SEE,* VADER? OUR GUEST *CAN* BE REASONABLE.

PROCEED WITH THE *OPERATION.* YOU MAY *FIRE* ON ALDERAAN *WHEN READY.*

WHAT!? BUT, YOU SAID--!

YOU ARE FAR TOO *TRUSTING.*

NO!!

PRINCESS LEIA, ARE YOU ALL RIGHT?! I HEARD YOU *CRY OUT!*

:*OH!*:

OH! CAPTAIN CHEDAKI! I'M SORRY-- I... MUST HAVE DOZED OFF...HAD A BAD DREAM.

WE'VE DROPPED OUT OF HYPERSPACE, RIGHT ON TARGET. WE'RE INSIDE THE SHIVA SYSTEM.

THIS IS ALMOST THE EDGE OF KNOWN SPACE, ABOUT AS *FAR* FROM THE EMPIRE AS A BODY CAN GET. WHY'D WE COME ALL THIS WAY, PRINCESS?

WE'RE INTERESTED IN SHIVA BECAUSE THE *EMPIRE* IS INTERESTED. THERE'S BEEN AN UN- USUAL AMOUNT OF TRAFFIC IN AND OUT OF THIS SECTOR RECENTLY.

PRELIMINARY SENSOR SCAN INDICATES SHIVA IV IS *IN- HABITED*. IF YOU'RE RIGHT ABOUT THAT IMPERIAL ACTIVITY, WE'LL HAVE TO DO OUR DETAILED, CLOSE- RANGE SCANS FROM A *SHUTTLE CRAFT.*

WE HAVE TO FIND OUT WHY.

YOU'RE THE *BOSS*, PRINCESS. I JUST DRIVE THE STARSHIP.

AND SHORT MINUTES LATER, ABOARD THE SHUTTLE...

INITIATE SEPARATION LAUNCH CHECKLIST.

I COPY. PRIMARY POWER SWITCH --ON.

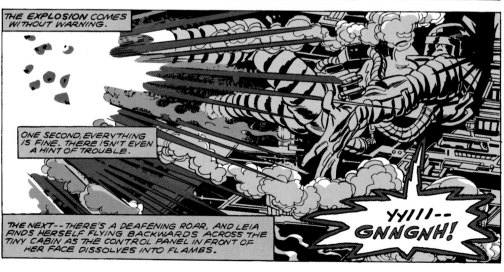

THE EXPLOSION COMES WITHOUT WARNING.

ONE SECOND, EVERYTHING IS FINE. THERE ISN'T EVEN A HINT OF TROUBLE.

THE NEXT--THERE'S A DEAFENING ROAR, AND LEIA FINDS HERSELF FLYING BACKWARDS ACROSS THE TINY CABIN AS THE CONTROL PANEL IN FRONT OF HER FACE DISSOLVES INTO FLAMBS.

YYIII-- GNNGNH!

ALMOST IMMEDIATELY, THE SHUTTLE AND ITS MOTHER SHIP FILL WITH SMOKE--AS THE EXPLOSION IGNITES THE SMALLER CRAFT'S FULL FUEL TANKS.

WE'RE *HIT*--BUT BY WHAT?! THE SCANNERS READ *CLEAR SPACE* FOR A MILLION KILO-METERS AROUND US!

JUBILEE, GET FORWARD TO THE SHUTTLE BAY! GIVE CHEDAKI AND THE PRINCESS A HAND, AND FLASH ME A STATUS REPORT--ON THE DOUBLE!

THE REST OF YOU-- INTO PRESSURE SUITS! WE'RE OPEN TO SPACE AND LOSING AIR! AND IF WE DON'T BRING THAT BLASTED FIRE UNDER CONTROL *FAST*--BEFORE ANY HOSTILE SENSORS PICK IT UP-- WE'RE AS GOOD AS *DEAD!*

ON A HUNCH, *ROAK*--THE FIRST OFFICER-- ORDERS THE REBELS' SENSORS REFINED TO THEIR FINEST CALIBRATION. WHAT THEY FIND CONFIRMS HIS WORST FEARS.

THE STARSHIP IS IN THE MIDDLE OF A *MINE-FIELD.*

THE BOMBS ARE SMALL -- A GRAIN OF *ANTI-MATTER* TUCKED IN-SIDE A MAGNAFIELD CASING -- SO SMALL THAT SENSORS SET FOR NORMAL SCAN WON'T REGISTER THEM, SO SMALL THAT THEY CAN SLIP THROUGH A SPACE-CRAFT'S METEOR SHIELDS-- YET THEY PACK A *FEAR-SOME* PUNCH.

LUCKILY, THE SHUTTLE ABSORBED MOST OF THE FORCE OF THE MINE--IT IS BADLY HURT, BUT DAMAGE TO THE STARSHIP ITSELF IS MINIMAL. THE CRITICAL PROBLEM IS THE FIRE, CREATING AN *INFRA-RED* HEAT SIGNATURE THAT THE BLOCKADE RUNNER'S DEFENSIVE SCREENS CAN'T HIDE, AN UNMISTAKABLE *BEACON* FOR ANY IMPERIAL WARCRAFT IN THE VICINITY.

LEIA, HAUL CHEDAKI OUT OF THERE! I'VE GOT ORDERS TO *JETTISON* THE SHUTTLE!

CHEDAKI'S *DEAD*, JUBILEE. I'M ON MY WAY.

HURRY-- *WAIT!* SAY AGAIN, ROAK? BY THE STARS, *NO!*

ROAK SAYS THE FIRING CIRCUITS ARE *INOPERATIVE*, THE EXPLOSION MUST HAVE FUSED THEM!

LEIA ACTS WITHOUT CONSCIOUS THOUGHT, IGNORING JUBILEE'S FRANTIC CRIES AS SHE SLAMS THE SHUTTLE'S HATCH SHUT AND LOCKS HERSELF IN.

THERE'S AN EMERGENCY BACK-UP TRIGGER. UNFORTUNATELY, IT'S INSIDE THE SHUTTLE.

FOR LEIA ORGANA, IT'S A SIMPLE CHOICE TO MAKE-- HER LIFE, IN EXCHANGE FOR THE LIVES OF HER COMPANIONS.

TRAILING A KILOMETER-LONG STREAMER OF CRIMSON FIRE, THE SHUTTLE CURVES DOWN AND AWAY FROM THE REBEL BLOCKADE RUNNER, TOWARDS THE BARREN, DESOLATE SURFACE OF SHIVA IV.

THAT'S SAVED THE STARSHIP. I THINK.

WITHOUT THE FIRE TO MARK ITS POSITION, IT CAN STAY HIDDEN BEHIND ITS SHIELDS AND, HOPEFULLY, WORK ITS WAY FREE OF THE MINEFIELD.

ANTI-MATTER MICROMINES-- THEY'RE *IMPERIAL* WEAPONS. BUT THAT'S SOMETHING TO WORRY ABOUT WHEN I'M ON THE GROUND.

I CAN'T BRAKE OR CONTROL MY DESCENT; I'LL BE MAKING A BALLISTIC APPROACH, HITTING THE ATMOSPHERE LIKE A *METEOR*. ALL I CAN DO IS PRAY THIS CRATE HOLDS TOGETHER UNTIL I REACH THE LOWER ATMOSPHERE...

...WHERE I CAN USE THE AIR RESISTANCE TO TRY TO MODIFY MY TRAJECTORY.

IT'S A SLIM CHANCE, BUT IT'S ALL LEIA HAS AS HER SHUTTLE TUMBLES TOWARD THE GROUND, TURBULENCE PUMMELING IT-- AND HER-- MERCILESSLY, WHILE FRICTION TURNS THE HULL RED-HOT, THEN WHITE-HOT.

STILL, LEIA REFUSES TO SURRENDER, FIGHTING FOR HER LIFE WITH ALL THE STRENGTH OF BODY AND WILL AT HER COMMAND -- RIGHT UP TO THE VERY END.

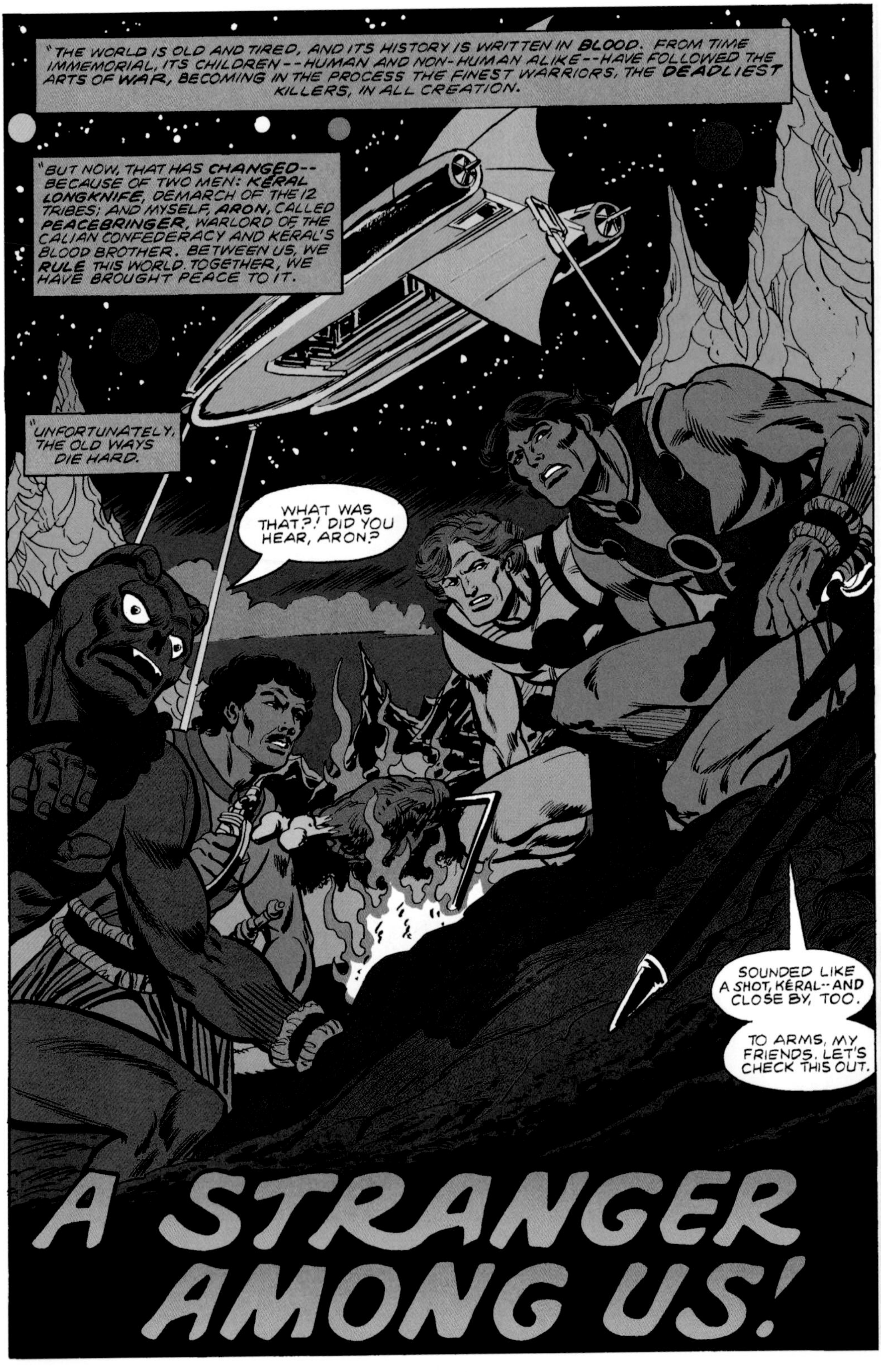
"THE WORLD IS OLD AND TIRED, AND ITS HISTORY IS WRITTEN IN BLOOD. FROM TIME IMMEMORIAL, ITS CHILDREN--HUMAN AND NON-HUMAN ALIKE--HAVE FOLLOWED THE ARTS OF WAR, BECOMING IN THE PROCESS THE FINEST WARRIORS, THE DEADLIEST KILLERS, IN ALL CREATION.
"BUT NOW, THAT HAS CHANGED--BECAUSE OF TWO MEN: KERAL LONGKNIFE, DEMARCH OF THE 12 TRIBES; AND MYSELF, ARON, CALLED PEACEBRINGER, WARLORD OF THE CALIAN CONFEDERACY AND KERAL'S BLOOD BROTHER. BETWEEN US, WE RULE THIS WORLD. TOGETHER, WE HAVE BROUGHT PEACE TO IT.
"UNFORTUNATELY, THE OLD WAYS DIE HARD.
WHAT WAS THAT?! DID YOU HEAR, ARON?
SOUNDED LIKE A SHOT, KERAL--AND CLOSE BY, TOO.
TO ARMS, MY FRIENDS. LET'S CHECK THIS OUT.
A STRANGER AMONG US!

AS I SUSPECTED--AN OUTCAST RAIDING PARTY. THEY'RE AFTER A LONE HUMAN WOMAN!

THEY ALMOST HAVE HER SURROUNDED. WE'LL HAVE TO MOVE *QUICKLY* IF WE'RE TO SAVE HER.

WITH THE MOONS DOWN, MILORD, WE CAN'T SEE VERY WELL. THE OUT-CASTS COULD HAVE AN *ARMY* OUT THERE.

THAT SWORD CUTS *BOTH* WAYS, DELOIS. FOR ALL THOSE OUT-CASTS KNOW...

...*WE COULD* BE AN ARMY. LET'S PLAY THAT PART TO THE HILT, COMRADES. STRIKE HARD AND FAST --DO AS MUCH DAMAGE AS WE CAN--AND GET THE WOMAN OUT OF HARM'S WAY.

"WITHOUT *BREAKING STRIDE*, I KICKED OFF FROM THE CREST OF THE RIDGE...

"...AND SLAMMED FULL-TILT INTO THE MIDST OF THE RAIDER BAND. WITH THE TERRIBLE, ELEMENTAL FEROCITY THAT IS MY HALLMARK...

"...I CUT A CRIMSON SWATHE THROUGH THE OUTCASTS' RANKS, GRANTING MY GIANT FOES THE SAME MERCY THEY WOULD GRANT ME.

"ALL THE WHILE, AS I FOUGHT, I THOUGHT OF THE WOMAN, AND REMEMBERED THE MANY TIMES I'D SEEN OUTCAST CAPTIVES--OR, RATHER, WHAT WAS *LEFT* OF THEM. IF THESE BUTCHERS ESCAPED WITH THEIR PRIZE, HER DEATH WOULD BE A SLOW, PAINFUL ONE.

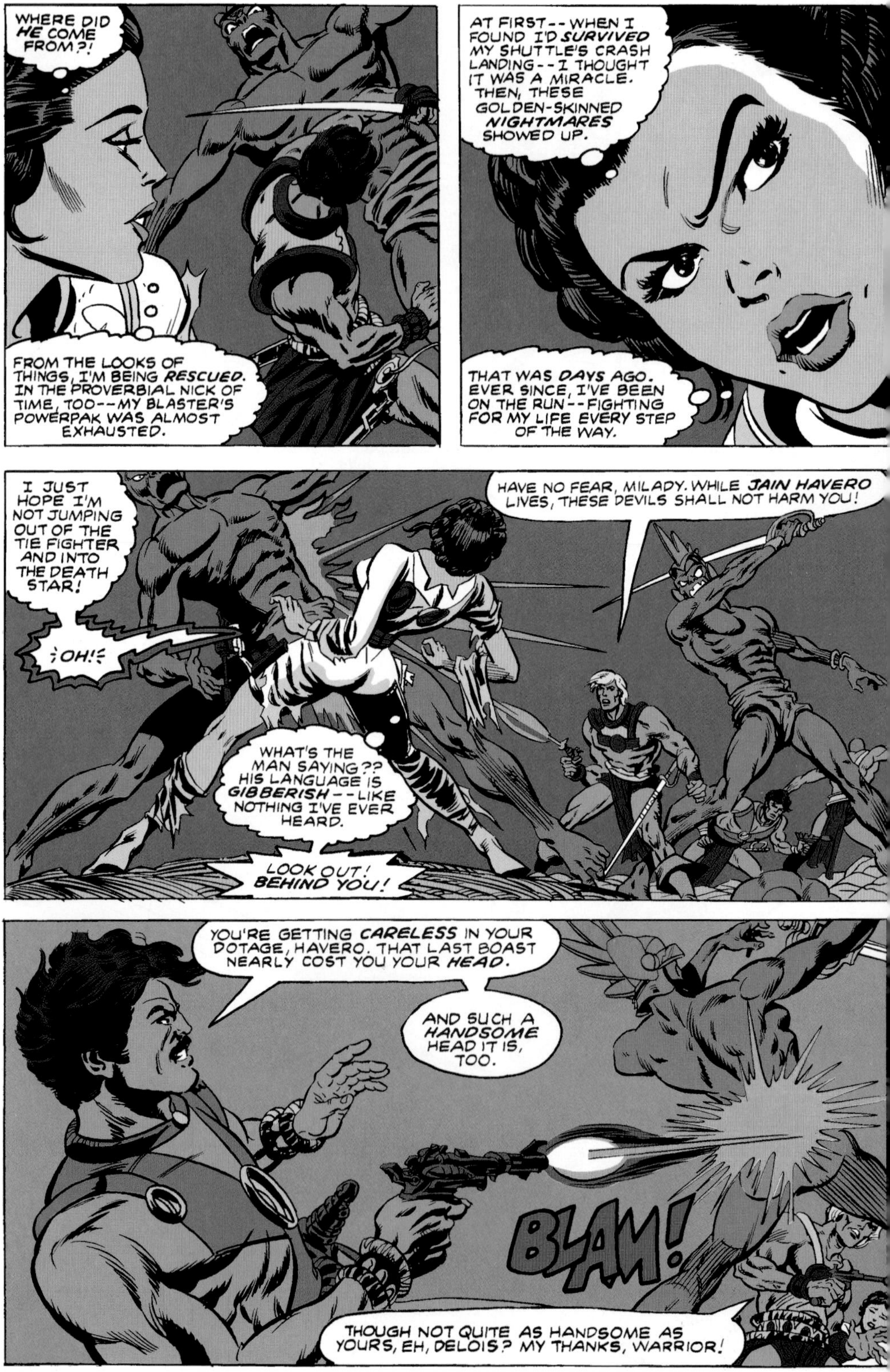

WHERE DID HE COME FROM?!
FROM THE LOOKS OF THINGS, I'M BEING RESCUED. IN THE PROVERBIAL NICK OF TIME, TOO--MY BLASTER'S POWERPAK WAS ALMOST EXHAUSTED.
AT FIRST--WHEN I FOUND I'D SURVIVED MY SHUTTLE'S CRASH LANDING--I THOUGHT IT WAS A MIRACLE. THEN, THESE GOLDEN-SKINNED NIGHTMARES SHOWED UP.
THAT WAS DAYS AGO. EVER SINCE, I'VE BEEN ON THE RUN--FIGHTING FOR MY LIFE EVERY STEP OF THE WAY.
I JUST HOPE I'M NOT JUMPING OUT OF THE TIE FIGHTER AND INTO THE DEATH STAR!
OH!
HAVE NO FEAR, MILADY. WHILE JAIN HAVERO LIVES, THESE DEVILS SHALL NOT HARM YOU!
WHAT'S THE MAN SAYING?? HIS LANGUAGE IS GIBBERISH--LIKE NOTHING I'VE EVER HEARD.
LOOK OUT! BEHIND YOU!
YOU'RE GETTING CARELESS IN YOUR DOTAGE, HAVERO. THAT LAST BOAST NEARLY COST YOU YOUR HEAD.
AND SUCH A HANDSOME HEAD IT IS, TOO.
BLAM!
THOUGH NOT QUITE AS HANDSOME AS YOURS, EH, DELOIS? MY THANKS, WARRIOR!

WE'RE DOING WELL AGAINST THIS *SMALL* BAND--EVEN THOUGH THEY'RE BETTER ARMED THAN USUAL, AND DISCIPLINED, TRAINED FIGHTERS TO BOOT. IT SEEMS THE INTELLIGENCE REPORTS I'VE BEEN RECEIVING FROM THE DRYLANDS MAY BE TRUE, AFTER ALL.

IF SOMEONE IS MASSING THE OUTCAST BANDS AND TURNING THEM INTO A COHESIVE COMBAT FORCE --*EH?!!*

BY THE DAWNSTAR --*OUTRIDERS!*

THE OTHERS HAVE THEIR HANDS FULL--IT'S UP TO *ME!*

FALL, VILLAINS!

"*WHILE HAVERO, DELOIS, AND KÉRAL BUSIED THEM-SELVES WITH THE MOUNT-LESS RAIDERS, I SINGLE-HANDEDLY TOOK ON THE OUTRIDERS. LUCK WAS WITH US ALL, AND SO...*

...*A FEW, FRANTIC, HARD-FOUGHT, MINUTES LATER...*

THEY'RE ON THE RUN, COMRADES. WE'VE BEATEN THEM!

AYE, BEATEN THEM --*THIS TIME.* WE FOUR ARE THE BEST OF OUR KIND THERE IS, AND WE HAD THE ADVANTAGE OF SURPRISE ON OUR SIDE. DESPITE THAT, THOSE OUTCASTS GAVE A *GOOD* ACCOUNT OF THEMSELVES.

I AM ASHAMED, MY BROTHER.

IN HAPPIER TIMES -- BEFORE OUR TWO RACES SIGNED THE CONCORDAT OF PEACE -- A WARRIOR OF THE 12 TRIBES WOULD *DIE* RATHER THAN FLEE FROM YOU NIGHTSKINS.

TIMES HAVE CHANGED, KÉRAL LONGKNIFE.

AND THESE CURSED WRETCHES ARE MERELY TRIBELESS SCAVENGERS, NOT YOUR PROUD *T'SYRIÉL.*

NOW THAT THE BATTLE'S WON, WARLORD, WE'D BEST SEE TO THE YOUNG WOMAN -- THERE SHE IS!

DON'T BE FRIGHTENED, LADY. WE MEAN YOU NO HARM.

THE NIGHT AIR IS TURNING COLD. GET HER A CLOAK FROM OUR CAMP, HAVERO, BEFORE SHE FREEZES.

HERE YOU ARE, LITTLE ONE. BUT TELL US -- WHAT BRINGS A LONE, UNESCORTED WOMAN TO THE HEART OF THE DRYLANDS?

I...I DON'T UNDESTAND YOUR LANGUAGE.

EH? YOUR TONGUE MAKES NO SENSE, GIRL.

WARLORD, LOOK AT HER SKIN-- IT'S SO *PALE!* AND HER CLOTHES! I'VE NEVER SEEN ANYTHING LIKE THEM!

BLAST! THEIR LANGUAGE IS COMPLETELY *UNKNOWN* TO MY TRANS-LATACOMP.

IT'LL BE A WHILE BEFORE IT CAN SORT THINGS OUT ENOUGH TO ENABLE ME TO TALK TO THEM.

LET ME TRY SOMETHING.

ARON. *ARON.* MY NAME IS ARON--DO YOU UNDERSTAND?

ARON?

YES! I AM ARON.

LEIA. I AM LEIA.

LEE-AH? LEIA-- SPLENDID! NOW WE KNOW OUR NAMES.

I RECOMMEND A SPEEDY DEPARTURE, ARON--BEFORE THOSE OUTCASTS RETURN WITH RE-ENFORCEMENTS.

CURIOUS -- THESE PEOPLE FIGHT WITH SWORDS, YET FLY ANTI-GRAVITY HOVERCRAFT! THE MIX DOESN'T MAKE SENSE.

I PASSED A RUINED CITY THE OTHER DAY. THE REMAINS WERE ANCIENT, BUT THEY INDICATED A NUCLEAR BOMB WAS RESPONSIBLE. A WAR WAS FOUGHT HERE, A LONG TIME AGO.

"LEIA REMAINED SILENT AS I TOOK HER GUN FROM HER--BUT HER EYES, HER DEMEANOR, SPOKE VOLUMES AS SHE EXAMINED US, OUR ATTIRE AND WEAPONS, OUR MACHINES. IN TRUTH, SHE WAS AS CUR-IOUS ABOUT US AS WE ABOUT HER.

"BY DAWN, WE WERE ONCE MORE RACING THE SUN WESTWARD. WE HAD COME HALFWAY AROUND THE WORLD FROM MY THRONE CITY, ILLŸRIAQUM...

"...AND THERE WAS STILL A FULL DAY'S TRAVEL AHEAD OF US BEFORE WE REACHED OUR DESTINATION, THE OUT-LANDS CITY OF K'AVOR.

"TWO DAYS AGO, ALL COMMUNICATIONS BETWEEN ILLŸRIAQUM AND K'AVOR HAD INEXPLICABLY BEEN CUT OFF. ALL FURTHER ATTEMPTS TO RAISE THE CITY HAD PROVED FRUITLESS.

"REPORTS SOON REACHED ME THAT--AT THE MOMENT WE LOST CONTACT--PEOPLE FOR SCORES OF MILES AROUND K'AVOR SAW A HUGE, BLINDING FLASH OF LIGHT.

"I, KÉRAL--AND MY TWO MOST TRUSTED AIDES-- LEFT ILLŸRIAQUM IMMEDIATELY FOR K'AVOR, TO LEARN THE TRUTH OF THESE MAD REPORTS FOR OURSELVES.

"THROUGHOUT THE DAY, I TALKED WITH LEIA--POINTING OUT VARIOUS OBJECTS IN THE FLIER AND GIVING HER THEIR NAMES, TRYING MY BEST TO GIVE HER SOME BASIC KNOW-LEDGE OF OUR LANGUAGE.

"SHE LEARNED QUICKLY.

WHY ARE YOU HERE, LITTLE ONE? WHY NOW? IS IT ACCIDENT-- COINCIDENCE--OR... DESIGN? ARE YOU FRIEND, OR FOE?

ARON DOESN'T TRUST ME.

HE AND HIS MEN ARE ALL TENSE, DEEPLY WORRIED. I'M A MYSTERY THEY CAN'T AFFORD RIGHT NOW.

"THEN, SOON AFTER SUNSET, WE REACHED K'AVOR--AND FOUND OURSELVES GAZING INTO THE GREAT PIT OF HELL!

"AHEAD OF US, THE GROUND HAD BEEN TURNED TO POLISHED BLACK GLASS--AS IF SOME GOD HAD TRANS-FORMED K'AVOR INTO A BROAD, SHALLOW, CERAMIC BOWL. THE SKY ABOVE THAT BOWL GLOWED LIKE SHIMMERING, FLAMELESS, INDIGO FIRE.

"A HALF-MILLION PEOPLE HAD CALLED THIS CITY HOME. THEY --LIKE THEIR CITY-- HAD BEEN REDUCED TO ASHES.

"BESIDE ME, LEIA GASPED.

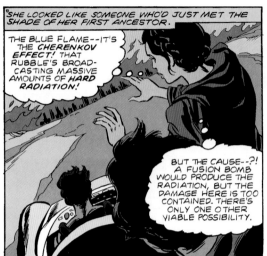

"SHE LOOKED LIKE SOMEONE WHO'D JUST MET THE SHADE OF HER FIRST ANCESTOR.

THE BLUE FLAME--IT'S THE *CHERENKOV EFFECT!* THAT RUBBLE'S BROAD-CASTING MASSIVE AMOUNTS OF *HARD RADIATION!*

BUT THE CAUSE--?! A FUSION BOMB WOULD PRODUCE THE RADIATION, BUT THE DAMAGE HERE IS TOO CONTAINED. THERE'S ONLY ONE OTHER VIABLE POSSIBILITY.

AN *ANTI-MATTER BOMB.*

ARON, YOU MUST *TURN AWAY.* THE RADIATION LEVELS ARE DEADLY. IF WE GO ANY CLOSER TO THAT CITY, WE'LL *DIE!*

HE DOESN'T UNDER-STAND -- AND MY TRANSLATACOMP STILL HASN'T ENOUGH DATA TO DO ME ANY GOOD.

WAIT--IF WORDS WON'T REACH HIM, PERHAPS ACTIONS --A *PANTOMIME* -- WILL DO THE TRICK?

WHAT IS THE FEMALE DOING, MY LORD?

I'M NOT...SURE, HAVERO. BUT I THINK... SHE DOESN'T WANT US TO ENTER K'AVOR.

IF WE DO, I THINK SHE'S SAYING WE'LL DIE.

A TRICK, WARLORD?

POSSIBLY, DELOIS.

BUT...I'M INCLINED TO *TRUST* HER.

TURN US ABOUT-- HEAD AWAY FROM K'AVOR.

EVERYONE'S REACTIONS-- THEY HAVE NO IDEA WHAT DESTROYED THIS CITY.

I CAN'T BE POSITIVE WITHOUT A COMPLETE SENSOR ANALYSIS, BUT I'LL STAKE ANY ODDS THAT IT WAS AN *IMPERIAL* WAR-HEAD. BUT WHY IS THE EMPIRE HERE-- WHAT DOES THIS WORLD OFFER IT?

WHATEVER THE REASON-- WHATEVER THE FORCE I'M FACING --IT'S UP TO ME TO *STOP* THEM.

MAGNIFICENT! THIS DEMON-STRATION IS ALL I WAS PROMISED AND MORE! ENJOY YOUR CROWN WHILE YOU CAN, WARLORD ARON--

--FOR YOU SHAN'T BE WEARING IT MUCH LONGER. SOON--VERY SOON NOW--CROWN, WIFE, CONFEDERACY, PLANET WILL BE *MINE!*

"WEEKS PASSED. BUT THOUGH MY AGENTS SCOURED THE LENGTH AND BREADTH OF THE PLANET, I CAME NO CLOSER TO DISCOVERING WHO WAS BEHIND THE DESTRUCTION OF K'AVOR THAN I'D BEEN THE NIGHT I'D FIRST BEHELD THE SHATTERED CITY.

"AND WITH EACH DAY, NEW, STEADILY MORE LURID TALES SPREAD THROUGH THE LAND-- K'AVOR WAS DESTROYED BECAUSE IT SERVED THE UPSTART, ARON PEACEBRINGER, WHO'D DARE TO SMASH THE ANCIENT WAR-GODS' DEATH CULTS AND SLAY THEIR PRIESTS. NOW, THOSE INSULTED DEITIES WERE EXACTING THEIR GRIM VENGEANCE--FIRST AGAINST TINY K'AVOR, AND SOON AGAINST PROUD ILLYRIAQUM ITSELF.

THE PATTERN IS AS PLAIN AS THE DESERT. SOMEONE IS LAYING THE FOUNDATION FOR A *COUP D'ETAT,* A *REVOLUTION.* AND THEIR POWER AND SUPPORT SEEMS TO BE GROWING.

I SHOULD HAVE EXPECTED THIS. TOO MANY STILL REMEMBER THE OLD WAYS. THEY MISS THE DRUMS OF WAR. I'VE GIVEN THEM PEACE. AND UNFORTUNATELY, MY PEOPLE HAVEN'T YET LEARNED TO LIKE IT.

GUESS WHO?

HM?!

WELLLL-- WITH THAT VOICE AND THAT PERFUME, WHO ELSE COULD IT BE BUT...

...KÉRAL LONGKNIFE!

NOT QUITE.

WHY-- ALISANDE! MY LADY, IT WAS AN HONEST MISTAKE.

OH? THEN CONSIDER THIS AN HONEST REMINDER, HUSBAND--

--BETTER LUCK NEXT TIME!

OW!

SLAP THE WARLORD OF THE CALIAN CONFEDERACY, WILL YOU, WENCH?

I'LL DO WORSE IF YOU'RE NOT CAREFUL!

PROMISES, PROMISES.

GARUMP!

SIR-- YOU SEEM TO HAVE ME AT A DISADVANTAGE.

MADAM -- I MEAN TO KEEP YOU THAT WAY.

"I LOVED ALISANDE WITH ALL MY HEART AND SOUL -- OUR YEARS TOGETHER SERVING ONLY TO DEEPEN AND ENRICH OUR FEELINGS FOR EACH OTHER.

"AND YET, AS WE KISSED, A NEW FACE FLASHED THROUGH MY MIND -- THE OUTWORLD STRANGER, OUR GUEST, LEIA.

"SHE WAS A FASCINATING, COURAGEOUS, BEAUTIFUL WOMAN. TOO FASCINATING -- TOO BEAUTIFUL.

LETTING ME UP FOR AIR, ARON? HOW KIND.

IT'S ONLY FOR A MOMENT. I THOUGHT WE MIGHT BETTER CONTINUE THIS WEIGHTY DISCUSSION...

...IN OUR CHAMBERS.

LATER...

I'D FORGOTTEN ABOUT TONIGHT'S GALA...

YOU'VE FORGOTTEN ABOUT A GREAT *MANY* THINGS OF LATE, ARON. EVER SINCE YOUR RETURN FROM K'AVOR, YOU'VE PRACTICALLY BECOME A *HERMIT.*

AND THE FEW TIMES YOU *HAVE* SHOWN YOUR FACE, YOU'VE BEEN ALMOST IMPOSSIBLE TO LIVE WITH.

I KNOW. I'M SORRY. I'M ...*AFRAID,* ALIS--FOR YOU, FOR OUR CHILDREN, FOR OUR WORLD.

WHINE?

HUSH, CHIBA. STOP BEING A PEST.

IS THE SITUATION THAT SERIOUS?

MORE SERIOUS--IN MORE WAYS--THAN YOU COULD POSSIBLY KNOW, MY WIFE. I LOOK AT YOU--LOVING YOU AS DEEPLY, AS PASSIONATELY, AS EVER--

--YET MY THOUGHTS STRAY EVER MORE FREQUENTLY TO LEIA. WHY? *WHY?!!*

I WISH YOU WOULD SPEAK TO LEIA, ARON. SHE'S TRIED OFTEN ENOUGH TO SEE YOU.

SHE'S TOLD ME OF A GALACTIC EMPIRE--VAST, MALEVOLENT, GREEDY--ALWAYS HUNTING FOR NEW CONQUESTS, EVER READY TO CRUSH ANY WHO OPPOSE IT.

DO YOU BELIEVE HER?

I DO NOT DISMISS HER TALE OUT OF HAND, AS YOU SEEM TO HAVE DONE.

ARON, I'VE SPOKEN WITH THE MASTER ARCHIVISTS--THEY SAY THAT *NO* WEAPON KNOWN TO CALIAN SCIENCE COULD HAVE DESTROYED K'AVOR. IF LEIA *IS* TELLING THE TRUTH, WE DARE NOT REFUSE HER AID.

SHE'S OUTSIDE, HUSBAND. AT LEAST *HEAR* HER.

THEN JUDGE FOR YOURSELF.

"HER ENTRANCE TOOK MY BREATH AWAY. IN A LITTLE OVER A MONTH, THE DESERT WAIF I'D RESCUED..."

LEIA...?

GREETINGS, WARLORD. BLESSED BE YOUR HOUSE, AND ALL WHO BEAR YOUR NAME.

...HAD BEEN TRANSFORMED INTO A BEAUTY WHOSE GRACE AND MAJESTY RIVALED THAT OF MY INCOMPARABLE WIFE.

"HER CALIAN WAS FLAWLESS, WITH A SLIGHT, DELIGHTFULLY EXOTIC ACCENT. ANGRILY I THRUST MY SUDDEN, DANGEROUS, THOUGHTS FROM MY MIND, AND SOUGHT DESPERATE REFUGE IN DIPLOMATIC CHIT-CHAT.

LEIA-- I NOW BELIEVE YOU ARE INDEED A PRINCESS-BORN.

STRANGE-- I'VE NEVER SEEN ARON SO ILL AT EASE. LEIA SENSES IT, TOO.

HUSBAND, LEIA-- SHALL WE GREET OUR GUESTS?

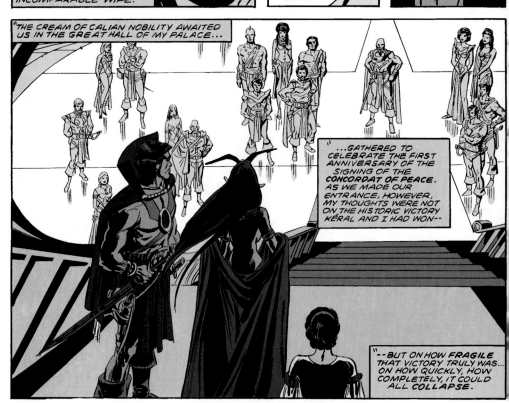

"THE CREAM OF CALIAN NOBILITY AWAITED US IN THE GREAT HALL OF MY PALACE...

...GATHERED TO CELEBRATE THE FIRST ANNIVERSARY OF THE SIGNING OF THE CONCORDAT OF PEACE. AS WE MADE OUR ENTRANCE, HOWEVER, MY THOUGHTS WERE NOT ON THE HISTORIC VICTORY KÉRAL AND I HAD WON--

--BUT ON HOW FRAGILE THAT VICTORY TRULY WAS... ON HOW QUICKLY, HOW COMPLETELY, IT COULD ALL COLLAPSE.

"MY FACE SHOWED *NONE OF THOSE* WORRIES..."

"...AS I INTRODUCED LEIA TO MY CHILDREN, FRIENDS, COMRADES. AT THE MOMENT, ALL I HAD TO GO ON WERE RUMORS, SUSPICIONS --AND LEIA'S WORD."

"I BELIEVED HER --BUT BEFORE I COULD TAKE ACTION, I HAD TO HAVE *PROOF.*"

M'LADY, PRINCE YGAL DELOIS--CAPTAIN OF THE WARLORD'S GUARD-- REQUESTS THE HONOR OF THE FIRST DANCE.

THE, AH, HONOR IS MINE...CAPTAIN.

"I WATCHED THEM WITH HOODED EYES, WISHING I STOOD IN DE-LOIS' PLACE--AND DESPISING MYSELF FOR IT."

HUSBAND, YOU GAZE AT LEIA AS YOU ONCE LOOKED AT ME.

AM I...THAT OBVIOUS, ALIS?

ONLY TO ONE WHO KNOWS YOU, *LOVES* YOU, AS I DO.

IT IS NO CRIME TO BE *TEMPTED,* ARON. TO SEE BEAUTY, AND WISH TO POSSESS IT. THAT MERELY MAKES YOU AS *HUMAN* AS THE REST OF US.

WHAT MATTERS IS WHAT YOU *DO* ABOUT IT. YOU HAVE A CHOICE TO MAKE, ARON. ABOVE ALL, BE *WISE* WHEN YOU MAKE IT.

I CARE FOR LEIA, TOO, AS A DAUGHTER, A FRIEND. I DO NOT WANT TO SEE HER HURT. ESPECIALLY BY YOU.

MILADY ALISANDE, I THINK SOMETIMES THAT THE *WRONG* ONE OF US WEARS MY WARLORD'S CROWN, AND RULES THIS LAND.

"SHE SMILED ENIGMATICALLY AND STARTED TO MOVE AWAY, BUT I CAUGHT HER ARM..."

"...AND, TOGETHER, THE WARLORD AND HIS LADY...

"...WHIRLED INTO THE CENTER OF THE STATE BALLROOM. USUALLY, WHEN OUR DANCE ENDED, WE WOULD SLIP AWAY TO SOME CONVENIENT, SHADOWED ALCOVE...

"...FOR AN EMBRACE, A KISS--LIKE LOVERS A FRACTION OF OUR AGE.

"TONIGHT, WITHOUT ANOTHER WORD-- AND WITH EYES FILLED WITH QUESTIONS, DOUBTS...PAIN-- WE PARTED.

"SEPARATELY, WE CIRCULATED AMONG OUR GUESTS, AND I NOTICED THAT MY YOUNG AIDE, DELOIS, NEVER LEFT LEIA'S SIDE, THOUGH SHE OCCASIONALLY TRIED TO LEAVE HIS.

"I WAS ABOUT TO INTERVENE WHEN LEIA GAVE A SMALL, STRANGLED CRY, AND BOLTED THROUGH THE CROWD TOWARDS A BALCONY OVERLOOKING THE CITY.

"DELOIS--MORE ANGRY THAN CONCERNED AT HER SUDDEN FLIGHT--STARTED AFTER HER. THE LOOK ON MY FACE AS I CUT HIM OFF FROZE HIM IN HIS TRACKS. I WOULD HANDLE THIS ALONE.

LEIA?

WHAT'S WRONG? I'D LIKE TO HELP.

CAN YOU WHISTLE UP A *STARSHIP*, WARLORD? CAN YOU SEND ME *HOME*?

NO.

THAT'S ALL RIGHT. I DON'T *HAVE* A HOME-- A TRUE HOME-- ANYMORE.

SO MUCH TIME HAS PASSED. MY SHIP SHOULD HAVE REACHED BASE-- AND A RESCUE PARTY RETURNED HERE TO LEARN WHAT HAPPENED TO ME-- LONG AGO. IF IT SURVIVED THE MINE-FIELD.

PART OF ME ...HOPES IT *WON'T* RETURN.

TONIGHT, ARON--DANCING, TALKING... FLIRTING-- I WAS *HAPPY*. I HAD NO CARES, NO RESPONSIBILITIES. I SAW A PART OF MYSELF I'VE *DENIED* EVER SINCE THE REBELLION BEGAN.

I WASN'T LEIA ORGANA--PRINCESS-SENATOR, REBEL LEADER, WARRIOR. I WAS A *WOMAN*--NO MORE, NO LESS-- ENJOYING MYSELF AT A FABULOUS PARTY.

I FORGOT... TOO MUCH.

NOT LONG AGO, I SAW MY WORLD, ALDERAAN, DE-STROYED. ITS PEOPLE--MY PARENTS, FAMILY, FRIENDS--BILLIONS OF LIVES SNUFFED OUT BEFORE MY EYES.

THEY DIED. BUT *I* LIVED.

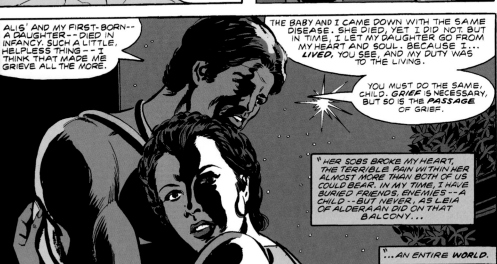

ALIS' AND MY FIRST-BORN-- A DAUGHTER--DIED IN INFANCY. SUCH A LITTLE, HELPLESS THING-- I THINK THAT MADE ME GRIEVE ALL THE MORE.

THE BABY AND I CAME DOWN WITH THE SAME DISEASE. SHE DIED, YET I DID NOT. BUT IN TIME, I LET MY DAUGHTER GO FROM MY HEART AND SOUL. BECAUSE I... *LIVED*, YOU SEE, AND MY DUTY WAS TO THE LIVING.

YOU MUST DO THE SAME, CHILD. *GRIEF* IS NECESSARY, BUT SO IS THE *PASSAGE* OF GRIEF.

" HER SOBS BROKE MY HEART, THE TERRIBLE PAIN WITHIN HER ALMOST MORE THAN BOTH OF US COULD BEAR. IN MY TIME, I HAVE BURIED FRIENDS, ENEMIES--A CHILD--BUT NEVER, AS LEIA OF ALDERAAN DID ON THAT BALCONY...

"...AN ENTIRE *WORLD*.

"I NEVER SAW THE BLACKGUARDS WHO STRUCK ME DOWN.

¡UNNNGNH!¿

ENORMOUS STORM-TROOPERS!

"IT WAS A *MASTERFUL* ATTACK--PERFECTLY EXECUTED.

" IN A MATTER OF SECONDS, LEIA AND I WERE BOUND AND GAGGED AND HAULED UP TO AN UNMARKED FLIER, HOVERING ABOVE THE PALACE.

" A MERE TOUCH OF THE THROTTLE SENT THE SUPER-SPEED SKYCRAFT ROCKETING OUT OF THE CITY--UNSEEN AND UN-CHALLENGED BY ILLYRIAQÜM'S VAUNTED AIR PATROL.

WHILE, BEHIND US, ON THE BALCONY...

ODD--I SAW PRINCESS LEIA RUN OUT HERE, FOLLOWED BY THE WARLORD. I'M SURE SHE WAS CRYING, THOUGH DELOIS INSISTS HE SAID NOTHING TO UPSET HER. IF HE HAS--FRIEND OR NO--I'LL CHALLENGE HIM TO A DUEL!

I'M ALSO SURE THAT, A MOMENT AGO, I HEARD THE PRINCESS *CRY OUT!*

BUT THE BALCONY'S *DESERTED!* HOW CAN THIS BE?!

I WAS WATCHING THE ONLY EXIT. I DIDN'T SEE EITHER OF THEM LEAVE. YET--THEY'RE *GONE!*

I DON'T LIKE THIS-- SOMETHING'S *WRONG.* I'D BEST ALERT LADY ALISANDE AND THE WAR COUNCIL!

"I AWOKE IN CHAINS, ALONE, IN THE DARK.

"AFTER A TIME, STRANGELY ARMORED GIANTS CAME AND MARCHED ME THROUGH THE CRUMBLING HALLS OF SOME ANCIENT FORTRESS.

"I DID NOT RESIST. I KNEW NOTHING OF WHERE I WAS, WHO HAD CAPTURED ME -- WHY I HAD BEEN TAKEN.

"CONSIDERING MY TOTAL IGNORANCE, I'D HAVE BEEN A FOOL TO TRY ANYTHING THEN.

"BUT LATER...

GREETINGS, WARLORD ARON.

IN THE NAME OF THE EMPEROR -- WELCOME.

WHO--?

WHO ARE YOU?!

I AM SK'AR!

I HAVE THE HONOR TO BE A GENERAL IN THE IMPERIAL STRIKE FORCE.

YOU -- YOUR CITY, YOUR PATHETIC LITTLE PLANET -- HAVE THE HONOR OF BEING MY NEXT TARGET.

LEIA...WAS RIGHT!

SOME HERE ARE OFF-WORLDERS, SOME OUTCASTS FROM THE NON-HUMAN TRIBES, SOME MY OWN CALIAN COUNTRYMEN. THIS "EMPIRE" MUST BE BEHIND THE UP-RISING IN THE WASTE, THE TALK OF UNREST IN THE CONFEDERACY.

AND PROBABLY BEHIND THE DESTRUCTION OF K'AVOR, AS WELL.

WE WILL FIGHT YOU, SK'AR, AND MAKE YOU RUE THE DAY YOU EVER SET EYES ON MY WORLD!

NEXT ISSUE:

STARFIRE, RISING

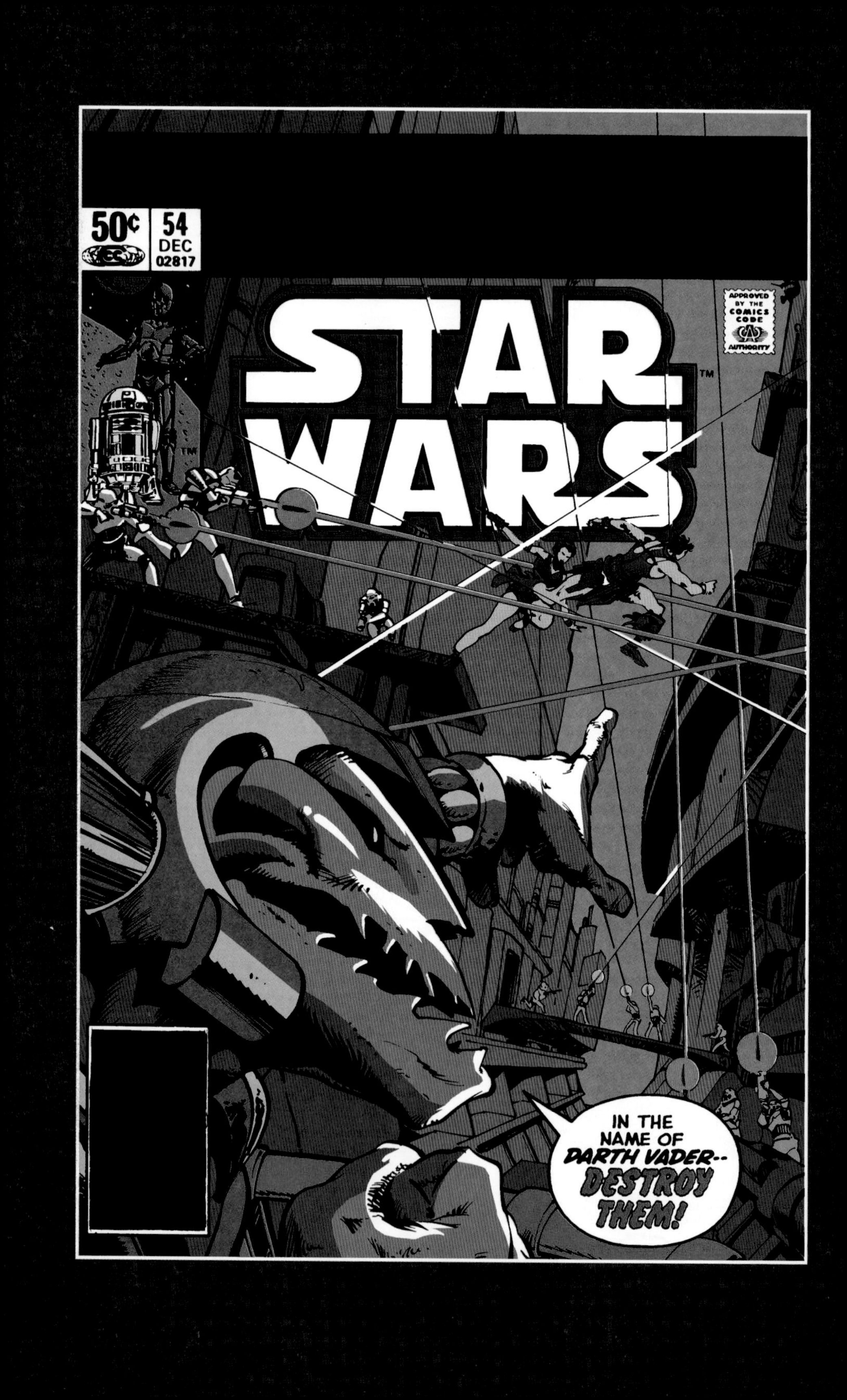
50¢
54
DEC
02817
STAR WARS
APPROVED BY THE COMICS CODE AUTHORITY
IN THE NAME OF DARTH VADER-- DESTROY THEM!

Lucasfilm PRESENTS: **STAR WARS** THE GREATEST SPACE FANTASY OF ALL!

CHRIS CLAREMONT — WRITER

CARMINE INFANTINO • WALT SIMONSON — PENCILERS

PALMER, GIACOIA & MILGROM — INKERS

BURZON — LETTERER
WEIN — COLORIST

JONES & FINGEROTH — EDITORS

JIM SHOOTER — ED-IN-CHIEF

"WEEKS AGO, *PRINCESS LEIA ORGANA*, ON A SCOUTING MISSION FOR THE REBEL ALLIANCE, CRASH LANDED ON MY HOMEWORLD, *SHIVA IV*, A SMALL PLANET ON THE EDGE OF KNOWN SPACE. I, *ARON PEACEBRINGER*, WARLORD OF THE CALIAN CONFEDERACY, RESCUED HER, AND SHE SOON DISCOVERED CIRCUMSTANTIAL EVIDENCE OF COVERT IMPERIAL OPERATIONS WITHIN MY REALM.

"SHE TOLD OF HER SUSPICIONS BUT BEFORE I COULD ACT, WE WERE BOTH CAPTURED BY IMPERIAL COMMANDO STORMTROOPERS AND TAKEN TO THE EMPIRE'S HIDDEN BASE. *

I AM-- SK'AR!

I HAVE THE HONOR TO BE A GENERAL IN THE IMPERIAL STRIKE FORCE. YOU-- YOUR CITY, YOUR PATHETIC LITTLE PLANET-- HAVE THE HONOR TO BE MY NEXT *TARGET*.

LEIA...WAS *RIGHT!* THIS "EMPIRE" SHE SPOKE OF MUST BE BEHIND THE UPRISING IN THE WASTE, AND THE GROWING TALK OF UNREST WITHIN THE CONFEDERACY.

WE...WILL *FIGHT* YOU, SK'AR.

STARFIRE RISING!

*FOR DETAILS, SEE LAST ISSUE-- L & D.

DON'T BE ABSURD, LORD ARON.

YOUR SWORDS AND CAVALRY AGAINST OUR BLASTERS AND ARMORED "WALKERS?"

YOUR FLIERS AGAINST OUR STAR DESTROYERS? THAT WON'T BE A FIGHT. IT WILL BE A *MASSACRE!*

WE DO NOT WANT YOUR PEOPLE SLAIN, MERELY THEIR SPIRITS BROKEN. THE EMPIRE NEEDS TROOPS. YOUR WORLD WILL PROVIDE THE FIERCEST FIGHTERS IN THE GALAXY.

ARON.

LEIA!

THE SWINE, THEY'VE TORTURED YOU!

THEY CALLED IT ... AN INTERROGATION. I'M ALL RIGHT ARON.

I'VE SURVIVED ...FAR WORSE.*

THERE'S SUCH A GRIEF AND PAIN-- IN HER VOICE. WHAT WAS *DONE* TO HER SO LONG AGO?!

THE WENCH WAS INSOLENT, ARON. I DECIDED TO TEACH HER A LESSON.

*: AT THE HANDS OF *DARTH VADER,* IN THE NOW LEGENDARY STAR WARS #2--LED

DELOIS!

TRAITOR!!

YOU WERE ONE OF MY MOST TRUSTED AIDES--!

I AM A *REALIST,* ARON.

I PREFER TO SERVE THE *WINNING* SIDE. WHEN THE EMPIRE WINS, I SHALL RULE HERE, IN THEIR NAME.

AND THAT VICTORY, WARLORD, IS CLOSE AT HAND.

114

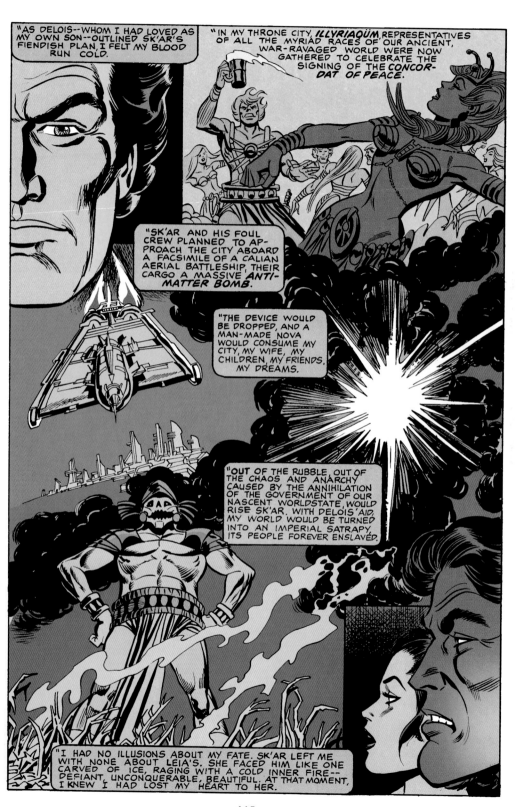

"AS DELOIS--WHOM I HAD LOVED AS MY OWN SON--OUTLINED SK'AR'S FIENDISH PLAN, I FELT MY BLOOD RUN COLD.

"IN MY THRONE CITY, *ILLYRIAQÜM*, REPRESENTATIVES OF ALL THE MYRIAD RACES OF OUR ANCIENT, WAR-RAVAGED WORLD WERE NOW GATHERED TO CELEBRATE THE SIGNING OF THE *CONCOR-DAT OF PEACE*.

"SK'AR AND HIS FOUL CREW PLANNED TO AP-PROACH THE CITY ABOARD A FACSIMILE OF A CALIAN AERIAL BATTLESHIP, THEIR CARGO A MASSIVE *ANTI-MATTER BOMB*.

"THE DEVICE WOULD BE DROPPED, AND A MAN-MADE NOVA WOULD CONSUME MY CITY, MY WIFE, MY CHILDREN, MY FRIENDS, MY DREAMS.

"OUT OF THE RUBBLE, OUT OF THE CHAOS AND ANARCHY CAUSED BY THE ANNIHILATION OF THE GOVERNMENT OF OUR NASCENT WORLDSTATE, WOULD RISE SK'AR. WITH DELOIS' AID, MY WORLD WOULD BE TURNED INTO AN IMPERIAL SATRAPY, ITS PEOPLE FOREVER ENSLAVED.

"I HAD NO ILLUSIONS ABOUT MY FATE. SK'AR LEFT ME WITH NONE ABOUT LEIA'S. SHE FACED HIM LIKE ONE CARVED OF ICE, RAGING WITH A COLD INNER FIRE-- DEFIANT, UNCONQUERABLE, BEAUTIFUL. AT THAT MOMENT, I KNEW I HAD LOST MY HEART TO HER.

REMOVE THEM TO HOLDING CELLS AND KEEP THEM UNDER GUARD UNTIL I RETURN.

PRINCESS LEIA IS NOT TO BE HARMED. THE EMPEROR RESERVES THAT PRIVILEGE FOR HIMSELF.

"SOON AFTER WE WERE LED AWAY, A BASSO RUMBLE SHOOK THE ANCIENT FORTRESS -- LOW FREQUENCY HARMONICS CAUSED BY THE TAKE-OFF OF SK'AR'S AIRSHIP.

"I TRIED TO APPEAR CALM AND UNCONCERNED...

"...BUT INSIDE I WAS DESPERATE. TIME WAS RUNNING OUT. THE GUARDS KNEW THIS AND EXPECTED ME TO MAKE SOME KIND OF MOVE. WITH A BRIEF WARNING GLANCE TO LEIA...

"...I GAVE THEM ONE. IT WAS CLUMSY -- DELIBERATELY SO -- AND QUICKLY DEALT WITH...

"...BUT FOR THAT MOMENT, ALL EYES WERE ON ME.

"LEIA UNDERSTOOD MY SILENT SIGNAL...

"...AND TOOK SWIFT ADVANTAGE OF MY DIVERSION.

"AS LEIA STRUCK, SO DID I. THE CLOSE CONFINES AND DIM LIGHTING OF THE CORRIDOR -- PLUS SK'AR'S ORDERS --

"-- WORKED IN OUR FAVOR. THE STORM TROOPERS WERE TOO FRIGHTENED OF INJURING THE PRINCESS TO USE DEADLY FORCE AGAINST US.

"THAT IS, UNTIL IT BECAME EVIDENT WE WERE INDEED ESCAPING.

LEIA -- BEHIND YOU!

"SHE LOOKED FOR A BLASTER, BUT NONE WAS AT HAND. I COULD NOT GO TO HER AID. AT THAT MOMENT, I WAS TOO BUSY FIGHTING FOR MY OWN LIFE.

"THE OFFICER HELD ONE OF MY DAGGERS. PERHAPS HE INTENDED TO LAY LEIA'S MURDER AT MY DOOR. I NEITHER KNOW NOR CARE.

"HE WAS LARGER THAN SHE, AND STRONGER.

"I SAW ONLY SCRAPS OF HER BATTLE--DURING THE FEW INSTANTS I DARED SHIFT MY EYES FROM MY OWN-- A MACABRE SHADOW-PLAY PROJECTED ON THE STONE WALLS OF THE CORRIDOR. I SAW THE KNIFE PLUNGE HOME. I HEARD LEIA'S CRY.

"THEN I WENT MAD.

"THE BATTLE MADNESS OF MY PEOPLE IS A FEARSOME, FEARFUL THING--A BERSERKER RAGE THAT TRANSFORMS ONE INTO A SUPER-HUMAN, NIGH-IRRESISTIBLE KILLING MACHINE--

"--AS THE IMPERIALS I FACED SOON LEARNED.

LEIA!

"WHEN SANITY RETURNED, ONLY I STOOD.

MY KNIFE--

--IMBEDDED IN THE OFFICER'S HEART!

LEIA, MY DEAR ONE, MY DARLING, ARE YOU ALL RIGHT?

WHEN I HEARD YOU CRY OUT, I THOUGHT...

HE... HE MISSED ME, BUT THE KNIFE...CAME SO CLOSE. I WAS SO... FRIGHTENED.

THEN, I... TURNED THE BLADE BACK AGAINST HIM. HE LOOKED SO SURPRISED WHEN IT STABBED HIM, ARON. I SAW THE LIGHT FADE FROM HIS EYES. I FELT HIS LAST BREATH! I'VE NEVER-- NOT LIKE THIS...I...I...

"HER VOICE TRAILED OFF INTO BROKEN SOBS. I HELD HER CLOSE AND COMFORTED HER AS BEST I COULD.

"ONLY A SKELETON FORCE REMAINED AT SK'AR'S BASE-- HE'D EVIDENTLY TAKEN MOST OF HIS COMMANDOS WITH HIM ON THE AIRSHIP, WITH SURPRISING EASE, WE STOLE A FLIER AND SET OFF IN PURSUIT.

"THROUGHOUT THE LONG FLIGHT, LEIA SPOKE ONLY WHEN NECESSARY, HER EXPRESSION SEVERE, HER THOUGHTS GRIM. IT WAS AS IF SHE HAD DIED AND NOT THE OFFICER. I KNEW WHAT SHE WAS GOING THROUGH. WAR, TO HER, HAD BEEN AN ABSTRACT CONCEPT, FOUGHT IN THE INFINITE VACUUM OF SPACE. WHEN A STARSHIP, OR A CITY, OR A PLANET IS DESTROYED, SO MANY ARE KILLED-- THE NUMBERS ARE SO HUGE, SO INCOMPREHENSIBLE-- THAT THE HUMAN MIND CANNOT RELATE TO THEM.

LEIA-- THE AIRSHIP!

THERE IT IS!

"BUT WHEN A SINGLE PERSON DIES-- AT ONE'S HANDS, BEFORE ONE'S EYES-- IT IS LIKE LOOKING INTO A MIRROR. A BOND HAS BEEN FORGED BETWEEN LIVING AND DEAD. A PRICE IS DEMANDED OF THE VICTOR-- THE TERRIBLE AWARENESS THAT HE OR SHE OR IT HAS TAKEN THE RAREST AND MOST PRECIOUS THING IN ALL CREATION: A SENTIENT LIFE.

"I WAS TWELVE YEARS OLD WHEN I MADE MY FIRST SUCH KILL, AND ON THAT DAY I SWORE I WOULD BRING THE KILLING ON SHIVA TO AN END!

"THE CONCORDAT OF PEACE FORGED BETWEEN MY CALIAN CONFEDERACY AND THE TWELVE TRIBES-- LED BY MY NON-HUMAN BLOOD BROTHER, KERAL LONGKNIFE-- FULFILLED THAT DREAM. I WOULD BRAVE THE ETERNAL PIT AND ALL ITS DEVILS BEFORE LETTING SK'AR-- OR ANYONE-- DESTROY IT!

GENERAL SK'AR-- UNIDENTIFIED CALIAN FLIER APPROACH-ING!

BASE REPORTS THAT PRINCESS LEIA AND THE BARBARIAN HAVE ESCAPED. IT'S PROBABLY THEM!

JAM ALL COMMUNICATIONS FREQUENCIES, TO PREVENT THEM FROM ALERTING THE CITY, ACTIVATE ALL DEFENSIVE WEAPONRY SYSTEMS AND LAUNCH A FIGHTER SCREEN.

I WANT THAT ANTIQUE KNOCKED OUT OF THE SKY.

COMPANY, ARON!

WHAT ARE THEY?

T.I.E. FIGHTERS-- THE EMPIRE'S STANDARD MILITARY WARCRAFT. BUT...

...THOUGH THE EMPIRE IS JUSTIFIABLY PROUD OF ITS TECHNOLOGY, THE QUALITY OF THE PERSON-NEL WHO USE THAT TECHNOLOGY...

...OFTEN LEAVES SOMETHING TO BE DESIRED.

BRAKOW

I'VE NEVER SEEN SUCH SKILL, LEIA! YOU WIELD THIS FLIER AS I DO MY SWORD!

COMING FROM YOU, THAT IS INDEED A COMPLI-MENT. THANK YOU.

"LEIA SPOKE SKYWALKER'S NAME WITH A SOFT--ALMOST UNCONSCIOUS--CARESS. SHE OBVIOUSLY CARED FOR HIM A GREAT DEAL. I HATED HIM.

BUT IF YOU THINK I'M GOOD, YOU SHOULD SEE THE YOUNG MAN WHO TAUGHT ME MOST OF WHAT I KNOW: LUKE SKYWALKER.

AND ON SK'AR'S AIRSHIP...

ALL BATTERIES-- *OPEN FIRE!*

BUT, GENERAL, WE COULD HIT OUR OWN SHIPS!

THEY ARE *EXPENDABLE,* MAJOR. AS ARE *YOU,* IF MY ORDERS ARE NOT OBEYED.

"THE HULL OF THE AIRSHIP GLOWED LIKE THE SUN, AND THE SKY AROUND US SIZZLED WITH FIRE AS HER ENERGY CANNONS FIRED A SIMULTANEOUS BROADSIDE.

"NOTHING COULD HAVE SURVIVED THAT BAR-RAGE. YET WE DID. VIRTUALLY UNSCATHED. LEIA SWEPT LOW OVER THE DECK, RAKING IT WITH OUR OWN CANNONS,

"HER FACE WAS SET IN A STOIC, EMOTIONLESS MASQUE.

"YET I SAW THE FLASH OF TEARS ON HER CHEEK, SENSED WHAT THIS ACTION WAS COSTING HER, INSIDE.

"HERS WAS AS GENTLE A SOUL AS I HAVE EVER KNOWN. I WONDERED HOW MUCH MORE OF THIS BUTCHERY IT COULD STAND.

LEIA-- WE'RE *HIT!*

SKIM LOW OVER THE AIRSHIP'S DECK AND *JUMP!*

"IN TRUE CALIAN TRADITION, WE TOOK OUR FIGHT INTO THE HEART OF THE ENEMY CAMP. OUR FATES WERE SEALED NOW AS SURELY AS IF WE HAD STAYED ABOARD OUR DOOMED FLIER, BUT AT LEAST THIS WAY, WE WOULD SELL OUR LIVES DEARLY, WITH HONOR. I LANDED SAFELY ON THE AIRSHIP'S DECK.

"LEIA MISSED.

NO.!!

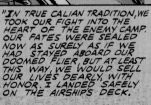

THIS PROJECTION-- WAS BARELY IN REACH!

I'M LUCKY I CAUGHT IT!

BUT MY ARM-- WRENCHED. I DON'T KNOW IF I'VE STRENGTH ENOUGH TO PULL MYSELF UP.

ARON!

TAKE MY HAND, MY LADY.

BY THE WAY, WHATEVER WEAPONS YOU MAY HAVE...

...I SUGGEST YOU DRAW THEM.

DON'T SOUND SO GLUM, WARLORD. PERHAPS THEY'RE HERE TO SURRENDER.

"ALAS, THEY WERE NOT.

"SK'AR CALLED MY PEOPLE THE FIERCEST, DEADLIEST WARRIORS IN KNOWN SPACE. THAT BLOODY MORNING, I LIVED UP TO OUR REPUTATION, AND LEIA ORGANA, PRINCESS OF ALDERAAN, FORGED ONE OF HER OWN. WE FOUGHT SIDE BY SIDE AND BACK TO BACK AGAINST A SEEMINGLY ENDLESS HORDE OF STORMTROOPERS.

ARON, WE HAVE TO REACH SK'AR'S BOMB. THIS SLAUGHTER-- OUR SACRIFICE-- MEANS *NOTHING* IF HE DETONATES IT.

I UNDER-STAND.

THIS AIRSHIP IS AS LARGE, IN ITS OWN WAY, AND AS COMPLEX AS A SMALL CITY. ITS VERY SIZE WORKS TO OUR ADVANTAGE.

IF WE CAN LOSE OUR PURSUERS...

...THEY'LL HAVE THE DEVIL'S OWN TIME FINDING US AGAIN.

FOOLS! THEY SLIPPED PAST YOU! FOLLOW THEM! FIND THEM! IMMEDIATELY!

YOU CALL YOURSELVES COMMANDOS, THE EMPEROR'S ELITE STRIKE FORCE. PROVE IT! I WANT THIS FARCE ENDED-- NOW! *ATTACK!!*

"*WITH THAT WE BEGAN A MADCAP, HELTER-SKELTER CHASE FROM ONE END OF THE GIANT VESSEL'S DECK TO THE OTHER-- WHICH FINALLY ENDED WHEN WE EMERGED, UNSEEN, BESIDE THE BOMB.*

"*IT HAD A GUARD DETACHMENT.*

"*...BUT NOT FOR VERY LONG.*

WHAT DO WE DO NOW? CAN THIS DEVICE BE DESTROYED?

NOT WITH THE WEAPONS WE'RE CARRYING. NOT SAFELY. IT CAN'T EVEN BE MOVED.

I'LL HAVE TO DISARM IT.

I WILL ENSURE THAT YOU REMAIN UNDISTURBED.

"*I* PROWLED THE CORRIDOR, ALMOST EAGER FOR OUR ENEMIES TO ROUND THE CORNER... BUT THE *ATTACK* CAME FROM *ABOVE*. DELOIS LEAPT FROM THE BATTLEMENTS, SWORD IN HAND, LUNGING AT *LEIA*.

"*DELOIS HAD NO CHANCE TO LAND ANOTHER.*

WHO--?!

LUKE!!

"*BUT AT THE LAST IN-STANT, LEIA SENSED HIS PRESENCE AND SLIPPED ASIDE, TURN-ING A FATAL BLOW INTO A WOUNDING ONE,*

"LUKE? COULD THIS YOUTH BE THE SKY-WALKER SHE HAD MENTIONED WITH SUCH AFFECTION IN HER VOICE?

YOU'RE PRETTY SHARP WHEN IT COMES TO STABBING SOMEONE IN THE BACK.

YOU'D BETTER HOPE YOU'RE AS GOOD IN A *FAIR* FIGHT...

...BECAUSE IF YOU AREN'T...

...THERE WON'T BE ANY REMATCH.

"*I* HEARD THUNDER OVERHEAD...

KERAL! IT IS GOOD TO SEE YOU, MY BROTHER!

"...AND AN ALIEN STARCRAFT SKIMMED THE DECK OF SK'AR'S AIRSHIP, SPITTING FIRE AT HIS GUN EMPLACEMENTS AND MEN...

BUT **WHAT** IS THAT FUZZY GIANT BY YOUR SIDE?!

"...AND DROPPING SOME WELL NEEDED REENFORCEMENTS.

HE IS A **WOOKIEE**, ARON, CALLED **CHEWBACCA**, AND HE IS AS FORMIDABLE A WARRIOR AS I HAVE EVER MET.

IT'S ALL RIGHT, LEIA. OUR SEARCH FOR YOU IS OVER-- THANK THE **FORCE**. BUT... YOU'RE HURT.

CHEWIE, RADIO LANDO! I NEED A MEDIKIT!

L-LATER...

THAT SLASH IS DEEP. YOU'RE LOSING A LOT OF BLOOD.

AND THAT BOMB IS **TICKING**! I HAVE TO DISARM IT!

LET ME!

YOU DON'T KNOW HOW! AND THERE ISN'T TIME TO TEACH YOU.

IF YOU WANT TO MAKE YOURSELF USEFUL, GO FIGHT STORMTROOPERS. JUST LEAVE ME BE. THIS IS SOMETHING *I* HAVE TO DO. ALONE.

IT'S...HARD. SO MUCH TO REMEMBER. I CAN'T AFFORD THE SLIGHTEST MISTAKE.

MY ARM HURTS. AND...I FEEL SO WEAK. MAKES IT...DIFFICULT TO CONCENTRATE.

NO! I WON'T YIELD. I WON'T FAIL. I HAD TO STAND BY HELPLESSLY AND WATCH AS MY HOMEWORLD, ALDERAAN, WAS DESTROYED. I WON'T LET A WORLD DIE AGAIN.

WITH A SUPREME EFFORT OF WILL, LEIA FORCED THE TREMBLING FROM HER HANDS, THE FATIGUE FROM HER LIMBS, AND STARTED TO WORK ON THE BOMB.

"NEARBY, LUKE, KERAL, CHEWBACCA AND I--AIDED BY A BARRAGE FROM THEIR SHIP, THE MILLENNIUM FALCON-- MADE SHORT WORK OF SK'AR'S COMMANDOS.

"AFTER A FINAL STRAFING RUN, THE CORELLIAN FREIGHTER SKIDDED INTO A PERFECT TOUCHDOWN ON THE AIRSHIP'S LANDING PAD...

...AND HER PILOT, LANDO CALRISSIAN, CHARGED FORTH TO AID IN THE MOPPING-UP OPERATIONS.

WELL, WHAT HAVE WE HERE?! AN IMPERIAL GENERAL, RUNNING OUT ON HIS MEN?

TYPICAL.

I HATE TO DISAPPOINT YOU, UGLY--

--BUT THIS IS AS FAR AS YOU GO!

SPOOW!

AHHRRR!

ON THE CONTRARY, REBEL.

UH-OH.

THOUGH ONE OF US WILL PERISH THIS DAY-- IT WILL NOT BE ME!

I'M HITTING HIM AT POINT-BLANK RANGE! BUT HE ISN'T STOPPING!

I HAVE A PERSONAL FORCE SHIELD, CRETIN. NO HAND BLASTER MADE CAN PENETRATE IT!

WHAP!

I WOULD RIP THE HEAD FROM YOUR BODY, HAD I THE TIME, BUT THAT SLAP WILL HAVE TO SUFFICE.

OHHH, BROTHER--THAT "SLAP" DARN NEAR DID THE TRICK. IF I HADN'T ROLLED WITH IT AT THE LAST INSTANT....!

I'LL PLAY DEAD FOR A FEW SECONDS, THEN GO AFTER THE GENERAL --AS FAST AS I CAN HOBBLE.

GENTLY, *GENTLY!* I'VE COME SO FAR-- I MUSTN'T BOTCH THINGS NOW!

ONE LAST WIRE TO CROSS...

IT'S DONE! THE BOMB IS DISARMED.

"*TEARS RAN FREELY DOWN LEIA'S FACE--TEARS OF FATIGUE, OF RELIEF, OF JOY. SHE HAD FACED HER INNER DEMONS AND TRIUMPHED. IN THAT MOMENT, THOUGH, SHE DID NOT TURN TO ME...*

...BUT TO LUKE SKYWALKER.

"*AND WITH THAT, I REALIZED THAT IT WAS MY DEMONS' TURN TO DIE.*

GENERAL SK'AR-- HE'S ABOARD THAT FLIER!

CHEWIE-- *STOP HIM!*

"*CHEWBACCA'S IMPROVISED MISSILE WAS A SOLID STEEL GUN MOUNT. ITS WEIGHT WAS AWESOME, YET HE LIFTED IT WITH CHILDISH EASE...*

"*...AND THREW IT WITH MURDEROUS ACCURACY.*

BOOM!

"*AS I SAW SK'AR'S AIRCRAFT EXPLODE, I FOUND MYSELF WISHING MY OWN FEELINGS, NEEDS AND DESIRES COULD BE LAID TO REST AS EASILY.*

"*I HAD LOVED LEIA--INSANELY, HOPELESSLY, HELPLESSLY--FROM THE MOMENT I MET HER. IT MATTERED NOT THAT I HAD A WIFE, WHOM I ADORED, AND A FAMILY. I SAW LEIA, AND MY HEART WAS HERS. BUT HER HEART WAS NOT MINE.*

"*IT WOULD NEVER BE MINE.*

"*AS I FINALLY ADMITTED THAT, MY MAD, ALL-CONSUMING NEED FOR HER FADED--LIKE THE SICKNESS IT HAD BEEN. I WOULD ALWAYS LOVE HER, BUT I COULD AT LAST LIVE WITHOUT HER.*"

THE NEXT HUNDRED HOURS WERE BUSY, AS THE CALIAN FLEET WAS MOBILIZED TO LATER DESCEND ON SK'AR'S BASE AND POUND IT INTO RUBBLE. SIMULTANEOUSLY, DELOIS' FELLOW CONSPIRATORS WERE ROOTED OUT. THOSE WHO WERE NOT SLAIN IN BATTLE WERE TAKEN INTO CUSTODY, TO BE TRIED FOR HIGH TREASON.

"ONCE THE CRISIS WAS PAST, ALL CONCERNED-- CALIAN NOBILITY AND REBEL STAR WARRIORS-- GATHERED IN THE GREAT HALL OF MY PALACE FOR ANOTHER GREAT CELEBRATION *, THIS ONE TO REVEL OVER THE SUCCESSFUL DEFENSE OF OUR PLANET FROM IMPERIAL CONQUEST.

*THESE CALIAN FOLKS SURE DO LIKE TO PARTY. LAST ISSUE, IT WAS FOR THE ANNIVERSARY OF THE CONCORDAT OF PEACE --LOUISE & DANNY.

THIS REMINDS ME OF THE CEREMONY ON YAVIN, AFTER WE DESTROYED THE DEATH STAR. THAT SEEMS... SO LONG AGO. I WAS SO YOUNG IN THOSE DAYS. LIFE WAS SO... SIMPLE.

LEIA AND I HAVE LOST SO MUCH, YET WE STILL HAVE EACH OTHER.

TRUE FRIENDS, UNTO DEATH. AND PERHAPS, ONE DAY...

...SOMETHING MORE THAN FRIENDS.

IT IS AN HONOR TO HAVE LUKE AND LEIA AS ALLIES. I HOPE FATE GRANTS THEM LIFELONG HAPPINESS--

--SUCH AS I HAVE FOUND WITH YOU, ARON.

YOU CAN SAY THAT, ALYS-- AFTER ALL THAT'S HAPPENED, AFTER WHAT I'VE THOUGHT AND DONE?

I KNOW YOU, ARON, AND I KNOW HER. YOU ARE TOO HONEST, TOO GOOD, A MAN TO DENY THE TRUTH ONCE YOU FINALLY PERCEIVED IT. WHEN THAT HAPPENED, AND YOU REALIZED WHERE YOUR HEART TRULY LAY, I KNEW YOU WOULD RETURN TO ME.

"ACROSS THE FLOOR, LANDO CALRISSIAN FOUND HIMSELF THE CENTER OF ATTENTION OF NEARLY EVERY UN- ATTACHED WOMAN AT COURT--AND MORE THAN A FEW DARING SOULS WHO WERE ATTACHED.

"OF COURSE, HE LOVED EVERY MINUTE OF IT.

127

"ON THE SIDELINES, CHEWBACCA IMPASSIVELY WATCHED THE FESTIVITIES, ACCOMPANIED BY SEE-THREEPIO AND ARTOO-DETOO.

AS A PROTOCOL DROID, I HAVE ATTENDED A GREAT MANY OF THESE FUNCTIONS, BUT THEY REMAIN A COMPLETE MYSTERY TO ME. HUMANS ENGAGE IN SUCH IRRATIONAL BEHAVIOR AT THEM...

...AND THEY ACTUALLY SEEM TO ENJOY IT!

BLRP!

EH? I'M SORRY, ARTOO, DID YOU SAY SOMETHING?

BLIP! A DIP! DIT!

I MUST INFORM OUR MASTERS AT ONCE! MASTER LANDO IS NEAREST-- BUT THERE'S TOO MUCH NOISE, HE CAN'T HEAR ME CALLING! AND THE CROWD KEEPS ME FROM REACHING HIM!

CHEWBACCA, DO YOU THINK YOU MIGHT HELP ME?

"THERE'S AN OLD CANTINA SAYING:'WHEN A WOOKIEE WANTS SOMETHING'--OR IN THIS CASE, SOMEONE--

HEY!

--'DON'T GET IN HIS WAY.'

SOMEBODY STOP THIS MONSTER!

I'M GAME, HOW?!

CHEWIE! WH--UNNGNH.!!

CRRAWK!

OKAY, OKAY, I GET THE MESSAGE. YOU WANT TO TALK TO ME, BUT IT HAD BETTER BE GOOD.

MASTER LANDO, ARTOO HAS BEEN SPEAKING TO THE SHIP'S LONG-RANGE SCANNERS.

THEY SAY THAT AN IMPERIAL STAR DESTROYER HAS JUST PHASED OUT OF HYPER-SPACE-- HEADING THIS WAY!

"WITHIN THE HOUR, THE *FALCON* WAS BOOSTING OUT OF SHIVA'S ATMOSPHERE AT MAXIMUM ACCELERATION, ON AN INTERCEPT COURSE WITH THE STAR DESTROYER. THEY WERE PLEDGED TO KEEP THE IMPERIALS FROM EXACTING THEIR FEARFUL RETRIBUTION FOR THE ANNIHILATION OF SK'AR'S COMMAND.

"ALL ABOARD KNEW THEY HADN'T A PRAYER OF SUCCESS--GOOD AS SHE WAS, THE *FALCON* WAS NO *MATCH* FOR AN IMPERIAL DREADNOUGHT--BUT THEY HAD TO AT LEAST MAKE THE ATTEMPT.

IT'S THE END OF ARON'S WORLD, LUKE,

THEY HAVE NO DEFENSE AGAINST AN ATTACK FROM SPACE. IF WE CAN'T FIND SOME WAY TO *STOP* IT, THAT STAR DESTROYER WILL RENDER THE PLANETARY SURFACE UNINHABITABLE.

IT'S SO... *UNFAIR!* AFTER ALL I--WE-- HAVE ENDURED, TO COME SO CLOSE TO VICTORY...

...AND THEN HAVE IT SNATCHED FROM OUR GRASP. I DIDN'T THINK ANYTHING COULD HURT SO MUCH.

LADY ALYSANDE, ARON'S WIFE, GAVE ME THIS WARCLOAK. IT WAS ORIGINALLY MEANT FOR THEIR DAUGHTER, TO BE WORN BY HER IN BATTLE. SHE... SHE CALLED ME HER "DAUGHTER IN SPIRIT."

SHE GAVE IT WITH LOVE, SHE SAID, KNOW- ING THAT I WOULD WEAR IT WITH *HONOR.*

LUKE, IT'S *ALDERAAN* ALL OVER AGAIN! PEOPLE--A WORLD --I CARE FOR ARE ABOUT TO DIE AND I'M POWERLESS TO PREVENT IT.

I'M EVEN-- *OH!!*

MAN THE GUNS, KIDS! THE IMPERIALS REACTED FASTER THAN WE ANTICIPATED.

THEY'RE GOOD SHOTS, TOO. THAT FIRST SALVO *BRACKETED* US.

"LUKE TOOK THE LOWER HULL QUAD-TURRET, WHILE LEIA CLIMBED INTO THE UPPER HULL POSITION.

I'M SET, LANDO. BUT MY SCOPE'S CLEAN.

WHERE'S THE OPPOSITION?

OPEN YOUR EYES, COMMANDER SKYWALKER, SIR.

I SCAN A QUINTET OF *TIE* FIGHTERS, COMING AT US HEAD ON!

MAKE THAT A *QUARTET*, LANDO.

VERY NICE, LEIA.

LANDO, FAR BE IT FOR ME TO TELL YOU HOW TO FLY THIS SHIP...

...BUT HOW ABOUT SHIFTING US INTO HYPER-SPACE?

OH, AND BY THE WAY, MAKE IT A *TRIO!*

WE'RE NEARLY THERE, KID. ANOTHER FEW SECONDS AND -- WILL YOU QUIT GRUMBLING, CHEWIE?! WHAT'S TO PREVENT US MAKING THE HYPER-SHIFT?!?

WRUNNK!

OH.

FORGET I ASKED.

THE *STAR DESTROYER--*!

THOSE *TIES* WERE HEADING US STRAIGHT TO IT!

LANDO, IS THERE ANYTHING WE CAN DO?!

WE'RE OUT OF RANGE OF THEIR TRACTOR BEAMS AND, SO FAR WE'RE KEEPING OUR DISTANCE, BUT SHE'S POUNDING US PRETTY HARD. OUR SHIELDS CAN'T TAKE MUCH MORE OF THAT KIND OF PUNISHMENT.

WHAT, CHEWIE?! REFINE THE FORWARD SENSOR SCAN!

RARWK!

GRAWWRK!

THAT'S IT, MY FRIENDS. WE'RE OUT OF OPTIONS.

THE STAR DESTROYER'S BEHIND US, WITH ITS *TIE'S* ON OUR FLANKS. AHEAD OF US IS A *BLACK HOLE.* EITHER WE SURRENDER-- OR THEY'LL RUN US RIGHT INTO IT.

LET ME OVER THERE, LANDO, I'LL TAKE THE CONTROLS.

I HAVE AN IDEA!

HEY! BE GENTLE WITH THE MATERIAL!

DO YOU HAVE ANY CONCEPTION OF WHAT THIS OUTFIT *COST*?!

RRUK?

YEAH, I THINK HE'S CRAZY, TOO.

LANDO CALRISSIAN, YOU'RE TALKING ABOUT THE MAN WHO DESTROYED THE DEATH STAR!

HANG ON, ALL OF YOU. I'M EXECUTING THE LAST MANEUVER THE IMPERIALS EXPECT--ACCELERATING TOWARDS THE BLACK HOLE!

LUKE, YOU *ARE* CRAZY!

CAPTAIN, WE'RE GETTING DANGEROUSLY CLOSE TO THE BLACK HOLE.

I PLAN TO ORBIT THE HOLE ALONG ITS PERIPHERY. WE'LL EMERGE WHERE WE WENT IN, BUT WITH A CONSIDERABLY HIGHER VELOCITY. BY THE TIME THE IMPERIALS REACT, WE'LL BE LONG GONE.

MAINTAIN COURSE AND SPEED. WHERE THEY CAN GO, WE CAN FOLLOW.

IT... COULD WORK--

"HUNTER AND HUNTED RUSHED HEADLONG TOWARDS THE ANCIENT, LONG-DEAD SUN-- A COLLAPSED STAR ONLY A FEW KILOMETERS IN DIAMETER, YET POSSESSED OF AN ALMOST IMMEASURABLE MASS WHOSE GRAVITY IS SO GREAT THAT EVEN LIGHT CANNOT ESCAPE.

--BUT THE RISK, LUKE.

THIS CLOSE TO THE HOLE-- OUR INSTRUMENTATION CAN'T BE TRUSTED! THE SLIGHTEST ERROR WILL THROW US IN AND DESTROY US!

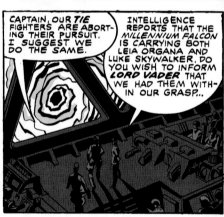

CAPTAIN, OUR TIE FIGHTERS ARE ABORTING THEIR PURSUIT. I SUGGEST WE DO THE SAME.

INTELLIGENCE REPORTS THAT THE MILLENNIUM FALCON IS CARRYING BOTH LEIA ORGANA AND LUKE SKYWALKER. DO YOU WISH TO INFORM LORD VADER THAT WE HAD THEM WITHIN OUR GRASP...

...AND LET THEM GO? I THOUGHT NOT.

I WON'T BE USING THE INSTRUMENTS, LANDO. I'LL GUIDE US THROUGH... WITH THE HELP OF THE FORCE.

"HE CLOSED HIS EYES, PULLED DEEP WITHIN HIMSELF, REACHED OUT TO THE UNIVERSE. ORDINARILY, A BLACK HOLE IS INVISIBLE TO THE NAKED EYE-- HENCE, ITS NAME--

--YET LUKE "SAW" IT CLEARLY IN HIS MIND, BECAME ONE WITH IT.

"THE FORCE LINKED HIM WITH THE AGES-OLD STAR, ALLOWING HIM TO PERCEIVE ITS CRUSHING GRAVITY FIELD AS AN INTRICATE, MULTICOLORED ENERGY MATRIX. IT WAS THE MOST BEAUTIFUL SIGHT HE'D EVER SEEN.

"GENTLY, HE FLEW ALONG THE NARROWEST OF PATHWAYS THROUGH THIS MONSTROUS, VIRTUALLY INSOLUABLE NATURAL MAZE, GUIDING THE FALCON WITH MINUTE, ALMOST UNNOTICEABLE COURSE ADJUSTMENTS. THE STRAIN WAS ALMOST UNENDURABLE-- FOR, ALTHOUGH THE TRANSIT WAS COMPLETED IN ONLY A FEW MINUTES, IT SEEMED TO LUKE LIKE YEARS--

--YET HE ENDURED.

"AND, AS HE ANTICIPATED, WHEN THE FALCON EMERGED FROM THE SCANNER INTERFERENCE FIELD BROADCAST BY THE BLACK HOLE, IT WAS TOO LATE FOR THE STAR DESTROYER TO STOP THEM!

"FOR THE IMPERIAL STARCRAFT, IT WAS TOO LATE, PERIOD.

"TOO CLOSE TO THE HOLE TO SAFELY MODIFY OR BRAKE HIS APPROACH, ITS CAPTAIN TRIED TO COPY LUKE'S MANEUVER. BUT NEITHER HIS COMPUTERS NOR HIS CREW WERE EQUAL TO THE TASK. THE GREAT WARSHIP SLIPPED A FRACTION OFF-COURSE, MOVED TOO CLOSE TO THE HOLE--AND HER FATE WAS SEALED.

"AS IT WAS DRAWN TOWARDS THE STAR, GRAVITY AROUND IT INCREASED AT A GEOMETRIC RATE. THE GRAVITY DIFFERENTIAL OVER THE LENGTH OF THE SHIP--THE DIFFERENCE IN STRESS BETWEEN THE BOW AND THE STERN--

"--A SINGLE GRAVITY AT THE END FARTHEST FROM THE HOLE, ONE MILLION-PLUS AT THE END NEAREST--INSTANTLY BECAME MORE THAN THAT VESSEL, OR ANY VESSEL, COULD WITHSTAND. AND SO, SHE DISINTEGRATED.

HRRRAWR!

BEAUTIFUL! LUKE, THAT WAS SOME OF THE *FINEST* THROTTLE JOCKEYING I HAVE EVER SEEN-- BUT IF YOU *NEVER* PULL A STUNT LIKE THIS AGAIN, IT'LL BE TOO SOON.

THOSE WERE MEN, LANDO--LIVING, SENTIENT BEINGS JUST LIKE OURSELVES. AND WE DESTROYED THEM. IS THAT REALLY A CAUSE FOR CELEBRATION?

I USED TO THINK IT WAS. THESE DAYS, I'M NOT SO SURE.

HELP ME CARRY LUKE BACK TO THE CABIN. AFTER HIS ORDEAL, HE NEEDS NOURISHMENT AND REST.

"LATER, LEIA RADIOED ME, INFORMING ME OF ALL THAT HAD HAPPENED AND OF THE DESTRUCTION OF THE IMPERIAL STARSHIP THAT HAD THREATENED MY WORLD. FOR A WHILE, AT LEAST, SHIVA IV WOULD REMAIN *FREE*."

WE BOUGHT ARON AND HIS PEOPLE SOME *TIME*, PRINCESS. THE REST IS UP TO *THEM*.

BUT THE CREW OF THE STAR DESTROYER-- I *FELT* THEM DIE. A MOMENT OF SUPREME TERROR, OF PAIN--THEN AN AWFUL, ALL-CONSUMING NOTHINGNESS.

THEY WERE MY ENEMIES, YET... I *GRIEVE* FOR THEM.

THE DAY WE LOSE THAT CAPACITY FOR GRIEF-- THE DAY WE KILL WITHOUT COMPUNCTION OR REMORSE--IS THE DAY WE GIVE THE TRUE, FINAL VICTORY IN THIS WAR TO *DARTH VADER*. WE MAY DEFEAT THE EMPIRE, BUT WE'LL HAVE LOST OUR SOULS IN THE PROCESS.

I...KNOW.

WE COULD... LEAVE YOU ON SHIVA, LIST YOU AS MISSING.

YOU'D AT LEAST HAVE A CHANCE TO FIND THE PEACE AND HAPPINESS YOU YEARN FOR. NO ONE WOULD EVER KNOW.

I WOULD KNOW.

I AM *PRINCESS OF ALDERAAN*, LUKE. FATE HAS CAST ME AS A LEADER OF THE REBELLION, FOR BETTER OR WORSE, WHATEVER THE OUTCOME...

...I'LL PLAY THAT ROLE TO THE FINISH.

AND I'LL STAND BY YOUR SIDE.

NEXT ISSUE: THE REBELS SEARCH FOR A NEW BASE, ONLY TO DISCOVER...

PLIF!

WHAT'S "PLIF"? FIND OUT NEXT MONTH, IN *SW #55!*

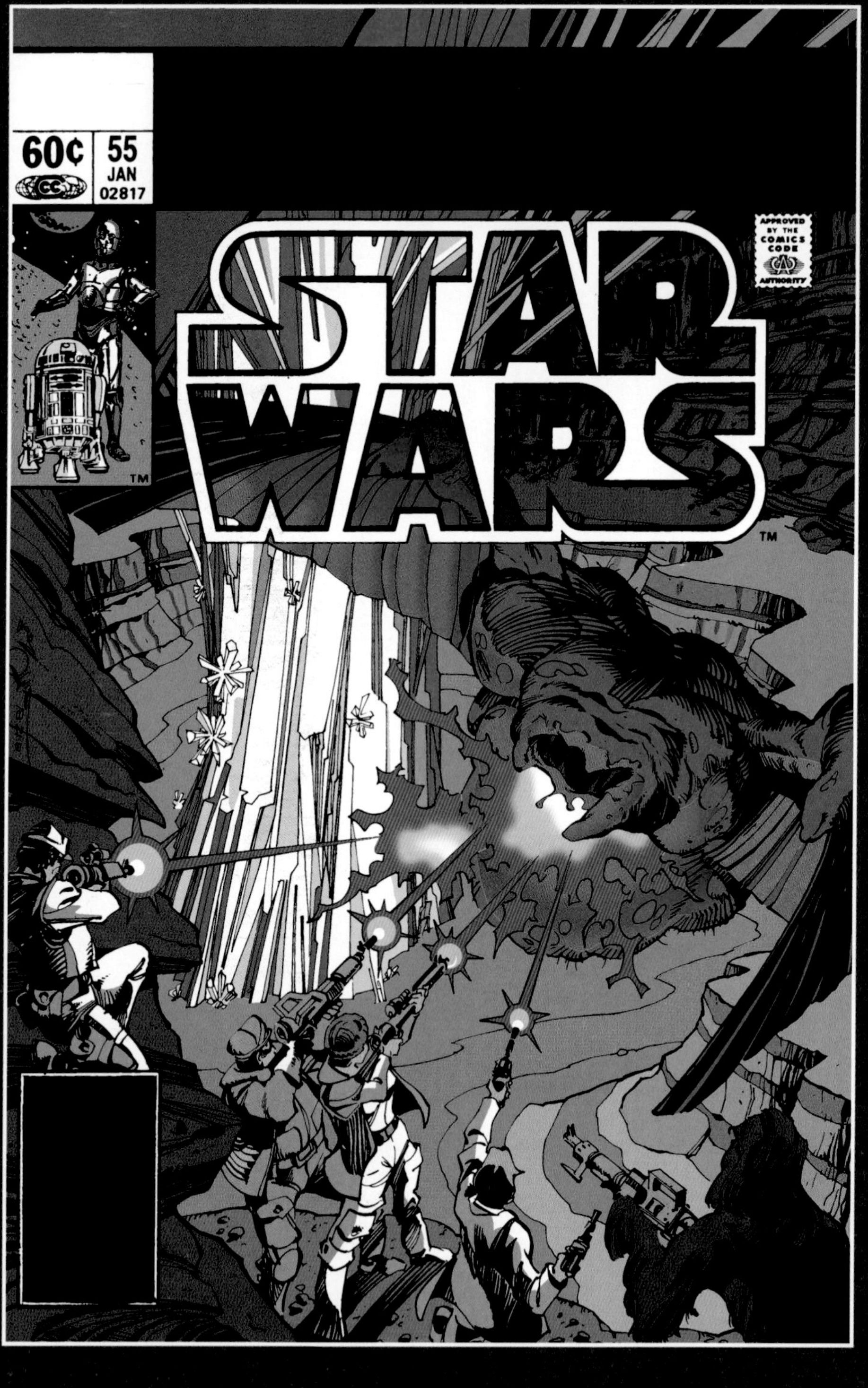
60¢
55
JAN
02817
APPROVED BY THE COMICS CODE AUTHORITY
STAR WARS
TM

ong ago in a galaxy far, far away. . .there exists a state of cosmic *civil war*. A brave alliance of *underground freedom fighters* has challenged the tyranny and oppression of the awesome *Galactic Empire*. This is their story!

Lucasfilm PRESENTS: **STAR WARS**™ THE GREATEST *SPACE FANTASY* OF ALL!

D. MICHELINIE	WALT SIMONSON	TOM PALMER	JOE ROSEN	D. WARFIELD	LOUISE JONES	JIM SHOOTER
WRITER	PENCILLER	INKER	LETTERER	COLORIST	EDITOR	EDITOR-AN-CHIEF

PLIF!

THE PLANET IS CALLED ARBRA, THOUGH SOME MEMBERS OF THE REBEL ALLIANCE SURVEY TEAM WENDING ITS WAY BETWEEN BOLES OF MILE-HIGH TREES HAVE NICKNAMED IT "SALVATION"--

--FOR INDEED, IT COULD WELL PROVE TO BE A PERFECT SITE FOR THE MAIN BASE THEY SO DESPERATELY NEED. COULD BE, THAT IS, IF PRINCESS LEIA ORGANA AND HER FELLOW REBELS ARE WILLING TO PAY...

...SALVATION'S PRICE!

THIS LOOKS LIKE A GOOD SPOT, TEAM--

--WE'LL CAMP HERE FOR THE NIGHT AND PUSH ON TO THE MOUNTAINS TOMORROW.

CARAVAN-- HALT!

--THINGS DO LOOK PROMISING. THE WAY THE BRANCHES OF THESE TREES INTERTWINE SO FAR OVERHEAD MAKES AN EXCELLENT SHELTER FROM VISUAL SURVEILLANCE.

THIS PLANET SEEMS PERFECT!

SNRRRK!

SOUNDS LIKE CHEWIE DISAGREES WITH YOU, THREEPIO. I SUPPOSE IT COULD BE A WOOKIEE'S DISTRUST OF ANYTHING NEW, BUT PERSONALLY--

--I THINK HE JUST DOESN'T LIKE HOOJIBS.

I MUST SAY, YOUR HIGHNESS--

"OH, REALLY? HOW ILLOGICAL."

"I ADMIT THAT OUR DATA ON NATIVE FAUNA IS LIMITED, AND THE HOOJIBS DO SEEM RATHER PROLIFIC--

"--BUT CERTAINLY THEY POSE NO THREAT TO SUCH A WELL-ARMED PARTY AS OURS."

AND BESIDES, THEY'RE CUTE!

THE REBEL RIDERS DISMOUNT; PORTABLE PLASTENTS ARE INFLATED...

...AND AS DUSK DESCENDS ON ARBRA, ALL IS WELL.

OR AT LEAST, ALMOST ALL...

LOOKS LIKE YOU'VE FOUND A FRIEND, CHEWBACCA. MAYBE HE THINKS YOU'RE HIS MOTHER?

GRLLARL

SORRY, LITTLE FELLA, I CAN'T PLAY WITH YOU JUST NOW.

I HAVE TO MAKE MY PRELIMINARY REPORT TO THE FLEET.

AND MOMENTS LATER, IN ORBIT SOME DISTANCE ABOVE ARBRA...

COMMANDER SKYWALKER? PRINCESS LEIA ON COMLINE SIX.

THANKS, BOSUN.

HELLO, LUKE? WE'RE PRETTY WELL SETTLED IN HERE, AND THERE HAVEN'T BEEN ANY PROBLEMS, SO I THINK IT'S A GOOD TIME TO TAKE THE FLEET OUT ON THE ELIPTIC WE DISCUSSED.

I SUPPOSE SO. BUT I STILL DON'T LIKE IT.

I MEAN, KEEPING OUR SHIPS IN ONE SPOT *IS* DANGEROUS, AND BY MOVING THEM IN A WIDE ARC AROUND THIS SYSTEM WE *CAN* MINIMIZE RISKS--

--BUT IT'S THE *REST* OF THE PLAN THAT WORRIES ME.

YOU KNOW, THE PART THAT SAYS THAT IF WE DON'T PICK UP A CODED SIGNAL FROM YOU ON OUR WAY BACK WE JUST KEEP GOING?

IT'S THE ONLY WAY, LUKE. THE EMPIRE CAN POP UP ANYWHERE, AND RESCUING ONE SURVEY TEAM ISN'T WORTH JEOPARDIZING THE ENTIRE FLEET.

I JUST HOPE THEY DON'T RUN INTO ANYTHING NASTY BEFORE --HUH?

YEAH, I KNOW --BLAST IT. OKAY, SEE YOU IN THREE DAYS.

SKY-WALKER OUT.

HEY! LANDO!

YOU'RE NOT LEAVING WITHOUT SAYING GOOD-BYE, ARE YOU?

SORRY, LUKE, I DIDN'T SEE YOU. I'VE BEEN KINDA PREOCCUPIED LATELY.

EVER SINCE WE LEFT *CLOUD CITY* UNDER IMPERIAL DOMINATION,* I'VE FELT UNEASY, LIKE THERE WAS SOMETHING I COULD'VE DONE TO HELP. I SUPPOSE THAT'S WHY I'M GOING *BACK*.

VA-DEET BLUP

I UNDERSTAND. AND SINCE ARTOO'S FINISHED CHECKING OUT THE FALCON, I GUESS THERE'S NOTHING LEFT TO SAY BUT--

*AS DETAILED IN STAR WARS #44.

--GOOD LUCK!

LANDO CALRISSIAN SEATS HIMSELF AT THE CONTROLS OF THE MODIFIED SPICE FREIGHTER, MILLENNIUM FALCON--

--AS AN ELEVATOR PLATFORM LOWERS THEM BOTH TO THE RAY-SHIELDED MOUTH OF A DARKENED LAUNCH BAY. AND THEN, MAJESTICALLY--

--THE FALCON SOARS!

I WISH I WAS GOING WITH HIM. HECK, I'D EVEN SETTLE FOR BEING WITH THE SURVEY CREW ON ARBRA. BUT THAT SKIRMISH WE FOUGHT ON *SHIVA* CAME SO SOON AFTER OUR ESCAPE FROM THE *TARKIN*--*

*IN ISSUES #53-54 AND #51-52 RESPECTIVELY.

--THAT NO ONE HAD TIME TO FILE A DETAILED DE-BRIEFING OF EITHER. AND GUESS WHO'S BEEN ELECTED?

BA-DRRRP!

THANKS, ARTOO. I CAN ALWAYS COUNT ON YOU TO LEND A SYMPATHETIC HEARING CAPACITOR.

NIGHTFALL ON ARBRA: SHY BREEZES RUSTLE THROUGH TREETOPS, STIRRING LEAVES, WHILE AT THE ENCAMP-MENT BELOW--

--A BAND OF TIRED REBELS RESTS, MANY TAKING PLEASURE IN THE FIRST FRESH AIR THEY'VE BREATHED IN MONTHS. THEIR SLUMBER IS DEEP...

...AND SO SOUND THAT NONE NOTICE THE FUR-COVERED SHADOWS THAT SKITTER ABOUT, CLIMBING BANKS OF DORMANT MACHINERY...

...UNTIL ONE SHADOW APPROACHES A SHUT-DOWN DROID--

--C-3PO, BY DESIGNA-TION--WHO DEFINITELY...

...DOES NOTICE!

OUCH!

WHAT--

--OH, MY WORD! I'M BEING EATEN ALIVE!

HELP! HELP!

SHOO!

ALARM CIRCUITS! ACTIVATING THE FLOOD LAMPS!

WHAT'S GOING--

--OFF?

WE'VE LOST POWER!

CORRECTION, BURTT-- THERE'S NO POWER TO *LOSE!* EVERYTHING'S DEAD!

IT'S THE HOOJIBS!

THEY'RE ENERGY EATERS! WE'VE GOT TO--

CLICK CLICK

--BLAST! THEY'VE EVEN DRAINED THE POWER PACKS ON OUR WEAPONS!

LOOK! THEY'RE GETTING AWAY!

STOP THEM, CHEWIE!

AND HE DOES!

RRRARHGG!

THOUGH HE FINDS THE AFTERMATH OF THAT ACTION SOMEWHAT--

PHFRRLL

-- UNANTICIPATED!

OH, DO PUT ME DOWN, WON'T YOU?

THERE'S A GOOD FELLOW.

HRF?

IT...IT TALKS! TELEPATHICALLY!

OF COURSE I TALK. MOST CIVILIZED BEINGS DO, YOU KNOW.

AND BY THE WAY, THAT'S PLIF-- NOT "IT"!

I'M THE SPOKESMIND FOR THOSE YOU CALL "HOOJIBS"!

BUT OUR SCANS SHOWED NO INTELLIGENT LIFE, NO TECHNOLOGY.

MY GOOD CREATURE, SINCE WHEN HAS INTELLIGENCE REQUIRED TECHNOLOGY? IT SEEMS TO ME THAT THE OPPOSITE CASE IS THE MORE ACCURATE.

ALL RIGHT, GRANTED. BUT THAT STILL DOESN'T ACCOUNT FOR YOUR MAKING A MIDNIGHT SNACK OF OUR POWER SUPPLIES!

OH... THAT.

"I SUPPOSE WE DO OWE YOU AN APOLOGY-- AND AN EXPLANATION.

"YOU SEE, THE REASON MY PEOPLE HAVE EXISTED FOR COUNTLESS CENTURIES WITHOUT TECHNOLOGY IS BECAUSE WE DON'T NEED TECHNOLOGY. WE'RE POWER FEEDERS--

"--MEANING THAT WE TAKE ENERGY DIRECTLY, RATHER THAN METABOLIZE IT FROM ANIMAL OR PLANT MATTER.

"SINCE EARLIEST RACIAL MEMORY WE'VE LIVED IN A CAVE, A DEN THAT HAS NOT ONLY SERVED AS OUR HOME--

"--BUT HAS BEEN THE SITE OF A FOOD SUPPLY AS ENDLESS AS IT IS

"--SPECTACULAR! THERE, CRYSTALS DRAW GEOTHERMAL ENERGY FROM THE PLANET'S CORE, TRANSFORM IT INTO ELECTRICITY AND RELEASE IT AS HARMLESS HIGH-ALTITUDE LIGHTNING.

"THAT WAY, PLANETARY PRESSURES ARE KEPT AT SAFE LEVELS, AND ALL WE NEED DO FOR NOURISHMENT IS GNAW ON THE POWER RODS!"

BUT WITH SO MUCH FOOD AT HOME, WHY HIT *US* FOR DINNER?

AH, YES, THAT WAS UN-FORTUNATE--

--BUT MADE NECESSARY, I REGRET TO SAY, BY THE *SLIVILITH.*

BY WHAT?

B-B-BY--

144

"--THAT!"

SKREEAWR

EEEEYAAH!

LOOK OUT!

OH, DEAR!

G-GET IT OFF ME! HELLLP!

CHEWIE! GRAB HIM!

BUT EVEN AN EIGHT FOOT WOOKIEE HAS LIMITATIONS--

--AS CHEWBACCA REALIZES AS HIS FEET RELUCTANTLY LEAVE THE GROUND!

BURTT AND I WERE ON GUARD WHEN THE HOOJIBS HIT, PRINCESS! OUR BLASTERS STILL WORK!

THEN STOP TALKING, MAN--

SACHOW

--AND GET OUT OF THE WAY!

HREEEEB

THBUMP

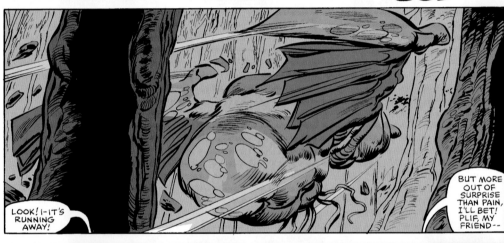

LOOK! I--IT'S RUNNING AWAY!

BUT MORE OUT OF SURPRISE THAN PAIN, I'LL BET! PLIF, MY FRIEND--

--I DON'T THINK YOU'VE TOLD US EVERYTHING.

NO, BUT I'M AFRAID THERE'S NOT A GREAT DEAL MORE.

"THE SLIVILITH DOESN'T HAVE MUCH OF A MIND, AS WE KNOW IT, BUT I WAS ABLE TO PICK UP SOME RATHER MUDDY TELEPATHIC IMAGES.

"APPARENTLY, THE MONSTER DRIFTED THROUGH SPACE IN A SORT OF HIBERNATING STATE FOR QUITE A NUMBER OF YEARS--

"--BEFORE BEING CAUGHT UP IN ARBRA'S GRAVITATIONAL PULL AND DRAWN PLANETWARD.

"ONCE WITHIN OUR ATMOSPHERE, IT GAINED MOBILITY--AND A GOAL.

"AFTER FLOATING SO LONG IN THE CONSTANT CHILL OF SPACE, IT SOUGHT *WARMTH.*

"UNFORTUNATELY, THE WARMEST SPOT ON THE PLANET, DUE TO THE GEOTHERMAL POWER RODS, WAS OUR CAVE!

"AND THUS THE MONSTER DROVE US AWAY, FORCING US TO FORAGE FOR WHATEVER FOOD WE COULD FIND. "

INCLUDING, I'M EMBARRASSED TO SAY, YOUR ENERGY STORES.

THAT'S ALL RIGHT, PLIF, WE UNDER- STAND-- AND WE'LL HELP YOU.

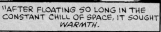

WE WILL?!

WE HAVE TO. THE HOOJIBS DIDN'T MEAN US ANY HARM. AND BESIDES, IF WE DON'T FIND ENERGY TO POWER OUR RADIO BY THE TIME THE FLEET RETURNS--

--THE SLIVILITH ISN'T GOING TO BE THE *ONLY* ALIEN STUCK ON THIS PLANET... MAYBE FOREVER!

147

THE REST OF THE NIGHT PASSES IN PREPARATION, IN THE FASHIONING OF MAKESHIFT WEAPONS AND DESPERATE PLANS.

AND AS MORNING ONCE MORE ARRIVES...

THAT'S IT?

YES, LEIA--

"--THAT'S OUR CAVE."

"GOOD. THEN ONCE WE'VE LURED THE SLIVILITH OUT, WE SHOULD BE ABLE TO RECHARGE OUR BLASTERS ON THE POWER RODS INSIDE. THAT WILL AT LEAST GIVE US A FIGHTING CHANCE!"

ALL RIGHT, SQUAD, THIS WILL BE DANGEROUS, BUT-- PLIF? JUST WHERE DO YOU THINK YOU'RE GOING?

THIS IS OUR BATTLE, TOO, LEIA--AND WE'RE GOING TO DO OUR PART! TO THE CAVE, HOOJIBS!

THE PROTESTS OF THE REBEL LEADER FALL ON LARGE, DEAF EARS--

--AND SOON, AT THE CAVERN ENTRANCE...

VERY WELL, FELLOWS, LET'S SHOW THAT GROTTO-GRABBING VILLAIN WHAT IT MEANS TO INCUR A HOOJIB'S WRATH!

SREE SREE SREE SREE SREE SREE SREE

SECONDS LATER...

WELL, WH-WHAT DO YOU KNOW? IT--

--WORKED?

148

THE CREATURE'S OUT! HIT 'IM!

YEAH--

"--FOR ALL THE *GOOD* IT'LL DO!"

THAK

SPETO

THE DISTRACTION'S WORKING, PRINCESS!

THEN LET'S GET THOSE DEAD BLASTERS TO THE CAVE, GEMMER-- AND FAST!

"WE'VE GOT TO RECHARGE THEM--

"--AND PUT THEM TO WORK BEFORE SOMEONE GETS--"

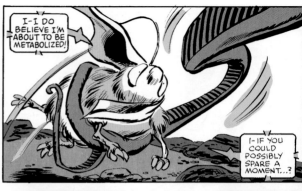

--KILLED...?

I-I DO BELIEVE I'M ABOUT TO BE METABOLIZED!

I-IF YOU COULD POSSIBLY SPARE A MOMENT...?

LEIA!

PUT *THAT HOOJIB* **DOWN!**

F-KOW

SRATCH

WH-WHY, THANK YOU! THAT WAS MOST KIND!

"KIND" MY EYE! IT WAS *STUPID!* NOW THE *SLIVILITH* KNOWS HE'S BEEN TRICKED! AND HE'S HEADING STRAIGHT FOR--

--ME!

TAKING THE ONLY ROUTE OPEN TO HER, PRINCESS LEIA RACES BACK INTO THE CAVE--

--WHERE SOON, AS COLD STONE WALLS GIVE WAY TO A SCENE OF CRYSTAL-LINE GRANDEUR...

THIS IS INCREDIBLE! I'VE NEVER SEEN ANY-THING LIKE IT!

YOU WON'T SEE ANYTHING AT ALL IF WE DON'T GET READY FOR WHAT'S RIGHT ON MY HEELS! SO STOP 'GAWKING AND LISTEN-- I'VE GOT A PLAN!

SORT OF...

AND, A FEW NERVOUSLY-BARKED DETAILS LATER...

CHEWIE, GET INTO POSITION! HERE IT COMES!

OKAY, GEMMER, LET HIM HAVE IT!

B-BUT, PRINCESS! THESE ARE OUR LAST CHARGED BLASTERS! IF WE USE THEM UP--

JUST DO AS I SAY, LIEUTENANT! IF THIS DOESN'T WORK, A THOUSAND BLASTERS WON'T SAVE US! JUST KEEP FIRING--

--UNTIL THAT FLYING SLUG GETS CLOSE ENOUGH...FOR...

...THIS! NOW, CHEWIE!

NOW!

FROM BEHIND THE SOLID ANCHOR OF A JUTTING STALAGMITE--

--A RAGING WOOKIEE RISES--

--REACHING TO GRAB A DOUBLE HANDFUL OF TRAILING TENTACLES--

152

--ENABLING HIM TO USE THE SLIVILITH'S MASS AND MOMENTUM AGAINST HIM--

--TO SLAM THAT STAR-SPAWNED MONSTER INTO--AND THROUGH--A NEARBY JUNGLE OF TOWERING, RAZOR-SHARP RODS!

KRINKATLESH

A SINGLE SCREAM LINGERS, THEN FADES, ABSORBED BY THE CRASHING DIN OF SHATTERING CRYSTAL... AND BY THE SAVAGE CRACKLE OF ENERGIES UNLEASHED!

IT... IT'S DEAD, ISN'T IT?

I'D SAY THAT'S A SAFE ASSUMPTION--

--WOULDN'T YOU, CHEWIE?

MRR-RRF

SECONDS LATER, THE REMAINING REBELS CAUTIOUSLY ENTER...

THEY DID IT!

NOW WE CAN RECHARGE THE RADIO!

WE CAN DO A LOT MORE THAN THAT, IF WE'RE SMART! JUST LOOK AT THIS PLACE! IT'S DEEP ENOUGH TO RESIST IMPERIAL PROBES, IT'S LARGE ENOUGH TO HOUSE OUR ENTIRE OPERATION, AND IT'S GOT A BUILT-IN SOURCE OF BOTH WARMTH AND POWER!

WE COULD SEARCH A DOZEN GALAXIES AND NOT FIND A BETTER BASE SITE THAN THIS!

:AHEM: MIGHT I REMIND YOU, SIR, THAT THIS IS OUR *HOME*? AND--

SORRY, LI'L GUY, WE LIKE YOU A LOT-- BUT WE'RE TIRED OF RUNNING.

YEAH, REAL TIRED.

THEN IT APPEARS, GENTLEMEN, THAT THE BATTLE IS NOT QUITE OVER...

STOP IT! PLIF'S RIGHT. THE EMPIRE'S TAKEN AWAY *OUR* HOMES-- AND WE WON'T STOOP TO THEIR LEVEL BY DOING THE SAME TO SOMEONE ELSE.

EVEN IF IT MEANS START-ING ALL OVER AGAIN.

FAREWELL, HOOJIBS. WE WISH YOU WELL.

THE REBELS TURN, BEGINNING THEIR DEPARTURE IN A THOUGHTFUL, DISAPPOINTED SILENCE...

...THAT IS SUDDENLY INTERRUPTED BY:

ON THE OTHER HAND, WHAT IS A HOME--

--WITHOUT GUESTS?

WHAT--?

IF YOU'D CARE TO *SHARE* OUR HOME, MY FRIENDS, TO WORK *WITH* US, I'M SURE WE'D BE DELIGHTED TO ACT AS YOUR HOSTS--

--INDEFI-NITELY.

PLIF...

...I THINK I LOVE YOU!

DAYS LATER, THE REBEL FLEET RETURNS, AND RECEIVES A NERVOUSLY-AWAITED SIGNAL CODE--AS WELL AS A BONUS--

--WORD THAT, AT LONG LAST, THEIR QUEST IS OVER.

AMIDST CELEBRATION, THE DE-SCENT TO ARBRA BEGINS.

EPILOGUE: HIGH ABOVE THE GAS PLANET, BESPIN, THERE HOVERS A MAN-MADE MIRACLE -- CLOUD CITY, A PASTEL-HUED METROPOLIS ONCE GOVERNED BY THE SAME MAN WHO NOW PILOTS A SPEEDING STARCRAFT TOWARDS IT. A MAN AS PROUD--

--AS HE IS CURRENTLY PUZZLED!

ODD. I HAVEN'T ENCOUNTERED A SINGLE BIT OF RESISTANCE. NOT EVEN A POD CAR MAKING A SECURITY CHECK!

SOMETHING'S WRONG HERE-- VERY WRONG!

AND, AFTER AN EXPERT FIVE-POINT LANDING--

--AND AN EXTENSIVE SEARCH OF SEVERAL LEVELS, LANDO CALRISSIAN DISCOVERS EXACTLY WHAT THAT "SOMETHING" IS!

EVERYONE'S GONE! THE WHOLE CITY'S DESERTED! BUT WHY? I'VE GOT TO FIND OUT--

--OR MY CURIOSITY'S GONNA KILL ME!

WHICH IT JUST MAY--IF THE SINISTER SHADOW THAT STALKS SILENTLY AND DETERMINEDLY TOWARDS HIM--

--DOESN'T DO THE JOB FIRST!

NEXT ISSUE: COFFIN IN THE CLOUDS!

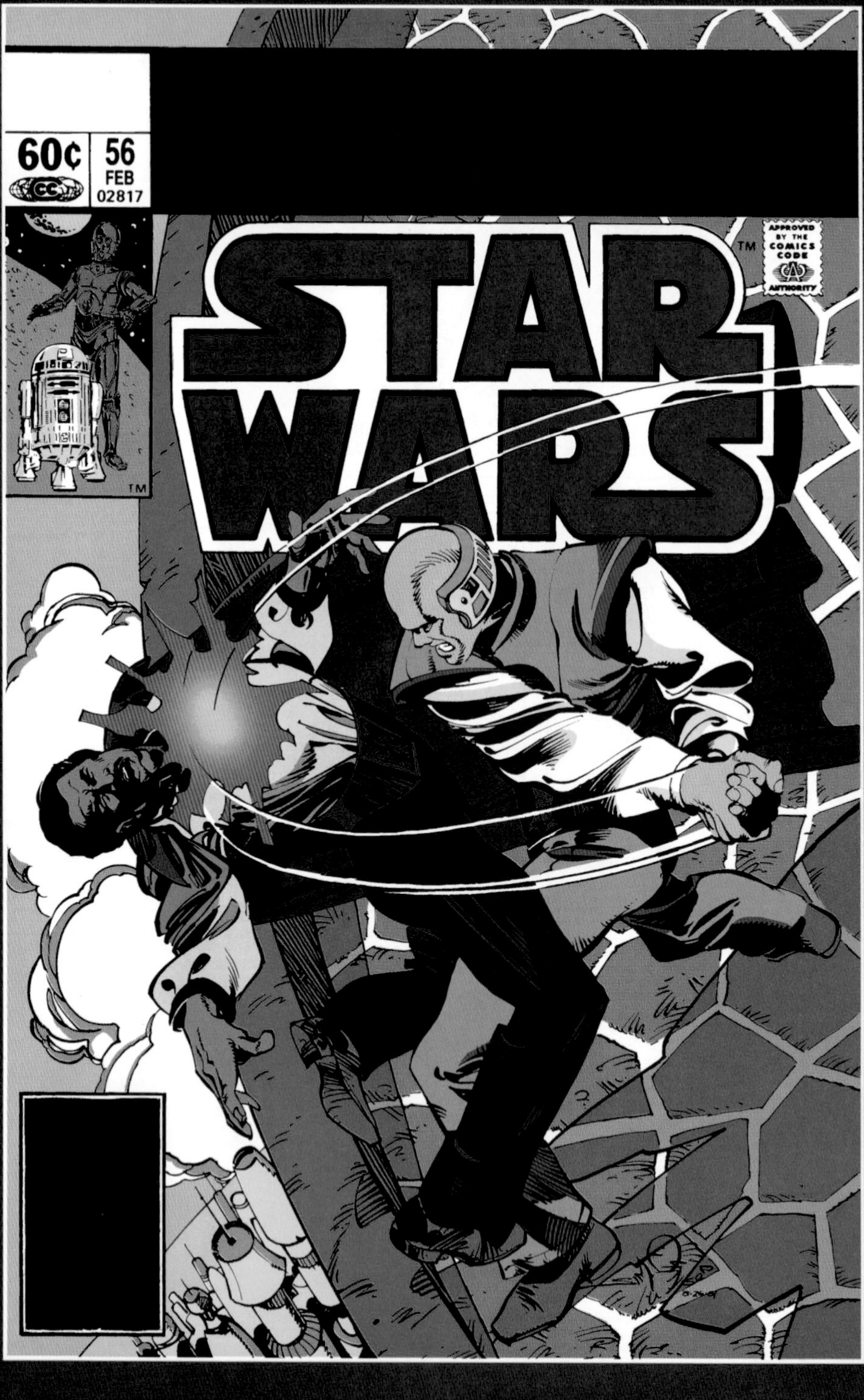

60¢
56
FEB
02817
STAR WARS
TM
APPROVED BY THE COMICS CODE AUTHORITY

ong ago in a galaxy far, far away. . .there exists a state of cosmic *civil war*. A brave alliance of *underground freedom fighters* has challenged the tyranny and oppression of the awesome *Galactic Empire*. This is their story!

Lucasfilm PRESENTS: **STAR WARS** — THE GREATEST SPACE FANTASY OF ALL!

| ID MICHELINIE | WALTER SIMONSON | TOM PALMER | JOE ROSEN | GLYNIS WEIN | LOUISE JONES | JIM SHOOTER |
| RITER / PLOT | PENCILS / PLOT | INKS | LETTERS | COLORS | EDITOR / PLOT | FAVORITE SUN |

THE UNIVERSE IS A PLACE OF PUZZLES-- AND FOR AN HABITUAL GAMESMAN LIKE LANDO CALRISSIAN, THE CHALLENGE OF THOSE PUZZLES IS THE SPICE OF LIFE.

BUT HERE ON CLOUD CITY, THE MAGNIFICENT PASTEL-SPIRED METROPOLIS HOVERING HIGH OVER THE GAS PLANET BESPIN, HE MAY FIND THAT SPICE--

--TURNING TO POISON!

E DON'T ET IT!

COFFIN IN THE CLOUDS

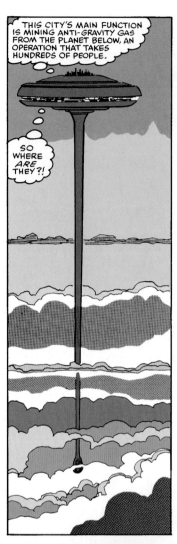

THIS CITY'S MAIN FUNCTION IS MINING ANTI-GRAVITY GAS FROM THE PLANET BELOW, AN OPERATION THAT TAKES HUNDREDS OF PEOPLE.

SO WHERE *ARE* THEY?!

I MEAN, I FIGURED THE EMPIRE'D MAKE SOME CHANGES WHEN THEY TOOK OVER,* BUT *TOTAL AUTOMATION*? THAT'S IMPOSSIBLE!

AND WHY DIDN'T I THINK OF IT WHEN *I* RAN THIS PLACE?

*IN ISSUE *44 -- LOUISE.

YEAH, THAT'S THE BOTTOM LINE, ISN'T IT? "WHEN I RAN..." AFTER ALL, I ONLY CAME *BACK* BECAUSE I FELT I SHOULD'VE DONE MORE TO KEEP THE EMPIRE OUT OF CLOUD CITY IN THE FIRST PLACE.

THOUGH FINDING A FLOATING *GHOST TOWN* WASN'T EXACTLY PART OF MY PLAN!

WELL, STANDING AROUND MOPING WON'T HELP ME SOLVE THAT LITTLE RIDDLE --

-- BUT MAYBE SOME WELL-CHOSEN QUESTIONS TO THE CITY'S CENTRAL COMPUTER BANK *WILL!*

INFORMATION

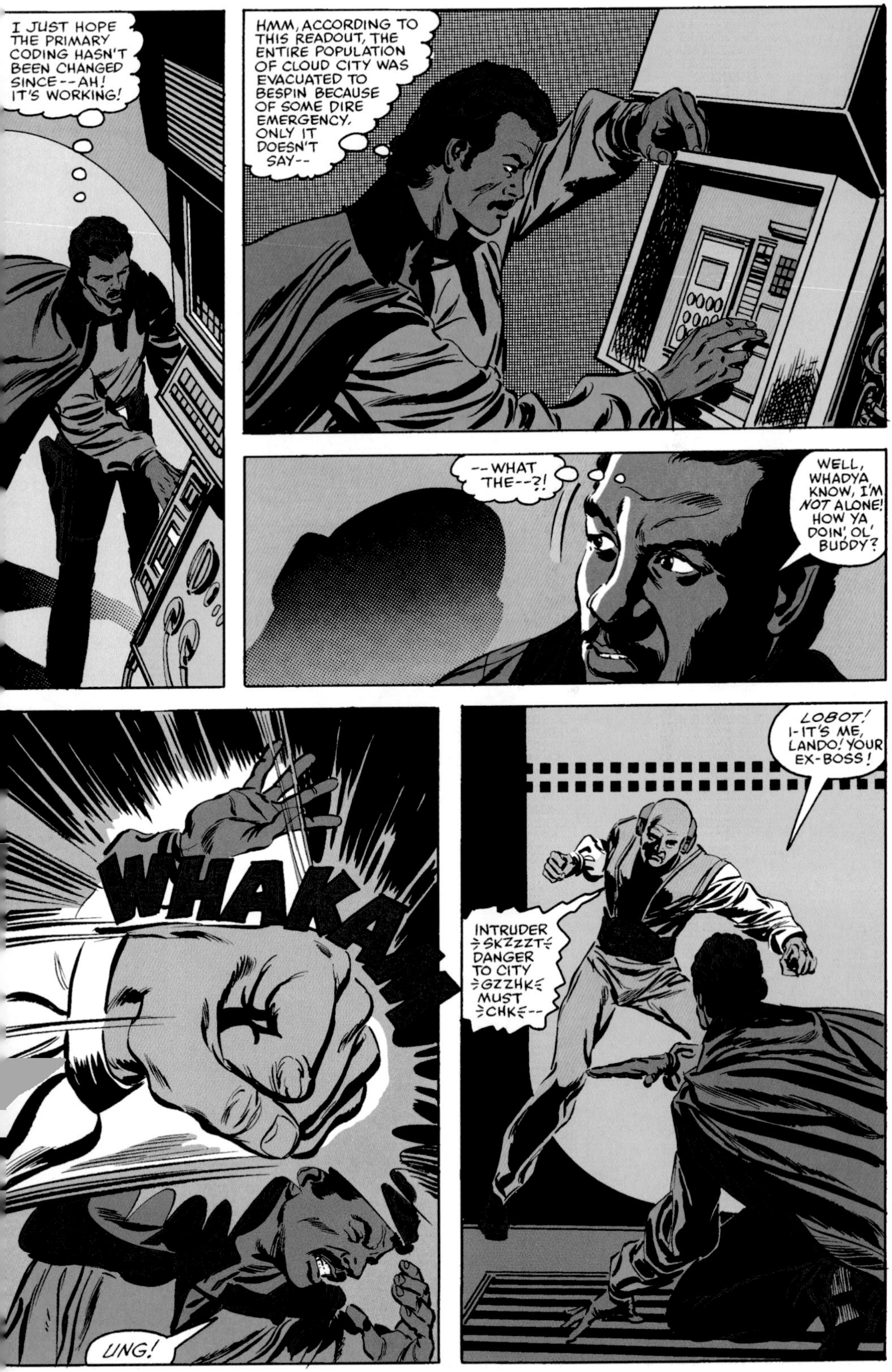
I JUST HOPE THE PRIMARY CODING HASN'T BEEN CHANGED SINCE--AH! IT'S WORKING!
HMM, ACCORDING TO THIS READOUT, THE ENTIRE POPULATION OF CLOUD CITY WAS EVACUATED TO BESPIN BECAUSE OF SOME DIRE EMERGENCY. ONLY IT DOESN'T SAY--
--WHAT THE--?!
WELL, WHADYA KNOW, I'M *NOT* ALONE! HOW YA DOIN', OL' BUDDY?
WHAKAM
UNG!
LOBOT! I-IT'S ME, LANDO! YOUR EX-BOSS!
INTRUDER ≷SKZZZT≷ DANGER TO CITY ≷GZZHK≷ MUST ≷CHK≷--

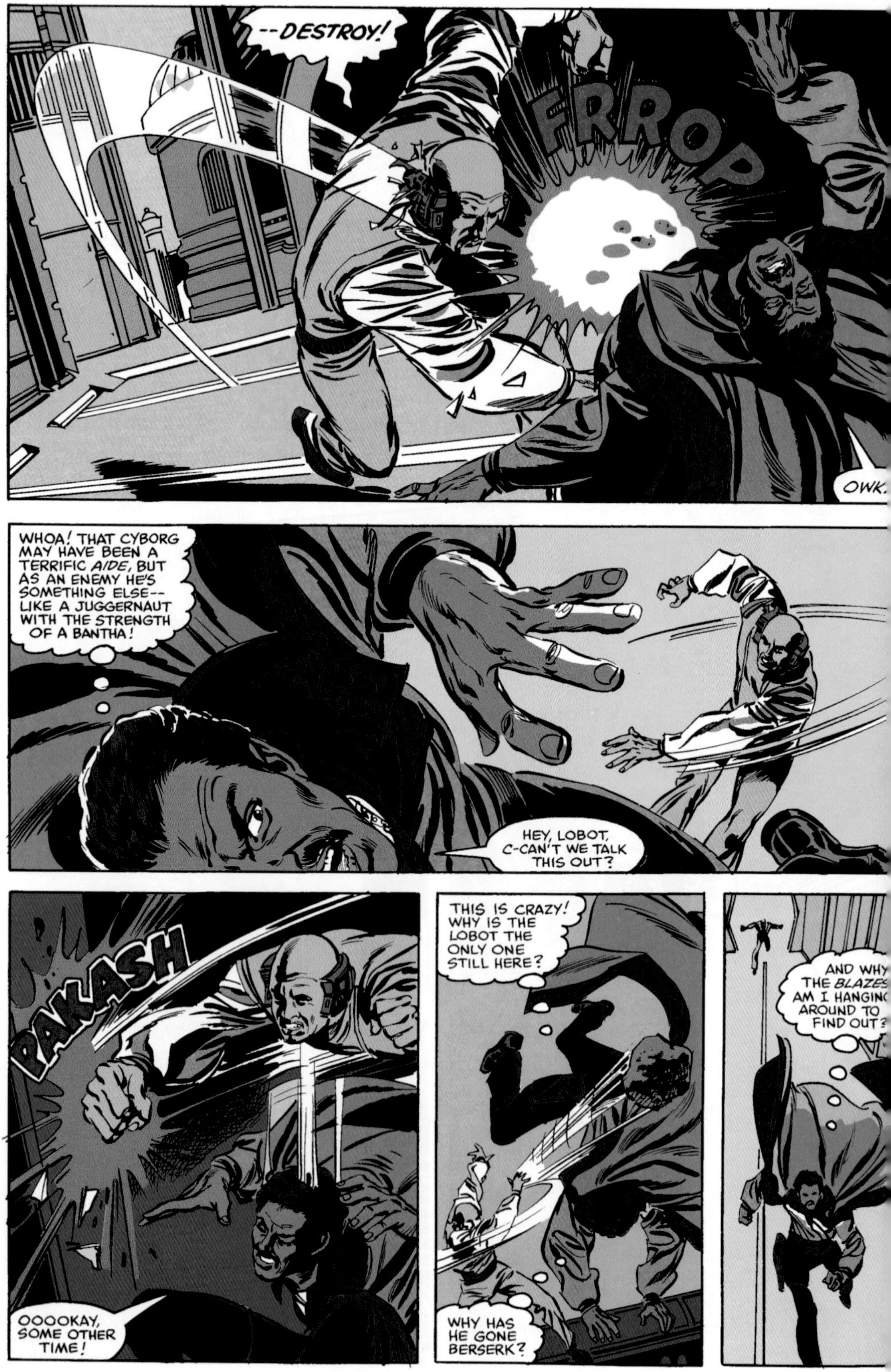

--DESTROY!
FRROP
OWK.
WHOA! THAT CYBORG MAY HAVE BEEN A TERRIFIC AIDE, BUT AS AN ENEMY HE'S SOMETHING ELSE-- LIKE A JUGGERNAUT WITH THE STRENGTH OF A BANTHA!
HEY, LOBOT, C-CAN'T WE TALK THIS OUT?
PAKASH
OOOOKAY, SOME OTHER TIME!
THIS IS CRAZY! WHY IS THE LOBOT THE ONLY ONE STILL HERE?
WHY HAS HE GONE BERSERK?
AND WHY THE BLAZES AM I HANGING AROUND TO FIND OUT?

MEANWHILE, AS LANDO CALRISSIAN SPRINTS FOR HIS LIFE, A SHIP IS APPROACHING THE OTHER SIDE OF CLOUD CITY.

A SHIP OF UNDENIABLY IMPERIAL *DESIGN*.

CUTTING ITS ENGINES, REPLACING THEM WITH DAMPENED RETROS, THE CRAFT GLIDES SLOWLY DOWNWARD--

--LANDS--

--AND RELEASES ITS FULL COMPLEMENT OF OMINOUSLY WELL-ARMED *PASSENGERS*.

STEP LIVELY, TROOPERS!

SERGEANT VOLLOT, IS YOUR *BOMB SQUAD* READY?

YES, SIR, CAPTAIN TREECE, WE'LL BEGIN ENERGY SCANS IMMEDIATELY. AS SOON AS WE'VE LOCATED THE EXPLOSIVES, WE SHOULDN'T HAVE ANY TROUBLE DISARMING THEM.

GOOD. THEN WE CAN CONCENTRATE ON FINDING THE *UGNAUGHT SCUM* THAT PLANTED THEM HERE!

SIR, THE UGNAUGHTS HAVE ALWAYS BEEN LAW-ABIDING WORKERS.

DID THEY GIVE ANY *REASONS* FOR SUDDENLY TURNING TRAITORS?

NONE THAT CONCERN YOU, SOLDIER. NOW, BEGIN SCANNING.

HOWEVER...

WELL, WELL, WELL... IMPERIALS!

THEY MUST BE THAT "DANGER TO CITY" THE LOBOT WAS BABBLING ABOUT!

WHICH MEANS THAT IF I WANT TO KEEP THE LOBOT FROM GETTING *ME*, I'VE GOT TO GET *THEM*!

ONLY FIRST, I'LL HAVE TO GET--

--THEIR *ATTENTION!*

SHOOT HIM!

AGH!

A REBEL ASSASSIN!

NO, YOU FOOLS, HE'S TOO FAR AWAY! GO AFTER HIM!

AND DON'T COME BACK UNTIL YOU'VE GOT THAT GRUBBER'S *ASHES* WITH YOU!

THE PURSUIT BEGINS-- WHILE SEVERAL STAR SYSTEMS AWAY, ANOTHER JOURNEY HAS RECENTLY ENDED ON THE PLANET CALLED ARBRA, A FOREST WORLD WHOSE GREEN, LEAFY FACADE IS BROKEN ONLY BY THE PEAKS OF JUTTING MOUNTAINS, AND THE GLITTERING SURFACE OF AN OCCASIONAL CLEARWATER LAKE.

IT IS TOWARDS THIS LATTER THAT A CAMOUFLAGED SKYSPEEDER NOW TURNS--

--FOR ARBRA HAS LATELY BECOME THE NEW BASE SITE FOR THE REBEL ALLIANCE, AND THIS SPEEDER IS ONE OF THEIRS.

SWOOPING LOW, IT SKIMS SWIFTLY OVER THE LAKE, AND THEN PLUNGES DEEP INTO A PRE-MAPPED PATH BETWEEN TOWERING TREES--

--MOVING INLAND PAST BRANCH-MOUNTED WATCH-POSTS --

--TO A MOUNTAINSIDE CAVERN WHERE OTHER SPEEDERS RECEIVE THEIR SPRAY-PAINTED PATTERNS OF CAMOUFLAGE.

THE SCOUT CRAFT LANDS--

--AND SURRENDERS ITS PILOT: REBEL LEADER AND ALDERAANIAN PRINCESS, LEIA ORGANA.

HAVE THIS SPEEDER RECHARGED IMMEDIATELY, CORPORAL, THERE'S AN ANOMALY ON THE NINTH PERIMETER I WANT TO CHECK OUT.

RIGHT AWAY, PRINCESS.

165

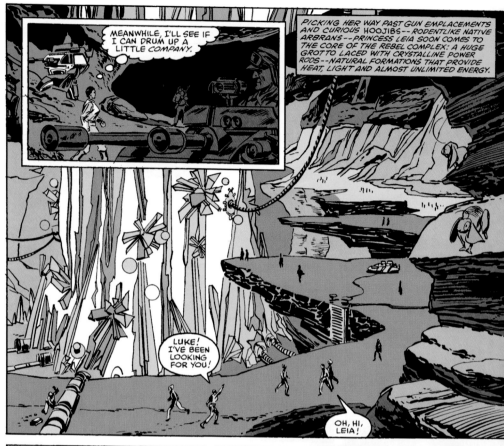

MEANWHILE, I'LL SEE IF I CAN DRUM UP A LITTLE *COMPANY.*

PICKING HER WAY PAST GUN EMPLACEMENTS AND CURIOUS HOOJIBS-- RODENTLIKE NATIVE ARBRANS-- *PRINCESS LEIA SOON COMES TO THE CORE OF THE REBEL COMPLEX: A HUGE GROTTO LACED WITH CRYSTALLINE POWER RODS--NATURAL FORMATIONS THAT PROVIDE HEAT, LIGHT AND ALMOST UNLIMITED ENERGY.*

LUKE! I'VE BEEN LOOKING FOR YOU!

OH, HI, LEIA!

I'M MAKING ANOTHER RUN ON THE PERIMETER, AND COULD USE A CO-PILOT. INTERESTED?

UH, WELL, I WOULD BE-- BUT LANDO HASN'T REPORTED IN FROM BESPIN YET, AND I'M A LITTLE WORRIED.

SO *SHIRA* AND I ARE GOING TO SEE IF HE'S OKAY.

OH? WELL, THAT WAS VERY KIND OF YOU TO VOLUNTEER, LT. BREI. I KNOW COMMANDER SKYWALKER WILL APPRECIATE YOUR COMPANIONSHIP.

I TRY TO PLEASE, PRINCESS.

YES, I'M SURE YOU DO.

THE TWO PILOTS LEAVE--

--AS THE CRYSTAL-WARMED CAVE GROWS EVER SO SLIGHTLY COOLER...

...WHILE ON CLOUD CITY, THINGS ARE GETTING DOWNRIGHT HOT!

SO MUCH FOR "DIVIDE AND CONQUER"! I MAY HAVE SPLIT THE ENEMY INTO TWO GROUPS--

--BUT NOW I HAVE TO STOP THIS ONE BEFORE IT SPLITS ME--

--INTO ATOMS!

FAKOW!

THAT SHOT BOUGHT ME ENOUGH TIME TO REACH THE CARBON-FREEZING ROOM, THE PLACE WHERE VADER FROZE HAN SOLO INTO A SOLID BLOCK OF CARBONITE!

AND WHERE I'VE JUST GOTTEN ONE DANGEROUS IDEA!

AS, ELSEWHERE...

GOOD WORK, SERGEANT. YOUR SCANS HAVE LOCATED THE FIRST BOMB. NOW TO--

HI, GUYS! COME TO DISARM ME, HAVE YA? HEY, THAT'S TERRIFIC!

WHA-- A TALKING *BOMB?!*

WHY NOT? THE UGIES PUT US TOGETHER WITH SPARE PARTS, AND THAT INCLUDED AUDIO COMPONENTS. SO DO YOU WANT SOME HELP, OR WHAT?

YOU? HELP *US?*

SURE! HEY, LOOK, PUT YOURSELF IN MY PLACE: WOULD *YOU* WANT TO EXPLODE? OF COURSE NOT! NOW C'MON, THIS THING'S ON A *TIME FUSE,* Y'KNOW!

WELL, I SUPPOSE IT COULDN'T HURT...

NOW YOU'RE COOKIN'! OKAY, GUYS, LET'S GET TO IT!

I'LL JUST STAND WAY OVER HERE AND, ER, WATCH FOR THAT REBEL GUNMAN. ;AHEM;

AND, SPEAKING OF WHOM...

SO FAR, SO GOOD. THOSE STORMTROOPERS FOLLOWED ME IN, JUST LIKE I HOPED. ONLY--

-- HOW DO I GET THEM *INTO* THE FREEZING CHAMBER? IF THIS WAS CARDS, OR DICE, OR SLIPLINE, I COULD RUN A BLUFF. BUT *VIOLENCE* ISN'T MY USUAL GAME!

SO NOW WHAT? SMOOTH TALK? CHICANERY?

BIRD IMPRESSIONS?

AW, HECK!

THERE'S NEVER A HERO AROUND WHEN YOU NEED ONE!

WHAT--? LOOK OU--

FFUPUMB

THEY'RE IN! ALL OF 'EM! BUT THEY'LL BE CLIMBING RIGHT *OUT* AGAIN IF I DON'T HIT THE FREEZE BUTTON--

--FAST!

INSTANTLY, A SHOWER OF SPARKING, CRACKLING LIQUID CASCADES FROM MULTIPLE NOZZLES, CHOKING OFF A SINGLE, PITIFUL SCREAM.

AND THEN...

THAT'S ONE FOR YOU, HAN.

AS...

ALMOST DONE, FELLAS, ONE MORE TWIST ON THAT GRATHOMETER AND EVERYTHING SHOULD BE HUNKY-DORY.

GOOD. THAT MAKES ONE DOWN AND--

SPING

--EH? THAT ALMOST SOUNDED AS IF WE'D *ACTIVATED* THE DETONATOR INSTEAD OF *DEACTIVATING* IT!

THAT'S PROBABLY BECAUSE YOU *DID*--

--SUCKERS!

FABOOOM

WHA--AN EXPLOSION! A-AND NOW THE WHOLE CITY'S LISTING!

WE MUST BE LOSING *TIBANNA* GAS!

I'VE GOT TO -- UH-OH! CENTRAL COMPUTER MUST'VE TOLD THE LOBOT SOMEONE WAS USING CARBON FREEZE!

AND SOMETHING TELLS *ME* I'D BETTER FIND ANOTHER WAY OUT!

170

GOOD THINKING! FOR SOON...

INTRUDER ⸚GZZT⸚ GONE!

MUST ⸚SKRRK⸚ SAVE CITY!

F-FIND INTRUDER ⸚FZZDT⸚ AND--

--KILL! KI⸚ZZZK⸚ KILL!

THAT EXPLOSION DIDN'T BLOW TOO BIG A HOLE --AND THE EMERGENCY DRONES ARE ALREADY SEALING IT UP!

WE SHOULDN'T DROP TOO FAR BEFORE--

--WELL, WELL! IMPERIALS! THEY MUST'VE BEEN THE ONES WITH THE EXPLOSIVES!

ONLY IT LOOKS LIKE THEY ALL GOT CAUGHT IN THEIR OWN TRAP!

K-TUNK

BETTER MAKE THAT--

--ALMOST ALL!

R...REBEL! Y-YOU ⸚KOFF⸚ ARE MY PRISONER!

171

SEEMS TO ME, FRIEND, THAT WE'RE *EACH OTHER'S* PRISONERS!

YES ÷KOFF÷ I SEE YOUR POINT. THEN MIGHT I SUGGEST WE CALL A TRUCE? FOR THE SAKE OF OUR *MUTUAL* SURVIVAL?

BAD ODDS... BUT I DON'T HAVE MUCH CHOICE.

ALL RIGHT.

A BAD SITUATION... BUT I CAN ALWAYS ALTER IT LATER.

EXCELLENT.

SO SUPPOSE WE START BY YOUR TELLING ME WHAT'S GOING *ON* HERE!

VERY WELL. I AM CAPTAIN TREECE, GOVERNOR OF CLOUD CITY, AND I AM LOOKING FOR TWELVE-- AH, *ELEVEN*--EXPLOSIVE DEVICES...

...PLANTED BY CREATURES CALLED *UGNAUGHTS*.

WHAT?!

"THOSE LACKEYS WORKED IN THE DISPOSAL ROOM, SEPARATING USEFUL COMPONENTS FROM SCRAP.

"BUT CLANDESTINELY, THEY EMPLOYED SOME OF THOSE COMPONENTS TO CONSTRUCT--

"--BOMBS! AND IF THE FIRST WAS TYPICAL, THEY'RE ALL EQUIPPED WITH DESTRUCT DEVICES THAT BLOCK ACCESS TO THEIR DETONATION CONTROLS.

"FORTUNATELY, THE UGNAUGHTS GAVE ENOUGH WARNING THAT WE WERE ABLE TO EVACUATE ALL CITIZENS TO BESPIN. BUT UNLESS WE FIND AND SHUT DOWN THE *REST* OF THOSE BOMBS..."

I KNOW--"SO LONG CITY!" BUT WHY WOULD THE UGNAUGHTS *PULL* A STUNT LIKE THAT?

QUITE SIMPLY, THEY ARE *JEALOUS!*

THEY WISH MINING OPERATIONS TO RETURN TO THE SURFACE OF THEIR HOME PLANET BELOW, SO THEY CAN ONCE MORE BE MINERS INSTEAD OF MENIALS!

I FIND THAT HARD TO BELIEVE, TREECE, BUT I GUESS MOTIVATIONS AREN'T IMPORTANT NOW.

WE CAN DISCUSS THEM *AFTER* WE'VE FOUND THE LOBOT!

THE LOBOT? B-BUT WHY--?!

JUST TRUST ME, CAPTAIN-- I HAVE A PLAN!

C'MON, LANDO, THINK OF A PLAN!

MOMENTS LATER, ON AN OUTER-RIM WALKWAY, A TREMBLING LOBOT STALKS, AND STAMMERS...

IN ≳KLIK≲ TRUDER...!

F-F-FIND...! ≳GZZHK≲

P-PRIME... DIRECTIVE! ≳SPT≲

PROTECT... ≳SSJJK≲... CITY!

M-MUST ≳K-KK≲--

--KILL?

HEY, LOBOT! THERE'S SOMETHIN' I FORGOT TO TELL YOU!

YOU'RE FIRED!

GRRRRAARR

LOOKS LIKE I STRUCK A NERVE!

AND UNLESS I WANT TO GET STRUCK *BACK*, I'D BETTER PUT SOME DISTANCE BETWEEN ME AN'--

--BLAST! LOBOT'S *SUPERHUMAN* STRENGTH TAKES HIM A DOZEN METERS IN A *SINGLE LEAP!* SO IT LOOKS LIKE *I'D* BETTER TAKE--

--A SHORT CUT!

THIS ACCESS TUBE SHOULD GET ME TO THE NEXT LEVEL IN NO TIME FLAT!

OUCH!

SLICK MOVE, CALRISSIAN-- BUT MAYBE *TOO* SLICK!

I DON'T SEE MY CYBORG PLAYMATE ANYWHERE!

COULD I POSSIBLY HAVE *LOST* HIM?

KAREEEESH

OFFHAND, I'D SAY "NO"!

THE CHASE CONTINUES, LEADING AT LAST TO THE FREIGHT-LOADING FACILITIES AT CLOUD CITY'S BASE, WHERE...

I NEVER SPENT MUCH TIME DOWN HERE! I JUST HOPE I CAN FIND THE RIGHT--

--DEAD END!

NOW ⸴SKIK⸴ DIE!

BOY, ARE YOU IN FOR A SURPRISE! OKAY, TREECE!

UH, TREECE?

TREEEEEECE!

SORRY, I'M NOT FAMILIAR WITH THIS TYPE OF LOADING CLAW. IT TOOK ME A WHILE TO GET THE MECHANISM WORKING!

⸴WHEW⸴ BETTER LATE THAN POST-MORTEM, I GUESS! JUST HOLD THE LOBOT UNTIL--

--"UNTIL" NOTHING! THAT CLAW'S NOT HOLDING HIM AT ALL! I'VE GOT TO PULL THE PLUG!

OR IN THIS CASE, THE MOTIVATIONAL PROGRAMMING CAPSULE!

UHH ⸴SKZZT⸴ UHHHHHHHH...

PUK

175

ALL RIGHT, TREECE, HE'S IMMOBILE--YOU CAN PUT HIM DOWN NOW.

WITH PLEASURE, REBEL.

I'M JUST GLAD THAT MY LITTLE PLOY WORKED.

HIS PLOY?! HMPH.

AND SOON...

THE WAY I FIGURE IT, THE UGNAUGHTS REALIZED THAT LOBOT WAS THE ONLY ONE WHO COULD DISARM THEIR BOMBS--SO THEY GAVE HIM A SHOT TO THE CIRCUITS AND LEFT HIM FOR DEAD.

ONLY THE DAMAGE DIDN'T KILL HIM--IT JUST MADE HIM A LITTLE CRAZY!

AND YOUR ADJUSTMENTS WILL "CURE" THAT INSTABILITY?

WELL, CAPTAIN, IF THEY DON'T--

--I DOUBT WE'LL REGRET IT FOR LONG!

YOU NEEDN'T BE CONCERNED, SIR. MY MENTAL PROCESSES ARE FUNCTIONING NORMALLY NOW.

TERRIFIC!

YOU CAN START BREATHING AGAIN, TREECE.

AND MOMENTARILY, AFTER AN ENERGY SCAN HAS LED SEARCHERS TO THE DARK BOWELS OF THE CITY...

SO, NOW THAT WE'VE FOUND THE SECOND BOMB, JUST HOW IS YOUR "FRIEND" HERE GOING TO DISARM IT?

VERY CAREFULLY, I HOPE, Y'SEE--

"--CYBORGS HAVE CERTAIN ABILITIES THE REST OF US LACK. FOR INSTANCE, THEY CAN FOCUS ENERGY TO MANIPULATE OBJECTS WITHOUT ACTUALLY TOUCHING THEM.

"WITH LUCK, THE LOBOT SHOULD BE ABLE TO USE THAT POWER TO GET PAST ANY SAFEGUARD MECHANISMS AND DETACH THE BOMB'S PRIMER CIRCUIT."

OH, W-WELL, IF IT'S THAT SIMPLE, P-PERHAPS I'D BEST START SCANNING FOR THE NEXT ONE! I-I'LL JUST--

TOO LATE, TREECE.

"IT'S STARTED!"

FROM THE MIND OF THE CONCENTRATING LOBOT, TENDRILS OF CYBERNETIC FORCE CAUTIOUSLY PROBE...

...SLIPPING PAST DEADLY TRIGGERS TO FIND A PRECISION-BALANCED PRIMER CONTROL...

...AND, WITH AN EFFORT OF DEXTERITY AND WILL BEYOND HUMAN CAPABILITY, TO FINALLY TURN THAT VITAL CONTROL--

--OFF!

--AND LATER, AFTER TEN "SOMETHING ELSES" HAVE BEEN LOCATED AND DISARMED...

THE DANGER'S OVER, TREECE. BUT BEFORE WE BRING THE CITIZENS BACK, I THINK YOU AND I SHOULD TALK.

OH? ABOUT WHAT?

HE... HE *DID* IT!

GOOD JOB, LOBOT!

I WAS MERELY PERFORMING MY ORDERED TASK, SIR. WILL THERE BE ANYTHING ELSE?

INDEED THERE WILL--

ABOUT UGNAUGHTS, IF THEY REALLY DID SET THOSE BOMBS TO PROTEST THEIR POSITION, MAYBE YOU SHOULD *CHANGE* THAT POSITION--

--BY TREATING THEM WITH THE SAME RES-PECT AND COURTESY *I* USED TO GIVE THEM.

MY GOOD MAN--

--I CAN ASSURE YOU THOSE LITTLE STUMP-WARTS WILL GET *PRECISELY* WHAT THEY DESERVE! IN FACT, I SUGGEST YOU GO TELL THEM SO!

WHA--

WHAT I'M SAYING, REBEL--

--IS THAT THE ARMISTICE IS *OVER!*

TREECE, YOU SLIME-LICKIN' SLIT-EARED SONOVA--!

LANDO CALRISSIAN'S RAGE LASTS PERHAPS A HUNDRED METERS, AT WHICH POINT IT IS RE-PLACED BY THE MORE IM-MEDIATE REALIZATION THAT--

178

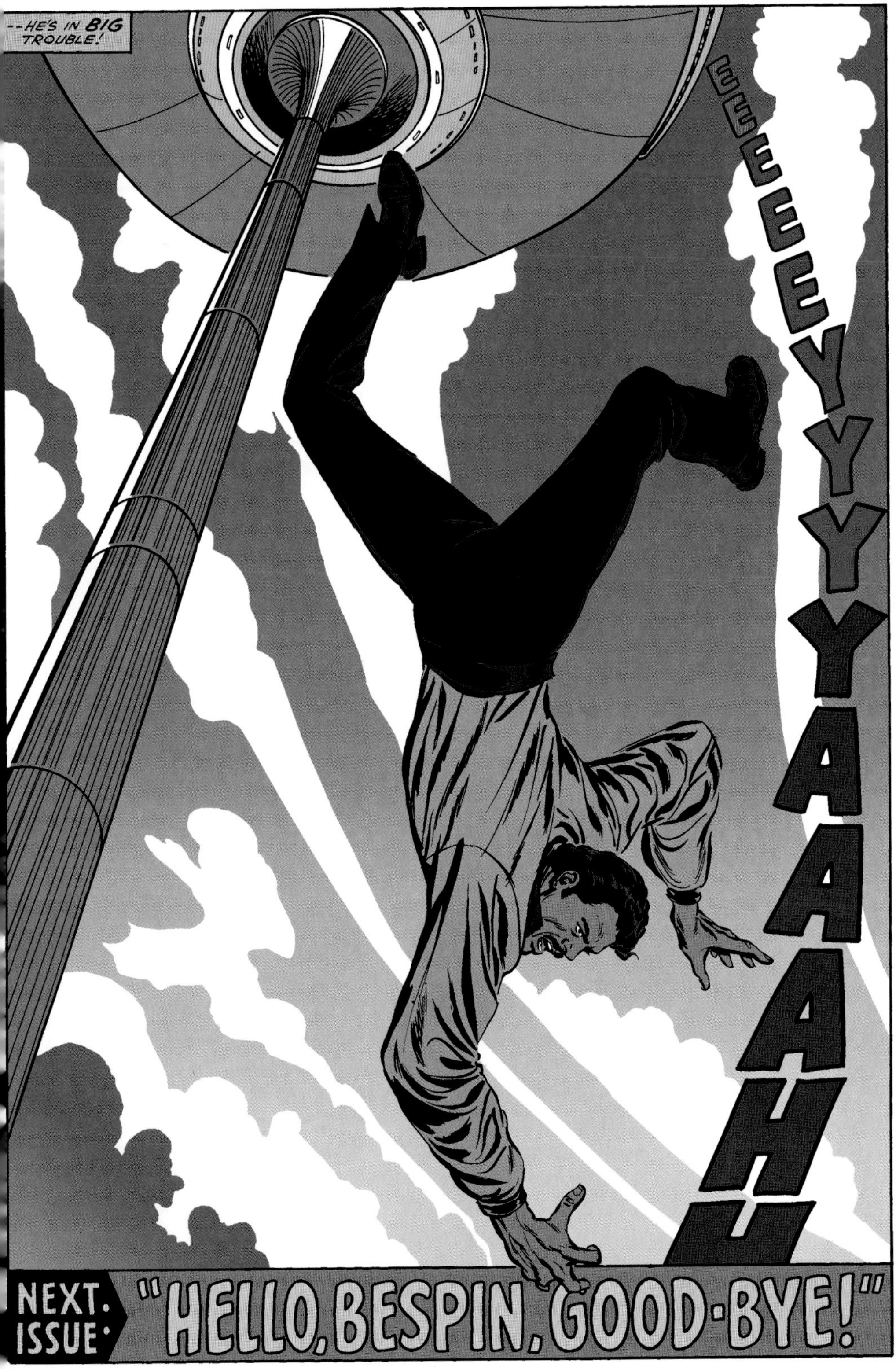
--HE'S IN BIG TROUBLE!
EEEEEEYYYYYAAAAAHH
NEXT ISSUE: "HELLO, BESPIN, GOOD-BYE!"

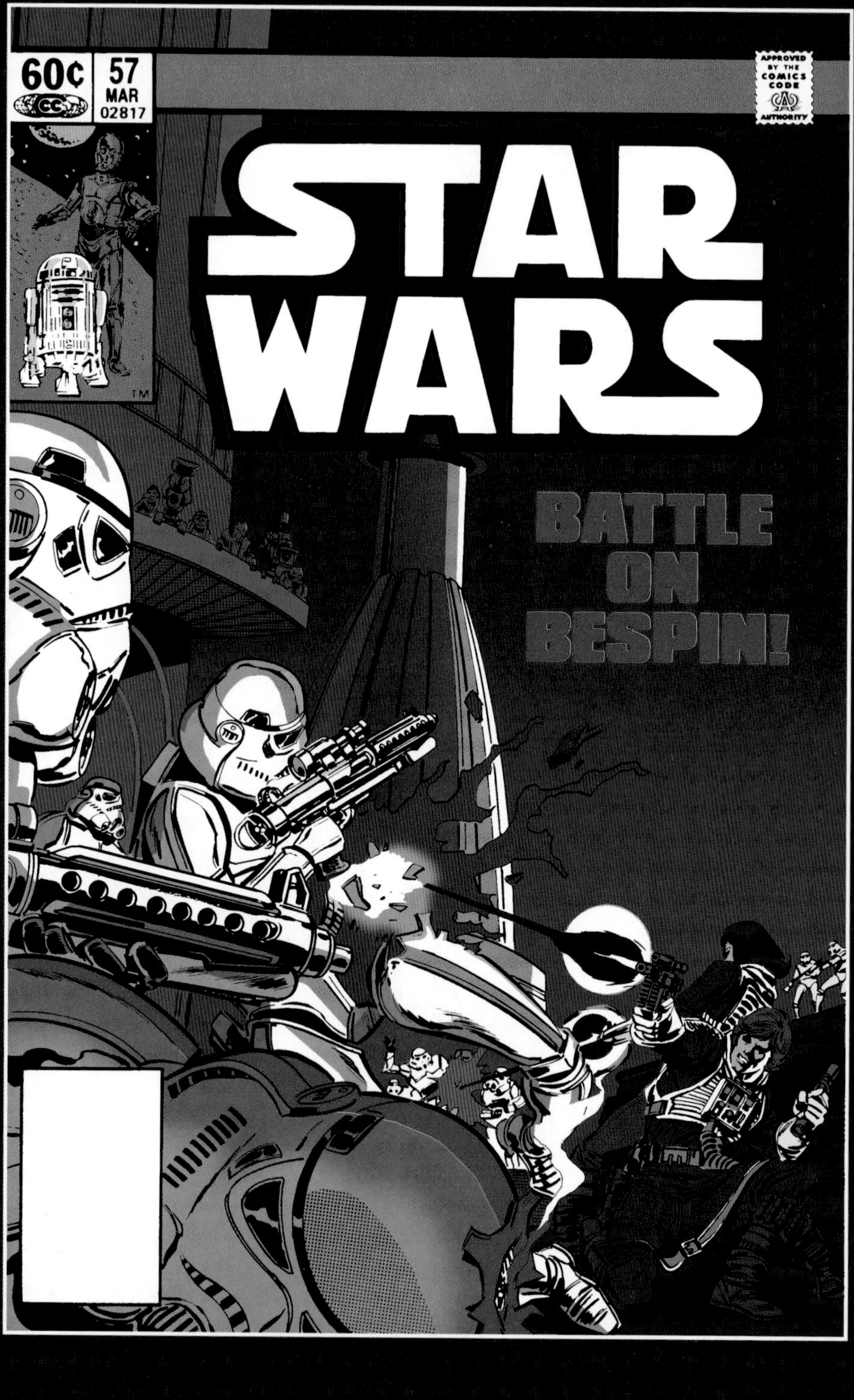

60¢
57
MAR
02817
APPROVED BY THE COMICS CODE AUTHORITY
STAR WARS
TM
BATTLE ON BESPIN!

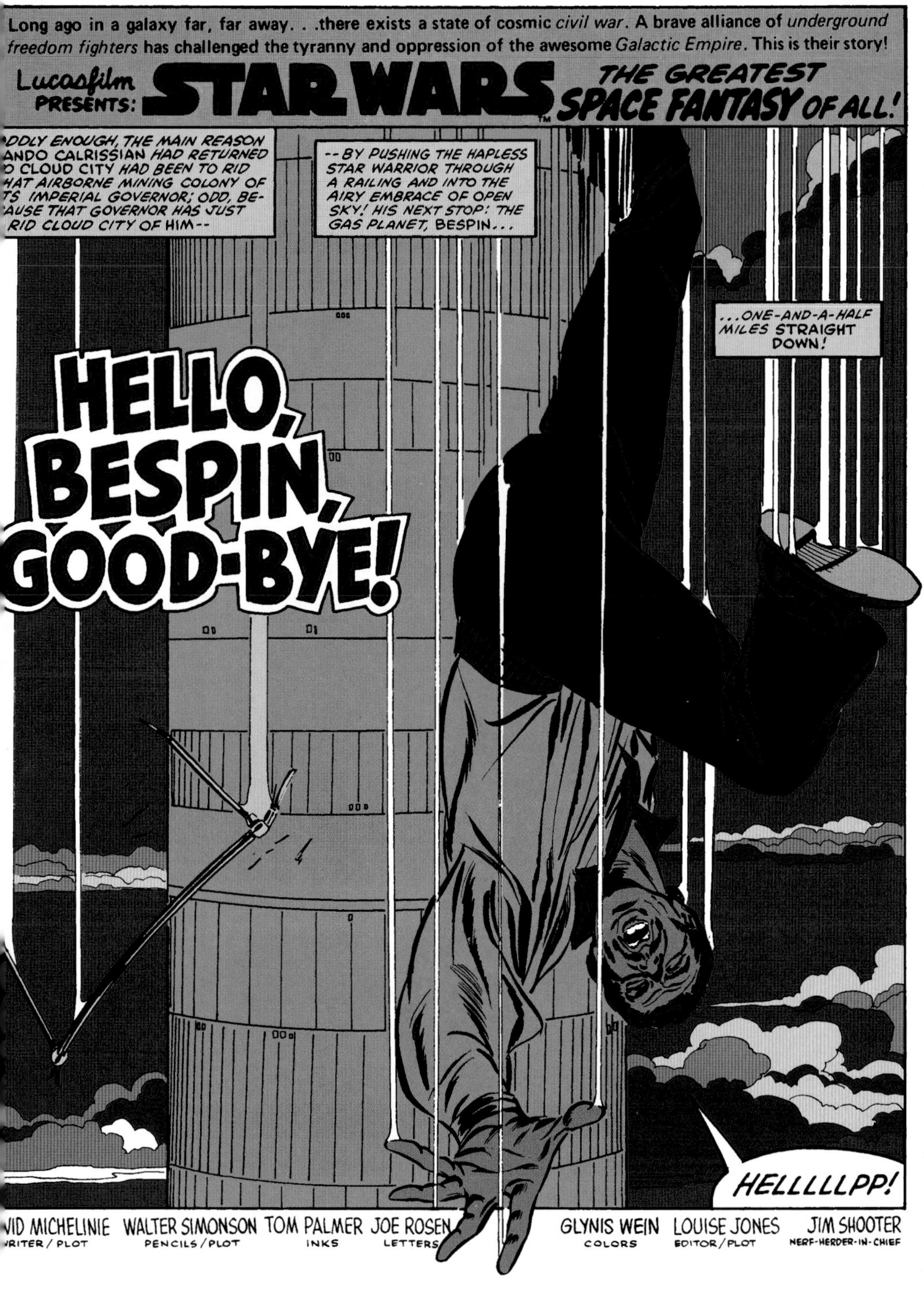
Long ago in a galaxy far, far away. . .there exists a state of cosmic civil war. A brave alliance of underground freedom fighters has challenged the tyranny and oppression of the awesome Galactic Empire. This is their story!
Lucasfilm PRESENTS: STAR WARS THE GREATEST SPACE FANTASY OF ALL!
DDLY ENOUGH, THE MAIN REASON ANDO CALRISSIAN HAD RETURNED O CLOUD CITY HAD BEEN TO RID HAT AIRBORNE MINING COLONY OF TS IMPERIAL GOVERNOR; ODD, BE-AUSE THAT GOVERNOR HAS JUST RID CLOUD CITY OF HIM--
--BY PUSHING THE HAPLESS STAR WARRIOR THROUGH A RAILING AND INTO THE AIRY EMBRACE OF OPEN SKY! HIS NEXT STOP: THE GAS PLANET, BESPIN...
...ONE-AND-A-HALF MILES STRAIGHT DOWN!
HELLO, BESPIN, GOOD-BYE!
HELLLLLPP!
VID MICHELINIE RITER / PLOT
WALTER SIMONSON PENCILS / PLOT
TOM PALMER INKS
JOE ROSEN LETTERS
GLYNIS WEIN COLORS
LOUISE JONES EDITOR / PLOT
JIM SHOOTER NERF-HERDER-IN-CHIEF

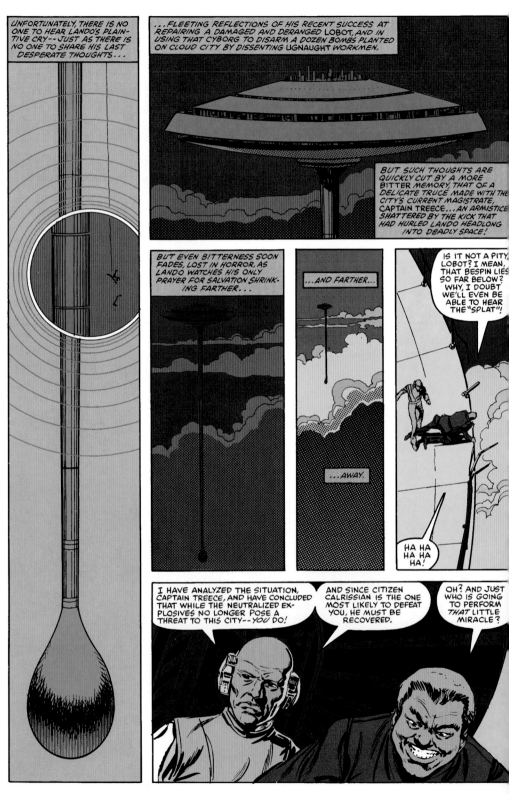

UNFORTUNATELY, THERE IS NO ONE TO HEAR LANDO'S PLAINTIVE CRY--JUST AS THERE IS NO ONE TO SHARE HIS LAST DESPERATE THOUGHTS...

...FLEETING REFLECTIONS OF HIS RECENT SUCCESS AT REPAIRING A DAMAGED AND DERANGED LOBOT, AND IN USING THAT CYBORG TO DISARM A DOZEN BOMBS PLANTED ON CLOUD CITY BY DISSENTING UGNAUGHT WORKMEN.

BUT SUCH THOUGHTS ARE QUICKLY CUT BY A MORE BITTER MEMORY, THAT OF A DELICATE TRUCE MADE WITH THE CITY'S CURRENT MAGISTRATE, CAPTAIN TREECE...AN ARMISTICE SHATTERED BY THE KICK THAT HAD HURLED LANDO HEADLONG INTO DEADLY SPACE!

BUT EVEN BITTERNESS SOON FADES, LOST IN HORROR, AS LANDO WATCHES HIS ONLY PRAYER FOR SALVATION SHRINKING FARTHER...

...AND FARTHER...

...AWAY.

IS IT NOT A PITY, LOBOT? I MEAN, THAT BESPIN LIES SO FAR BELOW? WHY, I DOUBT WE'LL EVEN BE ABLE TO HEAR THE "SPLAT"!

HA HA HA HA HA!

I HAVE ANALYZED THE SITUATION, CAPTAIN TREECE, AND HAVE CONCLUDED THAT WHILE THE NEUTRALIZED EXPLOSIVES NO LONGER POSE A THREAT TO THIS CITY--YOU DO!

AND SINCE CITIZEN CALRISSIAN IS THE ONE MOST LIKELY TO DEFEAT YOU, HE MUST BE RECOVERED.

OH? AND JUST WHO IS GOING TO PERFORM THAT LITTLE MIRACLE?

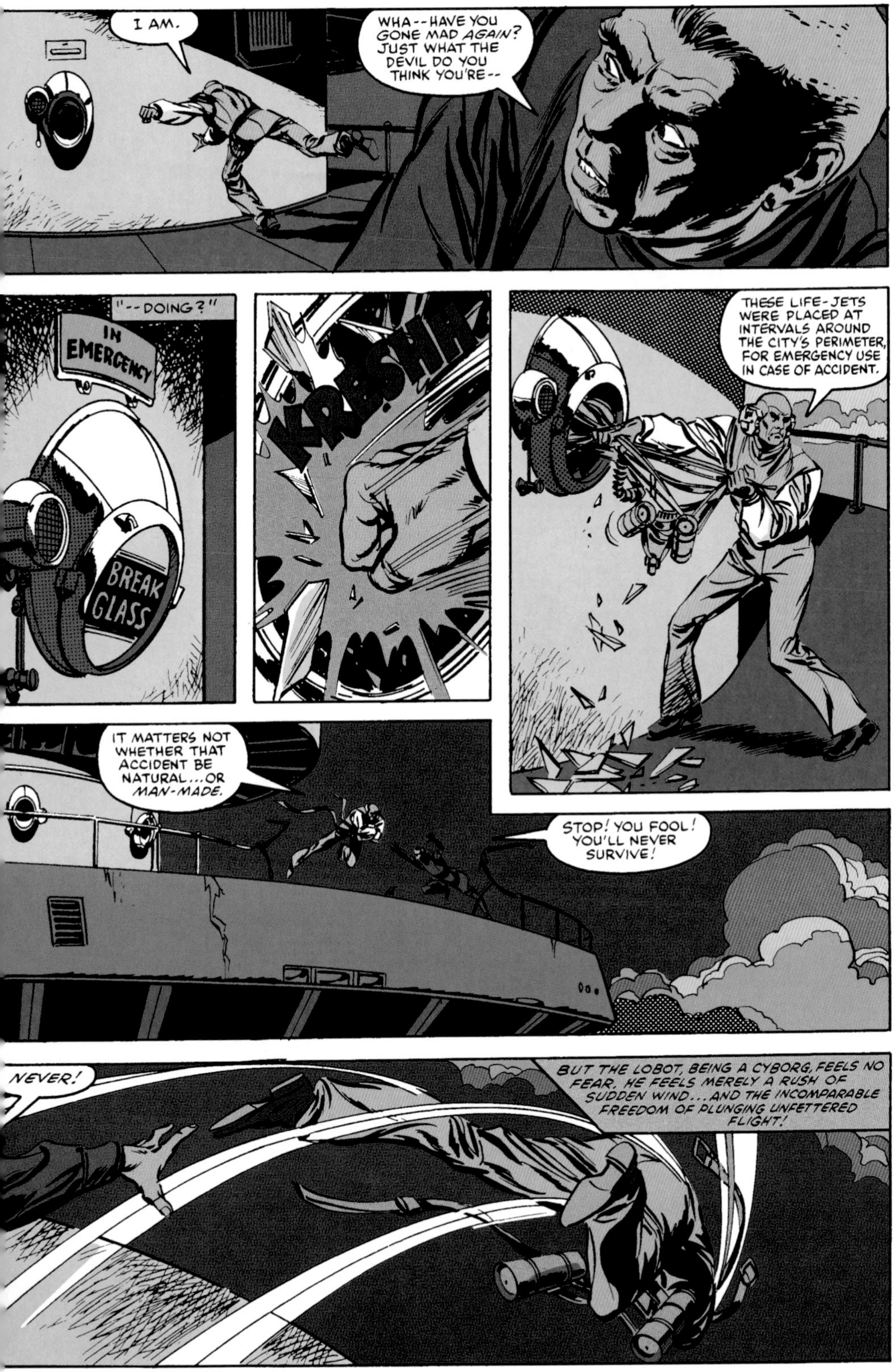

I AM.
WHA--HAVE YOU GONE MAD AGAIN? JUST WHAT THE DEVIL DO YOU THINK YOU'RE--
"--DOING?"
IN EMERGENCY
BREAK GLASS
KRESHH
THESE LIFE-JETS WERE PLACED AT INTERVALS AROUND THE CITY'S PERIMETER, FOR EMERGENCY USE IN CASE OF ACCIDENT.
IT MATTERS NOT WHETHER THAT ACCIDENT BE NATURAL...OR MAN-MADE.
STOP! YOU FOOL! YOU'LL NEVER SURVIVE!
NEVER!
BUT THE LOBOT, BEING A CYBORG, FEELS NO FEAR. HE FEELS MERELY A RUSH OF SUDDEN WIND...AND THE INCOMPARABLE FREEDOM OF PLUNGING UNFETTERED FLIGHT!

THIS LIFE-JET MAY NOT BE ABLE TO LIFT US BOTH BACK TO CLOUD CITY, BUT I SHOULD AT LEAST BE ABLE TO SLOW MR. CALRISSIAN DOWN--*IF* I CAN REACH HIM!

SIR! IT WILL BE NECESSARY FOR YOU TO DECREASE YOUR RATE OF DESCENT IN ORDER FOR ME TO CATCH UP TO YOU!

LIKE *HOW?!* I DON'T SKID TOO WELL ON CLOUDS!

NO, BUT YOU *CAN* TURN OVER AND EXTEND YOUR LIMBS, THEREBY CREATING GREATER WIND RESISTANCE.

OH.

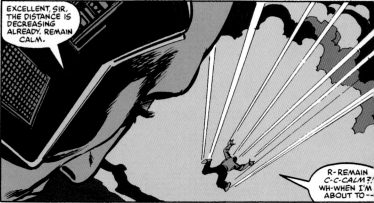

EXCELLENT, SIR. THE DISTANCE IS DECREASING ALREADY. REMAIN CALM.

R-REMAIN C-C-CALM?! WH-WHEN I'M ABOUT TO--

--HEY! HE WAS RIGHT!

HE *IS* GETTING CLOSER!

HE'S GOING TO--

--DO *IT!*

HIT THOSE ROCKETS, LOBOT--FAST!

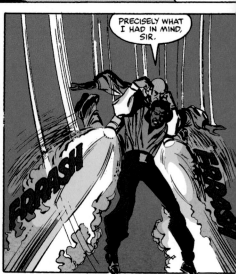

PRECISELY WHAT I HAD IN MIND, SIR.

FRRASH

FRRASH

184

WHILE BELOW, ON BESPIN, ALL IS QUIET ALONG A MIST-COVERED MARSH OF LIQUIFIED GAS--

--A HAZY SWAMP THAT HAS GIVEN RISE TO SOME OF THE MOST BIZARRE LIFE-FORMS IN THE GALAXY, BOTH PLANT--

--AND ANIMAL!

BE WE ROLLIN' LADS? FINE. ⸮AHEM⸮*

*TRANSLATED FROM THE UGNAUGHT TO GALAXY STANDARD.

GOOD AFTERNOON TO YE. THIS BE ARS FIVVLE REPORTIN' FOR "ACTION TIDINGS!"

WE BE IN PLEASANT MEADOW TODAY TO CAPTURE ON FILM A MOMENT O' HISTORY--THE ACTUAL SPLASHDOWN O' THAT DEN O' HUMAN INIQUITY, CLOUD CITY!

CALCULATIONS INDICATE THAT BOMBS PLANTED BY REVOLUTION'RY UGNAUGHT WORKERS HAVE ALREADY BLOWN, AN' THAT CLOUD CITY HAS STARTED ITS PLUMMET PLANETWARD. WITH LUCK, WE SHOULD BE SEEIN' THE RESULTS O' THAT DROP ANY MINUTE N--

PLOTCH

KI-YI! WE'RE LOSIN' TIBANNA GAS! S-SOMETHIN' HIT ONE O' THE LIFT BAGS!

THERE 'TIS! 'TWAS SOMETHIN' METALLIC!

AYE, AN' LOOK! SOMETHIN' ELSE IS FALLIN' THIS WAY! SOMETHIN'--

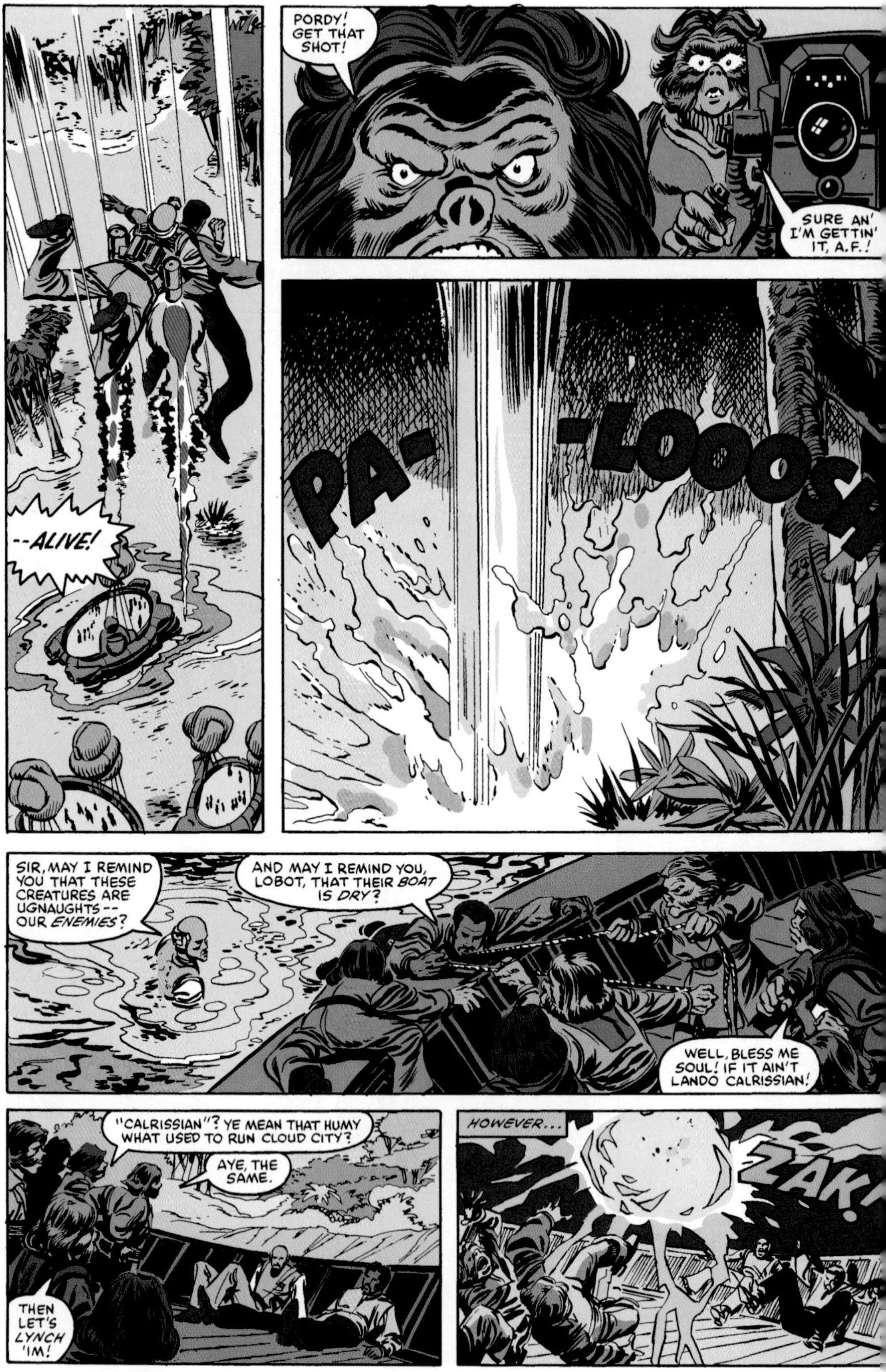

--ALIVE!
PORDY! GET THAT SHOT!
SURE AN' I'M GETTIN' IT, A.F.!
PA- -LOOOSH
SIR, MAY I REMIND YOU THAT THESE CREATURES ARE UGNAUGHTS -- OUR ENEMIES?
AND MAY I REMIND YOU, LOBOT, THAT THEIR BOAT IS DRY?
WELL, BLESS ME SOUL! IF IT AIN'T LANDO CALRISSIAN!
"CALRISSIAN"? YE MEAN THAT HUMY WHAT USED TO RUN CLOUD CITY?
AYE, THE SAME.
THEN LET'S LYNCH 'IM!
HOWEVER...
ZAK!

SORRY, FOLKS, THE WELCOME'S GONNA HAVE TO WAIT! WE'VE GOT COMPANY--

--RIDING IN ON *IMPERIAL SKIMMERS!*

'MUST BE THE STORMTROOPERS WHO WERE EVACUATED FROM CLOUD CITY-- PROBABLY TRACKED OUR FALL ON THEIR SCANNERS!

"SO UNLESS WE WANT TO END UP FEEDING THE SWAMP BUGS, I SUGGEST WE START SHOOTING BACK!"

AYE, LADDIE, YE HEARD THE MAN--

--GET THAT SHOT!

NO, DUMMY, I DON'T MEAN CAMERAS-- I'M TALKIN' ABOUT *BLASTERS!*

THEN YE'RE OUTTA LUCK, BUCKO. THIS HERE'S A NEWSBOAT-- WE GOT NO WEAPONS!

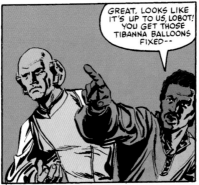

GREAT, LOOKS LIKE IT'S UP TO US, LOBOT! YOU GET THOSE TIBANNA BALLOONS FIXED--

--WHILE *I* FIX ME SOME *STORM-TROOPERS!*

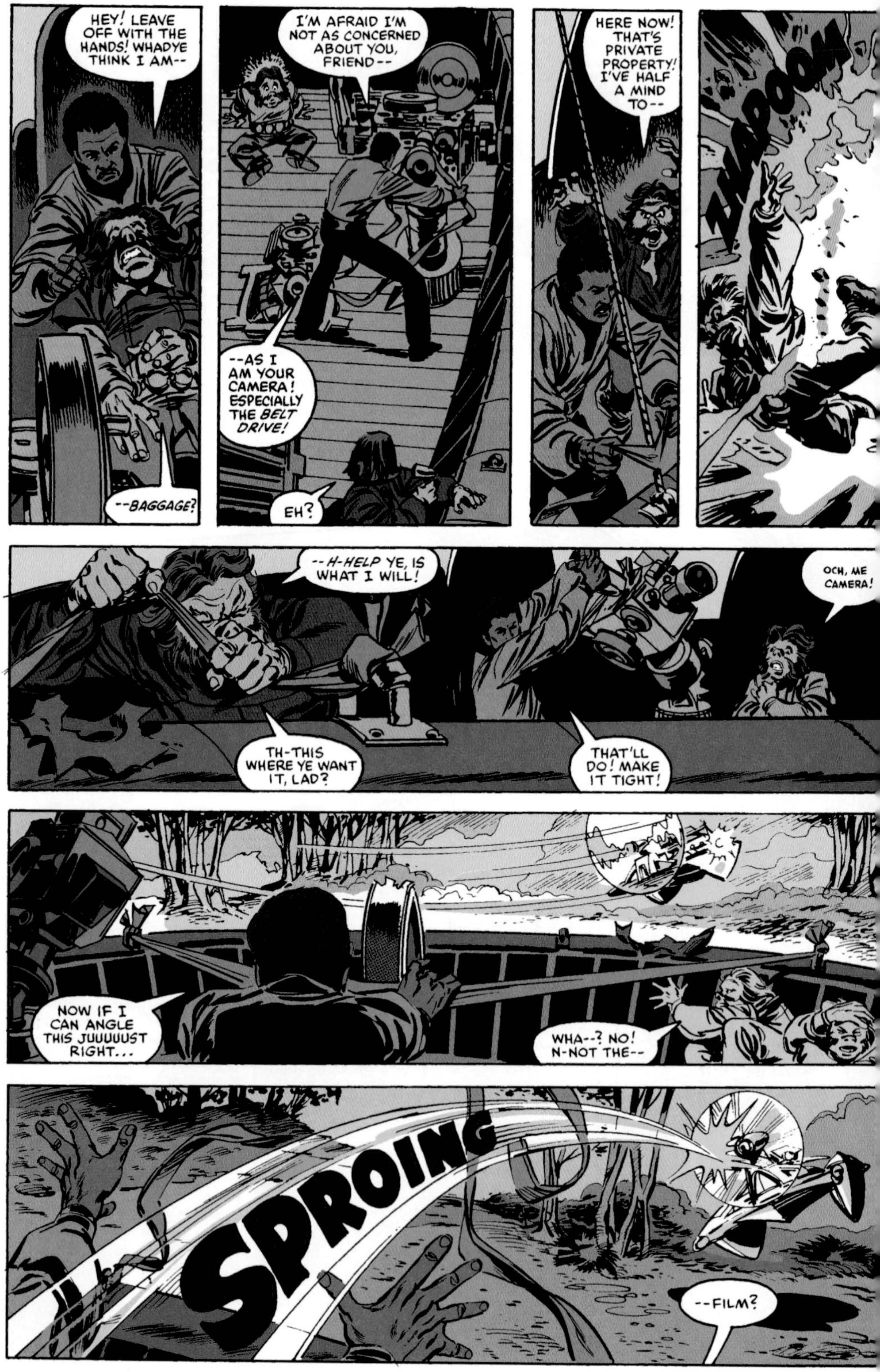

HEY! LEAVE OFF WITH THE HANDS! WHADYE THINK I AM--
--BAGGAGE?
I'M AFRAID I'M NOT AS CONCERNED ABOUT YOU, FRIEND--
--AS I AM YOUR CAMERA! ESPECIALLY THE BELT DRIVE!
EH?
HERE NOW! THAT'S PRIVATE PROPERTY! I'VE HALF A MIND TO--
ZHADOOM
--H-HELP YE, IS WHAT I WILL!
TH-THIS WHERE YE WANT IT, LAD?
THAT'LL DO! MAKE IT TIGHT!
OCH, ME CAMERA!
NOW IF I CAN ANGLE THIS JUUUUUST RIGHT...
WHA--? NO! N-NOT THE--
SPROING
--FILM?

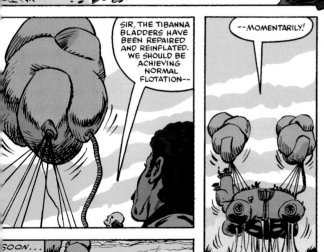

SIR, THE TIBANNA BLADDERS HAVE BEEN REPAIRED AND REINFLATED. WE SHOULD BE ACHIEVING NORMAL FLOTATION--

--MOMENTARILY!

THEN LET'S GET OUT OF HERE BEFORE THAT OTHER SKIMMER REALIZES OUR "SECRET WEAPON" WAS A FILM CAN--

--AND COMES BACK MAD!

THANKS. A LOT.

SOON...

CALRISSIAN, WE'VE BEEN TALKIN', AN' WE'RE ALL AGREED THAT WHILE YE WERE ONCE THE HIGH HUMAN O' CLOUD CITY--

--YE ALWAYS TREATED US FAIRLY.

SO, WE'VE DECIDED TO TAKE YE BACK TO OUR CAPITOL--

--AN' LET OUR LEADER CONDEMN YE T'DEATH!

WHILE HIGH ABOVE, IN A CITY KEPT ALOFT BY MYRIAD POCKETS OF ANTI-GRAVITY TIBANNA GAS...

THINGS ARE GOING BETTER THAN I'D HOPED. WITH CALRISSIAN DEAD--

--I CAN CLAIM *FULL CREDIT* FOR SAVING THIS INSTALLATION FROM-- EH? THAT SOUND! WHAT--

"--X-WING FIGHTERS! REBEL CRAFT!"

BUT WHAT THE BLAZES ARE THEY DOING *HERE*?!

APPARENTLY, THEY'RE LANDING

AND, AS LUKE SKYWALKER *AND HIS WING GUARD,* SHIRA BRIE, *DISEMBARK...*

NICE TOUCH-DOWN, ACE!

THANKS, SHIRA, BUT ARTOO DID MOST OF THE WORK.

TA-DOOT

HMM, KINDA QUIET.

YEAH, THE WHOLE PLACE SEEMS DESERTED. THAT COULD EXPLAIN WHY LANDO NEVER REPORTED BACK TO BASE.

THOUGH IT *DOESN'T* EXPLAIN WHERE HE *IS!*

ARTOO, PLUG INTO THE CITY'S CENTRAL COMPUTER AND TRY TO FIND US SOME ANSWERS, OKAY?

PADA-DIT

AND, IN SECONDS...

DA-DEET VROODA DOOT!

WELL, COMMANDER SKYWALKER, SOUNDS LIKE YOUR LITTLE BUDDY'S HIT THE JACKPOT!

SORT OF. HE SAYS A BUNCH OF BOMBS WERE PLANTED HERE, CAUSING THE ENTIRE POPULACE TO BE EVACUATED.

BUT THE BOMBS WERE RECENTLY NEUTRALIZED BY A LOBOT WORKING WITH A HUMAN. COULD BE LANDO.

"SKYWALKER," EH? IF THAT'S THE REBEL *LORD VADER* IS LOOKING FOR, MY SEAT IN THE IMPERIAL SENATE IS ASSURED!

TREECE TO GROUND TROOPS! RETURN TO CLOUD CITY IMMEDIATELY!

NOW WE HAVE TO --

-- WAIT A MINUTE! SOMETHING'S WRONG! I... I CAN FEEL...

DUCK!

≥WHUFF≤

FRRATCH

LOOKS LIKE THIS PLACE ISN'T *QUITE* DESERTED, AFTER ALL!

YEAH! WE'RE PINNED DOWN!

THEY'RE PINNED DOWN! CUT OFF FROM THEIR SHIPS! AND THEY'RE GOING TO STAY THAT WAY --

-- UNTIL MY TROOPS ARRIVE TO CART THEM OFF TO *VADER!*

WHILE BELOW, A DIFFERENT CARTING NEARS ITS END, AS FLOATING NEWS-BOATS APPROACH A PATCHWORK MAZE OF STILT-HOUSE DWELLINGS--

--THE CITY OF THE UGNAUGHTS!

AMIDST GROWING GAZES OF CURIOSITY AND AWE, THEY GLIDE THROUGH CITY GATES, DESCENDING TOWARDS A CENTRAL PLAZA,

WHERE SOON...

I USED TO DEAL WITH THE UGNAUGHTS AS A WORK FORCE, BACK WHEN I RAN CLOUD CITY. THEY WERE A BIT TEMPERAMENTAL, BUT GENERALLY SENSIBLE.

I ONLY HOPE THEIR GRAND MAJESTIC MUCKY-MUCK HAS STAYED THAT WAY!

A WORD OF ADVICE, LADDIE--

--WHEN ADDRESSIN' OUR LEADER, YE MIGHT TRY USIN' "KING" INSTEAD O'"MUCKY-MUCK."

I THINK YER NEXT O' KIN WOULD APPRECIATE IT.

RIIIIIGHT.

192

AND SO, A SHORT, SOBERING WALK LATER, AN EX-LEADER MEETS A CURRENT ONE, IN THE HIGH-CEILINGED HALL OF--

--KING OZZ.

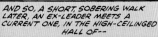

TELL YOU WHAT, KING, I'LL TRADE YOU *MY* EXPLANATION FOR *YOURS*. BECAUSE THE ONE TREECE GAVE--

--ABOUT YOUR CREATING AN INSURRECTION TO BRING TIBANNA MINING BACK TO THE PLANET'S SURFACE, JUST DOESN'T WASH!

GREETIN'S, LANDO, IT'S BEEN A WHILE. I HOPE YE'VE GOT A GOOD EXPLANATION FER ME.

YE KNOW HOW I FANCY TALL TALES...

HE SAID THAT, DID HE? WELL, IN A WAY, HE WAS RIGHT. GAS MININ' *WAS* GOOD ON BESPIN. BUT IT WAS *BETTER* ON CLOUD CITY! SHORTER HOURS, HIGHER PAY, GOOD TREATMENT.

THAT IS, UNTIL THE *EMPIRE* STUCK IN ITS UGLY NOSE!

THE EMPIRE?

AYE, THAT'S WHEN YER CAPTAIN STARTED SNEAKIN' A DOLE FROM THE PROFITS! AND SO'S HIS BOSSES WOULDN'T NOTICE--

--HE *DOUBLED* TIBANNA PRODUCTION, TAKIN' MORE GAS THAN BESPIN'S ECO-SYSTEM COULD SAFELY PRODUCE!

BUT HE WEREN'T JUST DESTROYIN' OUR HOME--

--HE WAS WORKIN' OUR PEOPLE 'TIL THEY WAS DROPPIN' LIKE MARNETS!

YOU MEAN TREECE TURNED *MY* CITY... INTO A *SLAVE CAMP?*

KING, YOU'VE JUST LOST YOURSELF AN ENEMY.

AND GAINED THE MEANEST, MADDEST *FRIEND* YOU'VE EVER HAD!

AN' THAT'S WHEN WE DECIDED TO DO SOMETHIN' *ABOUT* IT!

MEANTIME, ABOVE...

HEADS UP, ACE! WE'VE GOT TROUBLE!

I KNOW-- I'M SHOOTING AT IT!

"NO, I MEAN *MORE* TROUBLE, SILLY! THERE'S AN IMPERIAL TROOP TRANSPORT DIVING IN FROM THE HORIZON!"

"OH. I, UM, DON'T SUPPOSE THEY'VE JUST DROPPED BY FOR A REST STOP AND A COUPLE OF SANDWICHES...?"

FRRATCH

WHOOMP

BDAM

FRATOM

KROW

FRAM

GOSH, I LOVE A MAN WITH A SENSE OF HUMOR.

AT LEAST BETTER THAN THIS *LANDING!* ≳OOCH≲

IS NEARBY, AT THAT MOMENT...

RE YE SURE 'HIS PLAN O' ERS'LL WORK, UCKO? THERE'S LOT RIDIN' ON IT.

IT'LL WORK.

COME ON, LOBOT. WITH YOUR HELP, I SHOULD BE ABLE TO GIVE TREECE THE SAME SHAFT HE'S BEEN GIVING THE *UGNAUGHTS!*

SPEAKING OF WHOM, YOU GUYS STAY HERE--

--AND STAY OUT OF TROUBLE!

HMPH. THERE AIN'T NO NEWS HERE.

MAYBE NOT--

--BUT UNLESS ME EARS IS TELLIN' STORIES, THAT'S *GUNFIRE* COMIN' FROM OVER YONDER! AN' YE KNOW WHAT *THAT* MEANS.

AYE--

-- AN EXCLUSIVE!

LET'S GO, LADS!

AND AS THE "ACTION TIDINGS" NEWS TEAM ROUNDS A CARBON-SCORED CORNER--

--THEY ARE NOT DISAPPOINTED!

FAKAM

ZZLAT

EEEOW

LIGHT'S GOOD!

SPEED!

YER ON, ARS!

GOOD AFTERNOON. THIS BE ARS FIVVLE--

--BRINGIN' YE LIVE COVERAGE O' THE FIGHT FER CLOUD CITY! AN' A GALLANT STRUGGLE IT IS!

HNH?

WHAT THE--?

A PAIR O' COURAGEOUS, BUT WOEFULLY OUT-NUMBERED, REBELS IS SQUARED OFF AGAINST A HORDE OF IMPERIAL WAR DOGS! WE'RE HOPIN' TO HAVE INTERVIEWS AS SOON AS--

I DON'T BELIEVE THIS.

I DO-- BUT I DO WANT TO

WHUP! JUST A MOMENT! THERE SEEMS T'BE A *BREAK* IN THE FIGHTIN'! A BREAK APPARENTLY CAUSED BY--

LOOK! WE'RE BEING WATCHED!

--US?

KILL THEM.

I WOULDN'T DO THAT IF I WERE YOU, TREECE!

EH?!

WELL, I'LL BE! IT'S--

"--LANDO!"

IF YOU DON'T GET YOUR MEN OUT OF HERE FAST, I'LL HAVE LOBOT *RE-ARM* THE EXPLOSIVES--

--AND BLOW US *ALL* INTO THE NEXT STAR SYSTEM!

NO...

DAKOW

...I THINK *NOT!*

LOBOT--!

SSATCH

IT APPEARS, CALRISSIAN, THAT YOU'VE LOST THE ONLY BEING CAPABLE OF RE-ARMING THOSE BOMBS WITHOUT *TOUCHING* THEM--

--THEREBY SETTING OFF THEIR SELF-DE-STRUCT MECHANISMS. OR, TO PUT IT MORE SIMPLY: CHECK... AND *MATE!*

OH, GREAT. *NOW* WHAT'LL WE--

VRTADIT

--HUH? *OF COURSE!* WHY DIDN'T *I* THINK OF THAT?

HEY, *HOTSHOT!* YOU BLEW IT!

THE LOBOT WASN'T THE *ONLY ONE* WHO CAN MOVE THINGS WITHOUT TOUCHING THEM!

TAKE A LOOK!

M-MOTHER O' SAINTS! TH-THE CAMERA--IT MOVED BY *ITSELF!*

BUT LUKE SKYWALKER'S *BURGEONING* COMMAND OF THE FORCE-- THE ELEMENTAL ENERGY THAT *SURROUNDS* AND *PERMEATES* ALL THINGS-- IS *NOT* LIMITED TO *PARLOR TRICKS.*

FOR HE NOW USES THAT ABILITY TO *SEEK OUT* THE ELEVEN REMAINING BOMBS HIDDEN BY THE UGNAUGHTS ON CLOUD CITY, AND HAVING LOCATED THEM...

..ARMS *THEM!*

CLIK

HEY!

CLIK

WHAT--

CLIK

--WAS--

CLIK

OH-O

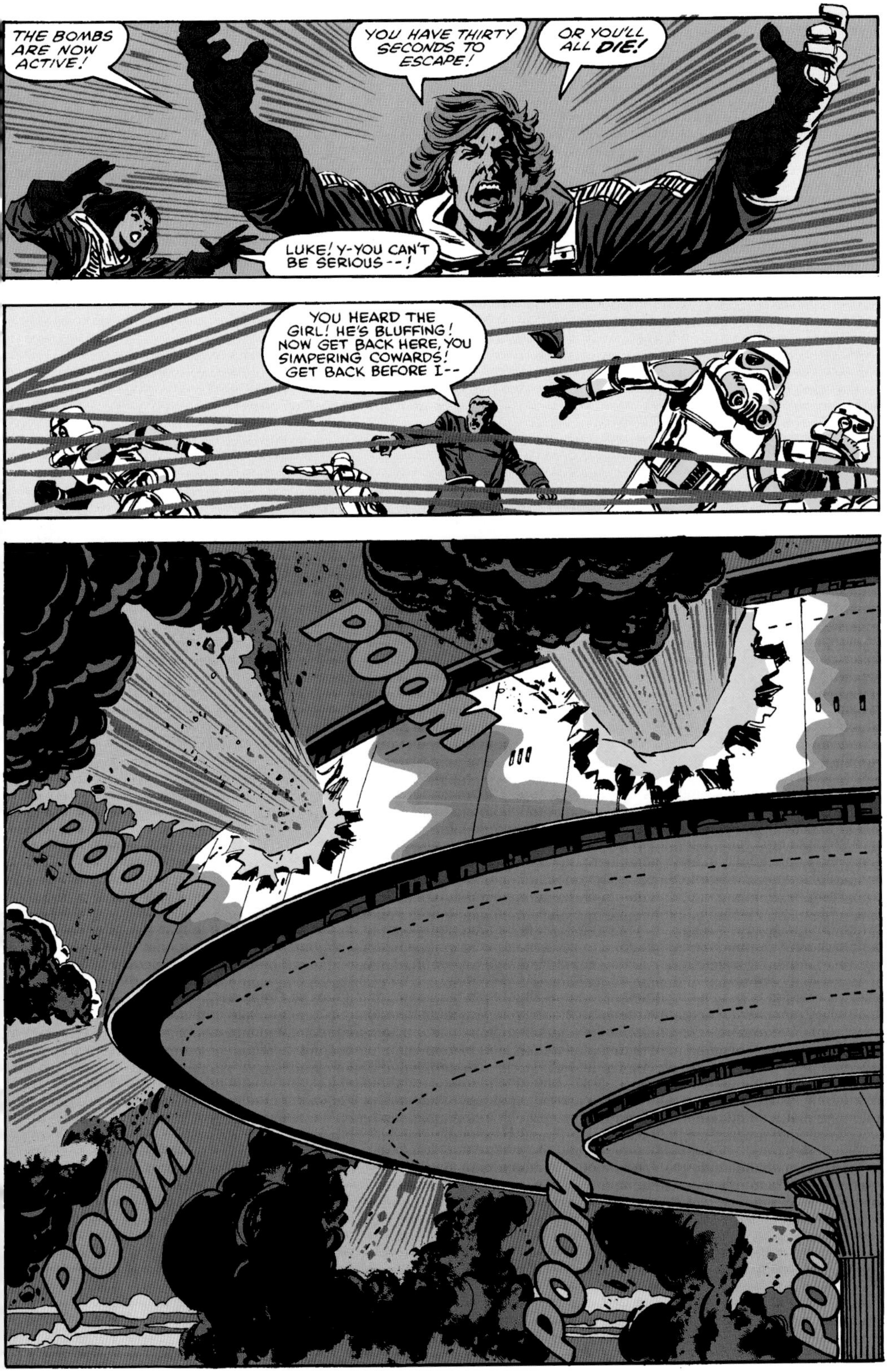
THE BOMBS ARE NOW ACTIVE!
YOU HAVE THIRTY SECONDS TO ESCAPE!
OR YOU'LL ALL DIE!
LUKE! Y-YOU CAN'T BE SERIOUS--!
YOU HEARD THE GIRL! HE'S BLUFFING! NOW GET BACK HERE, YOU SIMPERING COWARDS! GET BACK BEFORE I--
POOM
POOM
POOM
POOM
POOM

WITH A BANG...AND A WHIMPER...

...CLOUD CITY...

...SINKS!

LEAVING HER PLACE IN THE SKY TO BE FILLED BY A FLOCK OF CONFUSED, THOUGH HOPEFUL, CARRION BIRDS.

W-WAIT FOR M--

--I-I MEAN RETREAT!

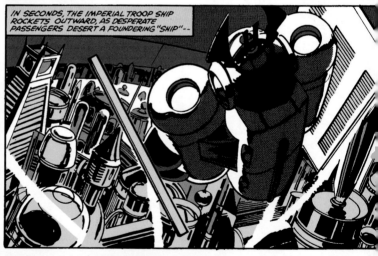

IN SECONDS, THE IMPERIAL TROOP SHIP ROCKETS OUTWARD, AS DESPERATE PASSENGERS DESERT A FOUNDERING "SHIP"--

-- LIKE THE DROVE OF TAIL-TUCKED RODENTS THEY ARE!

YOU'RE CRAZY, LUKE! I WAS JUST *KIDDIN'* ABOUT BLOWIN' THOSE BOMBS! WE GOTTA GET OUTTA HERE!

YE KNOW, IF WE HURRY, WE CAN STILL CATCH THE FALL O' CLOUD CITY ON FILM!

AYE, THERE COULD BE AN *AWARD* IN THIS YET!

WHOA! JUST HOLD ON A MINUTE! THERE'S NO RUSH.

÷OOPF÷

"NO RUSH"?! LOOK, BUDDY, JUST 'CAUSE YOU'RE *GOOD* FRIENDS WITH THE FORCE DOESN'T MAKE YOU A GOD! YOU'RE GONNA BREAK INTO AS MANY PIECES AS *WE* ARE IF YOU DON'T MOVE IT!

THAT'S TELLIN' 'IM, LANDO!

C'MON, RELAX! IT WAS A TRICK!

A WHAT?!

"I DIDN'T EXPLODE THE BOMBS-- I JUST BLEW THE *PRIMERS!* THAT WAY, THE HOLES THEY MADE LET OUT JUST ENOUGH TIBANNA GAS TO MAKE IT *SEEM* LIKE WE WERE DOOMED!

"HECK, THE EMERGENCY DRONES ARE PATCHING UP THOSE LITTLE HOLES ALREADY!"

SO YOU SEE, THERE NEVER WAS ANY *REAL* DANGER. ALL FLASH -- NO CRASH.

EVERYBODY HAPPY?

YOU WANT TO HIT HIM?

LADIES FIRST.

GRUDGINGLY, POTENTIAL FISTICUFFS GIVE WAY TO SIGHS OF RELIEF, AND AS A NEW DAY DAWNS, IT IS A FULLY RESTORED, FULLY FUNCTIONAL CLOUD CITY TO WHICH A GRATEFUL POPULACE RETURNS...

...AND WHERE, SPECTACULARLY, CELEBRATION REIGNS!

YAAY!

HURRAH!

LOOKS LIKE CLOUD CITY'S GOING TO BE OKAY. WITH LUCK, THE EMPIRE WILL THINK SHE CRASHED AND THEY'LL FORGET ALL ABOUT HER.

THE ONLY THING THAT BOTHERS ME IS THAT *TREECE* GOT AWAY.

OH, I WOULDN'T SAY HE GOT *CLEAN* AWAY. Y'SEE, WHILE YOU FOLKS WERE GETTING SHOT AT, LOBOT AND I HAD THE CITY'S FINANCIAL COMPUTER TRANSMIT A CHANGE OF ORDERS TO TREECE'S PRIVATE ACCOUNT ON *AARGAU.*

WE TRANSFERRED THE CAPTAIN'S LAST ILLEGAL DEPOSIT, ALONG WITH COMPLETE INFORMATION ON WHERE IT CAME FROM, TO A DIFFERENT ACCOUNT.

ONE SET UP BY A RATHER SEVERE FELLOW NAMED ...VADER!

UNDERSTANDING GROWS, SMILES FOLLOW, AND WITH A LAST WAVE OF FAREWELL--

--THE JOURNEY HOMEWARD BEGINS!

NEXT ISSUE: SUNDOWN!

60¢ | 58 APR 02817

STAR WARS

SPACE WALK... DEATH WALK!

.ong ago in a galaxy far, far away. . .there exists a state of cosmic *civil war*. A brave alliance of *underground*
reedom fighters has challenged the tyranny and oppression of the awesome *Galactic Empire*. This is their story!

Lucasfilm PRESENTS: STAR WARS

THE GREATEST SPACE FANTASY OF ALL!

DAVID	WALTER	TOM	JANICE	DON	LOUISE	JIM
ICHELINIE	SIMONSON	PALMER	CHIANG	WARFIELD	JONES	SHOOTER
CRIPT/PLOT	PENCILS/PLOT	INKS	LETTERS	COLORS	EDITRIX	EMPEROR

ELOW, ON THE FOREST WORLD CALLED
BRA, A BAND OF COURAGEOUS REBELS
S SET UP A PERMANENT BASE--A
PEN SANCTUARY FROM WHICH TO WAGE
EIR HIT-AND-RUN WAR AGAINST THE
RANNICAL EMPIRE.

HILE ABOVE, IN THE MODIFIED
PICE FREIGHTER, MILLENNIUM
LCON, THREE OF THE REBELLION'S
ST STALWART WARRIORS EMBARK
A MISSION THAT COULD CRIPPLE
E FACET OF IMPERIAL DOMINATION...

...IF THEY LIVE THROUGH IT!

SUNDOWN!

OKAY, LUKE, COORDINATES ARE PUNCHED IN.

AND IN RECORD TIME, I MIGHT ADD.

THANKS, LANDO. SORRY TO RUSH YOU, BUT I DON'T TRUST FERRET. THAT SAND-SLUG WOULD SELL THE GOODS OUT FROM UNDER US IF WE WERE EVEN A MINUTE LATE FOR OUR APPOINTMENT.

RIGHT NOW, THOUGH, YOU AND CHEWIE HAD BETTER STRAP IN. WE'RE ABOUT TO REACH--

"-- LIGHT SPEED!"

WITH A SILENT ROAR AND A FLASH OF TEMPORAL BRILLIANCE, THE MILLENNIUM FALCON VANISHES.

WHILE ON ARBRA, ALL CLUES TO THAT SHIP'S DEPARTURE POINT ARE ALSO SWEPT AWAY...

...AS GUARDS ARE MOTIONED BACK INTO A CAVE THAT SERVES AS BOTH HANGAR AND LAUNCH BAY...

...WHERE A ROCKLIKE BLAST DOOR IS SLOWLY LOWERED, KEEPING THE TUNNEL SAFE FROM PRYING EYES...

...AND FROM VAGRANT IMPERIAL SENSOR SCANS!

INSIDE, A LONE REBEL WALKS, HIS TENSIONS EASING, HIS SHIFT OVER.

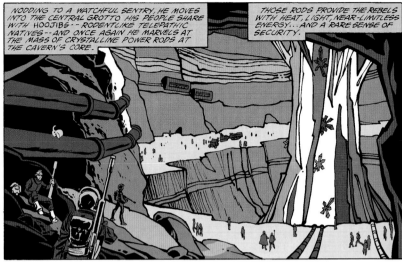

NODDING TO A WATCHFUL SENTRY, HE MOVES INTO THE CENTRAL GROTTO HIS PEOPLE SHARE WITH HOOJIBS-- RODENTLIKE TELEPATHIC NATIVES-- AND ONCE AGAIN HE MARVELS AT THE MASS OF CRYSTALLINE POWER RODS AT THE CAVERN'S CORE.

THOSE RODS PROVIDE THE REBELS WITH HEAT, LIGHT, NEAR-LIMITLESS ENERGY... AND A RARE SENSE OF SECURITY.

AS MUCH SECURITY, THE SOLITARY SOLDIER THINKS, AS ONE CAN EVER FIND--

--IN THE MIDDLE OF A WAR.

IF YOU ASK ME, IT'S THE ONLY WAY.

I AGREE, HILLY. PRINCESS LEIA'S PLAN IS SOUND.

AND IT'S NOT LIKE WE'VE NEVER DONE IT BEFORE.

I KNOW, BUT--

--HIDING THE ENTIRE FLEET INSIDE THE SUN?! ISN'T THAT A BIT CHANCY?

IT IS. BUT LEAVING THE SHIPS IN VARIABLE ORBIT WHERE ANY PASSING IMPERIAL COULD SPOT THEM IS TAKING AN EVEN GREATER CHANCE.

I JUST HOPE THAT THE PRINCESS KNOWS WHAT SHE'S DOING!

AND NEARBY, WHERE A STRATEGY MEETING HAS JUST ENDED, THOSE WORDS ARE VIRTUALLY BEING ECHOED.

ARE YOU CERTAIN THIS IS THE WISE THING TO DO, PRINCESS?

THE LOGIC OF YOUR PLAN IS IRREFUTABLE, BUT IT ALL SEEMS SO, WELL...

...DANGEROUS.

PERHAPS, THREEPIO. BUT IT IS STANDARD OPERATING PROCEDURE.

I KNOW, BUT I CAN'T HELP WISHING MASTER LUKE HAD STAYED BEHIND-- HE EXCELS AT RISKY VENTURES!

IF YOU WANT, PRINCESS, I'LL BE HAPPY TO GO AFTER LUKE AND OFFER TO TAKE HIS PLACE.

FAWEET?

THANK YOU, LT. BRIE, BUT THAT WON'T BE NECESSARY.

COMMANDER SKYWALKER'S PROJECT IS AS VITAL AS THIS ONE, AND HE'S NEEDED THERE.

THOUGH, I'M SURE YOU'D ENJOY MAKING YOUR OFFER TO HIM... PERSONALLY.

INDEED, PRINCESS--

--ALMOST AS MUCH AS LUKE WOULD.

'BYE.

WASN'T IT NICE OF SHIRA, ASKING TO HELP LIKE THAT? SHE'S SUCH A THOUGHTFUL PERSON.

YES. ISN'T SHE.

AND CUTE, TOO-- FOR A HUMAN.

THANKS, PLIF, I APPRECIATE THE SUPPORT.

BUT TO GET BACK TO SOOTHING YOUR NERVES, THREEPIO, NOT ONLY DO ACTIVE STARS MAKE IDEAL HIDING PLACES--

--BUT UNDER CONTROLLED CONDITIONS, THEY CAN BE QUITE SAFE.

"THROUGH PAST EXPERIMENTATION, WE'VE ESTABLISHED A PROCEDURE BASED ON THE LINKING OF FIVE *KERTS-BHRG* FIELD GENERATORS--

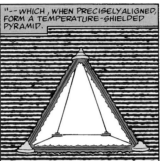

"--WHICH, WHEN PRECISELY ALIGNED, FORM A TEMPERATURE-SHIELDED PYRAMID.

"ONCE THE FLEET-- LESS WHAT FIGHTERS AND SUCH WE NEED FOR NORMAL OPERATIONS-- HAS BEEN SECURED *INSIDE* THE PYRAMID--"

-- THE TOTAL UNIT IS DIRECTED DOWN INTO THE STAR'S *CHROMOSPHERE*, A RELATIVELY COOL AREA BETWEEN THE CORONA AND THE SURFACE.

THE TEMPERATURE THERE RARELY EXCEEDS 8,000 DE-GREES, WELL WITHIN THE PYRAMID'S LONG-RANGE CAPACITY.

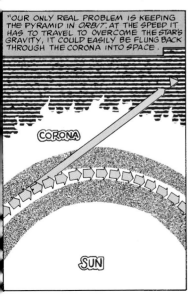

"OUR ONLY REAL PROBLEM IS KEEPING THE PYRAMID IN *ORBIT*. AT THE SPEED IT HAS TO TRAVEL TO OVERCOME THE STAR'S GRAVITY, IT COULD EASILY BE FLUNG BACK THROUGH THE CORONA INTO SPACE.

CORONA

SUN

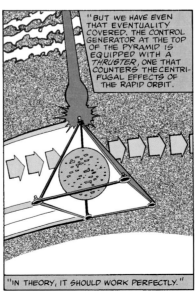

"BUT WE HAVE EVEN THAT EVENTUALITY COVERED. THE CONTROL GENERATOR AT THE TOP OF THE PYRAMID IS EQUIPPED WITH A *THRUSTER*, ONE THAT COUNTERS THE CENTRI-FUGAL EFFECTS OF THE RAPID ORBIT.

"IN THEORY, IT SHOULD WORK PERFECTLY."

"IN *THEORY*! OH, DEAR..."

209

AND SOON, THAT THEORY IS PUT TO THE TEST, AS A FINAL KERTS-BHRG GENERATOR IS TUGBOATED INTO PLACE ABOVE THE ARBRAN SUN--

--ITS BASE-MOUNTED SOLAR COLLECTOR READY TO ABSORB THE ENERGY REQUIRED TO POWER ITS VITAL FUNCTIONS.

WHILE IN THE CONTROL GENERATOR, HOVERING HIGH ABOVE ITS FOUR DRONELIKE COUNTERPARTS...

THAT'S CORRECT, GENERAL RIEEKAN, THE FLEET HAS BEEN MANEUVERED INTO ITS DESIGNATED POSITION.

"AND NOW THAT ALL FIVE GENERATORS ARE SET, THE ONLY THING LEFT TO DO IS--

"-- ENERGIZE!"

A BUTTON IS PRESSED, AND AT FIVE PRECISELY PREDETERMINED POINTS --

--SPACE CRACKLES--

--FORMING WALLS OF PROTECTIVE, TEMPERATURE-RESISTANT FORCE AROUND THE EVACUATED REBEL FLEET!

210

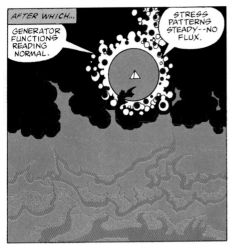

AFTER WHICH...

GENERATOR FUNCTIONS READING NORMAL.

STRESS PATTERNS STEADY--NO FLUX.

WE'VE GOT GREEN LIGHTS ACROSS THE BOARD, PRINCESS.

GOOD. THEN WE MIGHT AS WELL--

A HEARTBEAT--A BREATH SOFTLY HELD.

--TAKE 'ER DOWN!

SMALL ENGINES FIRE, AND THE GARGANTUAN PYRAMIDAL CONSTRUCT MOVES SLOWLY FORWARD, GAINING MOMENTUM AS IT ENTERS THE SUN'S GRAVITATIONAL PULL.

WHILE IN THE CONTROL GENERATOR, ALL IS SILENT AS EXTERIOR TEMPERATURES RISE TO TWO MILLION DEGREES...THREE MILLION... AND BEYOND.

211

UNTIL AT LAST...

WE MADE IT! WE'RE IN THE CHROMOSPHERE!

THEN ACTIVATE THE TOP THRUSTER--OR WE WON'T BE *STAYING* VERY LONG!

FLEET TEMPERATURE STABLE, WELL WITHIN ACCEPTABLE LEVELS.

NOT EVERYTHING, LAD. I'VE JUST RECEIVED A MESSAGE FROM ARBRA BASE.

LONG-RANGE SCANS HAVE PICKED UP SMALL CRAFT ENTER- ING THIS QUADRANT.

UNDENIABLY IMPERIAL.

THANKS, SHAHN.

LOOKS LIKE WE GOT THE FLEET UNDER WRAPS JUST IN TIME!

ORBIT ACHIEVED--

--AND HOLDING.

EVERYTHING'S A-OK.; WHEW!

ONLY NOW WE'D BETTER GET OUR- SELVES BACK TO ARBRA WHILE THERE'S ANY TIME *LEFT!*

212

ALL PERSONNEL EXCEPT THOSE ASSIGNED TO THE MAINTENANCE CREW REPORT TO THE SHUTTLE BAY--ON THE DOUBLE!

CAPTAIN MESA--

--GOOD LUCK. A LOT DEPENDS ON YOU.

DON'T WORRY, PRINCESS, WE'LL KEEP EVERYTHIN' SHIPSHAPE AN' RUNNIN' SMOOTH!

AND SOON...

ARE YOU POSITIVE THE SHUTTLE CAN GET US THROUGH, PRINCESS?

NO PROBLEM, LT. FALLTOWER. ITS SHIELDS AREN'T AS HEAVY AS THOSE ON THIS STATION--

--BUT THEY WERE DESIGNED TO PASS THROUGH THE CORONA AND BACK BEFORE REQUIRING RECHARGING.

THAT'S GOOD TO HEAR.

WILL YOU PLEASE HURRY ALONG, ARTOO? THERE'S ONLY ONE SHUTTLE, YOU KNOW, AND IF WE MISS THAT--

--WE'LL HAVE TO REMAIN FOR AN ENTIRE SIX DAY SHIFT!

I STILL DON'T UNDERSTAND WHY WE HAD TO COME ALONG IN THE FIRST PLACE.

I SUPPOSE IT IS FLATTERING THAT PRINCESS LEIA VALUES OUR OPINIONS, BUT SURELY THERE ARE OTHER--

B-DEEP!

EH?

ARTOO-DETOO, WHAT ARE YOU DOING?

213

COME BACK HERE, YOU IMPETUOUS ROLLER SKATE!

WE DON'T HAVE TIME TO INDULGE IN YOUR EXPLORATORY WHIMS! WE--

VADOOP-BRRRT

--WHAT'S THAT? YOU'VE SENSED AN UNCHARACTERISTIC SURGE IN THE GENERATOR'S POWER FEED? WELL, JUST DON'T STAND THERE! FIND OUT WHAT IT IS! IT MIGHT BE IMPORTANT!

FRA-DRRP

"KEEP MY SHIRT ON"?! DEAR FELLOW, I'LL HAVE YOU KNOW THAT EVEN IF I WORE A SHIRT, I WOULDN'T--

DIPADIT

--WHAT?! THE GENERATOR'S ABSORPTION CIRCUIT IS MALFUNCTIONING? I-IT'S ABOUT TO EXPLODE?

WELL, WHY DIDN'T YOU SAY SO? WE'VE GOT TO TELL THE PRINCESS! SHE'LL KNOW WHAT TO--

THE DOOR TO THE LAUNCH BAY! I-IT'S SEALING SHUT! BUT THAT CAN ONLY MEAN--

SHLANG

"--THAT THE SHUTTLE IS LAUNCHING!

"IT'S PROBABLY ACCELERATING THROUGH THE CORONA BY NOW!"

BUT THIS IS *DREADFUL!* THEY'VE GOT TO BE WARNED! SOMEONE HAS TO DO SOME-THING *BEFORE--*

PHOOF

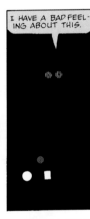

I HAVE A BAD FEEL-ING ABOUT THIS.

THANK GOODNESS! THE EMERGENCY POWER HAS COME ON! AT LEAST WE'LL BE ABLE TO SEE WHERE WE'RE GOING!

NOW WE MUST GET TO THE CONTROL ROOM!

I'M SURE THEY'LL HAVE EVERYTHING WELL IN HAND VERY *SOO--*

--OH, NO!

THE BURNING CIRCUITRY MUST HAVE PRODUCED NOXIOUS FUMES! THE ENTIRE MAINTENANCE CREW IS *UNCONSCIOUS!*

215

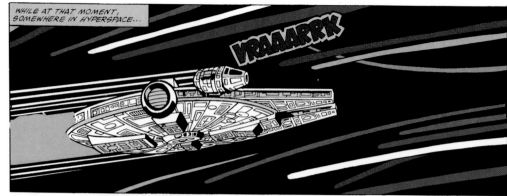

WHILE AT THAT MOMENT, SOMEWHERE IN HYPERSPACE...

VRAAARRK

I KNOW IT'S MY TURN AT THE STICK, CHEWBACCA, BUT I CAN'T COME UP RIGHT NOW.

I'M IN THE MIDDLE OF A GAME OF NOVACROWN.

YOU MEAN YOU'RE *LOSING* A GAME OF NOVACROWN.

THAT'S CALLED "STRATEGY", M'BOY. I'M LURING YOU INTO A SENSE OF FALSE CONFIDENCE.

WELL, IT'S SURE WORKING--THAT'S ANOTHER POINT FOR ME!

MRRF

EASY, CHEWIE.

I'VE GOT HIM ON THE RUN. THREE MORE MOVES AND--

GRRARRRAAARGG!

ALRIGHT! ALRIGHT! YOU DON'T HAVE TO SHAKE THE FALCON LOOSE AT THE SEAMS!

HEY--!

I'LL BE RIGHT THERE!

B-BUT, I WAS WINNING!

SORRY, LUKE. I GUESS WOOKIEES DON'T LIKE WAITING. { HEH {

THAT'S ONE I OWE YOU, CHEWIE!

THAT'S ONE I OWE YOU, CHEWIE!

MEANWHILE, BACK AT A SCENE OF PROBABLE DISASTER...

WE'RE THROUGH THE CORONA, PRINCESS--ALL SAFE AND SOUND!

YES, BUT JUST BARELY.

THAT PASSAGE DRAINED VIRTUALLY *ALL* OF THE ENERGY FROM OUR HEAT SHIELDS!

BEGGING YOUR PARDON, PRINCESS, BUT WE'RE RECEIVING A MESSAGE FROM C-3PO.

MESSAGE? BUT THREEPIO IS ON THIS SHUTTLE!

NOT ACCORDING TO HIS TRANSMISSION, MA'AM--

--IT'S COMING FROM THE CONTROL GENERATOR!

WHAT?!

HELLO? IS THIS THING WORKING? OH, GOOD.

I'M SORRY TO BE THE BEARER OF ILL TIDINGS, PRINCESS, BUT I'M AFRAID WE'RE EXPERIENCING A WIDESPREAD SYSTEMS BREAKDOWN! AND THE MAINTENANCE CREW HAS ALL BEEN RENDERED IMMOBILE!

NO!

THAT'S IMPOSSIBLE!

I SINCERELY WISH IT WERE, YOUR HIGHNESS!

"BUT MALFUNCTIONING CIRCUITRY HAS SEVERELY IMPAIRED THIS STATION'S ABILITY TO ABSORB SOLAR ENERGY! AS A RESULT, THE PROTECTIVE PYRAMID AROUND YOUR SHIPS IS WEAKENING."

"AND WORSE, THE THRUST UNIT ATOP THIS GENERATOR IS STARTING TO FLUCTUATE FROM LACK OF POWER, THREATENING THE STABILITY OF OUR ORBIT!"

AND I DON'T MIND ADMITTING, PRINCESS, THAT I'M BEGINNING TO GET A BIT WORRIED.

PARDON ME-- WE'RE BEGINNING TO GET WORRIED.

I HATE TO SOUND INSENSITIVE, BUT THOSE DROIDS ARE THE *LEAST* OF OUR PROBLEMS.

IF THAT PYRAMID PASSES THROUGH THE CORONA WITH-OUT THERMAL PROTECTION, WE COULD LOSE THE ENTIRE *FLEET!*

HOW TRAGIC!

MORE BAD NEWS, GENERAL. REMEMBER THE IMPERIAL SHIPS WE'VE BEEN TRACKING?

THEY'VE JUST ENTERED THIS SYSTEM!

BLAST! TAKE ELUSIVE ACTION IMMEDIATELY! BANK US BEHIND THE NEAREST MOON! WE'LL OBSERVE FROM THERE!

"UH-HUH. JUST AS I THOUGHT-- *TIE FIGHTERS*, FOUR OF THEM*!*"

ONLY FOUR? BUT WE COULD CALL A SQUAD OF X-WINGS UP FROM *ARBRA* AND TAKE THEM OUT WITH NO TROUBLE*!*

PERHAPS, LT. BRIE--

--BUT THEY'D BE *MISSED*. AND THAT COULD GIVE *DARTH VADER* A POTENTIALLY *DEADLY* CLUE TO OUR WHEREABOUTS. NO, WE'VE GOT TO STAY HERE AND BUILD UP OUR HEAT SHIELDS*!*

MEANWHILE, YEOMAN, CONTACT COMMANDER *SKYWALKER* AND HAVE HIM RETURN AT ONCE. PERHAPS HIS KNOWLEDGE OF *THE FORCE* CAN HELP US*!*

I DOUBT THERE'LL BE TIME FOR THAT, PRINCESS*!* OUR ORBIT IS BEGINNING TO DECAY*!*

IF SOMETHING DECISIVE ISN'T DONE SOON, THE FLEET--ALONG WITH ARTOO AND MYSELF--

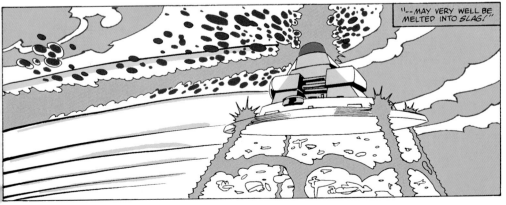

"--MAY VERY WELL BE MELTED INTO *SLAG!*"

AND OTHERWHERE, AS THE "FASTEST HUNK OF JUNK IN THE GALAXY" DROPS FROM LIGHT SPEED...

NICE JUMP, CHEWIE.

WE SHOULDN'T BE MORE THAN A STONE'S THROW FROM --

-- WHAT THE BLAZES IS THAT?

IT'S OUR DESTINATION, LANDO. OUR BEST HOPE OF HURTING THE EMPIRE AS BADLY AS THEY'VE HURT US. IT'S--

-- BAZARRE!

IT CERTAINLY IS!

WHILE WITHIN THE ARBRAN SUN, BITS OF SPARKING PLASMA BEGIN TO FLAKE FROM A WEAKENING THRUSTER--

--AS THE SCATHING CORONA DRAWS CLOSER... EVER CLOSER...

FAWEE-DOOP

PRINCESS! ARTOO SAYS HE HAS AN IDEA! HE'S CHECKING HIS DATA WITH THE GENERATOR EVEN AS I SPEAK!

WHAT'S THAT? THREEPIO, BOOST YOUR GAIN! WE'RE LOSING YOUR SIGNAL!

WE'RE LOSING SOMETHING ELSE, TOO--THOSE IMPERIAL BLOODHOUNDS!

THEY'RE LEAVING THE SYSTEM! LOOKS LIKE WE GOT BY WITHOUT BEING DISCOVERED!

YES, BUT IF WE DON'T THINK OF A SOLUTION SOON--

--WE WON'T HAVE MUCH LEFT TO BE DISCOVERED!

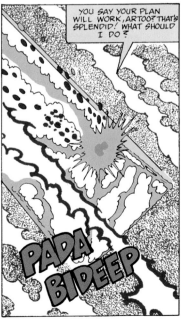

YOU SAY YOUR PLAN WILL WORK, ARTOO? THAT'S SPLENDID! WHAT SHOULD I DO?

PADA BIDEEP

OH, NO! Y-YOU CAN'T BE SERIOUS! I REFUSE! I'LL NEVER--

--KNOW HOW YOU TALKED ME INTO THIS! I REALIZE THAT LINKING THIS ENERGY CABLE TO THE REACTOR ABOARD ONE OF THE CRUISERS SHOULD PROVIDE ENOUGH POWER TO BOLSTER THE PYRAMID'S SHIELDING CAPACITY--

--BUT I HATE EVEN *BEING* IN SPACE, LET ALONE FLYING *THROUGH* IT!

STILL, BEING A HERO IN THE EYES OF ONE'S FELLOWS DOES HAVE ITS APPEAL.

PUP-PUP-PUP

IS THE REFLECTIVE FOIL I WRAPPED AROUND YOU KEEPING YOU COMFORTABLE, ARTOO?

I'M BEGINNING TO FEEL A BIT WARM, MYSELF.

BDRRP

OH? THE TEMPERATURE IS RISING BECAUSE WE'RE NEARING THE EDGE OF THE PYRAMID? BUT HOW COULD--

--GOOD GRACIOUS! THE HEAT IS MELTING MY ROCKET PACK! WE'RE LOSING MANEUVERABILITY!

AND WITHOUT IT, OUR MOMENTUM WILL CARRY US *PAST* THE CRUISER, *THROUGH* THE SHIELD... AND *INTO* THE CORONA!

WE'RE DOOMED.

WHILE IN ANOTHER PART OF THE GALAXY, THINGS ARE ALSO HEATING UP...

I DON'T LIKE IT, LUKE.

I HAD SOME DEALINGS WITH FERRET BACK WHEN I RAN CLOUD CITY-- AND I ALWAYS CAME AWAY FROM THEM FEELING LIKE I'D JUST SLEPT IN A SLIME PIT!

MEPPS.

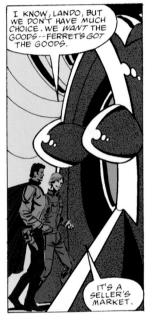

I KNOW, LANDO, BUT WE DON'T HAVE MUCH CHOICE. WE WANT THE GOODS-- FERRET'S GOT THE GOODS.

IT'S A SELLER'S MARKET.

AND, UH, SPEAKING OF MARKETS...

WOW.

GROOTONS! GROOTONS! FOUR CREDITS THE PAIR!

ONLY FLOWN ONCE BY A LITTLE OLD--

HAND MADE ON--

CAN LET YOU HAVE IT FOR--

MY WALLET--!

SWELL. HOW DO WE FIND FERRET IN ALL THIS?

I DOUBT THAT'LL BE A PROBLEM, LUKE.

I THINK HE'S FOUND US!

AND...

OKAY! THE SHIELDS AREN'T AT FULL STRENGTH, BUT THEY SHOULD HOLD FOR ONE PASS-THROUGH!

LET'S GO!

PRINCESS...

...IT WON'T DO ANY GOOD. ACCORDING TO COMPUTER CALCULATIONS, THE UNPROTECTED FLEET ENTERED THE CORONA--

--THIRTY SECONDS AGO!

NO! I-IT DIDN'T! IT COULDN'T HAVE! IT...I-I...

ALL RIGHT.

WE...WE'LL START OVER AGAIN. W-WE'LL BUILD... MORE SHIPS AND...

...AND...

HELLO? ARE YOU THERE? YOO-HOO!

WHA--

--THREEPIO!

224

I APOLOGIZE FOR NOT COMMUNICATING SOONER, PRINCESS. IF YOU WISH TO SCOLD ME, I FULLY UNDERSTA--

THREEPIO, I'VE NEVER BEEN HAPPIER TO SEE ANYONE IN MY LIFE! IF YOU'RE STILL ALIVE--

--THAT MUST MEAN THE *FLEET* HAS SURVIVED!

"OH YES, YOUR HIGHNESS! THE LINK-UP BETWEEN THE CONTROL GENERATOR AND ONE OF THE CRUISERS IS TEMPORARY--

-- BUT IT DOES ENABLE THE THRUST UNIT TO KEEP US IN ORBIT UNTIL MORE PERMANENT REPAIRS CAN BE MADE."

BUT HOW DID YOU DO IT?

I MUST ADMIT, PRINCESS, THAT ARTOO-DETOO PROVIDED OUR SALVATION.

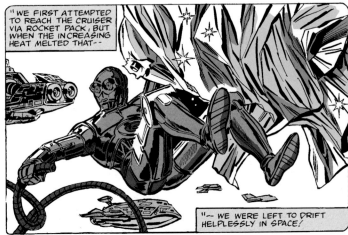

"WE FIRST ATTEMPTED TO REACH THE CRUISER VIA ROCKET PACK, BUT WHEN THE INCREASING HEAT MELTED THAT--

"-- WE WERE LEFT TO DRIFT HELPLESSLY IN SPACE!

"THAT IS UNTIL ARTOO MADE A BRILLIANT, IF OBVIOUS, SUGGESTION.

"FOLLOWING IT, I TORE A SECTION OF THE PROTECTIVE FOIL FROM HIS UPPER TORSO--

"-- IN ORDER TO ALLOW HIS BUILT-IN FIRE EXTINGUISHER TO POP THROUGH.

"WE THEN USED THAT EXTINGUISHER AS A MINIATURE PROPULSION SYSTEM TO GUIDE US TO THE CRUISER--

"-- WHERE WE MADE THE PROPER CONNECTION WITH AT LEAST FOUR OR FIVE SECONDS TO SPARE!"

YOU'LL BOTH GET MEDALS FOR THIS--AS WELL AS THE LONGEST, WARMEST *LUBE BATHS* WE CAN MUSTER!

OH, I COULD *USE* ONE, MADAME!

ALL RIGHT, SECURE FROM EMERGENCY STATIONS-- WE'RE GOING IN AT NORMAL SPEED.

AND YEOMAN, YOU CAN CANCEL THAT MESSAGE TO COMMANDER SKYWALKER.

I'M AFRAID THERE'S NOTHING TO CANCEL, PRINCESS.

WHAT?

I'VE BEEN TRYING TO RAISE THE MILLENNIUM FALCON EVER SINCE YOUR FIRST ORDER, BUT I'VE GOTTEN NO RESPONSE! IT'S LIKE--

--THEY'VE SIMPLY DROPPED OUT OF EXISTENCE!

NEXT ISSUE: *BAZARRE!*

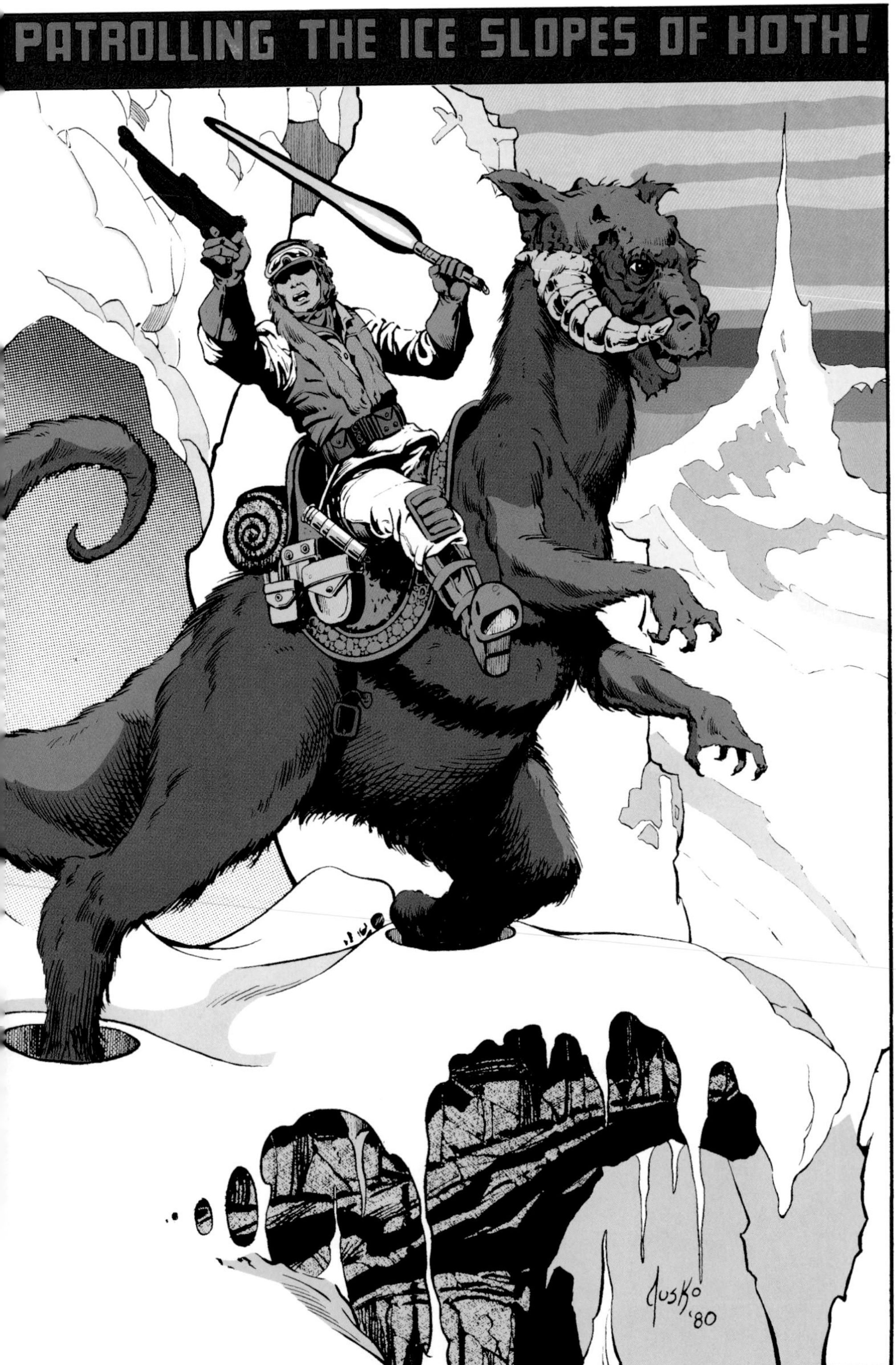
PATROLLING THE ICE SLOPES OF HOTH!
Jusko '80

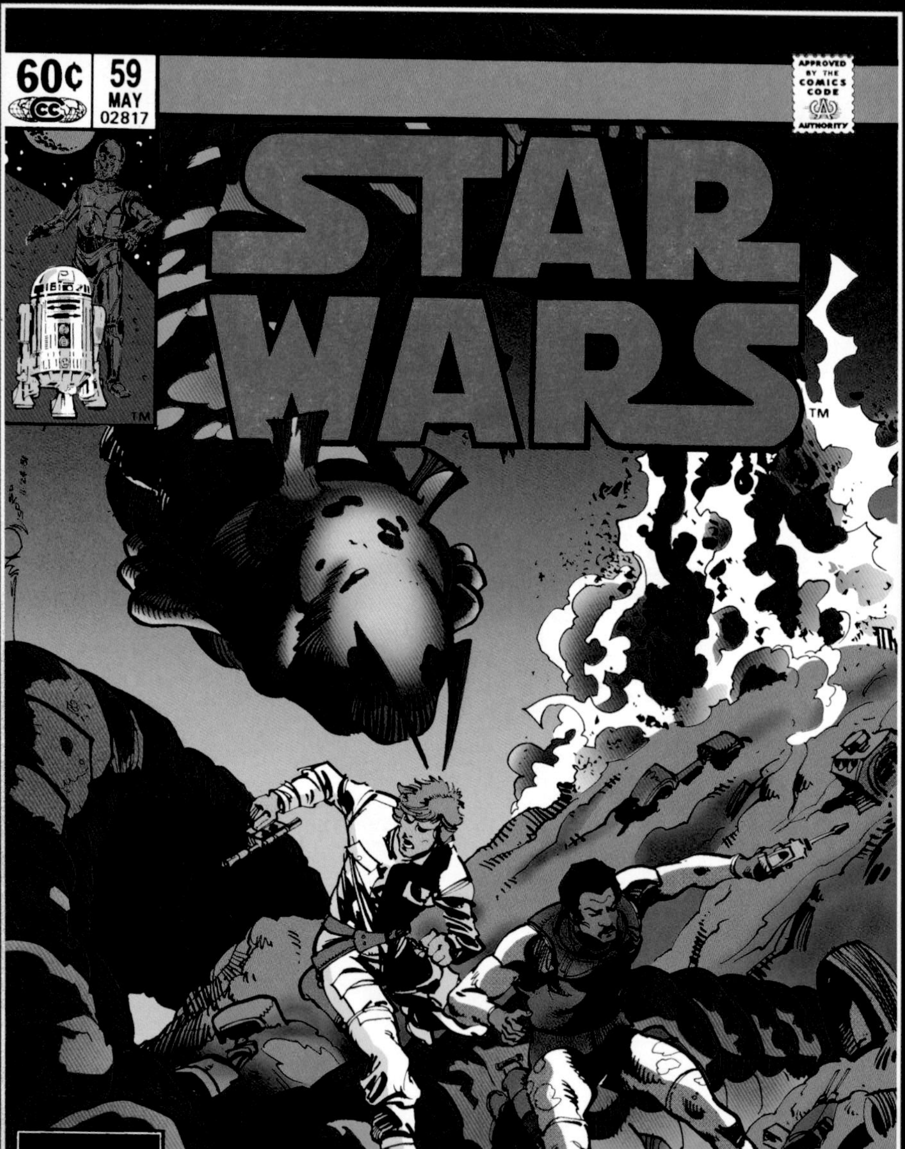
60¢
59
MAY
02817
APPROVED BY THE COMICS CODE AUTHORITY
STAR WARS™

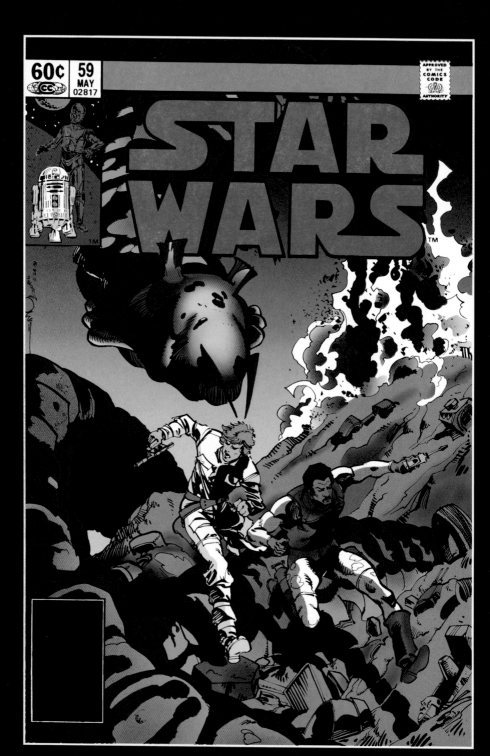

Long ago in a galaxy far, far away. . .there exists a state of cosmic *civil war*. A brave alliance of *underground freedom fighters* has challenged the tyranny and oppression of the awesome *Galactic Empire*. This is their story!

Lucasfilm PRESENTS: **STAR WARS** ™ THE GREATEST **SPACE FANTASY** OF ALL!

DAVID MICHELINIE — WRITER / PLOT

WALTER SIMONSON — PENCILS / PLOT

TOM PALMER — INKS

JOE ROSEN — LETTERS

DON WARFIELD — COLORS

AL MILGROM — EDITOR

JIM SHOOTER — HIGH ROLLER

THIS IS...

BAZARRE

...A FLOATING MARKET IN SPACE WHERE ANYTHING MAY BE BOUGHT, BARTERED OR SOLD, AND IT IS HERE THAT LANDO CALRISSIAN AND LUKE SKYWALKER HAVE COME ON A MISSION FOR THE REBEL ALLIANCE, ONLY TO DISCOVER THAT BAZARRE'S SPECIAL-OF-THE-DAY APPEARS TO BE--

--DEATH AT BARGAIN PRICES!

ONE MOVE, GRUBBERS, AND YOU'RE ASHES!

MM, NOT MUCH MEAT ON THIS ONE. I COULDN'T POSSIBLY GIVE YOU MORE THAN TEN CREDITS.

LOOK, BUDDY, CAN'T YOU SEE THIS IS AN AMBUSH?! NOW BEAT IT! I'M NOT FOR SALE!

HMPH. BELLIGERENT, TOO.

EIGHT CREDITS.

I'M SORRY, QUAD-LO, BUT I'M AFRAID THE FELLOW'S RIGHT. THESE GENTLEMEN AREN'T MERCHANDISE--

--THEY'RE MY GUESTS!

WELL, AS I LIVE AND BREATHE! IF IT ISN'T--

ORION FERRET, DEAR BOY, AT YOUR SERVICE.

SKEK

ALLOW ME TO APOLOGIZE FOR YOUR RATHER CRUDE WELCOME. SECURITY IS VITAL IN RUNNING AN OPERATION LIKE BAZARRE, AND MY GUARDS OCCASIONALLY GET OVER-ZEALOUS.

YOU COULD HAVE TOLD THEM WE'D BE ARRIVING, FERRET.

I DID.

SKEK

NOW, SHALL WE ADJOURN TO MY OFFICE?

230

AND SOON, IN AN EXECUTIVE WING OF THE CELESTIAL SHOPPING MALL...

YOU HAVE THE GOODS, FERRET?

LANDO, DEAR LANDO, HAVE I EVER LET YOU DOWN?

YOU WANT A LIST?

AH, DROLL AS EVER, I SEE. BUT WORRY NOT. YOU REQUESTED FOUR *TIE FIGHTERS*--

--AND IT'S FOUR YOU SHALL HAVE.

I'VE BEEN SUCCESSFUL IN PURCHASING PARTS OF DAMAGED IMPERIAL CRAFT FROM VARIOUS BATTLEFIELD SCAVENGERS--

--AND HAVE USED THESE PARTS TO RE-CONSTRUCT THE SHIPS YOU ORDERED.

NOT THAT I KEEP THEM *HERE*, OF COURSE, AS I MENTIONED--

--I'M VERY KEEN ON SECURITY.

THEN WHERE *ARE* THEY, FERRET? WE HAVEN'T GOT ALL DAY!

PRINCESS LEIA AND THE OTHERS ARE HIDING OUR FLEET IN THE SUN NEAR ARBRA, AND THEY MIGHT NEED OUR HELP! *

TUT-TUT, YOUNG MAN, EVERYTHING IS ARRANGED. THE SHIPS ARE HIDDEN ON *PATCH-4*, A DISPOSAL PLANET SOME PARSECS FROM HERE. THEY'VE BEEN CLEVERLY BLENDED WITH THE OTHER, UM, REFUSE.

* THIS STORY TAKES PLACE DURING *LAST ISSUE'S* STORY. TRUST US.
--ELUCIDATIN' AL.

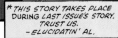

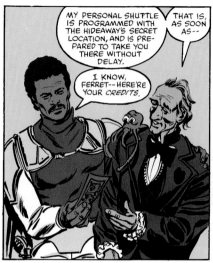

MY PERSONAL SHUTTLE IS PROGRAMMED WITH THE HIDEAWAY'S SECRET LOCATION, AND IS PREPARED TO TAKE YOU THERE WITHOUT DELAY.

THAT IS, AS SOON AS--

I KNOW, FERRET--HERE'RE YOUR *CREDITS*.

YOU'RE *SO* UNDERSTANDING, DEAR BOY. HAVE A NICE TRIP!

ONCE THEY'VE LEFT, MY LITTLE FRIEND, I'LL ACTIVATE THE SHUTTLE'S REMOTE *EJECTION* SYSTEM AND CAST THEM BOTH INTO SPACE!

THAT WAY WE'LL HAVE THE MONEY, THE FIGHTERS *AND* THE REBELS' SHIP!

SKEK-HEK-HEK

OH, BY THE WAY, FERRET, IT SEEMS I NEGLECTED TO INTRODUCE THE *THIRD* MEMBER OF OUR PARTY.

"THIRD" MEMBER?

YES, I'D LIKE YOU TO MEET--

-- MY ASSOCIATE, *MR. CHEWBACCA*.

GRRARRRK

WHA-- A WOOKIEE?!

SKEK?

YES, I THOUGHT YOU MIGHT APPRECIATE SOME *COMPANY* WHILE WE WERE GONE.

YOU WILL KEEP THE MAN AMUSED, WON'T YOU, CHEWIE?

AND IF WE DON'T REPORT BACK SAFELY IN ONE HOUR--

--RIP *HIS HEAD* OFF!

WHAT--?!

WAIT! Y-YOU CAN'T DO THIS--!

SKEK-EK-EK-EK-EK!

SO LONG, FERRET! SEE YOU IN AN HOUR!

I REALIZE THAT WAS A DIRTY TRICK, LUKE, BUT I HAD DEALINGS WITH FERRET BACK WHEN I RAN CLOUD CITY--

--AND BE-LIEVE ME, HE'S *USED* TO DIRT!

MASTER?

YES, YES, WHAT *IS* IT, P'LOR?

A MESSAGE, SIR.

A SCRAMBLED EMERGENCY TRANSMISSION FOR THE REBELS, FROM SOMEONE NAMED "LEIA." SHALL I HAVE THEM RETURN?

OF COURSE NOT. WHY MAKE A DIFFICULT SITUATION EVEN MORE--

WHAT? OH, NO, DEAR FELLOW, IT'S NOTHING THAT CONCERNS YOU.

BY THE BY, DON'T YOU GET *DIZZY* WAY UP THERE?

MOMENTS LATER, AS A *WELL-KEPT* SHUTTLE MOVES FROM A *PRIVATE DOCK SLOT* ON THE *ARTIFICIAL WORLD* CALLED BAZARRE...

I STILL DON'T *TRUST* FERRET.

NEITHER DO I, BUT WE SHOULD BE OKAY AS LONG AS *CHEWIE'S* ON THE JOB. FERRET MAY BE A *GREEDY SLUG*--

-- BUT HE'S NOT A *STUPID* GREEDY SLUG!

I'D FEEL A LOT BETTER IF WE HAD MORE THAN *SHORT-RANGE* MANUAL CONTROL OVER THIS THING.

SPEED BUILDS, PEAKS, AND AUTO-MATIC SWITCHES THROW, SENDING THE LITTLE CRAFT INTO HYPER-DRIVE--

--AND THEN PULLING IT BACK OUT AFTER A *SHORT*, TIMELESS VOYAGE HAS BROUGHT IT TO--

--PATCH 4, DEAD AHEAD!

YEAH, I KNOW, I CAN *SMELL* IT ALREADY!

NOW, LANDO, YOU KNOW THERE HAS TO BE SOME-PLACE WHERE PEOPLE CAN DUMP UNRECYCL-ABLE MACHINE PARTS.

I KNOW, AND *MACHINES* DON'T BOTHER ME.

IT'S THE COFFEE GROUNDS AND BANTHA TRIPE *I* CAN'T TAKE! ≥PHEW≤

NEVERTHELESS, AN EXPERT LANDING IS MADE ON THE PLANET'S RUNNY, JELLYLIKE SURFACE.

AFTER WHICH...

OKAY, SOON AS I STRAP ON THIS RADIO AND THESE BINOCS, WE'LL BE ALL SET.

UH, SAY, LUKE, I'VE BEEN THINKING...

...MAYBE ONE OF US SHOULD STAY HERE, Y'KNOW, TO GUARD THE SHIP? I'D BE HAPPY TO--

SORRY, LANDO--

--BUT IT'LL TAKE BOTH OF US TO RIG THOSE TIES TO A TRACTOR BEAM. THAT IS, IF WE CAN EVER *FIND* THE--

--HOLD IT!

235

THERE THEY ARE! HIDDEN UNDER CAMOUFLAGE NETTING, JUST LIKE FERRET SAID! LET'S GO!

BLAST! I *KNEW* I SHOULDN'T HAVE WORN NEW BOOTS!

AMIDST THE SLURPING SOUNDS OF RELUCTANT FOOTSTEPS, THE JOURNEY BEGINS...

...AND WITH THE ADDITION OF SURPRISING NEW SOUNDS, IT ABRUPTLY ENDS!

HEY! YOU HEAR THAT?

Y'MEAN THAT WEIRD RUMBLING? SORT OF LIKE A GALACTIC FREIGHTER SLIPPIN' A GEAR?

SRRREEAARRG!

O-OR MAYBE ≶GULP≶ TH-THE GROWLING OF A VERY *BIG* STOMACH?

HOLY--!

ANOTHER BONUS FROM FERRET, NO DOUBT!

I SHOULD'VE FIGURED HE WOULDN'T LEAVE THOSE SHIPS UNGUARDED!

BUT THAT'S NOT THE BIGGEST SHOCK!

OH, GREAT! WHAT THE HECK COULD TOP A MONSTER LIKE THIS?

HOW 'BOUT THE FACT THAT OUR BLASTERS AREN'T DOIN' BEANS AGAINST IT!

AGH! THE SLIME-LICKER ALMOST NAILED ME!

HANG ON, LANDO!

MAYBE MY LIGHTSABER CAN DO WHAT THE BLASTERS COULDN'T!

THANKS, LUKE! YOU SAVED MY LIFE!

I'M AFRAID IT WAS JUST A STAY OF EXECUTION, LANDO--

--UNLESS WE CAN FIND SOME WAY BACK TO THE SHUTTLE!

AND *THIS* ISN'T IT!

THE PASSAGE WAY'S BLOCKED!

I TELL YA, IF I EVER LAY MY HANDS ON FERRET AGAIN...!

GET IN LINE, BROTHER!

AND, SPEAKING OF THE DEVIL...

BY NOW, MY WATCHBEAST ON PATCH-4 HAS UNDOUBTEDLY RID ME OF THOSE ANNOYING REBELS.

AND, IF P'LOR PICKS UP THE *MENTAL SIGNAL* I'M SENDING, THEIR FURRY COMPATRIOT HERE SHOULD ALSO CEASE TO BE A PROBLEM!

WHILE ON THE SUBJECT OF PROBLEMS...

GET FERRET ON THE HORN, LUKE! MAYBE WE CAN *BUY* OUR WAY OUT OF THIS!

RIGHT!

WRONG! THE TRANSCEIVER'S DEAD! WE CAN'T LINK UP WITH THE SHUTTLE TO CALL BAZARRE!

FERRET'S STUCK IT TO US AGAIN!

I SWEAR, I'M GONNA COME BACK AN' *HAUNT* THAT SONOVA--

PSST! HEY! OVER HERE!

HUH?

COME THIS WAY! YOU'LL BE SAFE!

IS HE KIDDIN'? FOLLOW SOMEONE WE CAN'T EVEN *SEE?*

IT'S GOTTA BE A TRAP!

SRRAARRGH

THEN AGAIN...

...WE WOULDN'T WANT TO BE IMPOLITE!

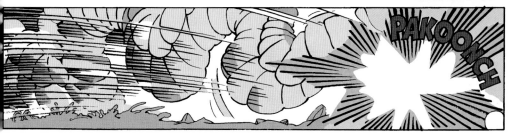

PAKOONCH

≥WHEW≤ THAT WAS CLOSE!

I KNOW, BUT IT'S AWFUL DARK IN HERE. I JUST HOPE WE HAVEN'T MADE A BIG--

CLICK

--MISTAKE?

COVER MY FLANK, LUKE!

YOU'RE COVERED! IF THESE JOKERS WANT A FIGHT, THEY'LL GET MORE THAN THEY--

WELCOME!

 I AM SERJA KESSELROOK, AND I AM WELCOMINK YOU TO OUR HUMMEL HOME!

ER, H-HI THERE, SERJA. I'M LANDO. AND WE APPRECIATE YOUR HELP.

PHOOEY! YOU ARE VERY MUCH--

 --WELCOME!

I ≥ULP≤ G-GET THE PICTURE!

 AND, AFTER FURTHER HUGS AND INTRODUCTIONS...

YOU MEAN, SERJA, THAT YOU FOLKS *LIVE* DOWN HERE?

YOU'RE BEINK CORRECT, BUDDY!

 THE EMPIRE IS EACH OF US TAKINK OUR HOMES, LEAVINK US NOTHINK BUT TO WANDER. WE HOP FREIGHTERS, STOW AWAY, GET NAME "HOBOES"!

IN TIME, WE ALL COME HERE, MAKE FRIENDS, DECIDE TO STAY. AND IS GOOD HOME. LITTLE SMELLY, BUT NOT BAD--

--UNTIL CRUMB-BUM *FERRET* SHOW UP!

240

IN MATTER FACT, WHEN YOU COME DOWN IN FERRET'S SHIP, WE ARE GOINK TO *KILL* YOU. BUT THEN CEASAR ATTACK YOU, SO WE KNOW YOU OKAY.

CEASAR?

YA-YA, FERRET'S BEAST. THE WATCHER. HE MAKE LIFE MISERABLE, KEEPINK US ALL UNDERGROUND.

BUT SURELY FERRET HAS SOME WAY OF CONTROL-LING THE MONSTER?

THAT HE DOES, LAD. THERE'S A *SONIC PACIFIER* IN THE VERY SHIP YOU CAME IN-- WE SEEN HIM USE IT BEFORE, MAKES THE WATCHER ACT LIKE AN OBEDIENT CHILD. BUT UNFORTUNATELY, TO GET TO IT--

--YA GOTTA GO *THROUGH* THE BEAST!

WHILE ON BAZARRE...

COME

TOK TOK

MASTER, THERE'S A PROBLEM AT BERKI'S SPICE BOOTH. HE'D LIKE TO SPEAK WITH YOU.

RIGHT ON TIME!

THANK YOU, P'LOR. I'LL CALL HIM IMMEDIATELY.

MRRLL

OH, DON'T BE SILLY, DEAR FELLOW. I'VE NOTHING UP MY SLEEVE.

I MERELY HAVE A BUSINESS TO RUN.

AND TO *PROTECT!*

SHHHISH

GRRRRARGG.

EXCELLENT! THE LIQUID HAS ALREADY SOLIDIFIED INTO ROCK-HARD CRYSTAL! THAT SPRITZER UNIT MAY BE A *MESSY* SAFE-GUARD, BUT IT'S MOST EFFECTIVE.

PRRRRRR

241

AND, ON PATCH-4... SOME OF THE BOYS TRIED TO STOP THE BEAST BEFORE, BUT ONLY SUCCEEDED IN BEIN' ITS AFTERNOON *SNACK!*

THEN MAYBE WE CAN HELP.

WE HAVE TO. AFTER ALL, WE DIDN'T COME TO *FEED* CEASAR...

...WE CAME TO *BURY* HIM!

HUH?

WHAT?

BEG PARD?

LUKE EXPLAINS-- AND SOON, ON THE SLIPPERY SURFACE NEAR THE HOBOES' REFUGE...

IT'S A GOOD THING YOU GUYS HAD AN EMERGENCY EXIT-- THAT BEASTIE'S STILL PARKED AT YOUR FRONT DOOR!

WHICH, AMONG OTHER THINGS, MAKES HIM A PERFECT TARGET!

YOU ARE BEINK TOO KIND.

NOT REALLY, SERJA. WE'VE AS MUCH AT STAKE IN STOPPING CEASAR AS YOU DO!

OKAY, LANDO, AIM YOUR BLASTERS AT THAT MOUNTAIN OF JUNK ACROSS THE GORGE, GOT IT? THEN--

--FIRE!

FRATCH

SZAKT

ZAKOW

ZHADAW

WE DID IT! THE MONSTER'S COMPLETELY COVERED!

SURE LOOKS THAT WAY, BUT MAYBE WE'D BETTER HOLD OFF A COUPLE OF MINUTES, JUST IN CASE--

WE DON'T *HAVE* A COUPLE OF MINUTES! LEIA MIGHT BE IN--

"--TROUBLE...?"

SRRREEAARRGH

I-IT'S CEASAR! HE WASN'T EVEN STUNNED!

RUN, LUKE! GET OUTTA THE WAY BEFORE-- LUKE?

LUKE!

ZTOW

I NOT BE SEEINK HIM!

THE BOY'S A GONER, THAT'S FER SURE.

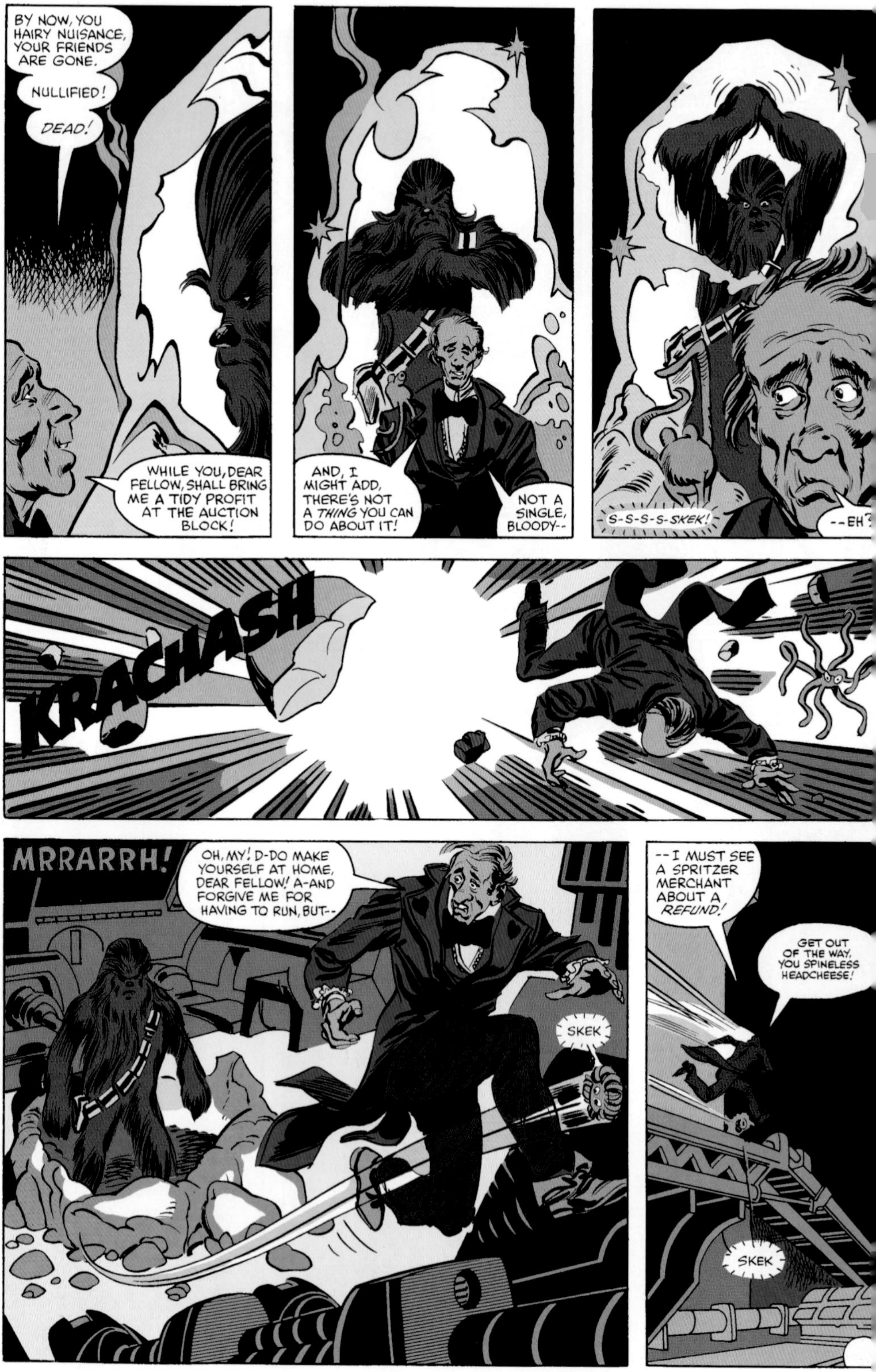
BY NOW, YOU HAIRY NUISANCE, YOUR FRIENDS ARE GONE.
NULLIFIED!
DEAD!
WHILE YOU, DEAR FELLOW, SHALL BRING ME A TIDY PROFIT AT THE AUCTION BLOCK!
AND, I MIGHT ADD, THERE'S NOT A THING YOU CAN DO ABOUT IT!
NOT A SINGLE, BLOODY--
S-S-S-S-SKEK!
--EH?
KRACHASH
MRRARRH!
OH, MY! D-DO MAKE YOURSELF AT HOME, DEAR FELLOW! A-AND FORGIVE ME FOR HAVING TO RUN, BUT--
SKEK
--I MUST SEE A SPRITZER MERCHANT ABOUT A REFUND!
GET OUT OF THE WAY, YOU SPINELESS HEADCHEESE!
SKEK

GO ON, GET OUTTA HERE! I'LL TRY TO HOLD THIS MAN-EATER OFF!

NOT HAVINK TO SAY TWICE, BUDDY!

LET'S GO!

CEASAR'S GOING AFTER LANDO AND THE HOBOES! DIDN'T EVEN NOTICE I'D DUCKED UNDER THIS RUBBLE!

BUT I'VE GOT TO MAKE THE MOST OF MY LUCK, GET TO THE SHUTTLE AND ACTIVATE THAT SONIC PACIFIER--

--BEFORE SOMEONE GETS KILLED!

BLAST! I'VE GIVEN THAT SLITHERING NIGHTMARE EVERYTHING I'VE GOT, AND IT'S NOT EVEN SLOWING DOWN!

EXCEPT MAYBE TO TAKE AIM!

CHOONCH

YIKE!

MADE IT! NOW TO REV UP THAT SONIC PACIFIER!

ER, THAT IS... IF I CAN *FIND* THE THING!

PRRATCH

NAGH!

THAT LAST LUNGE... KNOCKED ME FOR A LOOP! H-HEAD SPINNING! CAN'T...RUN!

BUT THAT MONSTER'S GONNA LEARN...THERE'S NO SUCH THING AS A *FREE* LUNCH!

'SPECIALLY IF IT'S *LANDO CALRISSIAN!*

ZLADOW

FUMP

HUH?!

HEY, LANDO! YOU OKAY?

LOOKS LIKE I FOUND THAT *SONIC SWITCH* JUST IN TIME!

HUH? OH, UH, YEAH! I-I FIGURED THAT'S WHAT HAPPENED! NUTS.

I *DID* IT! WITH ONE SHOT! I-I MUST'VE HIT A VITAL ORGAN!

THAT HAD TO BE THE GREATEST SHOT IN THE GALAXY! I'LL BE A *LEGEND* FOR THIS! THEY'LL WRITE *SONGS* ABOUT ME! THEY'LL--

WHAT MARVELOUS FORESIGHT I HAD, INSISTING THAT A FUELED SPACER BE KEPT IN MY PRIVATE HANGAR AT ALL TIMES!

HOWEVER, NEARBY, A WOOKIE WATCHES...REACHES INTO A UTILITY POUCH...AND BEGINS ASSEMBLING A CURIOUSLY FAMILIAR DEVICE.

NOTHING CAN STOP ME NOW!

KLK

—SKEK—

JUST STOP FRETTING, WILL YOU? AS SOON AS THE IGNITION CIRCUITS ARE PRIMED, WE'LL LEAVE THIS SORDID BATTLEFIELD!

"THEN ALL WE NEED DO IS CONDUCT BUSINESS FROM SPACE FOR A WHILE--"

CHK

--AND THEN RETURN WHEN OUR PERSECUTORS HAVE LOST INTEREST. IT'S ALL SO SIMPLE, REALLY--

"--WHEN ONE DEALS WITH RUFFIANS OF INFERIOR CALIBER!"

FRACHOW

SEE? ALREADY WE'RE LIFTING OFF. AND IN SECONDS WE'LL BE--

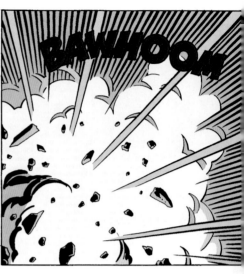

BAWHOOM

DRAT! THE SALESMAN WHO PEDDLED THIS SPACER MUST BE IN LEAGUE WITH THAT *SPRITZER* MERCHANT! I'VE HALF A MIND TO--

--EH?!

WELL, HEL*LO*, DEAR FELLOW! I- I WAS JUST GOING TO SEE IF YOUR FRIENDS WERE SAFE ON--

--WHAT? W-WELL, YES, I *DO* REALIZE THAT MY HOUR IS UP, B-BUT SURELY YOU CAN'T MEAN TO--

GRRARRLL

MOTHER *SAID* THERE'D BE DAYS LIKE THIS..

CHEWIE!

HWRFF?

I HATE TO SPOIL YOUR FUN-- I MEAN, I *REALLY* HATE TO--BUT I'M AFRAID EVERYTHING WORKED OUT OKAY.

AND NO THANKS TO *YOU,* FERRET!

WH-WHY, WHATEVER DO YOU MEAN, DEAR BOY?

I MEAN THAT DESPITE YOUR TRICKS--

"--THE *TIES* WE PAID FOR ARE MOORED WITH THE *FALCON* BELOW BAZARRE.

"AND SINCE WE LEFT YOUR SONIC DEVICE WITH THE HOBOES, SO THAT *THEY* HAVE CONTROL OVER CEASAR--

"-- I DON'T THINK YOU'LL BE USING PATCH-4 AGAIN!"

WHUUP?!

FRRGG!

THAT'S RIGHT, CHEWIE, YOU CAN GET RID OF FERRET NOW.

I THINK WE'VE HAD ENOUGH TO DO WITH *GARBAGE* FOR ONE DAY!

SKEK

OH, DO SHUT UP!

249

AND THUS IT IS THAT, SOMETIME LATER OVER THE LUSH FOREST W̲CALLED ARBRA, A MODIFIED SPICE FREIGHTER TOWS FOUR IMPERIAL WAR CRAFT BEHIND IT VIA TRACTO⸻ BEAM, DROPPING ITSELF AND ITS CARGO EVER LOWER--

--UNTIL, AT LAST, ALL SETTLE IN THE HIDDEN CAVERN FORTRESS THAT SERVES AS HEADQUARTERS FOR THE REBEL ALLIANCE. AND THERE...

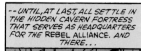

LUKE!

LEIA! HOW'D IT GO WITH THE FLEET?

OH, WE HAD A LITTLE PROBLEM WITH ONE OF THE FIELD GENERATORS,* BUT WE FIXED IT UP IN TIME.

I'M JUST GLAD TO SEE THAT YOU AND LANDO ARE SAFE.

*AGAIN, LAST ISSUE.

WE'RE ALL GLAD, ACE. IN FA⸻WE'RE THROWING A PARTY ⸻CELEBRATE YOUR SUCCESS⸻

SHIRA'S RIGHT. BUT DO YOU THINK YOU COULD DO ME A FAVOR BEFORE ASKING FOR THE FIRST DANCE, LUKE?

WHAT, PRINCESS?

CHANGE YOUR UNIFORM?

RIGHT, PRINCESS.

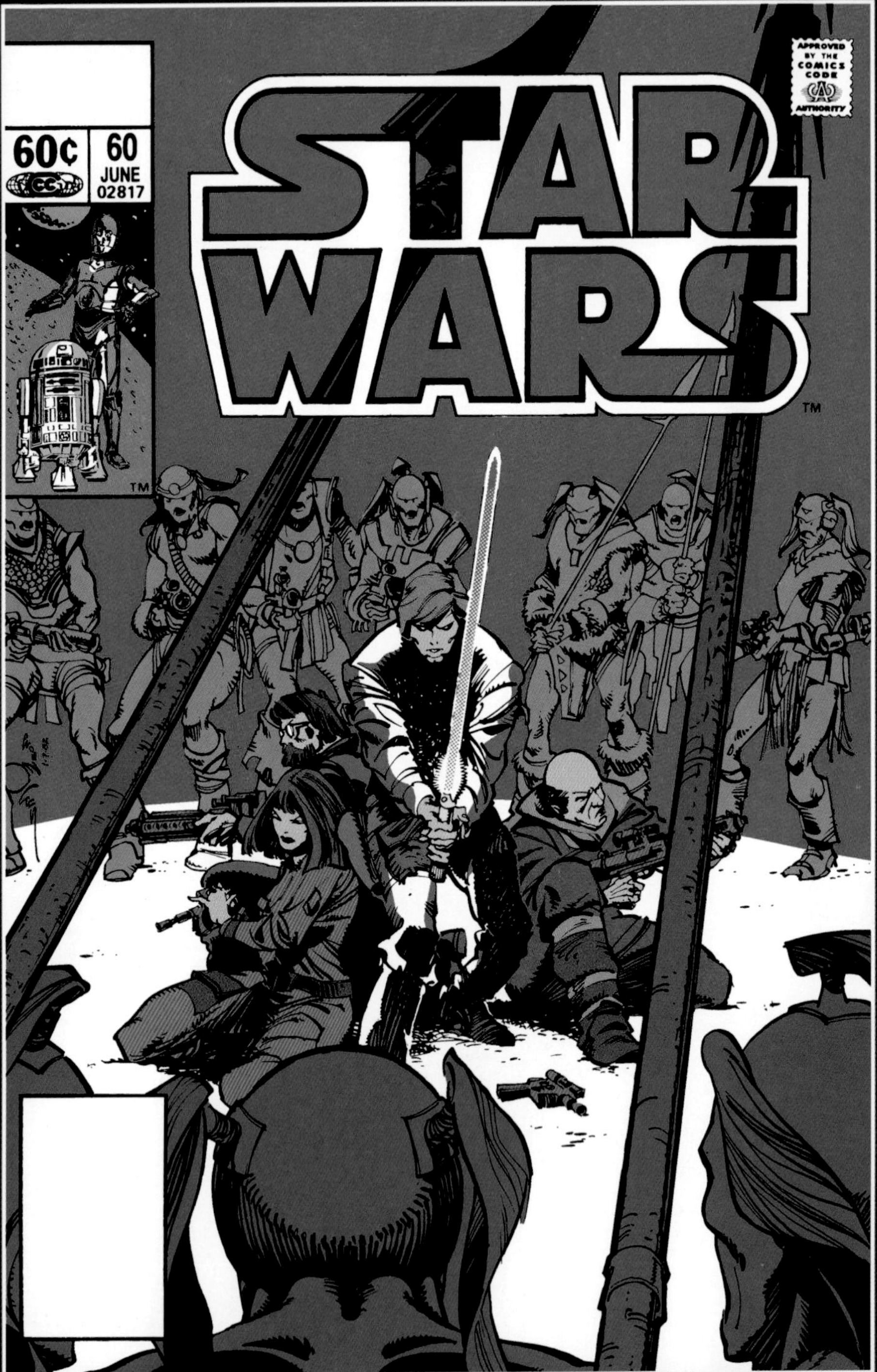

60¢
60
JUNE
02817
APPROVED BY THE COMICS CODE AUTHORITY
STAR WARS

Lucasfilm PRESENTS: STAR WARS

THE GREATEST SPACE FANTASY OF ALL!

VID MICHELINIE SCRIPTER/PLOT	WALTER SIMONSON PENCILS/PLOT	TOM PALMER INKS	JOE ROSEN LETTERS	GLYNIS WEIN COLORS	AL MILGROM EDITOR	JIM SHOOTER GRAND MOFF

AND THE ISOLATED IMPERIAL OUTPOST CALLED SPINDRIFT *IS* BATHED IN FLAME! LONG AGO, THE SOLDIERS HERE HAD BEEN WARNED OF POSSIBLE ATTACK BY THE EMPIRE'S ARCH ENEMIES, THE REBEL ALLIANCE, BUT THESE ATTACKERS ARE START-LINGLY, DEVASTATINGLY--

-- THEIR OWN KIND!

CH CHOWM

SHIRA'S STORY

W-WE LET THOSE *TIE FIGHTERS* THROUGH BECAUSE THEY WERE "FRIENDLIES," MAJOR! WH-WHY ARE THEY OPENING FIRE?!

"AND NOW THEY'RE STRAFING OUR MAIN DEFENSE BATTERY!"

I WISH WE COULD *ASK 'EM,* GERDY--BUT THEY JUST TOOK OUT THE *COMMUNICATIONS* TOWER!

SOMEONE HIGH UP MUST BE *REAL MAD!*

DARTH VADER! IT'S GOTTA BE!

"BLAST IT, GERDY! I *TOLD* YOU NOT TO USE PRIORITY FREQUENCIES TO CALL THAT FEMALE ON ADUBA-4!"

WHUMP

"B-BUT, THAT'S CRAZY, MAJOR! *NO ONE* WOULD DESTROY AN ENTIRE OUTPOST BECAUSE OF ONE LITTLE INFRACTION OF THE RULES!"

"*NO ONE"?* YOU FORGET WHO WE'RE *TALKING* ABOUT, GERDY!

OH, YEAH. VADER...

BUT WHATEVER REASON, WE'VE GOTTA SAVE OUR SKINS! EVERYONE GET TO THE SHUTTLECRAFT AND--

"WH-WHAT SHUTTLE-CRAFT?!"

"NEVER MIND! WE'LL TAKE THE SUB-TER ROVER!"

ONCE WE'RE UNDERGROUND, A FLEET OF *STAR DESTROYERS* COULDN'T HARM US! ALL WE HAVE TO DO IS CROSS THIS BRIDGE AND THEN HEAD FOR--

PABOOM

"MAJOR! TH-THEY BLEW THE BRIDGE! WHAT'LL WE DO NOW?"

"THERE'S ONLY ONE THING WE *CAN* DO-- INSTIGATE *EMERGENCY STRATEGIC OPTION SIX!*"

"WH-WHAT'S THAT, MAJOR?"

"IT'S A COMPUTER-DERIVED LOGIC RESPONSE TO A COMBAT SITUATION IN-VOLVING EXCESSIVELY UNEVEN ODDS. BASICALLY, IT MEANS--"

--GIVE UP!

THE BATTLE IS OVER, AND DEFEATED IMPERIAL EYES CAN BUT WATCH PASSIVELY AS A QUARTET OF TWIN ION ENGINE FIGHTER CRAFT DROPS SLOWLY DOWNWARD...

...LANDS...

...AND REVEALS ITS SECOND SURPRISE OF THE DAY.

THE PILOTS. TH-THEY'R ...REBELS

KEEP THOSE HANDS HIGH! STAY IN LINE THERE!

GEMMER, CALL DOWN THE TRANSPORT!

THEN IT WASN'T VADER!

≥WHEW≤

WITHIN MOMENTS, A CARBON-SCORED TROOP TRANSPORT SETS DOWN ON THE STILL-SMOLDERING BATTLEFIELD...

256

...THERE TO ACCEPT A GRUMBLING CARGO OF FORCIBLY DOCILE PASSENGERS.

AND ONLY THEN CAN THE LEADER OF THE RAID, COMMANDER LUKE SKYWALKER, GRATEFULLY RELAX...

WELL, SHIRA, WE DID IT.

AND WITH MINIMAL LOSS OF LIFE, ACE. NICE GOIN'!

AT LEAST WE KNOW THOSE REBUILT TIES WE BOUGHT FROM *FERRET* * ARE GOOD ENOUGH TO PASS FOR IMPERIAL ISSUE. NOW FOR THE *SECOND* PART OF THE MISSION.

CAPTAIN THORBEN, I BELIEVE YOU KNOW WHAT TO LOOK FOR?

*LAST ISSUE.

AYE, COMMANDER, AN' I'LL BE FETCHIN' IT RIGHT BACK FOR YA.

GOOD.

'CAUSE I'LL FEEL A WHOLE LOT BETTER ONCE WE'VE CONFIRMED THAT THOSE *ROUTE COORDINATES* WE CAME FOR ARE THE REAL THING.

DON'T WORRY, LUKE, WE'VE STILL GOT *THE FORCE* ON OUR SIDE--

--NOT TO MENTION THE BEST DARNED FLIGHT COMMANDER IN THE GALAXY!

257

THANKS, SHIRA, BUT IF THAT *SECRET ARMADA* WE'VE HEARD THE EMPIRE IS BUILDING IS FOR REAL, WE'LL NEED A LOT MORE THAN THAT.

SO WHAT'S THE PROBLEM? CAN'T WE JUST GO IN AND BLOW THEM OUT OF THE SKY?

NO, WE'D LOSE TOO MANY WARRIORS. A DIRECT ASSAULT WOULD BE MADNESS.

WHICH IS WHY WE GOT HOLD OF THOSE TIE FIGHTERS. IF WE CAN INFILTRATE THE ARMADA, WE MIGHT BE ABLE TO DESTROY IT FROM *WITHIN.*

BUT ONLY IF OUR REPORTS ABOUT THIS RELAY POST HAVING THE ARMADA'S ROUTE CO-ORDINATES WERE TRUE.

THAT THEY WERE, COMMANDER!

AN' I'VE GOT THE CODED CARTOGRAPH MODULE TO PROVE IT!

THEN WE'RE ON OUR WAY, ACE!

UH... RIGHT! ⌐HEH⌐

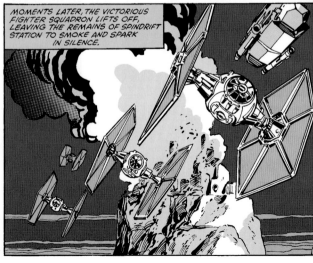

MOMENTS LATER, THE VICTORIOUS FIGHTER SQUADRON LIFTS OFF, LEAVING THE REMAINS OF SPINDRIFT STATION TO SMOKE AND SPARK IN SILENCE.

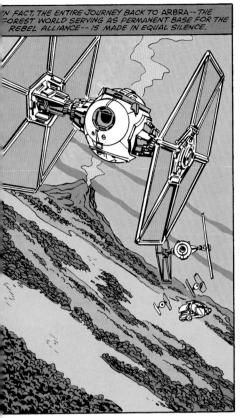

IN FACT, THE ENTIRE JOURNEY BACK TO ARBRA--THE FOREST WORLD SERVING AS PERMANENT BASE FOR THE REBEL ALLIANCE-- IS MADE IN EQUAL SILENCE.

UNTIL...

TIE SQUAD, IDENTIFY YOURSELVES-- OR BE BLASTED INTO THE NEXT QUADRANT!

THIS IS COMMANDER SKYWALKER! CODE PHRASE--

--"FLYING BANTHAS NEVER SLEEP"!

ALL RIGHT, COMMANDER, YOU'RE CLEARED.

YOU AND YOUR MEN CAN PASS.

AND THEY DO, LOOPING DOWN THROUGH LASER-HEWN PATHS IN THE DENSE FOREST GROWTH, GLIDING PAST NERVOUS SENTRIES--

I'LL NEVER GET USED TO SEEIN' THOSE THINGS IN HERE!

--AND ARRIVING AT THEIR MOUNTAIN CAVERN HEADQUARTERS, TO BE GREETED BY...

PRINCESS LEIA!

I READ THE REPORT YOU TRANSMITTED, LUKE-- CONGRATULATIONS.

THANKS.

NOW ALL WE HAVE TO DO IS GET THAT MAP PLAN DECODED, AND THEN WAIT FOR THE RIGHT MOMENT TO STRIKE!

IN THAT CASE, YOUR HIGHNESS, I'D LIKE PERMISSION TO SPEND A LITTLE TIME OFF-PLANET. I'LL NEED THE RETURN COORDINATES FOR ARBRA, OF COURSE, AND--

I'M SORRY, LIEUTENANT BRIE, BUT I'M AFRAID THAT WON'T BE POSSIBLE.

AS YOU KNOW, ARBRA'S EXACT COORDINATES ARE DIVULGED ONLY TO KEY PERSONNEL, TO REDUCE THE RISK OF A SECURITY BREACH IN THE EVENT OF CAPTURE.

AND ANYWAY, WHY DO YOU WANT TO LEAVE NOW?

THAT'S... PERSONAL, PRINCESS. BUT IT'S ALSO VERY IMPORTANT. COULDN'T YOU--

AS I SAID, LIEUTENANT, I'M SORRY-- BUT NO.

THEN I'M AFRAID YOU LEAVE ME NO CHOICE. I'M GOING-- I HAVE TO GO.

EVEN IF I CAN'T COME BACK.

HEY, I HAVE AN IDEA! SINCE I KNOW ARBRA'S MAP SPECS, AND I'VE GOT NOTHING ELSE SCHEDULED BEFORE WE TACKLE THAT ARMADA, WHY DON'T I GET AN ESCORT TOGETHER AND TAG ALONG?

BUT--

AFTER ALL, SHIRA'S A GOOD WARRIOR-- A GOOD FRIEND. AND WE WOULDN'T WANT TO LOSE HER, WOULD WE?

UHHHH... NO. OF COURSE NOT.

THANKS, LUKE.

'BYE, PRINCESS!

ARMADA: THE VERY WORD CONJURES AN IMAGE OF VAST NUMBERS OF RUGGED, POWERFUL VESSELS, ALL DEDICATED TO THE SINGLE PURPOSE OF MAKING WAR.

AND AT A SECRET LOCATION AT THE EDGE OF THE GALAXY, THANKS TO RECENT IMPERIAL DECREE, THAT IMAGE HAS BECOME REALITY!

AS, IN THE LEAD WARSHIP...

I BUILT THIS FLEET! FORMED IT FROM THE BEGINNING! AND BY PALPATINE, I'LL RUN IT ANY WAY I BLOODY WELL CHOOSE!

NEED I REMIND YOU, GENTLEMEN, THAT A MISSION AS VITAL AS OURS CAN HAVE BUT *ONE* LEADER? *ONE* DECISION-MAKER?

B-BUT, *ADMIRAL GIEL*, I WAS MERELY SUGGESTING--

YOU WERE "SUGGESTING," COLONEL--

IT IS MY POLICY TO *SQUASH* THEM!

BUT, SIR, THIS REPORT--!

IF THE REBELS *DECIPHER* THAT CLASSIFIED INFORMATION THEY STOLE FROM SPINDRIFT, THEY COULD *ATTACK!*

--THAT I'M NOT SHOWING ENOUGH CONCERN OVER A SCRAGGLY BAND OF HIT-AND-RUN AMATEURS! I ASSURE YOU, SIR, THAT IT IS NOT MY POLICY TO WORRY OVER GNATS!

THEN *LET* THEM!

THE ONLY THING THEY'LL LEARN FROM ATTACKING *MY* FLEET--

--IS THAT THERE ARE *EASIER* WAYS OF COMMITTING *SUICIDE!*

262

THE IMPERIAL ARMADA HOVERS ON-- WHILE MANY PARSECS AWAY, ABOVE A BACKWATER WORLD CALLED SHALYVANE, A MUCH SMALLER GROUP OF STARCRAFT ARRIVES...

THAT'S RIGHT, ARTOO. THIS IS WHERE SHIRA WAS BORN.

THOUGH WHY SHE WANTS-- OR *NEEDS*-- TO RETURN... WELL...I GUESS WE'LL LEARN SOON ENOUGH.

RED LEADER TO PACK-- BEGIN DESCENT!

AND SOON...

THIS PLACE LOOKS LIKE IT WAS HIT HARDER THAN WE HIT *SPINDRIFT*, COMMANDER. WHAT HAPPENED?

BEATS ME, WALD. *NOBODY* KNOWS MUCH ABOUT THIS REGION--ITS HISTORY OR OTHERWISE.

THE X-WING FIGHTERS LAND. AND MOMENTS LATER, THEIR PILOTS MOVE CAUTIOUSLY TOWARDS THE CRUMBLING RUINS OF AN ANCIENT CITY--

263

--WHERE THEIR ARRIVAL DOES NOT GO TOTALLY *UNREGARDED*...

YOU MOVE AROUND LIKE YOU KNOW WHERE YOU'RE GOING, SHIRA.

I DO. I GREW UP HERE. AND IF MEMORY SERVES, WHAT I'M LOOKING FOR IS RIGHT--

--THERE! THE CIRCLE OF *KAVAAN!* A VERY... *SPECIAL* PLACE.

ALL RIGHT, THEN.

WE'LL JUST POST A GUARD AND GO ON TO--

NO, LUKE, PLEASE, UNDER-STAND...

...THIS IS SOMETHING I HAVE TO DO ALONE.

WHAT DO YOU MEAN, "DO I FEEL LEFT OUT?" SHIRA'S A BIG GIRL, ARTOO. SHE CAN DO WHAT SHE WANTS.

SEE IF *I* CARE...

BUT WHAT LUKE SKYWALKER CARES SEEMS UN-IMPORTANT IN THE FACE OF WHAT SHIRA BRIE DOES--

--AS SHE KNEELS, RESPECTFULLY, BEFORE A CHIPPED STONE ALTAR--

--AND REMOVES FROM HER BELT A GLINTING LENGTH OF SHINY STEEL.

A KNIFE?

BUT WHAT'S SHE GOING TO DO WITH--

OH, NO! SH-SHE'S--

"--CUT HERSELF!"

SLOWLY, WITH MEASURED MOVEMENTS, THE KNEELING WOMAN TURNS HER HAND, ALLOWING A SINGLE DROP OF LIFE'S BLOOD TO FALL FROM THE SHALLOW WOUND. SHE FOLLOWS IT WITH A GLANCE... A NOD...

...AND A PRAYER.

A PRAYER THAT IS SUDDENLY SHATTERED BY...

G'HRINGYAAA!

WHA--?

LOOK! COMING FROM THE RUINS!

WHAT ARE THEY?

I DON'T KNOW--

"--BUT I THINK THEY'D LIKE TO BE OUR EXECUTIONERS!"

ZATT

ZATT-ATT

ZATT

G'HRING GHOSAII!

GHA, JHODAHD!

FABOOOM

THEY'VE GOT EXPLOSIVES!

TAKE COVER!

AND THAT MEANS *YOU*, SHIRA!

LUKE, I-I'M SORRY! I DIDN'T THINK THIS WOULD HAPPEN!

YOU MEAN, YOU *KNEW* ABOUT THESE CHARACTERS?!

I-I KNEW THEY *EXISTED*, LUKE--

--BUT I DIDN'T THINK THEY'D STILL BE AROUND *HERE*! THERE'S NO *REASON*--!

LOOK, KID, IF YA'VE HAD *EXPERIENCE* WITH THESE GUNDARKS, YA'D BETTER TELL US! IT MIGHT SAVE OUR *LIVES*!

OH, I'VE HAD EXPERIENCE, ALL RIGHT! THOSE BARBARIANS ARE FROM THE SAME HORDE THAT DESTROYED THIS CITY--

--ALONG WITH MY ENTIRE *FAMILY!*

IN A NUTSHELL...

"...BACK WHEN I WAS A LITTLE GIRL, THIS PLACE WAS CALLED *CHINSHASSA.* MY TRIBE LIVED HERE, AND THEY WERE AN INDUSTRIOUS, PEACEFUL PEOPLE. THAT IS, WHEN THEY WERE *ALLOWED* TO BE.

"BECAUSE A BAND OF *NOMADS* ALSO WANDERED THE WORLD-- BARBARIANS WITH AN ANCIENT, RACIAL HATRED OF ANYONE DIFFERENT FROM THEMSELVES.

"AND WHILE NO ONE KNOWS WHY, THEIR GREATEST GOAL IN LIFE WAS TO WIPE MY PEOPLE FROM THE FACE OF THE PLANET!

"SO THEY KEPT OUR SOLDIERS EMBROILED FOR YEARS IN A SERIES OF USELESS, SENSELESS BATTLES...

"...FOR NO OTHER REASON, IT APPEARS, BUT THAT THEY *ENJOYED* THEM.

"AND THUS IT WAS THAT WE ACCEPTED, GRATEFULLY, AN UNEXPECTED PEACE QUERY FROM THE NOMADS. WE THOUGHT, WE HOPED, THAT THEY'D GROWN AS TIRED OF THE CONTINUAL COMBAT AS WE HAD.

"WE WERE FOOLS.

"FOR WHEN WE GATHERED AT THE CIRCLE OF KAVAAN, OUR MOST HOLY SHRINE, TO AWAIT THE NOMAD EMISSARIES WHO WERE TO SIGN THE PACT OF PEACE--

"--WE FOUND OURSELVES GREETED INSTEAD BY *OTHER* VISITORS...

"...BY BIRDS THAT SCREAMED DOWN FROM OUT OF THE SUN...

"...AND RAKED THE COURTYARD WITH TALONS OF FIRE!

"I KNOW NOW THAT THOSE 'BIRDS' WERE TIE SHIPS, AND THE 'HOLLOW-EYED GHOSTS' THAT SPEWED FROM THEM WERE IMPERIAL STORMTROOPERS.

"BUT AS I WATCHED MY FATHER BEING CUT DOWN, AND SAW MY MOTHER DIE WHILE CRADLING HIS STILL-WARM CORPSE, I DIDN'T CARE *WHAT* THEY WERE.

"A PLACE I FOUND--

"--IN THE DRAINAGE SYSTEM THAT RAN BENEATH THE CITY, WHERE I HAD PLAYED MANY TIMES WITH THE OTHER CHILDREN.

"I WAS IN SHOCK, TERRIFIED, AND ALL I WANTED WAS A PLACE TO HIDE.

"ONCE INSIDE, I RAN...AND RAN ...AND KEPT ON RUNNING.

"AFTER THAT, I LIVED BY MY WITS--

"--DOING WHAT I HAD TO TO SURVIVE.

"AND IT WAS ONLY MANY YEARS LATER THAT A LOOSE-TONGUED COMPANION, AN EX-FIGHTER PILOT, BRAGGED ABOUT A MISSION HE'D FLOWN ON SHALYVANE... AND I LEARNED WHAT *REALLY* HAPPENED."

I FOUND THAT THE NOMADS HAD TOLD THE EMPIRE THAT MY TRIBE WAS IN LEAGUE WITH THE REBEL ALLIANCE. MY DRUNKEN FRIEND SAID *THAT* WAS WHY THEY HAD KILLED THEM ALL: MEN... WOMEN...CHILDREN.

AND SO I JOINED THE REBELLION.

EVERY YEAR SINCE THEN, ON THE ANNIVERSARY OF THE SLAUGHTER, I'VE RETURNED TO THIS SPOT, TO ADD *MY* BLOOD TO THEIRS...

THAT'S QUITE A STORY, LASS! TOO BAD IT DON'T DO *BEANS* ABOUT GETTIN' US OUTTA THIS SCRAPE!

I WOULDN'T BE SO SURE, THORBEN.

...AND TO RENEW MY OATH OF *VENGEANCE* AGAINST THE EMPIRE!

IF WE COULD FIND THE DRAINAGE SYSTEM SHIRA TALKED ABOUT, WE MIGHT BE ABLE TO *ESCAPE* THE SAME WAY

BUT, LUKE, THAT WAS A *LIFETIME* AGO! I DON'T REMEMBER WHERE THE TUNNELS ARE!

MAYBE NOT--

--BUT MAYBE YOU DON'T *HAVE* TO! ARTOO, USE YOUR SENSORS!

SEE IF YOU CAN FIND A *DENSITY ANOMALY* IN THE GROUND BELOW!

PIDI-BEEP

WHRRR

KLIK

HMMMMM

VADEET! VADEET!

HE'S FOUND SOMETHING!

IT BETTER BE SOMETHIN' *GOOD*! OUR *BLASTERS* ARE RUNNIN' LOW!

MUST BE ⸗MMF⸗ UNDER THIS BROKEN COLUMN! I-IF I CAN JUST...MOVE IT...AH!

THERE! IT'S ONE OF THE TUNNELS!

YEAH, BUT IT DOESN'T LOOK TOO *STABLE.*

THORBEN, YOU'RE IN COMMAND. IF I DON'T COME BACK, DO THE BEST THAT YOU--

SORRY, LUKE, BUT THIS IS *MY* TERRITORY! I'LL SEND YOU A CARD FROM THE OTHER SIDE!

WHA-- SHIRA! NO--!

HRRRUMMBALOOOM

A CAVE-IN! TH-THE TUNNEL COLLAPSED!

SHIRA!

"WE CAN'T HELP 'ER NOW, COMMANDER! THE BAR-BARIANS ARE *CHARGIN'!*"

271

THEN MOW 'EM DOWN!

"THOSE SCUM WERE THE CAUSE OF ALL THIS!"

AND WE'RE GOING TO MAKE THEM PAY!

"IN BLOOD!"

BUT...

IT'S NO GOOD, LUKE! OUR BLASTERS ARE DRY!

THEN THERE'S ONLY ONE THING TO DO!

WE TAKE SOME OF THEM WITH US!

AND THE FIRST ONE'S FOR SHIRA!

HOWEVER...

KRAKAKAROOOM

WHAT THE--?!

272

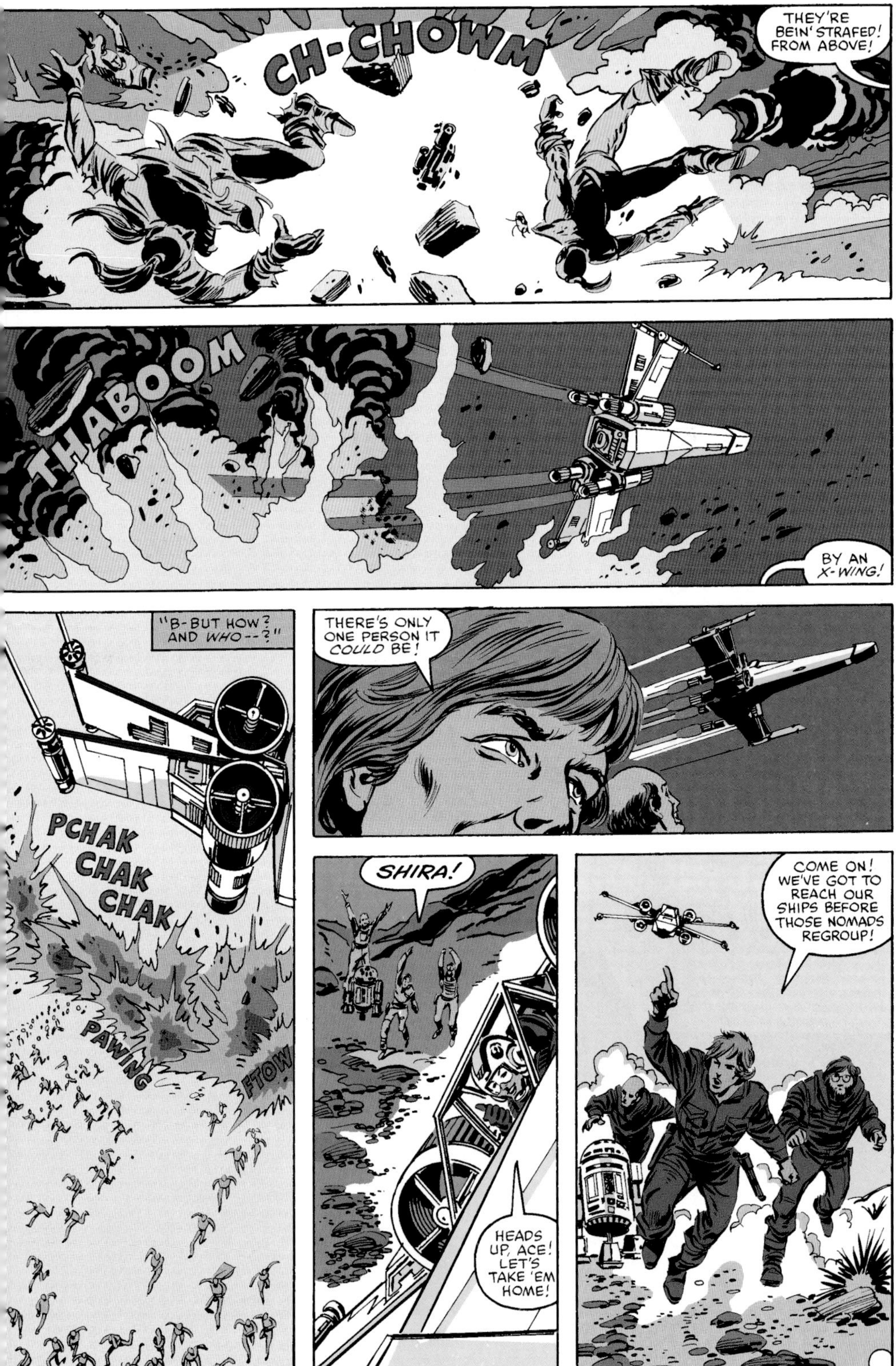
CH-CHOWM
THEY'RE BEIN' STRAFED! FROM ABOVE!
THABOOM
BY AN X-WING!
"B-BUT HOW? AND WHO--?"
PCHAK CHAK CHAK
PAWING
FTOW
THERE'S ONLY ONE PERSON IT COULD BE!
SHIRA!
HEADS UP, ACE! LET'S TAKE 'EM HOME!
COME ON! WE'VE GOT TO REACH OUR SHIPS BEFORE THOSE NOMADS REGROUP!

AND, MOMENTS LATER, ON THE OUTSKIRTS OF CHINSHASSA...

YOU FELLAS OKAY?

WE'RE FINE!

AND YOU'RE TERRIFIC! HOW'D YOU DO IT?

OH, EXCEPTIONAL SKILL, EXTRAORDI-NARY TALENT...

...AND A WHOLE BUNCH OF LUCK!

THAT TUNNEL COLLAPSED BEHIND ME, BUT THE REST OF THE PASSAGE WAS CLEAR. SO I WAS ABLE TO MAKE MY WAY PAST THE NOMADS AND GET TO MY FIGHTER.

AND BOY, ARE WE GLAD YOU DID!

BUT WE'RE EVEN MORE GLAD THAT YOU'RE STILL ALIVE.

"WE LUKE OR...

..."I

BOTH.

CONVERTERS FIRE, AND FOUR SLEEK SHIPS TAKE TO THE STARS. BEHIND THEM, THE PAST LIES MOLLIFIED, WITH OLD DEMONS PUT TO ROUT. WHILE AHEAD--

-- THE FUTURE WAITS!

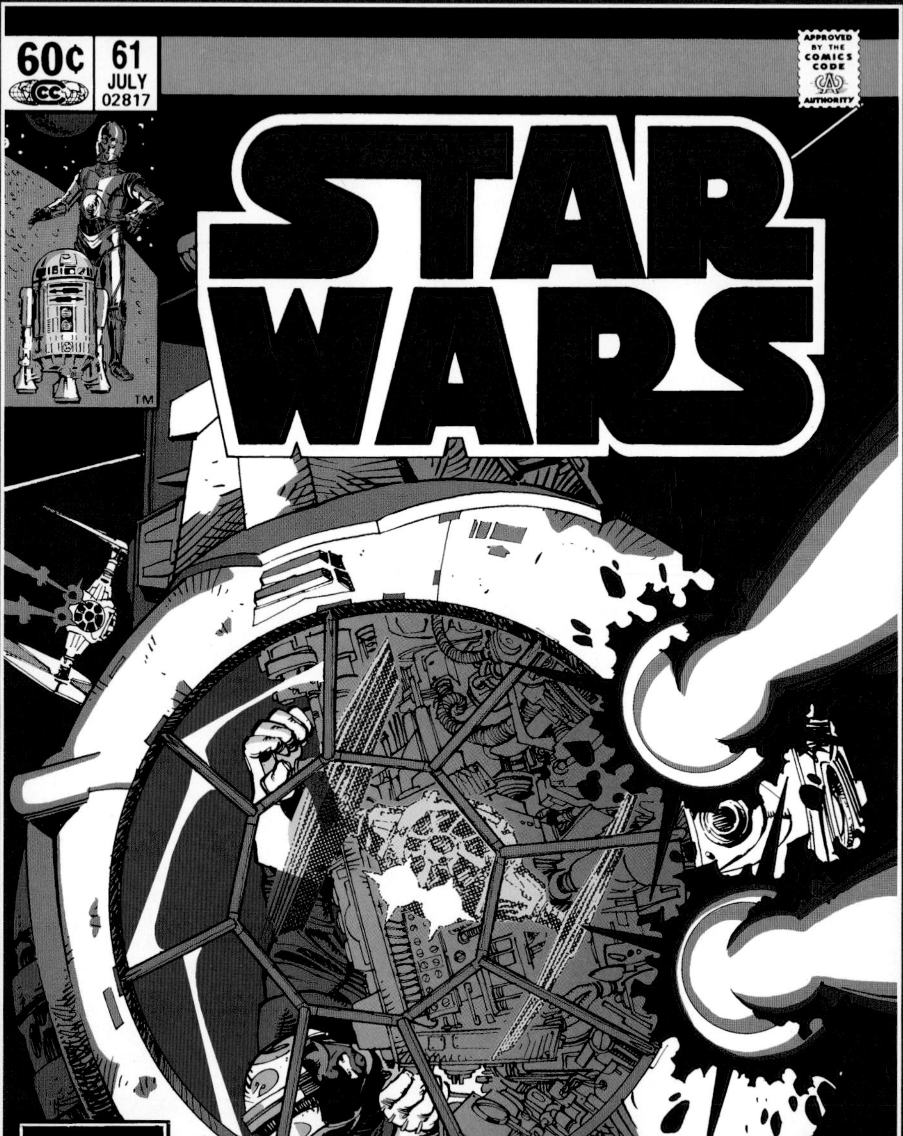
60¢
61
JULY
02817
APPROVED BY THE COMICS CODE AUTHORITY
STAR WARS
TM

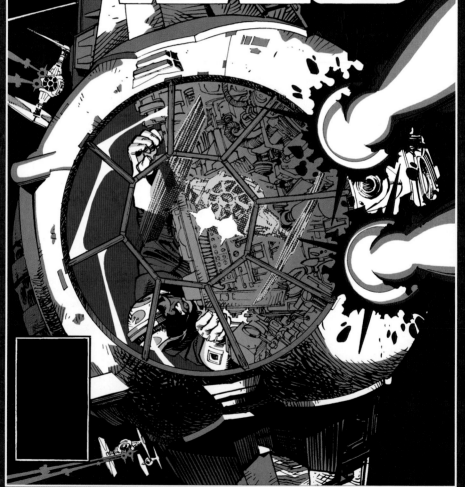

Long ago in a galaxy far, far away. . .there exists a state of cosmic *civil war*. A brave alliance of *underground freedom fighters* has challenged the tyranny and oppression of the awesome *Galactic Empire*. This is their story!

Lucasfilm PRESENTS: **STAR WARS** THE GREATEST SPACE FANTASY OF ALL!

DAVID MICHELINIE — SCRIPTER / PLOT
WALTER SIMONSON — BREAKDOWNS / PLOT
TOM PALMER — FINISHES
JOE ROSEN — LETTERS
GLYNIS WEIN — COLORS
AL MILGROM — EDITOR
JIM SHOOTER — FATHER FIGURE

SCREAMS IN THE VOID

IN RECOGNITION OF YOUR RECENT ACTS OF HEROISM ON THE PLANET *SHALYVANE,* YOU ARE HEREWITH AWARDED THE BURDINE CLUSTER, ALONG WITH THE TRADITIONAL ADVANCEMENT IN RANK--

--CAPTAIN BRIE.

*LAST ISSUE.

YOUR EFFORTS TO SAVE THE LIVES OF *COMMANDER SKYWALKER* AND THE REST OF YOUR SQUAD HAVE EARNED YOU THE GRATITUDE OF THE ENTIRE ALLIANCE. AND TO THAT I'D LIKE TO ADD--

--MY PERSONAL APPRECIATION.

PRINCESS...

...THE PLEASURE WAS MINE.

HER MOUTH CURLING INTO A HINT OF A SELF-ASSURED SMILE, SHIRA BRIE FILES PAST THE ROWS OF ASSEMBLED STAR WARRIORS, FELLOW SOLDIERS WHO CATCH THAT SMILE--

--AND RETURN IT AS A ROAR OF SPONTANEOUS, HEARTFELT AFFECTION!

Y'KNOW, WITH A FEW MORE LIKE HER, WE'D HAVE THIS WAR *WON!*

I KNOW WHAT YOU MEAN, LANDO.

UH, LUKE, NOW THAT THE CEREMONY IS OVER, I THOUGHT WE MIGHT--

SORRY, LEIA--

--CAN'T TALK NOW.

I HAVE TO GO CONGRATULATE SHIRA!

BUT--!

YOUR HIGHNESS, IS EVERYTHING ALL RIGHT? YOU LOOK RATHER PALE.

I'M...FINE, THREEPIO.

JUST FINE.

HOWEVER, AS SHE TURNS TO LEAVE, PRINCESS LEIA ORGANA'S SHOULDERS SAG, HER GAIT SLOWS TO A SOFT, LACKLUSTER SHUFFLE...

...UNTIL AT LAST, ALONE IN HER PRIVATE QUARTERS, SHE TENDERLY LIFTS A CHERISHED HOLOSPHERE, THE WARMTH OF HER TOUCH BRINGING A THREE-DIMENSIONAL IMAGE INTO FOCUS.

AN IMAGE BOTH RAKISH--

--AND FAMILIAR.

HAN...OH, HAN, I WISH YOU WERE HERE WITH ME, I MISS YOU...

...AND I *NEED* YOU.

279

YOU COULD HELP ME UNDERSTAND WHY I'M SO CONFUSED, WHY I FEEL SO STRANGE WHEN LUKE AND SHIRA ARE TOGETHER. I MEAN, I LIKE LUKE--A LOT! HE'S A VERY SPECIAL PERSON, BUT IT'S *YOU* THAT I *LOVE!*

SO I SHOULD BE HAPPY THAT LUKE'S FOUND SOMEONE TO CARE ABOUT.

SHOULDN'T I...?

OH, I DON'T KNOW *WHAT* I--

WHY, I'M SORRY, PRINCESS. I THOUGHT YOU WERE ALONE.

MY GOODNESS. YOU *ARE* ALONE!

UH, RIGHT, THREEPIO! I-I WAS JUST... ER...

...GOING OVER THE ATTACK PLANS FOR THAT IMPERIAL ARMADA! YES! IT, AH, HELPS ONE'S MEMORY TO TALK OUT LOUD.

OF COURSE, PRINCESS, I QUITE UNDERSTAND.

HER REGAL COMPOSURE REGAINED, THE REBEL LEADER WALKS BRISKLY TO A NEARBY BRIEFING ROOM.

AS BEHIND HER, THE HOLO-GRAPHIC IMAGE OF HAN SOLO FLICKERS STUBBORNLY...

...AND FADES.

MEANWHILE, HALF-A-GALAXY AWAY, THE LARGEST ARMADA *IN EMPIRE HISTORY* CONTINUES ITS LONG JOURNEY TO THE IMPERIAL CAPITOL, MOVING STEADILY UNDER THE COMMAND OF --

--ADMIRAL GIEL, THE TRANSPORT CAGE IS READY FOR YOUR INSPECTION!

EXCELLENT, COLONEL MALKA. IF THE LAST HALF OF THIS MISSION GOES AS SMOOTHLY AS THE FIRST, WE SHOULD--

--JUST A MOMENT.

OH, DECK OFFICER? MIGHT I HAVE A WORD WITH YOU?

WHY, UH, SURE, ADMIRAL. ANYTHING WRONG?

NO--

--NOT IF THE EMPIRE HAS STARTED ISSUING *PARTY HATS* TO ITS COMBAT TROOPS!

THAT'S TEN LAPS AROUND THE SHIP, GRUBBER-- NOW!

T-T-*TEN?!* ~GULP~

Y-YES, SIR!

R-RIGHT AWAY, SIR!

NATURALLY, HE'LL STOP RUNNING AS SOON AS HE ROUNDS THE FIRST CORNER-- BUT I'LL WAGER HE WEARS HIS REGULATION *CAP* IN THE FUTURE!

~SIGH~ I DO DISLIKE DISCIPLINING THE CREW, MALKA. BUT IT'S A JOB THAT MUST BE DONE.

YES, SIR--

--ESPECIALLY WHEN WE'RE TRANSPORTING SOMETHING AS IMPORTANT AS THE *SCREAMER.*

PLEASE, COLONEL, I PREFER THAT YOU USE THE CORRECT TERMINOLOGY. IT'S NOT A "SCREAMER." IT'S A "TEEZL." OR, TO BE MORE PRECISE--

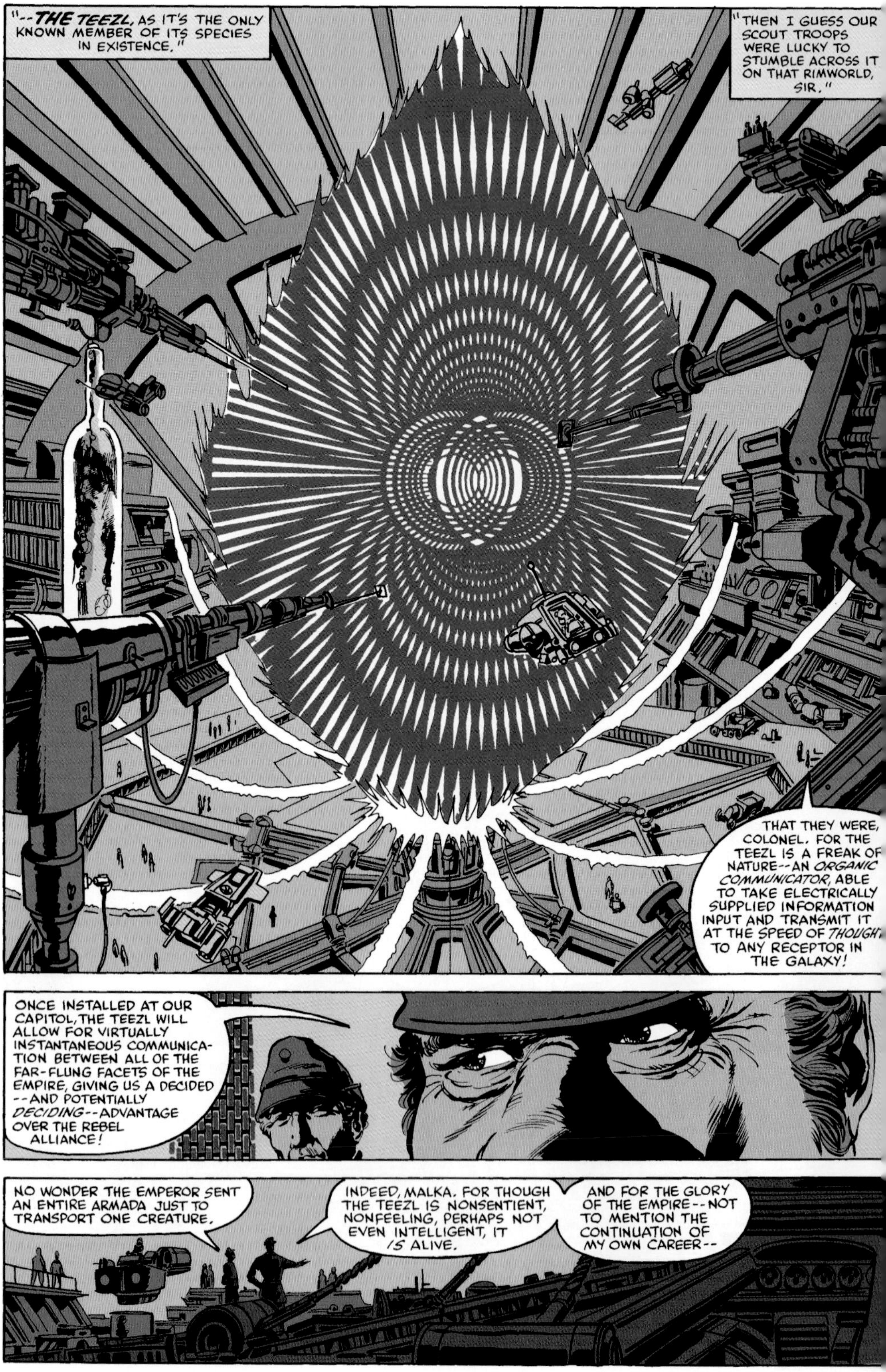
"--THE TEEZL, AS IT'S THE ONLY KNOWN MEMBER OF ITS SPECIES IN EXISTENCE."
"THEN I GUESS OUR SCOUT TROOPS WERE LUCKY TO STUMBLE ACROSS IT ON THAT RIMWORLD, SIR."
THAT THEY WERE, COLONEL. FOR THE TEEZL IS A FREAK OF NATURE--AN *ORGANIC COMMUNICATOR*, ABLE TO TAKE ELECTRICALLY SUPPLIED INFORMATION INPUT AND TRANSMIT IT AT THE SPEED OF *THOUGHT* TO ANY RECEPTOR IN THE GALAXY!
ONCE INSTALLED AT OUR CAPITOL, THE TEEZL WILL ALLOW FOR VIRTUALLY INSTANTANEOUS COMMUNICATION BETWEEN ALL OF THE FAR-FLUNG FACETS OF THE EMPIRE, GIVING US A DECIDED --AND POTENTIALLY *DECIDING*--ADVANTAGE OVER THE REBEL ALLIANCE!
NO WONDER THE EMPEROR SENT AN ENTIRE ARMADA JUST TO TRANSPORT ONE CREATURE.
INDEED, MALKA. FOR THOUGH THE TEEZL IS NONSENTIENT, NONFEELING, PERHAPS NOT EVEN INTELLIGENT, IT *IS* ALIVE.
AND FOR THE GLORY OF THE EMPIRE--NOT TO MENTION THE CONTINUATION OF MY OWN CAREER--

-- I FULLY INTEND TO *KEEP* IT THAT WAY!

BUT, AT THAT MOMENT, IN A GROTTO HANGAR ON ARBRA...

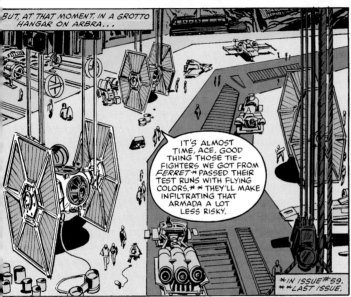

IT'S ALMOST TIME, ACE. GOOD THING THOSE TIE-FIGHTERS WE GOT FROM *FERRET* ✱ PASSED THEIR TEST RUNS WITH FLYING COLORS.✱ ✱ THEY'LL MAKE INFILTRATING THAT ARMADA A LOT LESS RISKY.

✱IN ISSUE #59.
✱✱LAST ISSUE.

I KNOW, SHIRA, AND IF REPORTS ABOUT THE ARMADA'S *CARGO* ARE ACCURATE, THERE'S A LOT RIDING ON THIS RAID.

SERGEANT! HAVE THE MODIFICATIONS BEEN COMPLETED?

THEY HAVE, SIR. THESE *SIGNAL TRANS-CEIVERS* WILL LET YOU TELL YOUR OWN SHIPS FROM ANY IMPERIALS YOU MIGHT RUN ACROSS.

ALSO, YOUR GUNS HAVE BEEN ALTERED TO FIRE ONLY A HALF-DOZEN BURSTS AT STANDARD STRENGTH.

AFTER THAT, THEY RELEASE THEIR ENTIRE ENERGY STORES IN ONE SHOT, WITH ENOUGH POWER TO CUT THROUGH EVEN THE STRONGEST SHIELDS! I SUGGEST YOU CHOOSE YOUR TARGETS CAREFULLY, SIR.

GOOD LUCK.

I GUESS THAT TAKES CARE OF THE PRELIMINARIES. WE MIGHT AS WELL SUIT UP AND--

283

LUKE! CAN I TALK WITH YOU A MINUTE?

HUH? UH, CERTAINLY, SHIRA, IS THERE A PROBLEM?

NO, IT'S JUST THAT, WELL, THIS IS GOING TO BE A DANGEROUS MISSION-- MORE DANGEROUS THAN MOST. AND I JUST WANTED YOU TO KNOW THAT ...WELL...

...WHAT I MEAN TO SAY IS, IN CASE ONE OF US DOESN'T MAKE IT BACK...

SOMETIME LATER--

--UNFILTERED STARLIGHT SHINES THROUGH A SMALL PLANETARY SYSTEM NEAR THE ROUTE OF THE IMPERIAL ARMADA--

--WHERE A FAR RECON PATROL OF TWIN ION ENGINE FIGHTERS PICKS UP--

A DISTRESS SIGNAL!

BETTER CHECK IT OUT. IF IT'S ONE OF OURS, THEY MIGHT NEED HELP. AND IF IT'S A REBEL--

--WELL, WE COULD ALL USE A LITTLE BONUS COME PAYDAY, EH?

THERE IT IS!

AND IT'S A TIE-- OR WHAT'S *LEFT* OF ONE!

THE ATMOSPHERE'S BREATHABLE!

I'LL RUN A LIFE SCAN TO SEE IF--

--WAIT A SECOND! I'M PICKING UP READINGS FROM *BEHIND* US! AND THEY LOOK LIKE--

--REBELS!

IT'S A TRA-- AAAGGHH!

SRRRATCH

BLAST! THE OTHERS ARE FINISHED! BUT MY SHIP'S JUST CRIPPLED! I STILL HAVE TIME TO--

-- EJECT!

CHOOSH

THAT WAS A GREAT IDEA, COMMANDER, USING TIE WRECKAGE AS A LURE. THEY FELL FOR IT COMPLETELY!

NOW IF THEY'LL JUST COOPERATE...

HI! AS YOU MAY HAVE NOTICED, YOU'RE OUR PRISONER. AND UNLESS YOU TELL US THE *RECOGNITION CODES* FOR ENTRANCE INTO THE IMPERIAL ARMADA, YOU'RE ALSO GOING TO NOTICE A VERY LARGE *HOLE* IN YOUR HEAD!

CARE TO TALK?

NEVER! I WAS TRAINED TO WITHSTAND TORTURE, AND I'M NOT AFRAID TO DIE!

SO THERE'S *NOTHING* YOU REBEL SCUM CAN DO TO INTIMIDATE ME!

NO? *TCH* WHAT A PITY.

CHEWBACCA...?

MRRARRGH!

KRRRRIP!

HNH?!

A-A WOOKIEE?! Y-YOU DIDN'T *SAY* YOU HAD A WOOKIEE!

UH, WH-WHAT WAS THAT QUESTION AGAIN? ÷HEH÷

THE ARMADA MOVES ON -- SLOWLY, SURELY, CONFIDENT THAT THE SHEER POWER IT REPRESENTS WILL KEEP IT SAFE FROM ATTACK.

SO CONFIDENT THAT IT TAKES LITTLE NOTICE OF A RETURNING RECONNAISSANCE PATROL.

UNTIL... TIE PATROL, IDENTIFY YOUR-SELVES --AT ONCE!

WELL, HERE GOES NOTHING!

THIS IS DELTA LEADER! I. D, #76-19!

HMM, THAT'S CAPTAIN MILNN'S CODE. BUT YOUR VOICE SOUNDS STRANGE, CAPTAIN.

I THINK I'M ≈ SNIFF ≈ CATCHING A COLD. MY COOLING UNIT'S MALFUNCTIONING AGAIN.

AH! I KNOW WHAT YOU MEAN.

MAINTENANCE HAS REALLY GONE DOWN-HILL LATELY.

ALL RIGHT, DELTA GROUP --

--PASS!

AND, SWITCHING TO AN OBSOLETE TRADING FREQUENCY ONCE INSIDE THE SPRAWLING ARMADA...

OKAY, GANG, THIS IS IT! EVERYONE READY?

ALPH?

ALL SET, COMMANDER!

THORBEN?

SYSTEMS AT "GO," SIR!

SHIRA?

FLYIN' HIGH, ACE!

THEN CROSS YOUR FINGERS, FOLKS-- AND LET'S DO IT!

CASUALLY, THE BOGUS TIE FIGHTERS SEPARATE...

...EACH SINGLING OUT A SUITABLE, UNSUSPECTING TARGET.

--ALL THAT AWAITS IS THE FINAL COMMAND--

NOW!

-- FOR THE BATTLE TO BEGIN!

ZZRAK

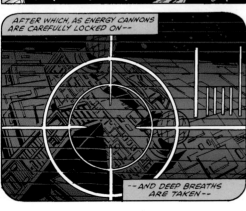

AFTER WHICH, AS ENERGY CANNONS ARE CAREFULLY LOCKED ON--

--AND DEEP BREATHS ARE TAKEN--

288

M-MAJOR VOSS! WE'RE UNDER ATTACK!

FAKOWM

I'M AWARE OF THAT, IDIOT! BUT FROM WHERE? AND BY WHOM?

I--I DON'T KNOW, SIR--

"--BUT SOME OF THE OTHER SHIPS ARE BEING HIT AS WELL! AND THEIR ATTACKERS SEEM TO BE--"

--TIE FIGHTERS!

THEN SET DEFENSIVE BATTERIES AND RE-TURN FIRE IMMEDIATELY!

"B-BUT, SIR! WE'RE SUR-ROUNDED BY OUR OWN FLEET! IF WE MISS, WE COULD--"

AN ATTACK ALWAYS WARRANTS A COUNTER-ATTACK, BOSUN!

NOW CARRY OUT YOUR ORDERS!

BEEN NICE KNOWIN' YA, ERL.

LIKE-WISE.

289

MEANWHILE, ON ADMIRAL GIEL'S FLAGSHIP...

WHAT THE BLOODY BLAZES IS GOING ON?!

I'M NOT SURE, SIR! OUR DESTROYERS HAVE OPENED FIRE, APPARENTLY SHOOTING RANDOMLY AT FIGHTERS!

"EVEN OUR OWN SHIELDS ARE TAKING STRAY LASER BOLTS! I-IT'S ALMOST LIKE--

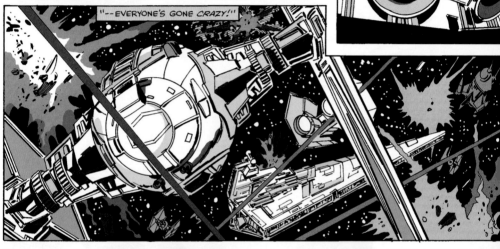

"--EVERYONE'S GONE *CRAZY!*"

AND NEARBY, WITH LUKE SKYWALKER...

BULL'S-EYE!

BUT THAT ONLY LEAVES ME WITH TWO STANDARD-POWER SHOTS LEFT! AND THERE'S ANOTHER TIE COMING IN FROM--

-- ÷WHEW÷ ACCORDING TO THE TRANSCEIVER SIGNAL, THAT'S *ALPH'S* SHIP!

GOOD THING I DIDN'T-- HUH?

S-SOMEONE *ELSE* NAILED HIM! THEY GOT *ALPH!*

VERY CLEVER--AND VERY OBVIOUS! SOME REBELS MUST HAVE ENTERED OUR RANKS WITH COUNTERFEIT FIGHTERS!

AND THEY'RE USING THEM TO THROW THE ENTIRE ARMADA INTO CHAOS!

BUT THEY'RE NOT THE *ONLY* CLEVER ONES!

CONTACT THE TRANSPORT CAGE! HAVE THE TEEZL TRANSMIT *INTERFERENCE* ON ALL FREQUENCIES BUT THE IMPERIAL WAR BAND!

THAT WAY THE REBELS WILL BE FORCED TO USE THAT WAVELENGTH AND WE'LL BE ABLE TO PICK UP THEIR SIGNALS, THEN ISOLATE THEIR CRAFT-- AND DESTROY THEM!

YES, SIR!

IN THE TRANSPORT CAGE, HIGH TO THE REAR OF THE COMMAND MODULE, THE ADMIRAL'S ORDERS ARE RECEIVED, THEN QUICKLY TRANSFERRED TO THE PULSING, MANY-SPINED TEEZL--

--WHICH OBEDIENTLY SENDS FORTH A PSYCHIC SHRIEK, A POWERFUL BLANKET OF STATIC THAT BLOCKS ALL WAVELENGTHS SAVE THE PRE-SELECTED WAR BAND!

AS A RESULT OF WHICH...

COMMANDER, THIS IS THORBEN! COMMANDER--?

BLAST! COMMUNICA- TIONS ARE OUT! I'LL HAVE TO--

FRRATCH

--NO! ONE OF MY SOLAR PANELS HAS BEEN HIT!

I'LL BE LUCKY TO GET AWAY *ALIVE*, LET ALONE REACH THE FLAGSHIP!

IT'S UP TO THE OTHERS NOW!

291

AND AMONG THOSE "OTHERS": LUKE SKYWALKER!

THE RADIO'S OUT! AND WORSE, THE TRANSCEIVER'S BEING JAMMED! I CAN'T TELL WHICH TIES ARE FRIENDLY!

BUT I DON'T HAVE ANY CHOICE! I'VE GOT TO KEEP THE EMPIRE FROM USING THAT SCREAMER AGAINST THE ALLIANCE!

AND I CAN'T LET DEFECTIVE EQUIPMENT--

-- OR ANYTHING ELSE STOP ME!

-- OR ENEMY GUNS--

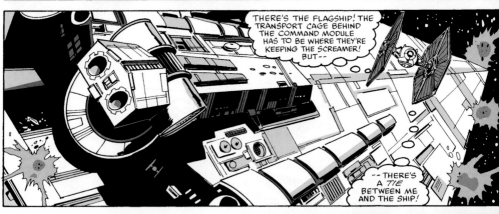

THERE'S THE FLAGSHIP! THE TRANSPORT CAGE BEHIND THE COMMAND MODULE HAS TO BE WHERE THEY'RE KEEPING THE SCREAMER! BUT--

-- THERE'S A TIE BETWEEN ME AND THE SHIP!

ADMIRAL! WE'VE GOT TWO FIGHTERS IN THE VICINITY OF THE TRANSPORT CAGE! NO TRANSMISSIONS FROM EITHER!

WE CAN'T TAKE CHANCES-- BLOW THEM BOTH TO ATOMS!

THOSE CANNONS COULD BE SHOOTING AT THE OTHER TIE-- OR PROVIDING COVER FIRE FOR IT! THERE'S ONLY ONE WAY TO FIND OUT...

CLEARING HIS MIND, LUKE CALLS UPON *THE FORCE*--

--THAT ELEMENTAL ENERGY THAT IS A PART OF ALL THINGS--

PLIK

-- AND USES IT TO PROBE *THE ONCOMING SHIP*, SEARCHING FOR AN INDICATION WHETHER THE PILOT IS FRIEND OR FOE... SEEKING AN ANSWER...

...AND FINDING ONE!

KACHOOM

I'VE ONLY GOT THE ULTRA-POWER BLAST LEFT! SO I'D BETTER MAKE DARNED SURE IT--

"--COUNTS!"

SHRAKOW

LIKE A LANCE OF RIGHTEOUS FIRE, THE BOOSTED ENERGY BOLT CUTS THROUGH IMPERIAL SHIELDS--

--THROUGH THICK WALLS AND MULTIPLE CIRCUIT PANELS--

--CREATING AN EXPLOSIVE CHAIN REACTION THAT TAKES THE UNKNOWING TEEZL --

--THE LIFE-SUSTAINING TRANSPORT CAGE--

--AND A GREAT DEAL OF ADMIRAL GIEL'S FLAGSHIP WITH IT!

PA-BA-FAWHOOOM

~WHEW~

W-WE'VE SUSTAINED SEVERE DAMAGE, ADMIRAL! AND *THERE'S* THE SLIME-LICKER THAT CAUSED IT!

PLEASE, MALKA, THERE'S NO NEED TO GET EXCITED, MERELY DISPATCH A SQUAD OF OUR OWN FIGHTERS, HAVE THEM CHASE THE REBEL DOWN--

--AND *BRING ME HIS HEAD!!*

THIS IS SORT OF LIKE RUNNING BEGGAR'S CANYON BACK ON TATOOINE! 'COURSE, BEGGAR'S CANYON DIDN'T SHOOT *BACK*--

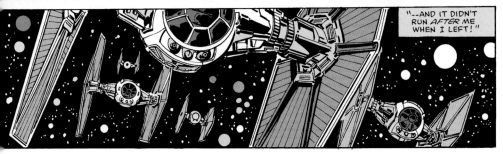

"--AND IT DIDN'T RUN *AFTER* ME WHEN I LEFT!"

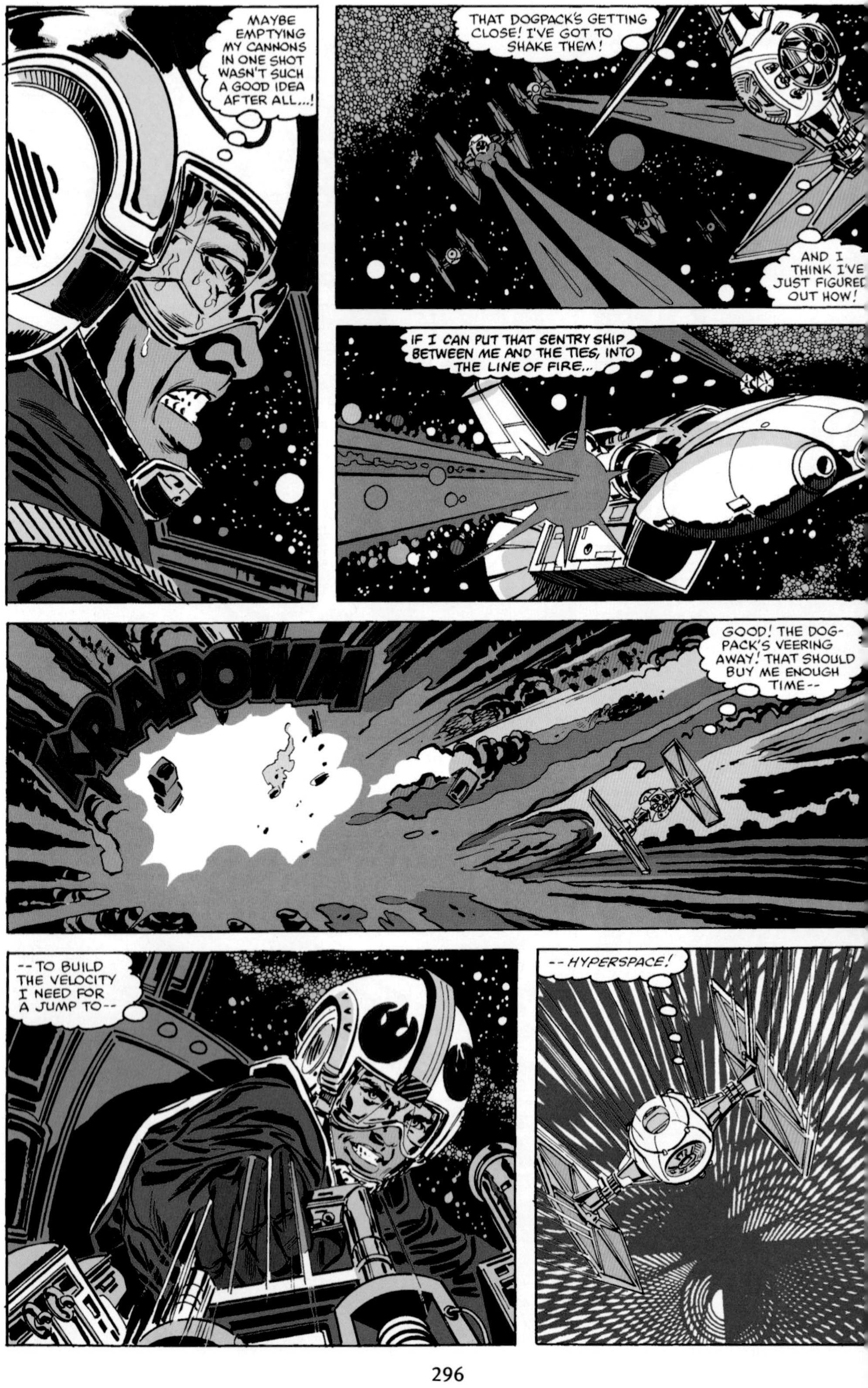

MAYBE EMPTYING MY CANNONS IN ONE SHOT WASN'T SUCH A GOOD IDEA AFTER ALL...!
THAT DOGPACK'S GETTING CLOSE! I'VE GOT TO SHAKE THEM!
AND I THINK I'VE JUST FIGURED OUT HOW!
IF I CAN PUT THAT SENTRY SHIP BETWEEN ME AND THE TIES, INTO THE LINE OF FIRE...
KRAPOWM
GOOD! THE DOG-PACK'S VEERING AWAY! THAT SHOULD BUY ME ENOUGH TIME--
--TO BUILD THE VELOCITY I NEED FOR A JUMP TO--
--HYPERSPACE!

THANKFULLY, THE RETURN TO ARBRA IS MADE WITHOUT INCIDENT. AND AS LUKE SKY-WALKER TURNS HIS SPENT FIGHTER TOWARDS THE REBELS' MOUNTAIN BASE--

--AND GIVES THE PROPER SECURITY CODE FOR PASSAGE THROUGH A HIDDEN CAVERN ENTRANCE--

--HE FULLY EXPECTS TO BE GREETED BY AN AIR OF WELL-EARNED CELE-BRATION...

WE DID IT, GUYS! NOW THE EMPIRE WILL HAVE TO GO BACK TO SMOKE SIGNALS AND SHOUTING!

DIDN'T YOU HEAR ME? I SAID WE GOT THE SCREAMER!

PRINCESS LEIA WOULD LIKE TO SEE YOU IN THE BRIEFING ROOM, SIR.

HMPH. I GUESS THERE'S ONE SOUR-PUSS IN EVERY CROWD, BUT I'M NOT GOING TO LET THAT SPOIL MY DAY!

ARTOO! THREEPIO! DID YOU HEAR THE GOOD NEWS?

WE...HEARD, MASTER LUKE. CONGRATULATIONS.

I THINK.

I DON'T GET IT. SOMEONE MUST'VE HAD A SALE ON GLOOM PILLS!

HEY, THORBEN! I'M GLAD YOU MADE IT BACK! WHERE'S--

EXCUSE ME, COMMANDER, I HAVE TO RUN THE HOLOJECTOR.

LUKE, WILL YOU PLEASE HAVE A SEAT?

SURE, LEIA. BUT I DON'T UNDER-STAND--

AS YOU KNOW, WE EQUIP ALL WAR VESSELS WITH HOLOGRAPHIC CAMERAS FOR USE IN FUTURE TACTICAL STUDIES.

RIGHT. BUT WHAT'S THAT GOT TO DO WITH--

CAPTAIN THORBEN, YOU MAY RUN THE PROGRAM FROM YOUR TIE SHIP NOW.

SAY, ISN'T THAT THE LAST FIGHTER I TAGGED? THE ONE NEAR THE FLAGSHIP?

IT IS.

FREEZE THAT IMAGE, CAPTAIN, AND BRING UP THE MAGNIFICATION.

LOOK, I STILL DON'T-- WAIT A MINUTE! THAT'S NO IMPERIAL! THAT PILOT'S WEARING *REBEL* GEAR! IT'S--

--OH, NO! NO! I-IT COULDN'T BE!

SHIRA!

NEXT ISSUE: PARIAH!

DANGER! UGNAUGHTS AT WORK!

KEEP-AWAY PLAYED CLOUD CITY STYLE, AS CHEWBACCA TRIES TO RESCUE SEE-THREEPIO FROM A FIERY FINISH. RENDERED BY *IRON MAN* EMBELLISHER *BOB LAYTON.*

BOB LAYTON

60¢ | **62** AUG 02817

STAR WARS

LUKE SKYWALKER: PARIAH!

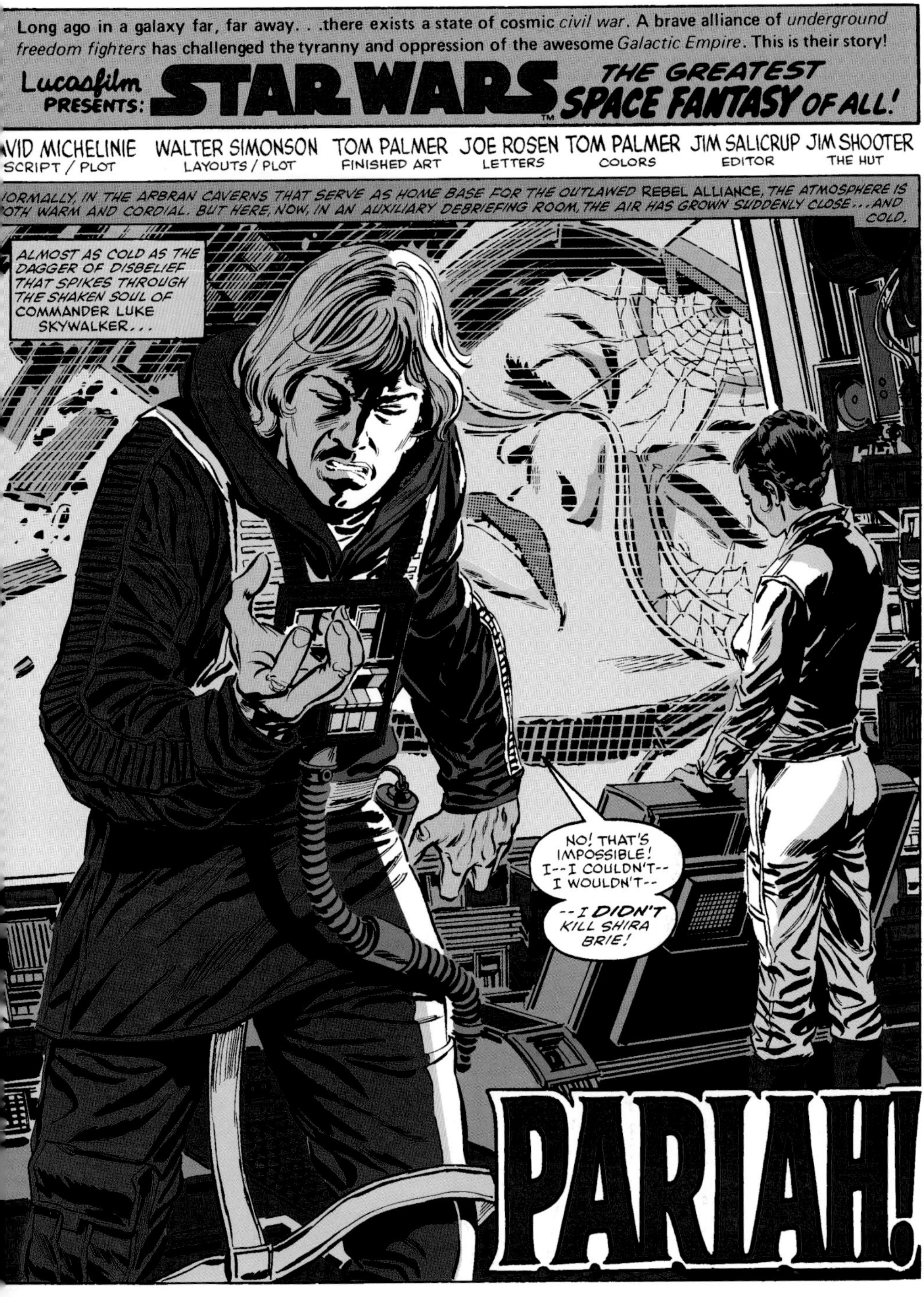

Long ago in a galaxy far, far away. . .there exists a state of cosmic *civil war*. A brave alliance of *underground freedom fighters* has challenged the tyranny and oppression of the awesome *Galactic Empire*. This is their story!
Lucasfilm PRESENTS: STAR WARS™ THE GREATEST SPACE FANTASY OF ALL!
VID MICHELINIE SCRIPT / PLOT
WALTER SIMONSON LAYOUTS / PLOT
TOM PALMER FINISHED ART
JOE ROSEN LETTERS
TOM PALMER COLORS
JIM SALICRUP EDITOR
JIM SHOOTER THE HUT
ORMALLY, IN THE ARBRAN CAVERNS THAT SERVE AS HOME BASE FOR THE OUTLAWED REBEL ALLIANCE, THE ATMOSPHERE IS OTH WARM AND CORDIAL. BUT HERE, NOW, IN AN AUXILIARY DEBRIEFING ROOM, THE AIR HAS GROWN SUDDENLY CLOSE . . . AND COLD.
ALMOST AS COLD AS THE DAGGER OF DISBELIEF THAT SPIKES THROUGH THE SHAKEN SOUL OF COMMANDER LUKE SKYWALKER . . .
NO! THAT'S IMPOSSIBLE! I--I COULDN'T--I WOULDN'T--
--I *DIDN'T* KILL SHIRA BRIE!
PARIAH!

MY MEMORY IS CLEAR-- *ICE CLEAR!* I REMEMBER MY SQUAD ATTACKING THAT IMPERIAL ARMADA, USING BOGUS *TIE FIGHTERS!*

I'D BROKEN THROUGH AND WAS DIVING ON THE FLAGSHIP WHEN ANOTHER TIE CUT BETWEEN ME AND MY TARGET!*

*LAST ISSUE, -- J.S.

BUT SINCE THE SIGNAL DEVICES WE WERE USING TO DISTINGUISH OUR SHIPS FROM THE EMPIRE'S HAD GONE OUT--

-- I HAD TO USE *THE FORCE* TO TELL ME IF THE BLOCKADING TIE WAS FRIEND OR FOE!

AND, LEIA... THE FORCE TOLD ME TO SHOOT! *IT TOLD ME TO SHOOT,* BLAST IT!

BUT ACCORDING TO THE HOLOGRAPHS TAKEN BY OUR OTHER SURVIVING FIGHTER, THE PILOT OF THE TIE I SHOT DOWN WAS SHIRA! MY OWN WING GUARD!

IT'S IMPOSSIBLE!

I BELIEVE YOU, LUKE, I DON'T KNOW WHAT HAPPENED, BUT I BELIEVE YOU. HOWEVER, I...

...I'M AFRAID I CAN'T SUPPORT YOU!

I KNOW.

YOU DO?

SHIRA WAS WELL-LIKED, PRINCESS, BY A LOT OF PEOPLE. AND I...APPEAR TO HAVE KILLED HER.

AS A LEADER OF THE ALLIANCE, YOUR SIDING WITH ME COULD ONLY CAUSE DISSENSION-- A SPLIT IN RANKS THAT COULD THROW OUR WHOLE ORGANIZATION INTO CHAOS! AND THE *REBELLION'S* MORE IMPORTANT THAN *EITHER* OF US!

I UNDERSTAND THAT, LEIA, AND I'LL TRY TO HELP YOU ANY WAY I CAN...

AND SO, MOMENTS LATER, AFTER SAD FAREWELLS AND A FINAL TOUCHING OF HANDS...

OKAY, YOUR HIGH-AND-MIGHTINESS, IF THAT'S THE WAY YOU WANT IT, YOU CAN JUST *HAVE* MY LOUSY COMMISSION!

I DIDN'T WANT TO BE AN *OFFICER* ANYWAY!

MY GOSH! THE PRINCESS BUSTED LUKE SKYWALKER--THE MOST HONORED WARRIOR IN THE ALLIANCE!

SHE MUST REALLY BE CONVINCED THAT HE'S GUILTY!

WHICH IS JUST WHAT I *WANTED* YOU TO THINK!

AW, GOOD RIDDANCE, IF YOU ASK ME!

AND GOOD *LUCK,* LUKE. MAY THE FOR...WELL...

...GOOD LUCK.

CORRIDOR 14, MODULE 3: BETTER KNOWN AS "THE MESS."

IT IS HERE THAT HUNGRY REBELS GATHER TO EAT, TO COMMUNE WITH NATIVE, RODENTLIKE HOOJIBS, AND TO RELAX. IT IS A BUSTLING HALL WHERE THE CLATTER OF PLASTICWARE AND THE LOW RUMBLE OF CONVERSATION NEVER FLAG.

HEY! LOOK!

WELL, ALMOST *NEVER...*

I HAVEN'T HEARD SO MUCH *QUIET* SINCE MY LAST SOLO FLIGHT IN DEEP SPACE!

IT'S ALMOST LIKE TIME HAD STOPPED BETWEEN HEARTBEATS!

303

I'D PROBABLY GET A KINDLIER RECEPTION BY KICKING A SLEEPING *WAMPA*!

UM, I'LL HAVE A BANTHA STEAK, PLEASE.

SORRY, NO MORE BANTHA.

NOPE.

FRESH OUT.

OKAY, HOW ABOUT SOME FLANGTH?

BALKA GREENS?

I SEE.

MR. SKYWALKER, WE THINK IT MIGHT BE BEST IF YOU ATE IN YOUR OWN QUARTERS FOR THE TIME BEING. I HOPE YOU UNDERSTAND.

OH, COME ON! I'VE *FOUGHT* WITH YOU GUYS! EVEN SAVED SOME OF YOUR *LIVES*!

WE KNOW, SIR, AND MOST OF US DON'T LIKE THIS ANY MORE THAN YOU DO. WE'RE JUST TRYING TO AVOID TROUBLE.

TOO BAD SKYWALKER DIDN'T THINK O' THAT BEFORE HE *MURDERED* CAPTAIN BRIE WITH THAT *HOCUS-POCUS* O' HIS!

WATCH IT, MILO! THERE'S NO NEED TO GET PHYSICAL--!

PHYSICAL, EH? MAYBE *THAT'S* WHY HE DID IT! MAYBE SHIRA WASN'T *FRIENDLY* ENOUGH FOR 'IM!

IS THAT IT, LOVER-BOY?

"LOVER--"?!

-- YOU'RE *SLIME*!

MILO--

KATHRAK

EASY, LUKE!

SEE? WH-WHAT'D I TELL YA! NO ONE DECKS *MILO FOURSTAR* THAT FAST!

HE MUSTA USED *THE FORCE!* HE'S A SORCERER! HOW CAN WE *TRUST* A MAN LIKE THAT?

HE MIGHT EVEN BE IN LEAGUE WITH *VADER!*

I THINK YOU'D BETTER LEAVE, MR. SKYWALKER. I'M...SORRY THIS HAPPENED.

YEAH. SO AM I.

AND SOON, IN THE YOUNG REBEL'S PRIVATE QUARTERS...

SHIRA--SOMEONE I REALLY CARED ABOUT--IS DEAD. I SHOULD BE IN MOURNING, I SHOULD BE *COMFORTED* BY MY FRIENDS.

INSTEAD, I'M TREATED LIKE SOMETHING YOU SCRAPE OFF THE BOTTOM OF YOUR BOOT!

AND THE WORST PART IS--

--THERE'S NO *REASON* TO IT! THERE'S NO SENSE, NO SANITY, NO--EH?

THAK

MY MEDAL, THE ONE I GOT FOR THE BATTLE OF THE *DEATH STAR.* IT'S THE HIGHEST HONOR THE ALLIANCE GIVES.

MAYBE I SHOULD'VE TAKEN BETTER CARE OF THE THING.

IT'S STARTING TO LOOK A LITTLE TARNISHED...

PARDON ME, MASTER LUKE. MIGHT ARTOO AND I HAVE A WORD WITH YOU?

HOOWEET?

I'M NOT IN A CONVERSATIONAL MOOD RIGHT NOW, THREEPIO.

I SYMPATHIZE, SIR, BUT WE'VE JUST RECEIVED INFORMATION THAT I THOUGHT YOU MIGHT FIND ENCOURAGING.

IT SEEMS THAT THE SPIES WHO WERE SENT TO FIND *BOBA FETT*--THAT LOATHESOME BOUNTY HUNTER WHO CAPTURED HAN SOLO--HAVE UNCOVERED SOME PROMISING CLUES! ISN'T THAT *WONDERFUL*?

MASTER LUKE? SIR?

THE FORCE HELPED ME DESTROY THE DEATH STAR--BUT IT WAS THAT *SAME* FORCE THAT TOLD ME TO KILL SHIRA!

COULD BEN KENOBI HAVE *LIED* TO ME? WAS EVERYTHING THAT YODA TAUGHT ME ABOUT THE FORCE A *SHAM*?

HAVE I BASED MY LIFE, MY ENTIRE PURPOSE FOR THE LAST SEVERAL YEARS, ON A *DELUSION*?

NO! THERE HAS TO BE SOMETHING ELSE! ANOTHER FACTOR IN ALL THIS! AND I'M GOING TO FIND IT--

--OR I'M GOING TO *DIE* TRYING!

OH, DEAR!

LATER, IN THE MAIN STARCRAFT HANGAR WITHIN THE CAVERNS OF ARBRA...

I'M SORRY, LUKE, I JUST CAN'T.

THAT'S NOT MY PROBLEM.

YOU'VE ADMITTED TO BLOWING SHIRA BRIE OUT OF THE SKY, AND AROUND HERE THAT MAKES YOU ABOUT AS POPULAR AS PLAGUE! IF I TOOK YOUR SIDE, I'D HAVE THE WHOLE *REBELLION* AGAINST ME.

AND THOSE ARE BAD ODDS IN ANY BOOK.

BUT, LANDO, YOU *HAVE* TO LET ME TAKE THE *FALCON!* WITHOUT MY COMMISSION, I CAN'T GET ACCESS TO MILITARY SHIPS!

MATTER OF FACT, I'VE RECEIVED SPECIFIC IN-STRUCTIONS NOT TO LET YOU ANYWHERE *NEAR* THE FALCON. AND THAT'S EXACTLY WHAT I PLAN TO DO--

-- JUST AS SOON AS I PICK UP MY SPARE CAPE AT THE BASE LAUNDRY. SHOULDN'T TAKE MORE THAN...

FIFTEEN MINUTES?

...FIFTEEN IT IS.

I HATED PUTTING LANDO ON THE SPOT LIKE THAT, AND I HOPE HE DOESN'T CATCH ANY FLAK FROM IT. BUT I'VE JUST GOT TO GET OFF-PLANET IF I WANT TO FIND--

COMMANDER? I- I MEAN, "MR. SKYWALKER"? I'M AFRAID I'LL HAVE TO ASK YOU TO HALT, SIR.

WHAT--?

NON-RANKING PERSONNEL AREN'T ALLOWED FLIGHT PRIVILEGES WITHOUT SPECIFIC PERMISSION, SIR. SO UNLESS YOU'VE GOT A PASS, YOU'D BETTER STEP AWAY FROM--

--HUH?! WH-WHAT'RE YOU DOING? THAT'S MY *WEAPON!* YOU'RE NOT AUTHORIZED TO--

SKRAK

O-ON SECOND THOUGHT, I CAN ALWAYS GET AN-OTHER WEAPON! I-IN FACT, I THINK I'LL GO LOOK FOR ONE *NOW!*

CHEWBACCA! THANKS, OLD BUDDY! BUT I THINK I'D BETTER USE THE TIME YOU'VE BOUGHT ME TO GET OUT OF--

SNRRRGGH!

"*WE'D*" BETTER GO?! UH-UH, CHEWIE. I CAN'T LET YOU GET INTO HOT WATER BECAUSE OF ME. I APPRECIATE IT, BUT--

--HNGH?! HEY! L-LEGGO! THAT'S AN ORDER, BLAST IT!

PUT ME DOWN! *PUT ME--*

--OH, WHAT THE HECK...

MOMENTS LATER, THE HIGHLY MODIFIED SPICE FREIGHTER MILLENNIUM FALCON, BLASTS OFF FROM PLANET ARBRA, BUILDING QUICKLY TO LIGHT SPEED--

-- FOR A JOURNEY THAT EVENTUALLY TAKES IT TO A SMALL, BACKWATER WORLD HALF-A-GALAXY AWAY...

THIS IS *SHALYVANE*, CHEWIE-- IT WAS SHIRA'S HOMEWORLD.

SHE RETURNED HERE A FEW DAYS AGO TO PERFORM SOME SORT OF TRIBAL RITUAL.* AND I'M HOPING THAT THAT-- OR *SOMETHING* HERE --WILL SHED SOME LIGHT ON WHY SHE HAD TO... WELL... LET'S SET DOWN OVER THERE.

*IN STAR WARS #60. --J.S.

THE FALCON LANDS-- ALLOWING LUKE SKYWALKER AND HIS WOOKIEE COMPANION TO MAKE THEIR WAY CAUTIOUSLY TO THE RUINED CITY OF CHINSHASSA.

WHERE...

FRRHF

I KNOW. THE PLACE SMELLS OLD. AND DEAD.

BUT THIS IS THE ONLY WAY TO GET TO THE *CIRCLE OF KAVAAN,* THE PRINCIPAL SHRINE OF SHIRA'S TRIBE.

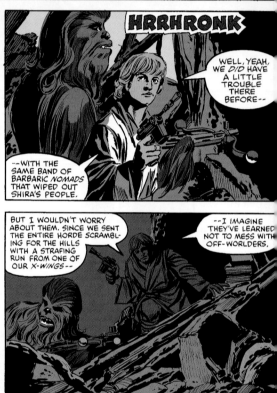

HRRHRONK

WELL, YEAH, WE *DID* HAVE A LITTLE TROUBLE THERE BEFORE--

--WITH THE SAME BAND OF BARBARIC *NOMADS* THAT WIPED OUT SHIRA'S PEOPLE.

BUT I WOULDN'T WORRY ABOUT THEM, SINCE WE SENT THE ENTIRE HORDE SCRAMBL-ING FOR THE HILLS WITH A STRAFING RUN FROM ONE OF OUR *X-WINGS*--

--I IMAGINE THEY'VE LEARNED NOT TO MESS WITH OFF-WORLDERS.

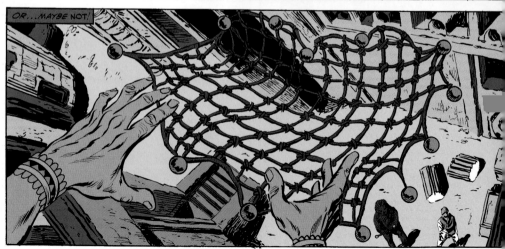

OR...MAYBE NOT!

MRRYYARGGH!

HANG ON, CHEWIE! I'LL GET YOU--

--FREE?

CHUD

CHEWIE--!

LOOKS LIKE I WAS *WRONG* ABOUT THOSE BARBARIANS! THEY'VE GOT NERVE--

--AND THEY WANT *BLOOD!*

G'HRING GHOSA!!!

SHRAK

CHN-G'HIIAVO!

THIS NET IS ELASTIC-- PULLING TIGHTER WITH EVERY MOVEMENT! CAN'T GET TO MY BLASTER!

BUT MAYBE... I CAN STRETCH THE BINDING ENOUGH...TO REACH MY...

...LIGHTSABER!

VRRRRANCH

DID IT! AND NOT A MOMENT TOO SOON!

"THOSE NOMADS ARE COVER- ING GROUND FASTER THAN A HOTHIAN BLIZZARD!"

AND WE'D BETTER GET MOVING BEFORE THEY COVER US-- WITH A SHROUD!

C'MON, CHEWIE!

G'HO-JAHD GHRAVAIIG!

JAHD! JAHD!

312

P-CHOW!

QUICK! BEHIND THIS RUBBLE!

AND SO...

THIS BURNT-OUT BUILDING IS DARK, BIG AND OUT-OF-THE-WAY. IT SHOULD BE PERFECT!

G'HRAVAAR!

ALL RIGHT! THEY BOUGHT IT!

BLAST! THEY'RE GAINING ON US! WE'LL HAVE TO GIVE 'EM THE SLIP!

NOW WE JUST NEED TO GO BACK THE WAY WE CAME AND--

--NO GOOD! THEY'VE GOT BOTH ENDS OF THE ALLEY COVERED! WE'D BETTER FIND SOMEPLACE TO HIDE AND WAIT 'EM OUT!

THAT IS, EXCEPT FOR ONE SLIGHT PROBLEM. I DON'T THINK IT'S ENTIRELY --

313

--DESERTED! YOU! COME OUT OF THERE!

G'HRING JHALA-MOS! PALA...AH... ≥AHEM≤

IS THIS THE TONGUE YOU ARE MORE SPEAKING LIKE, YES?

WE UNDER-STAND YOU.

GOOD! THEN I AM G'HINJI, AND I AM REPEATING WHAT I SAY, YES? I SAY--

--"DON'T HURT ME-- I'M OLD!" YES?

DON'T WORRY, OLD MAN, WE WON'T HURT YOU-- IF WE DON'T HAVE TO.

CHEWIE! CHECK THE ALLEYWAY!

MRRFRFF!

OKAY, I GUESS WE'RE SAFE FOR NOW.

SO MAYBE I CAN TURN THIS SITUATION TO OUR ADVANTAGE. I'M LOOKING FOR INFORMATION, G'HINJI-- ABOUT ONE OF THE HUMANS WHO USED TO INHABIT THIS CITY.

HUMANS? IN CHINSHASSA?

BUT THERE ARE NEVER HUMANS IN CHINSHASSA, YES?

WHAT?! B-BUT, THAT CAN'T BE!

"OH, BUT *IS,* YES? IN MATTER OF TRUTH, UNTIL THREE CYCLES AGO, CITY WAS BEING LIVED IN BY MY OWN PEOPLE! YES! WAS GREAT MAJESTY, AND WONDERFUL COMFORT. BUT THEN, ONE DAY--

"--CITY *DIE!*

"BOMBS FALL FROM SHIPS FLOWN BY PEOPLE CALLED '*EMPIRE,*' YES? NO REASON THEN-- NO REASON NOW. BUT BOMBS TURN CITY TO RUINS, AND TURN MY PEOPLE TO HOMELESS NOMADS.

"YES..."

BUT THAT'S CRAZY! IF YOUR STORY REALLY HAPPENED, THEN EVERYTHING SHIRA TOLD ME WAS A LIE! AND IF SHIRA LIED... WHAT *IS* TRUE?!

OH-OH. YOU ARE HAVING THE PROBLEM, YES?

315

I'M AFRAID SO, G'HINJI. I CAME LOOKING FOR ANSWERS, AND ALL I'VE FOUND ARE DIFFERENT *QUESTIONS!*

WHICH MAKES IT EVEN MORE VITAL THAT I REACH--

--THE CIRCLE OF *KAVAAN!*

OOOOOO, YOU SEEK *HOLY* PLACE, YES?

MY PEOPLE SEE CIRCLE DESECRATED BY UN-BELIEVERS THREE CYCLES AGO!

THEY NOT LET YOU REACH IT EASY!

BUT THERE IS A WAY, YES? IF YOU PASS... *TRIAL BY ORDEAL!*

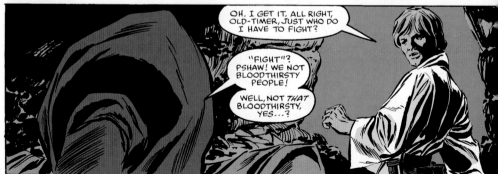

OH. I GET IT. ALL RIGHT, OLD-TIMER, JUST WHO DO I HAVE TO FIGHT?

"FIGHT"? PSHAW! WE NOT BLOODTHIRSTY PEOPLE!

WELL, NOT *THAT* BLOODTHIRSTY, YES...?

ALL YOU DO IS TELLING ME WHICH DRINKING VESSEL HIDES STONE, YES? IF GODS WITH YOU, THEY HELP YOU FIND STONE. IF YOU'RE BEING UNBELIEVER, YOU NOT FIND STONE.

THEN MY *PEOPLE* FIND YOU!

YEEESSSS...

VRRARGGH!

EASY, CHEWIE. I MAY NOT BE THE GAMESMAN LANDO IS, BUT I DO HAVE A FEW TRICKS UP MY SLEEVE!

OKAY, G'HINJI-- YOU'RE ON!

I DON'T LIKE THIS.

I HAVEN'T CALLED ON THE FORCE SINCE ...SHIRA DIED.

BUT I DON'T SEE THAT I'VE GOT MUCH CHOICE!

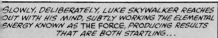

SLOWLY, DELIBERATELY, LUKE SKYWALKER REACHES OUT WITH HIS MIND, SUBTLY WORKING THE ELEMENTAL ENERGY KNOWN AS THE FORCE, PRODUCING RESULTS THAT ARE BOTH STARTLING...

...AND UPLIFTING!

OFFHAND...

...I'D SAY IT WAS...

...THAT ONE!

317

HMMMM, NOT EXPECTING TO DO THAT.

HA! YOU GOT SOME PRETTY STRONG GODS THERE! HA!

YOU OKAY!

SO COME! WE BE TAKING YOU TO CIRCLE OF KAVAAN NOW, NO MORE TROUBLE.

"WE"?

OH, YES-

SNAP

--WE!

WHA--NOMADS! A-ALL OVER THE PLACE! THEY WERE HIDING IN THE RUINS!

HIDE GOOD, YES HERD YOU HERE FOR ME TO TEST--THEN KILL YOU AFTER!

BUT SINCE YOU HAVE SWELL GODS, WE NOT KILL AT ALL, YES?

UH, Y-YES! YES!!

318

-- COMING AT LAST TO THE FAMILIAR STONY CLUTTER OF THE CIRCLE OF KAVAAN!

YOU'D BEST HAVE YOUR TRIBESMEN WAIT AT THE PERIMETER, G'HINJI.

AH, YES, THEY ARE STILL BEING SOMEWHAT WARY.

I DON'T BLAME THEM. I'M A LITTLE NERVOUS MYSELF.

THAT ALTAR WAS THE SPECIFIC SPOT THAT SHIRA PICKED TO PERFORM HER RITUAL.

AND THOUGH IT WAS PARTLY DESTROYED IN THE FIGHT THAT FOLLOWED, IT'S STILL OUR BEST BET FOR FINDING OUT WHAT'S BEEN GOING ON!

AND SO, NOT KNOWING WHAT THEY'LL FIND-- OR EVEN WHAT THEY'RE LOOKING FOR-- THE THREE FIGURES STRIDE FORWARD, SEARCHING.

UNTIL...

FHRRG!

THERE!

YES! SOMETHING AT ALTAR, REFLECTING BACK THE SUN!

IS SOME SURPRISE, OH BOY, YES?

BUT...THINGS ARE BEING TOO STRANGE! *STONE* NOT REFLECTIVE, YES?

NO, G'HINJI, BUT WHAT WAS HIDDEN *INSIDE* THE STONE IS! THERE'S MACHINERY HERE, WHAT APPEARS TO BE A HIGHLY SOPHISTICATED *TRANSMITTER!*

IT LOOKS LIKE SHIRA WAS TRYING TO *CONTACT* SOMEONE!

AND I'VE GOT TO FIND OUT *WHO!* IF I CAN JUST SEND A BLANK TRANSMISSION, THEN TRACE THE BEAM TO--*BLAST!* THERE ISN'T A POWER SWITCH! NO WAY TO ACTIVATE THE MECHANISM! SO HOW DID--

--WAIT! IF I REMEMBER RIGHT, SHIRA NEVER ACTUALLY *TOUCHED* THE ALTAR!

SHE JUST LET A DROP OF HER *BLOOD* SPILL ON IT, SAYING IT WAS HOMAGE TO HER SLAIN FAMILY! AND THAT MUST MEAN...

CHEWIE.

LEND ME YOUR KNIFE.

NEARBY, SILENT EYES OBSERVE GRIMLY AS THE FAIR-HAIRED HUMAN DRAWS SHARPENED STEEL ACROSS HIS NAKED PALM--

--LETTING FLOW A THIN STREAM OF LIFE'S BLOOD, A TRICKLE OF CRIMSON THAT DROPS SWEET AND WARM, TO THE DUSTY STONE OF THE SHATTERED ALTAR.

AND THEN, FOR THE RIVETED WATCHERS, THERE IS NOTHING LEFT BUT TO WAIT...

...AND WAIT...

...AND...

...WAIT.

HMPH. DON'T KNOW FOR YOU--

--BUT FOR ME, THIS NOT BIG EXCITEMENT, YES?

I DON'T UNDERSTAND. I PUT MY BLOOD IN THE SAME PLACE THAT SHIRA PUT HERS-- BUT NOTHING HAPPENED!

YOUR GODS ARE SOMETIME SLEEPING, YES? MAYBE THIS TIME. COME-- WE EAT.

BUT I WAS SO CERTAIN! I MEAN, MY BLOOD MAY BE DIFFERENT FROM SHIRA'S, IN COMPOSITION, BUT I WAS SURE THERE'D BE SOME REACTION, THAT SOMETHING WOULD HAPPEN--!

AND IT DOES!

LUKE!

WHA--? OH, NO! N-NOT HERE! NOT...

...HIM!

LUKE--

321

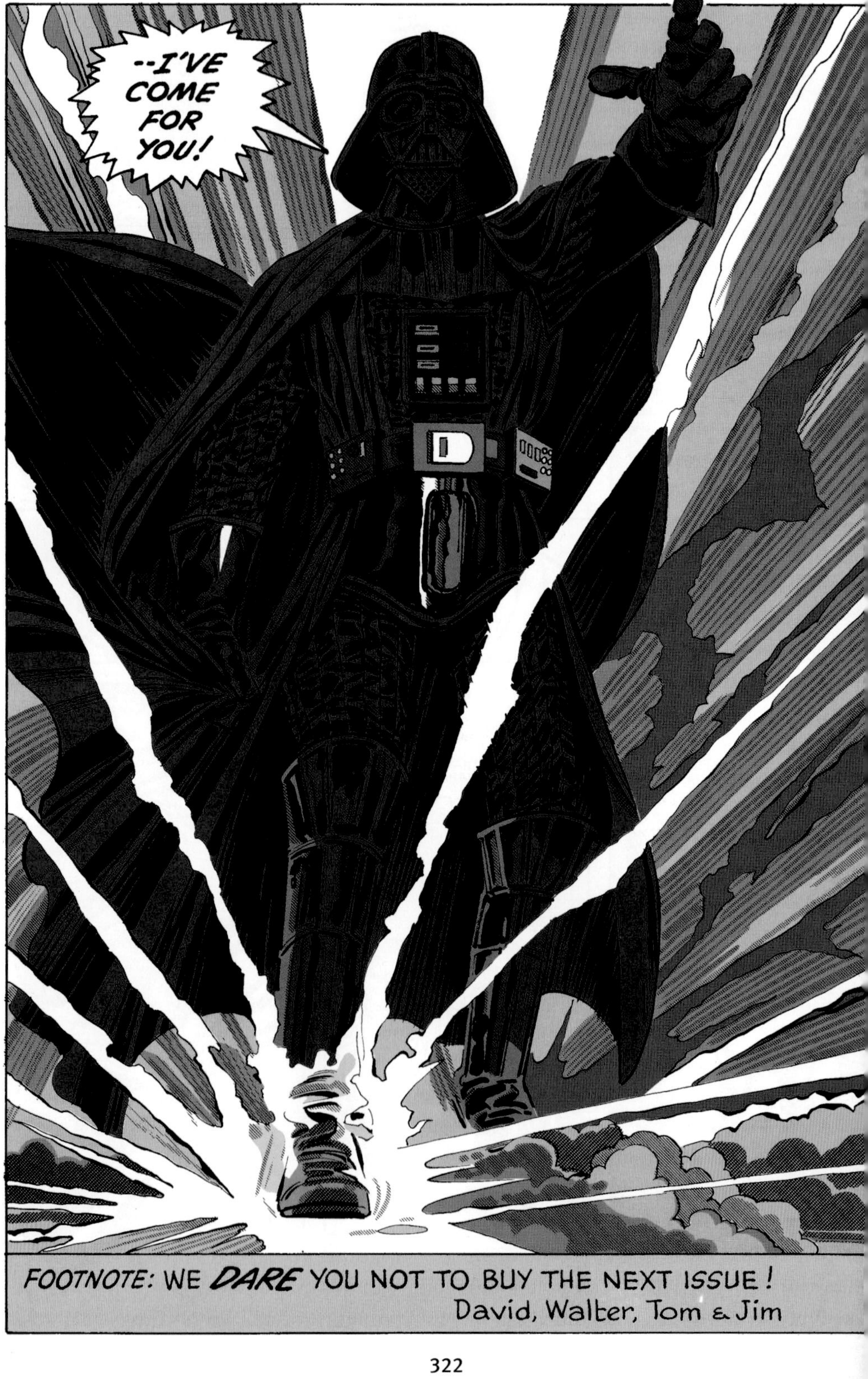
--I'VE COME FOR YOU!
FOOTNOTE: WE DARE YOU NOT TO BUY THE NEXT ISSUE!
David, Walter, Tom & Jim

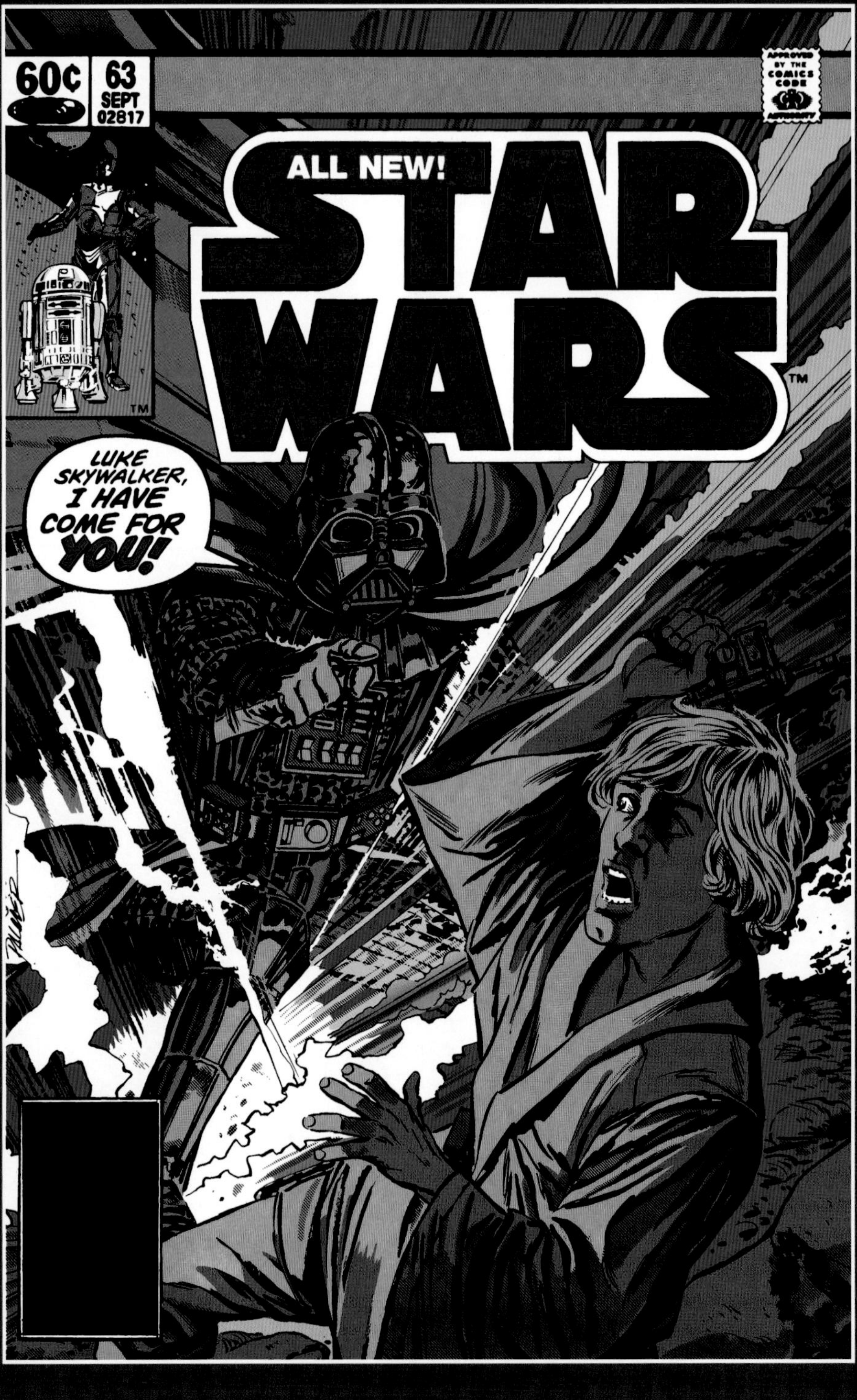

60¢
63
SEPT
02817
APPROVED BY THE COMICS CODE AUTHORITY
ALL NEW!
STAR WARS™
LUKE SKYWALKER, I HAVE COME FOR YOU!

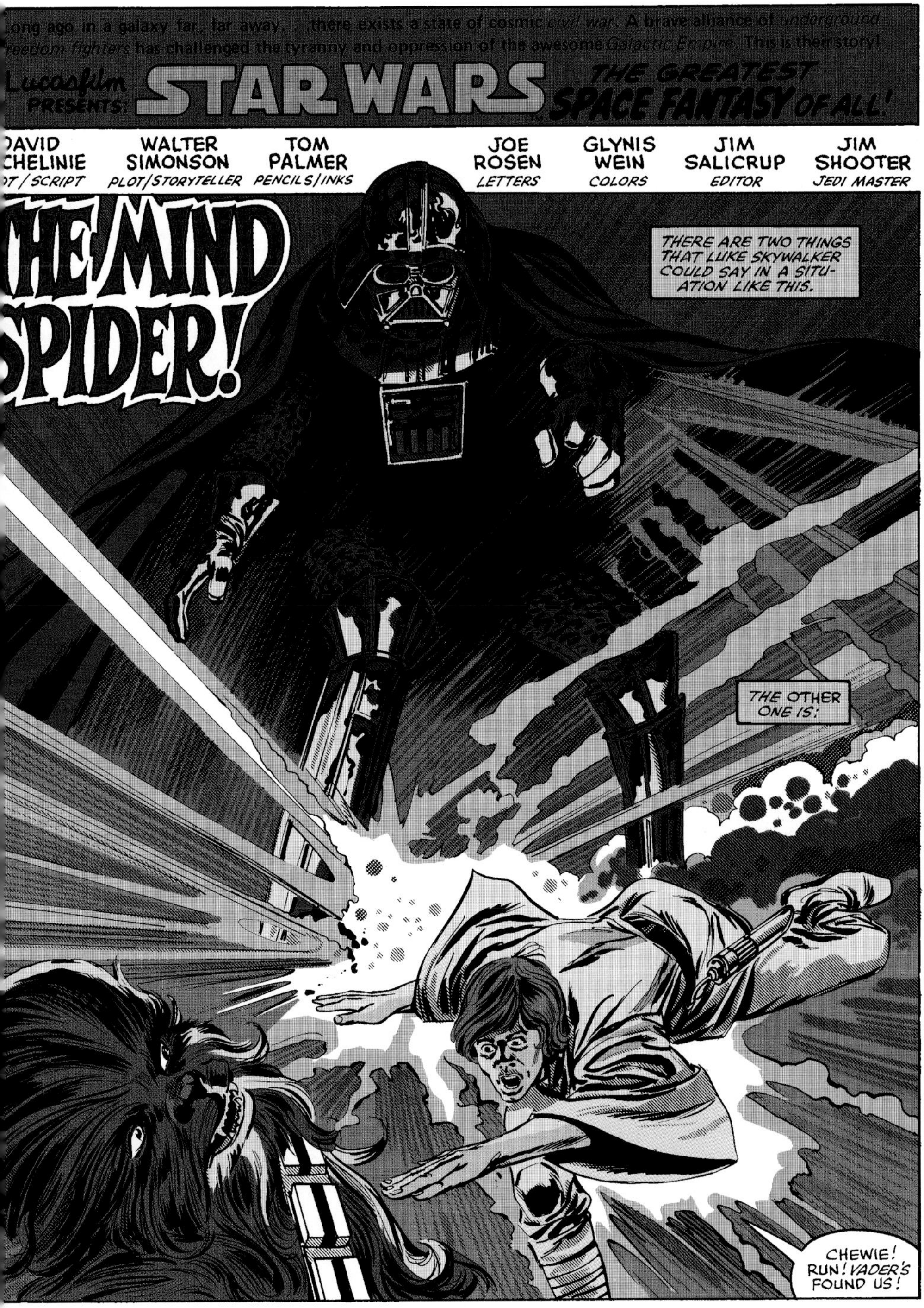
ong ago in a galaxy far, far away. . .there exists a state of cosmic civil war. A brave alliance of underground reedom fighters has challenged the tyranny and oppression of the awesome Galactic Empire. This is their story!
Lucasfilm PRESENTS: STAR WARS
THE GREATEST SPACE FANTASY OF ALL!
AVID CHELINIE T / SCRIPT
WALTER SIMONSON PLOT/STORYTELLER
TOM PALMER PENCILS/INKS
JOE ROSEN LETTERS
GLYNIS WEIN COLORS
JIM SALICRUP EDITOR
JIM SHOOTER JEDI MASTER
HE MIND SPIDER!
THERE ARE TWO THINGS THAT LUKE SKYWALKER COULD SAY IN A SITU- ATION LIKE THIS.
THE OTHER ONE IS:
CHEWIE! RUN! VADER'S FOUND US!

BLAST! WE CAME HERE TO *SHALYVANE* TO FIND OUT WHY *THE FORCE* STEERED ME WRONG, WHY IT MADE ME KILL SHIRA BRIE, A FELLOW REBEL!

AND WHEN WE STUMBLED ACROSS THAT BLOOD-ACTIVATED TRANSMITTER HIDDEN IN THE ALTAR SHIRA USED FOR HER RELIGIOUS RITUALS, I THOUGHT WE'D DONE IT!

BUT NOW IT LOOKS LIK THE WHOLE THING WAS A SET-UP! A TRAP!

AND *DARTH VADER'S* BEHIND IT ALL--

Z-HRAK

--HUH? MY LASER BOLT! I-IT WENT RIGHT *THROUGH* HIM!

BY NOW, YOUNG SKYWALKER, YOU'VE REALIZED THAT I AM BUT A *HOLOGRAPHIC IMAGE*--

--A MIRAGE TRIGGERED BY YOUR SPECIFIC BLOOD CHEMISTRY COMING INTO CONTACT WITH THE KAVAAN TRANSMITTER--

--THE SAME DEVICE USED TO MAINTAIN CONTACT WITH MY MOST TRUSTED OPERATIVE--

--SHIRA BRIE!

SHIRA? AN IMPERIAL *AGENT*?!

MAJOR BRIE WAS TRAINED WELL, AND WAS PLANTED IN THE REBEL ALLIANCE YEARS AGO FOR A SINGLE PURPOSE; TO BRING ABOUT--

--YOUR *DESTRUCTION.*

ACCORDING TO ORDERS, WERE SHE UNABLE TO FACIL TATE YOUR DIRECT DEMISE SHE WAS TO DESTROY YOU CREDIBILITY, THEREBY UNDER MINING YOUR WORTH TO THE REBELLION.

AND SINCE YOU ARE HERE, OBVIOUSLY ALIVE, I MUST ASSUME THAT THE LATTER OPTION HAS BEEN EFFECTED--

--THAT YOU ARE NOW AN OUTCAST, A PARIAH, UNTRUSTED AND QUITE POSSIBLY LOATHED BY THOSE YOU CARE ABOUT MOST.

THUS THERE IS BUT ONE ENTITY WHO WILL ACCEPT YOU, TRUST YOU, TREAT YOU AS AN EQUAL.

LUKE, I'VE COME FOR YOU.. AND NOW...

...YOU MUST COME...

...TO ME!

OOOOOO! THAT'S SOME NASTY FRIEND YOU'RE HAVING THERE, YES?

NO, G'HINJI.

DARTH VADER IS NOBODY'S FRIEND.

THOUGH HE DOES MAKE ONE HECK OF AN *ENEMY!*

CHEWIE, GET DOWN! THAT TRANSMITTER'S GOING TO--

"--BLOW!"

FAHLAMM

I HATE IT.

VADER *KNEW* I WOULDN'T GET TAGGED BY THAT EXPLOSION!

HE'S KNOWN EVERY MOVE I'VE MADE BEFORE I KNEW THEM MYSELF!

SO I GUESS HE MUST KNOW WHAT I HAVE TO DO NEXT!

COME ON, CHEWIE, WE'RE HEADING FOR THE IMPERIAL DATA VAULT ON *KRAKE'S PLANET.*

WE SHOULD BE ABLE TO GET WHAT WE NEED THERE,

BUT YOU ARE JUST SAYING ROTTEN HUMAN KNOWS YOUR MOVINGS, YES? SOUNDS PRETTY RISKY TO ME!

THAT CAN'T BE HELPED, G'HINJI.

I NEED HARD PROOF TO CONVINCE THE REBELLION-- AND MYSELF-- THAT SHIRA WAS A TRAITOR.

AND IF THAT BLACKHEARTED SITH LORD WANTS TO STOP ME--

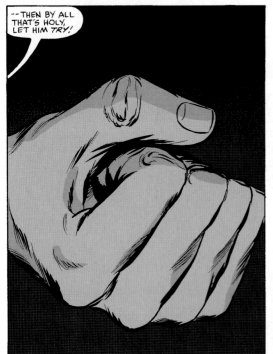

--THEN BY ALL THAT'S HOLY, LET HIM *TRY!*

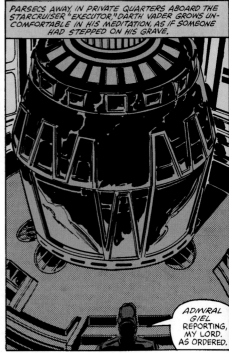

PARSECS AWAY, IN PRIVATE QUARTERS ABOARD THE STARCRUISER "EXECUTOR," DARTH VADER GROWS UN-COMFORTABLE IN HIS MEDITATION, AS IF SOMEONE HAD STEPPED ON HIS GRAVE.

ADMIRAL GIEL REPORTING, MY LORD. AS ORDERED.

PNEUMATIC LOCKS HISS SMOOTHLY OPEN, AND...

AH, YES. GIEL. FRESH FROM YOUR LATEST TRIUMPH--

--THAT OF LOSING THE ONE-OF-A-KIND *TEEZL* TO A BAND OF HIT-AND-RUN REBELS!*

*IN STAR WARS #61.--J.S.

THE ENEMY FORCES USED STOLEN TIE FIGHTERS TO GET PAST SENTRY POSTS, SIR. NO PRECAUTIONS COULD HAVE PREVENTED THAT.

NEVERTHELESS, THE TEEZL COULD HAVE INCREASED IMPERIAL COMMUNICATIONS CAPACITY A *THOUSAND-FOLD.*

I DO NOT TAKE ITS DESTRUCTION LIGHTLY.

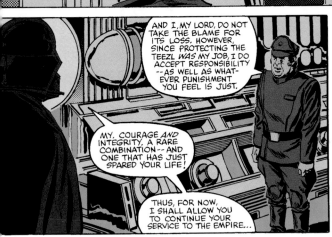

AND I, MY LORD, DO NOT TAKE THE BLAME FOR ITS LOSS. HOWEVER, SINCE PROTECTING THE TEEZL *WAS* MY JOB, I DO ACCEPT RESPONSIBILITY --AS WELL AS WHATEVER PUNISHMENT YOU FEEL IS JUST.

MY. COURAGE *AND* INTEGRITY. A RARE COMBINATION-- AND ONE THAT HAS JUST SPARED YOUR LIFE!

THUS, FOR NOW, I SHALL ALLOW YOU TO CONTINUE YOUR SERVICE TO THE EMPIRE...

THE DEMOTED OFFICER LEAVES, STIFFLY, AS ANOTHER CREWMAN ENTERS...

WE'VE RECEIVED A TERMINATION SIGNAL FROM SHALYVANE, LORD. APPARENTLY, THE TRANSMITTING UNIT THERE HAS SELF-DESTRUCTED!

EXCELLENT! THEN ALL IS PROCEEDING AS PLANNED! HAVE THE HELMSMAN RESET OUR COURSE, CAPTAIN--

...LEFTENANT GIEL!

"LEF--?!"

AS YOU WISH, MY LORD. GOOD DAY.

-AHEM-

-- WE GO TO *KRAKE'S PLANET* AT ONCE!

SLOWLY, THE IMPERIAL WAR FLEET TURNS, AND MOVES OUT. THEIR DESTINATION: *KRAKE'S PLANET--*

--A SMALL, GRACELESS WORLD WHERE, MERE MOMENTS BEFORE, A HIGHLY-MODIFIED SPICE FREIGHTER CALLED THE MILLENNIUM FALCON *HAD SET DOWN ON AN ISOLATED PLAIN, ALLOWING ITS TWO PASSENGERS TO SPRINT TO THE ENTRANCE OF A NEARBY CAVE. A CAVE BOTH DARK--*

--AND VERY NARROW!

MRRGH!

I KNOW IT'S CLOSE IN HERE, CHEWIE, BUT THIS IS THE ONLY WAY.

THE DATA VAULT IS LIKE A FORTRESS, AND WE'D NEVER GET IN WITH A FRONTAL ASSAULT.

WE'RE JUST LUCKY THE FALCON'S COMPUTERS HAD INFO ON THESE TUNNELS--SEEMS THEY WERE USED FOR SMUGGLING IN THE OLD DAYS.

NOW, THEY'RE FORGOTTEN AND DESERTED.

UH, E-EXCEPT FOR--

--THAT!

FR-KK-FR-KK

-- WHEW-- LOOKS LIKE HE'S MORE AFRAID OF US THAN WE ARE OF HIM!

VRROWK!

WELL... ALMOST!

BUT DON'T WORRY, I SEE DAYLIGHT AHEAD AND THAT'S GOTTA BE--

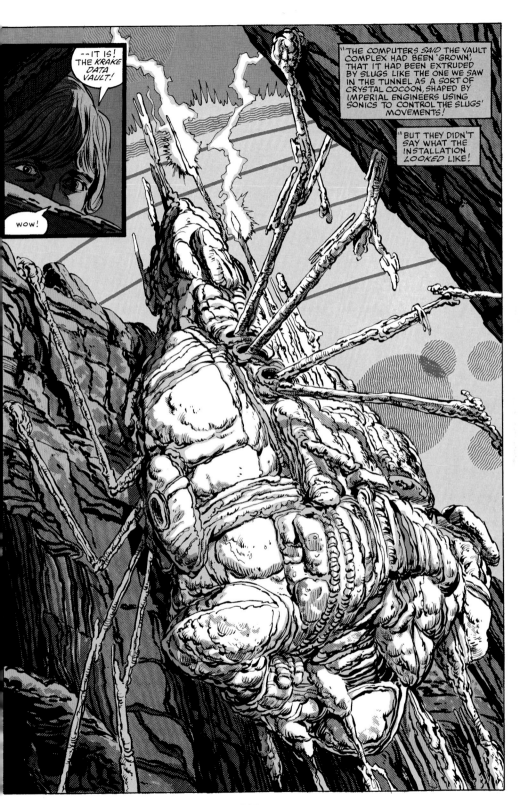

--IT IS! THE *KRAKE DATA VAULT!*

WOW!

"THE COMPUTERS *SAID* THE VAULT COMPLEX HAD BEEN 'GROWN', THAT IT HAD BEEN EXTRUDED BY SLUGS LIKE THE ONE WE SAW IN THE TUNNEL AS A SORT OF CRYSTAL COCOON, SHAPED BY IMPERIAL ENGINEERS USING SONICS TO CONTROL THE SLUGS' MOVEMENTS!

"BUT THEY DIDN'T SAY WHAT THE INSTALLATION *LOOKED* LIKE!

"YOU'D THINK THAT POSITIONING THE VAULT IN THE MIDDLE OF A RAVINE AND COVERING THAT RAVINE WITH AN IMPREGNABLE FORCE FIELD WOULD BE SECURITY ENOUGH!

NOT THAT THEY NEED ONE FOR US-- WE'VE GOT *ENOUGH* PROBLEMS!

IF VADER'S AS FAR AHEAD OF US AS HE SEEMS, HE MUST'VE FIGURED WE'D COME HERE, THAT WE'D SNEAK IN THROUGH AN AIR SHAFT OR SOMETHING AND TRY TO REACH THE CENTRAL STORAGE COMPUTER.

"SO WE'VE GOT TO OUTTHINK HIM, WE'VE GOT TO FIND SOME OTHER WAY TO GET SHIRA'S FILE. A WAY SO SIMPLE, SO COMMON, THAT IT'D BE BENEATH THE DARK LORD'S DIGNITY TO EVEN CONSIDER IT.

"AND CHEWIE, OLD BUDDY...I THINK I'VE JUST *FOUND* IT!"

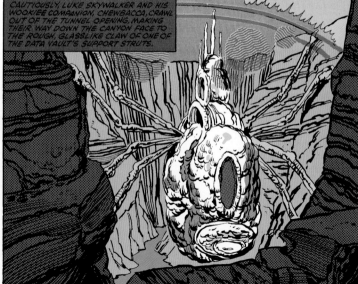

CAUTIOUSLY, LUKE SKYWALKER AND HIS WOOKIEE COMPANION, CHEWBACCA, CRAWL OUT OF THE TUNNEL OPENING, MAKING THEIR WAY DOWN THE CANYON FACE TO THE ROUGH, GLASSLIKE CLAW OF ONE OF THE DATA VAULT'S SUPPORT STRUTS.

"BUT I GUESS WHEN YOU'VE GOT WHAT AMOUNTS TO A UNIVERSAL *MIND* HOLDING PERSONNEL DATA FOR THE ENTIRE EMPIRE--

"--SHAPING THE WHOLE THING LIKE A GIANT *CRAWLY* MUST BE AN ADDED DETERRENT FACTOR!"

WHILE SEVERAL STAR SYSTEMS AWAY, ON A FOREST WORLD CALLED ARBRA, IN A CAVERN USED AS HOME BASE BY THE OUTLAWED REBEL ALLIANCE...

...A PRINCESS WAITS.

YOU'RE WORRIED ABOUT LUKE, AREN'T YOU, LEIA?

YOU DON'T NEED TO BE A TELEPATHIC *HOOJIB* TO GUESS THAT, PLIF.

I'VE GOT A FEELING ...I DON'T KNOW WHY, BUT I THINK WE'RE GOING TO NEED LUKE, AND SOON. IF HE DOESN'T CLEAR HIMSELF AND RETURN TO THE REBELLION--

--I'M AFRAID OUR CAUSE COULD SUFFER A DISASTER OF *GALACTIC* PROPORTIONS!

OH, OH, MY!

LEIA AND PLIF RETURN TO SOLEMN THOUGHT --AS ON KRAKE'S PLANET...

LET'S SEE, ONE MORE SCOOP TO GET THE GREASE OFF THE TOP AND--

--÷SNIFF÷ AHHH! PERFECT!

OKAY, CAP'N, SOUP'S ON!

THANKS, FARLIE. I APPRECIATE YOUR LETTING ME EAT IN HERE-- THE MESS HALL GETS KIND OF CRAZY ON PAYDAY!

HMMM. ÷SLUP÷ NOT BAD.

USING A DIFFERENT STOCK THESE DAYS?

IT'S THE SEASONING.

HNH?!

S-SORRY, CAP'N! TH-THEY CAME OUTTA NOWHERE!

REBELS! WH- WHAT DO YOU WANT?

INFORMATION. SPECIFI-CALLY, ANY FILE DATA LISTED UNDER THE NAME, "SHIRA BRIE"!

I KNOW THIS KITCHEN COMPUTER CONSOLE IS USED MAINLY FOR RECIPES AND SUPPLY CALCULATIONS, BUT WITH THE PROPER SECURITY CODE IT SHOULD BE ABLE TO TAP INTO THE CENTRAL DATABANK!

HMPH. AND WHAT MAKES YOU THINK THAT I'LL SUPPLY THAT CODE?

OH, HOW ABOUT--

-- THE FOUR GRAINS OF SILICARTHA I DUMPED IN YOUR SOUP?

ON TATOOINE, THAT'S ENOUGH TO KILL A 50-POUND SAND-BORER!

'COURSE, IT MAY WORK A LITTLE SLOW ON HUMANS, BUT...

AGGH! M-MY STOMACH! I CAN FEEL THE POISON WORKING ALREADY!

QUICK! HELP ME TO THE CONSOLE! I-I'LL PROGRAM ANYTHING YOU WANT!

AND FOUR LEVELS AWAY, AT THE ENTRANCE TO THE DATA VAULT'S CENTRAL COMPUTER AREA...

YOU SURE THIS IS WHERE WE'RE SUPPOSED TO WAIT?

THAT'S WHAT LORD VADER ORDERED. WE'RE TO CAPTURE THE REBEL WHEN HE TRIES TO ENTER THE COMPUTER ROOM.

OH. THEN I GUESS WE SHOULD IGNORE THE ALERT I'M PICKING UP, HUH? THE ONE ABOUT THE TOP SECRET INFORMATION THAT'S JUST BEEN ILLEGALLY CHANNELED TO THE KITCHEN TERMINAL?

ALERT

WHAT?!

THERE! THE PROGRAM'S LOCKED IN AND SET TO RECORD ON ONE OF FARLIE'S RECIPE CHIPS!

NOW, PLEASE! GIVE ME THE ANTIDOTE!

YOU HEARD THE MAN, CHEWIE--

--GIVE IT TO HIM!

WHOKK

B-BUT, THE POISON--! HE'LL DIE!

ONLY OF EMBARRASSMENT, FARLIE. ALL I PUT IN HIS DINNER WERE SOAP FLAKES FROM THE DISHWASHING DROID!

NOW, IF I PUNCH IN "RECORD" AND "PLAYBACK" AT THE SAME TIME, THAT SHOULD--

WORKING! FILE PROGRAM TO FOLLOW. SUBJECT:

SHIRA ELAN COLLA BRIE.

CURRENT RANK: MAJOR, IMPERIAL SPECIAL FORCES.

PERSONAL HISTORY JUDGED IDEAL. BORN IN EMPIRE CAPITOL. RAISED IN PALACE OF EMPEROR PALPATINE AS PART OF EXPERIMENT IN ADOLESCENT INDOCTRINATION.

EXPERIMENT TOTALLY SUCCESSFUL.

GAINED EXPERT RATING IN ALL KNOWN FORMS OF COMBAT. INTELLIGENCE AND COORDINATION BOTH EXTRAORDINARY.

BIOLOGICALLY ALTERED TO REJECT PAIN, AND TO ACCELERATE PHYSICAL HEALING PROCESS.

GRADUATED WITH TOP HONORS IN HISTORY OF ACADEMY. RECORD UNEQUALLED SINCE.

PERSONALLY SELECTED BY LORD DARTH VADER FOR INFILTRATION INTO BANNED ORGANIZATION KNOWN AS "REBEL ALLIANCE"--SEE REFERENCE LOG #49734.

VADER PROJECT REQUIRED TOTAL RAZING OF CITY OF *CHINSHASSA* ON PLANET SHALYVANE TO ESTABLISH CREDIBLE BACKGROUND FOR SUBJECT.

PROJECT'S PURPOSE: THE ELIMINATION-- EITHER ACTUAL OR EFFECTUAL-- OF REBEL COMMANDER, *LUKE SKYWALKER.*

PROJECT STATUS: OPEN.

END OF PROGRAM.

THEN... THE FORCE WAS RIGHT. SHIRA MUST HAVE BEEN COMING AFTER *ME* WHEN I BLEW HER AWAY!

I CAN'T BELIEVE IT. THERE'S *GOT* TO BE MORE TO IT THAN THAT!

FRRRRPH!

I KNOW, CHEWIE. IT'D BE TOO DANGEROUS TO HANG AROUND AND LOOK FOR MORE INFORMATION NOW.

WE'LL HAVE TO MAKE DO WITH THE DATA ON THIS RECORD-ING CHIP UNTIL--

--HUH?!

ZZZATCH

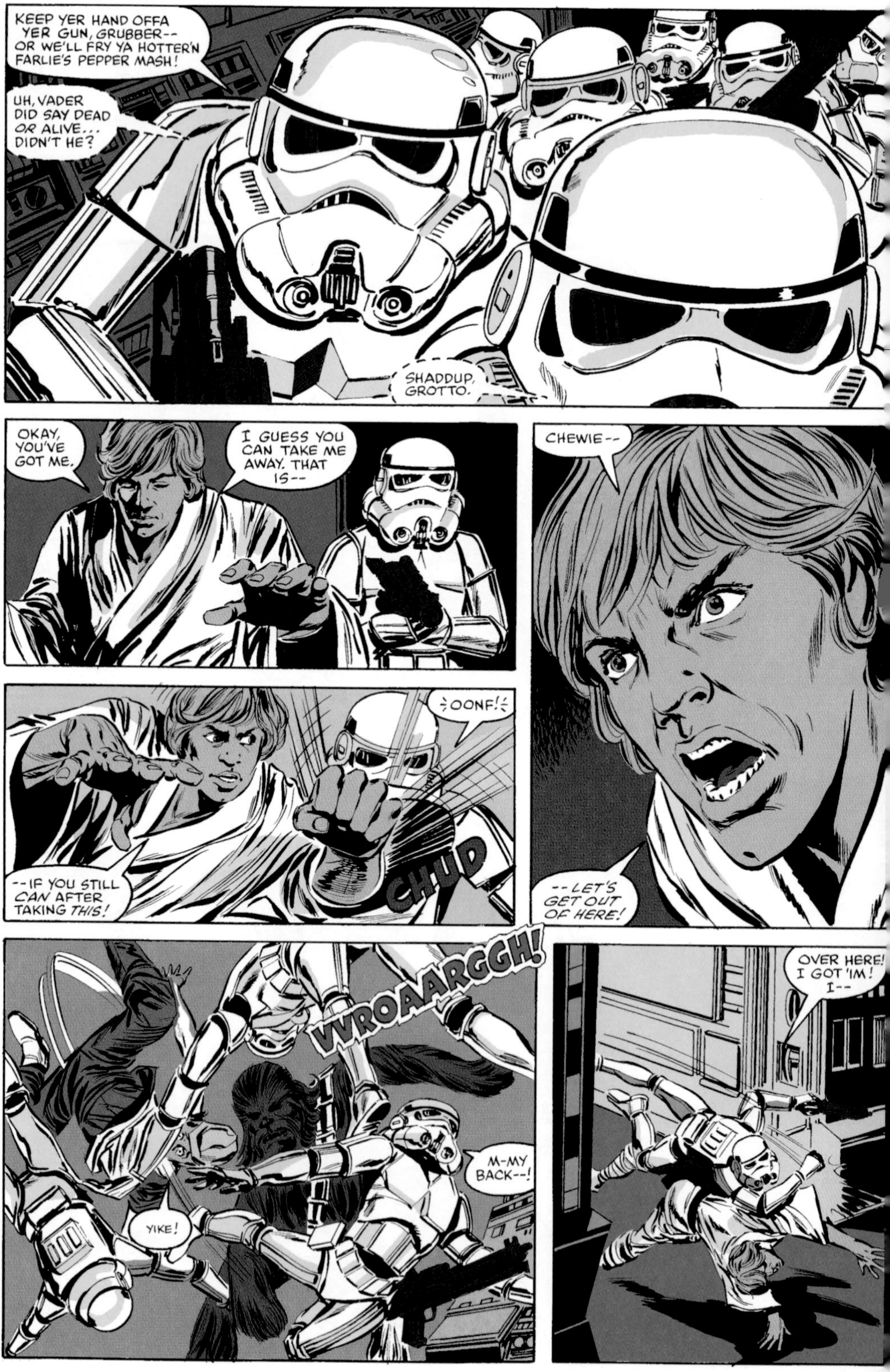

KEEP YER HAND OFFA YER GUN, GRUBBER-- OR WE'LL FRY YA HOTTER'N FARLIE'S PEPPER MASH!
UH, VADER DID SAY DEAD OR ALIVE... DIDN'T HE?
SHADDUP, GROTTO.
OKAY, YOU'VE GOT ME.
I GUESS YOU CAN TAKE ME AWAY. THAT IS--
OONF!
--IF YOU STILL CAN AFTER TAKING THIS!
CHUD
CHEWIE--
--LET'S GET OUT OF HERE!
VVROAARGGH!
M-MY BACK--!
YIKE!
OVER HERE! I GOT 'IM! I--

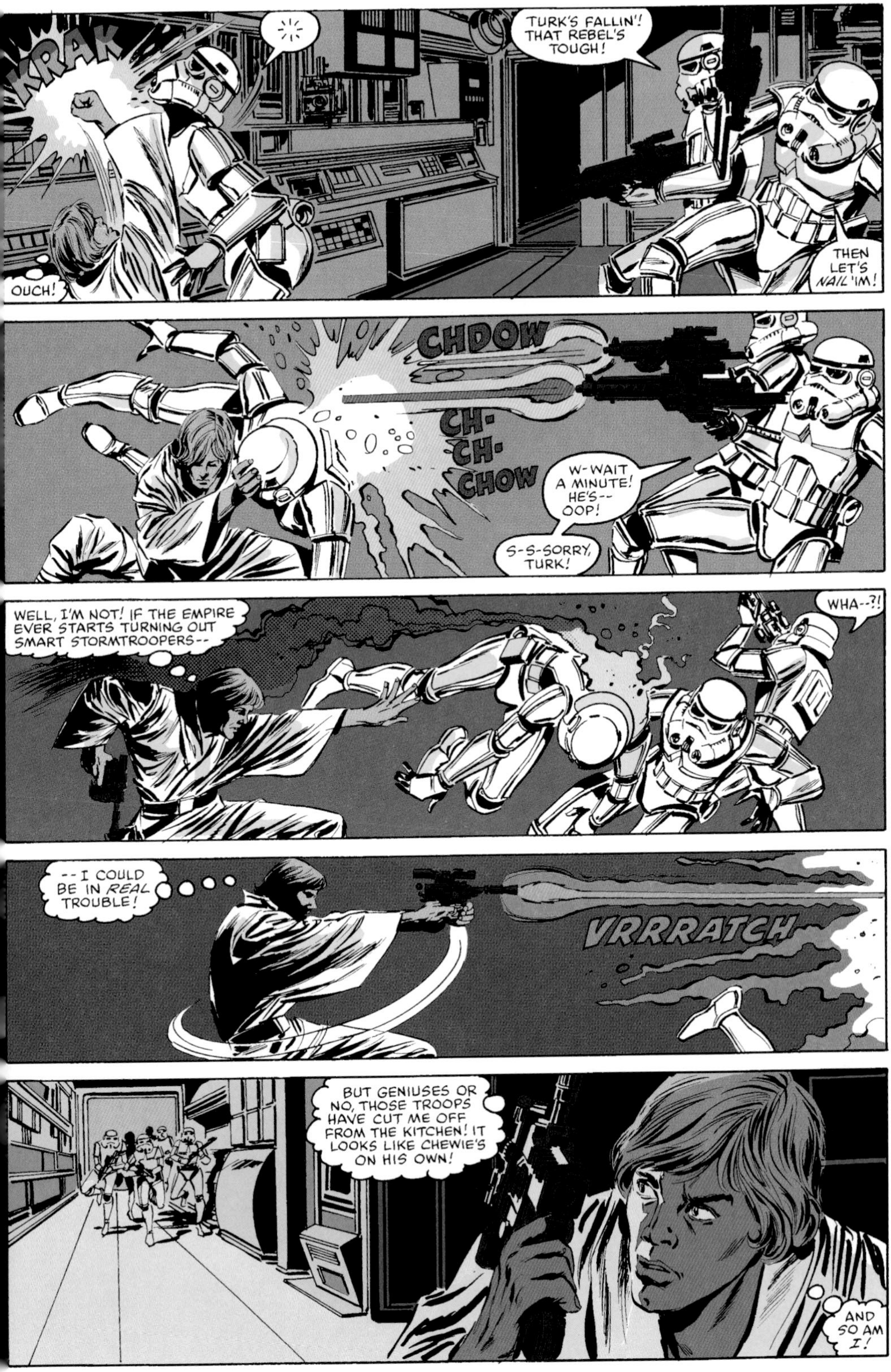
KRAK
!
TURK'S FALLIN'! THAT REBEL'S TOUGH!
OUCH!
THEN LET'S NAIL 'IM!
CHDOW
CH-
CH-
CHOW
W-WAIT A MINUTE! HE'S-- OOP!
S-S-SORRY, TURK!
WELL, I'M NOT! IF THE EMPIRE EVER STARTS TURNING OUT SMART STORMTROOPERS--
WHA--?!
--I COULD BE IN REAL TROUBLE!
VRRRATCH
BUT GENIUSES OR NO, THOSE TROOPS HAVE CUT ME OFF FROM THE KITCHEN! IT LOOKS LIKE CHEWIE'S ON HIS OWN!
AND SO AM I!

MEANWHILE, KILOMETERS ABOVE...

WE'RE APPROACHING KRAKE'S PLANET, MY LORD. AND WE'VE JUST RECEIVED WORD THAT A SKIRMISH HAS BROKEN OUT AT THE MAIN DATA COMPLEX.

I KNOW. FORWARD OUR LANDING REQUIREMENTS TO FORCE FIELD CONTROL AT ONCE--AND BEGIN DESCENT!

YES, SIR!

AND, AS THE GIANT STARSHIP DIPS LOWER OVER THE HORIZON...

I'M OUT!

BUT I'M *NOT* OUT OF DANGER!

THOSE TROOPERS AREN'T CRACK SHOTS--

--BUT THERE'S ALWAYS THE CHANCE THAT A STRAY BLAST COULD STRIKE HOME!

WHICH, WITH THE HELP OF THIS EMERGENCY LIFE-LINE CABLE--

--IS EXACTLY WHERE *I'M* GOING!

BUT "HOME" IN THIS CASE LIES AT THE FAR END OF A FAMILIAR MAZE OF SMUGGLERS' TUNNELS--

--AND TAKES THE FORM OF A BATTERED, THOUGH MUCH BELOVED, SPICE FREIGHTER!

GOTTA GET TO THE FALCON AND RUN A FAST LIFE SCAN!

SINCE CHEWIE'S THE ONLY WOOKIEE ON THIS PLANET--

--HE SHOULDN'T BE TOO HARD TO--

"--OH, NO! HE DIDN'T MAKE IT! HE'S STILL AT THE DATA VAULT!"

AND THERE'S ONLY ONE WAY TO GET HIM OUT...!

ONCE AGAIN TRUSTING THE ELEMENTAL POWER KNOWN AS THE FORCE, LUKE SKYWALKER REACHES OUT WITH HIS MIND--

--AND REACHES INTO THE DATA VAULT SECURITY CENTER...

THERE'S DUST ON THAT CONSOLE, MISTER! HOW MANY TIMES HAVE I TOLD YOU--

--TO...

DISENGAGE... PROTECTIVE... ENERGY... SHIELD...

...IMMEDIATELY!

341

HEARTBEATS LATER...

WRROWKK

WHA--THE ENERGY SHIELD IS DOWN! PUT IT BACK UP, YOU FOOLS!

B-BUT, SIR, YOU SAID--

DO IT NOW!

SHRRRING

AND THEY DO!

BUT NOT BEFORE SEVEN-AND-A-HALF FEET OF FUR AND TENSING MUSCLE DROPS GRACEFULLY TO THE TOP OF A HOVERING SPACECRAFT!

WHERE, ONCE INSIDE...

STRAP YOURSELF DOWN, CHEWIE--

--THIS IS GOING TO BE ROUGH!

THAT ENERGY SHIELD IS KEEPING US IN AS EFFECTIVELY AS IT KEEPS EVERYTHING ELSE OUT!

342

WHICH MEANS THAT WE'VE GOT TO SHUT DOWN THE VAULT'S POWER GENERATOR! AND SINCE WE DON'T HAVE TIME TO RUN A LOCATION PROBE TO FIND IT--

--OUR ONLY OPTION IS TO BOOST THE FALCON'S DEFLECTOR SCREENS--

"--AND TAKE OUT THE WHOLE COMPLEX!"

SHRRAPASH

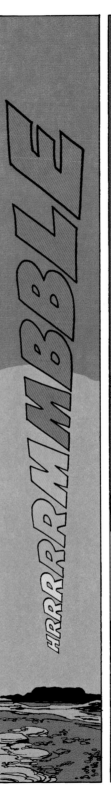

HRRRRRMMBBBLE

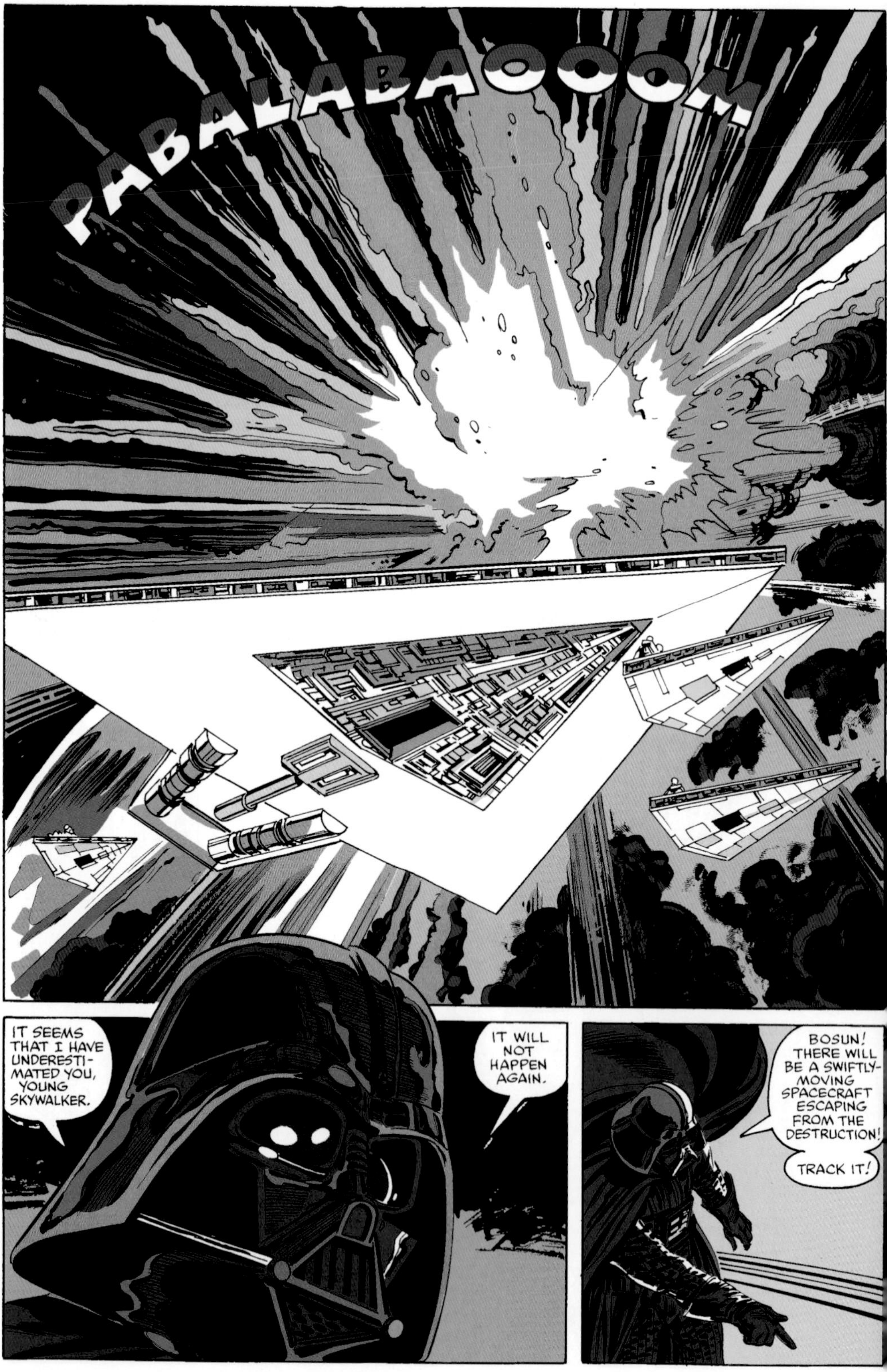
PABALABAOOOM
IT SEEMS THAT I HAVE UNDERESTIMATED YOU, YOUNG SKYWALKER.
IT WILL NOT HAPPEN AGAIN.
BOSUN! THERE WILL BE A SWIFTLY-MOVING SPACECRAFT ESCAPING FROM THE DESTRUCTION!
TRACK IT!

I'VE GOT IT, SIR-- BUT IT LOOKS LIKE WE'RE TOO LATE!

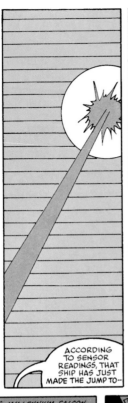

ACCORDING TO SENSOR READINGS, THAT SHIP HAS JUST MADE THE JUMP TO--

"--HYPERSPACE!"

ON THE BRIDGE OF THE "EXECUTOR," LORD DARTH VADER CURLS FINGERS INTO FIST...THEN TURNS... AND WALKS SILENTLY, DANGEROUSLY AWAY.

WHILE ABOARD THE WARP-HOPPING MILLENNIUM FALCON...

TERRIFIC. I DISCOVER THAT A WOMAN I CARED ABOUT WAS REALLY A TRAITOR, ONE WHO TRIED TO KILL ME.

BUT I DON'T GET THE EVIDENCE I NEED TO USE THAT INFORMATION TO CLEAR MY NAME!

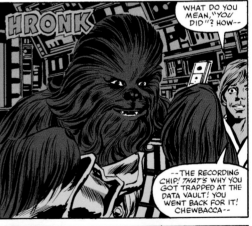

HRONK

WHAT DO YOU MEAN, "YOU DID"? HOW--

--THE RECORDING CHIP! THAT'S WHY YOU GOT TRAPPED AT THE DATA VAULT! YOU WENT BACK FOR IT! CHEWBACCA--

--YOU'RE ONE IN A MILLION!

HRF·HRF

EPILOGUE: A MEDICAL LAB DEEP WITHIN THE BOWELS OF THE "EXECUTOR"...

HOW IS THE PATIENT, FX9?

ALIVE, BARELY.

PATIENT HAS SUFFERED MULTIPLE TRAUMA, EXTREME LOSS OF VITAL FLUIDS, EXTENSIVE STRUCTURAL FRACTURE. SURVIVAL TO DATE DUE SOLELY TO EXCEPTIONAL RESTORATIVE CAPABILITIES.

RECUPERATION PROCESS WILL BE LONG, AND AT BEST UNCERTAIN, BUT ACCORDING TO PROJECTION DATA: POSSIBLE.

GOOD. BECAUSE NOW, MORE THAN EVER, I HAVE NEED OF--

--SHIRA BRIE!

THE WARSHIPS MOVE ON, AS THE ICY CHILL OF SPACE--

--FOR A FLEETING MOMENT--

-- SEEMS COLDER STILL...

Next Issue: THE TROUBLE WITH GOLRATH

346

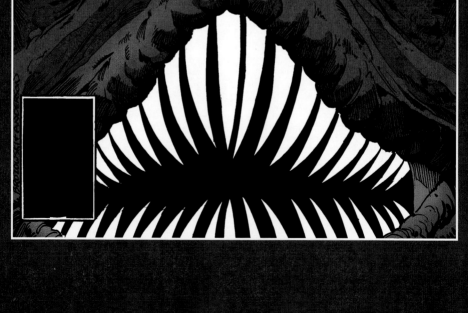

60¢ 64 OCT 02817

STAR WARS

"SERPHIDIAN EYES"

Long ago in a galaxy far, far away. . .there exists a state of cosmic *civil war*. A brave alliance of *underground freedom fighters* has challenged the tyranny and oppression of the awesome *Galactic Empire*. This is their story!

Lucasfilm PRESENTS: **STAR WARS** THE GREATEST **SPACE FANTASY** OF ALL!

| MICHAEL EISHER PLOT | DAVID MICHELINIE SCRIPT | JOE BROZOWSKI PENCILS | VINCE COLLETTA INKS | JOE ROSEN LETTERS | GLYNIS WEIN COLORS | JIM SALICRUP EDITOR | JIM SHOOTER EDITOR-IN-CHIEF |

DEEP IN THE BOWELS OF A MOUNTAIN STRONGHOLD ON THE PLANET *ARBRA*, IN A ROOM WHERE MEMBERS OF THE REBEL ALLIANCE *PLAN THEIR UNTIRING STRUGGLE AGAINST THE EVIL* GALACTIC EMPIRE, A MEETING CONTINUES...

YOU MEAN, PRINCESS, THAT WE'VE GOT TO MAKE FRIENDS WITH...*THAT?*

WE DO, BERL-- IF WE WANT TO *SURVIVE!*

SERPHIDIAN EYES

349

AS YOU KNOW, WE'VE RECEIVED WORD OF INCREASED IMPERIAL PRESENCE IN THE *BELIAL* SYSTEM. BUT SINCE WE HAVE NO BASES OR ALLIES IN THAT SECTOR, OUR INFORMATION IS DANGEROUSLY INCOMPLETE.

TO PROTECT OURSELVES FROM IMPERIAL SNEAK ATTACK, WE NEED INFORMANTS, OR "EYES," IN THAT AREA.

AND THAT'S WHERE YOURSELF, COMMANDER SKYWALKER AND CAPTAIN TARHEEL COME IN.

OUR BEST HOPE LIES WITH *SERPHIDI*, THE FOURTH PLANET FROM BELIAL. THE NATIVES--*SERPS*, SUCH AS THE ONE PICTURED HERE--ARE GENERALLY SYMPATHETIC TO THE REBELLION.

BUT THEIR CURRENT MONARCH, *KING S'SHAH*, IS A TYRANT WHO RULES WITH AN IRON HAND-- AND DEFINITE IMPERIAL LEANINGS!

SO IT'S UP TO YOU TO GO TO SERPHIDI AND CHANGE A FEW MINDS--BEFORE IT'S TOO LATE!

WHAT A PITY ARTOO AND I ARE DUE FOR OUR ANNUAL WORN PARTS REPLACEMENT. WE MIGHT HAVE BEEN OF HELP.

GOSH, THREEPIO, IF YOU'RE REALLY THAT DISAPPOINTED, I'M SURE WE COULD PULL A FEW STRINGS AND--

O-OH, NO! I- I MEAN, I COULDN'T LEAVE ARTOO TO FACE SURGERY ALONE! I- I *COULDN'T--*!

DON'T WORRY, THREEPIO, I THINK BERL, CINDA AND I CAN HANDLE THIS MISSION.

IT SEEMS SIMPLE ENOUGH.

PA-DRPP?

THE BRIEFING SESSION ENDS.

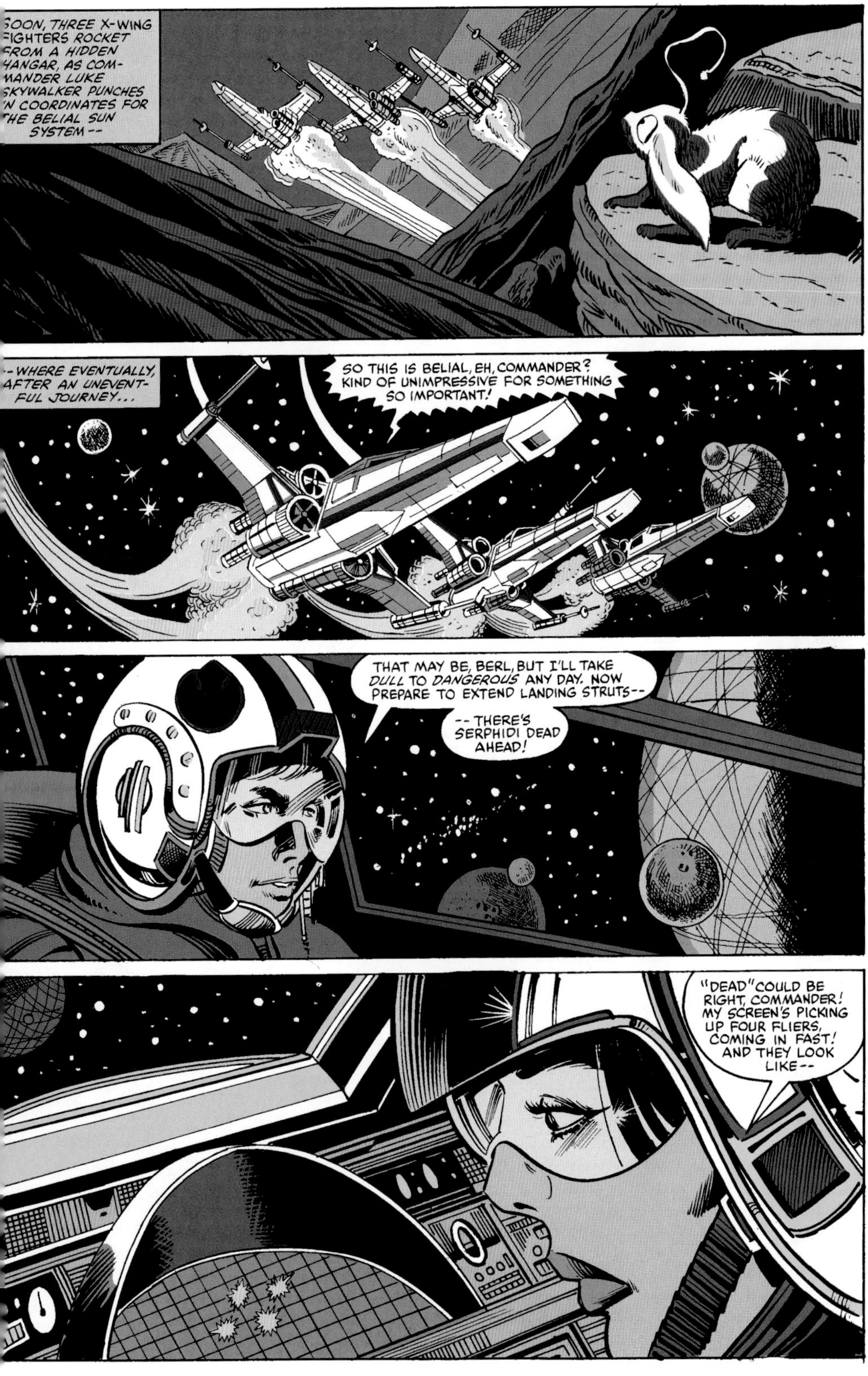
SOON, THREE X-WING FIGHTERS ROCKET FROM A HIDDEN HANGAR, AS COMMANDER LUKE SKYWALKER PUNCHES IN COORDINATES FOR THE BELIAL SUN SYSTEM--
--WHERE EVENTUALLY, AFTER AN UNEVENTFUL JOURNEY...
SO THIS IS BELIAL, EH, COMMANDER? KIND OF UNIMPRESSIVE FOR SOMETHING SO IMPORTANT!
THAT MAY BE, BERL, BUT I'LL TAKE DULL TO DANGEROUS ANY DAY. NOW PREPARE TO EXTEND LANDING STRUTS--
--THERE'S SERPHIDI DEAD AHEAD!
"DEAD" COULD BE RIGHT, COMMANDER! MY SCREEN'S PICKING UP FOUR FLIERS, COMING IN FAST! AND THEY LOOK LIKE--

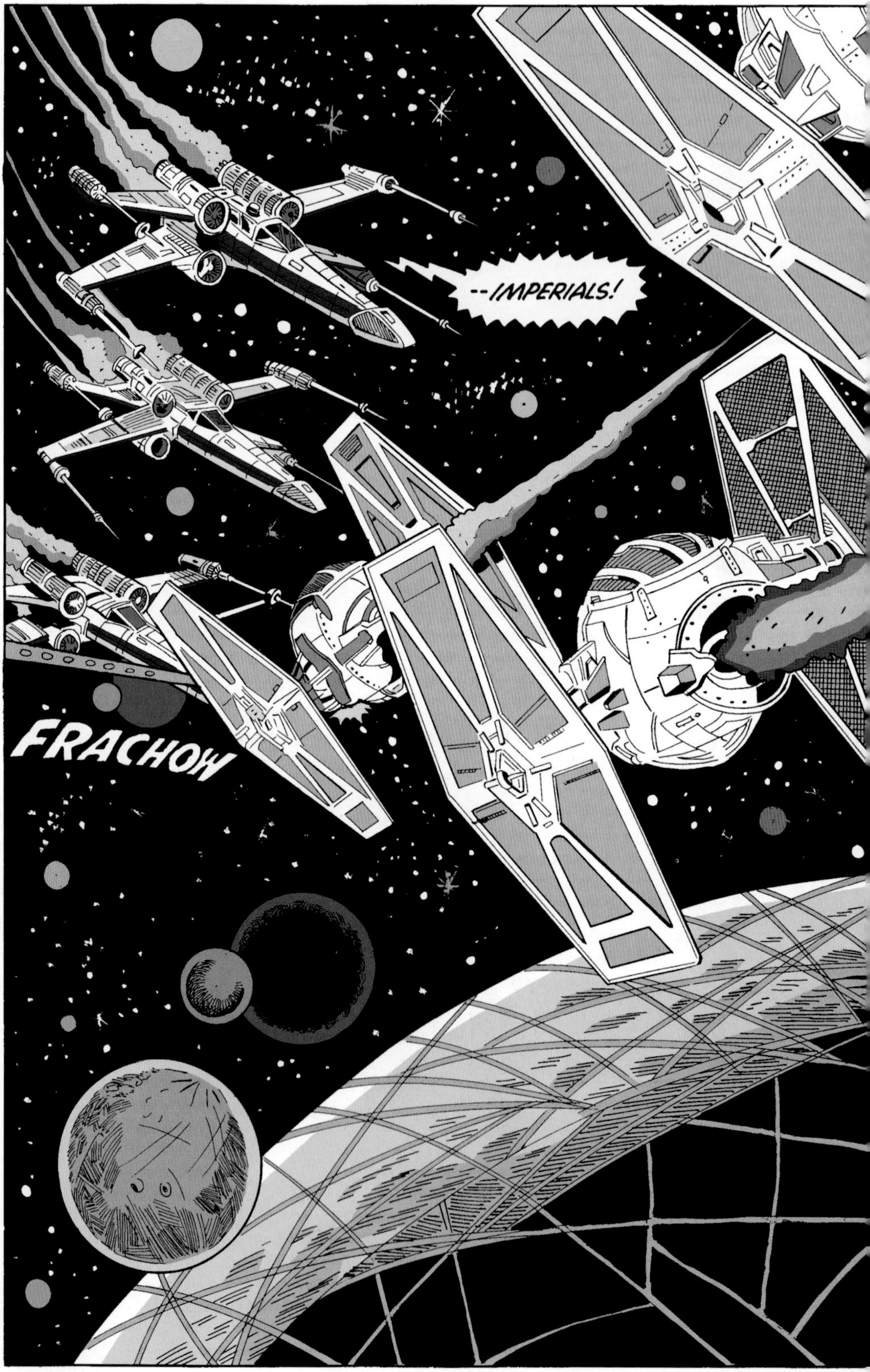
--IMPERIALS!
FRACHOW

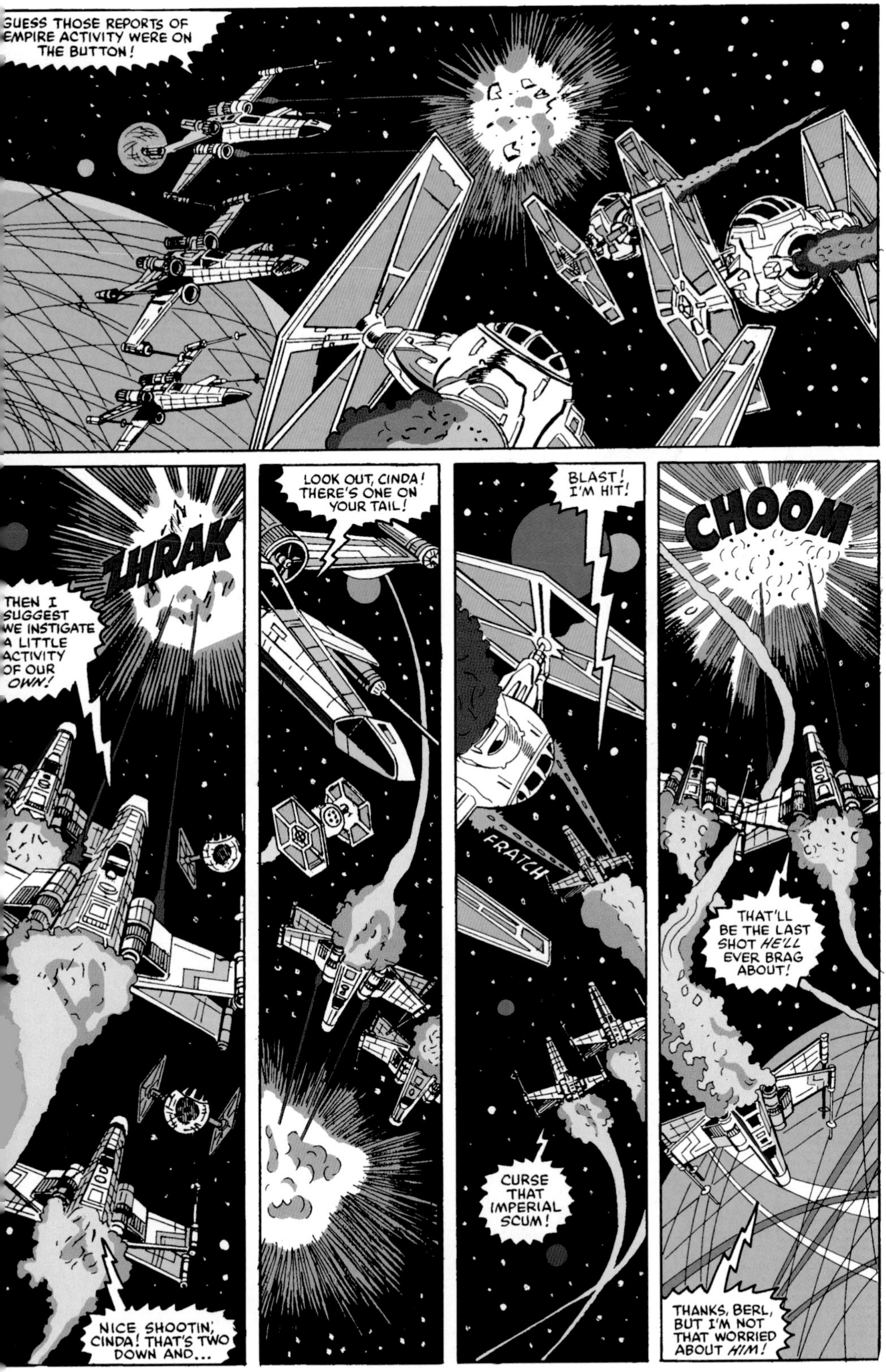
GUESS THOSE REPORTS OF EMPIRE ACTIVITY WERE ON THE BUTTON!
ZHRAK
THEN I SUGGEST WE INSTIGATE A LITTLE ACTIVITY OF OUR OWN!
NICE SHOOTIN', CINDA! THAT'S TWO DOWN AND...
LOOK OUT, CINDA! THERE'S ONE ON YOUR TAIL!
BLAST! I'M HIT!
FRATCH
CURSE THAT IMPERIAL SCUM!
CHOOM
THAT'LL BE THE LAST SHOT HE'LL EVER BRAG ABOUT!
THANKS, BERL, BUT I'M NOT THAT WORRIED ABOUT HIM!

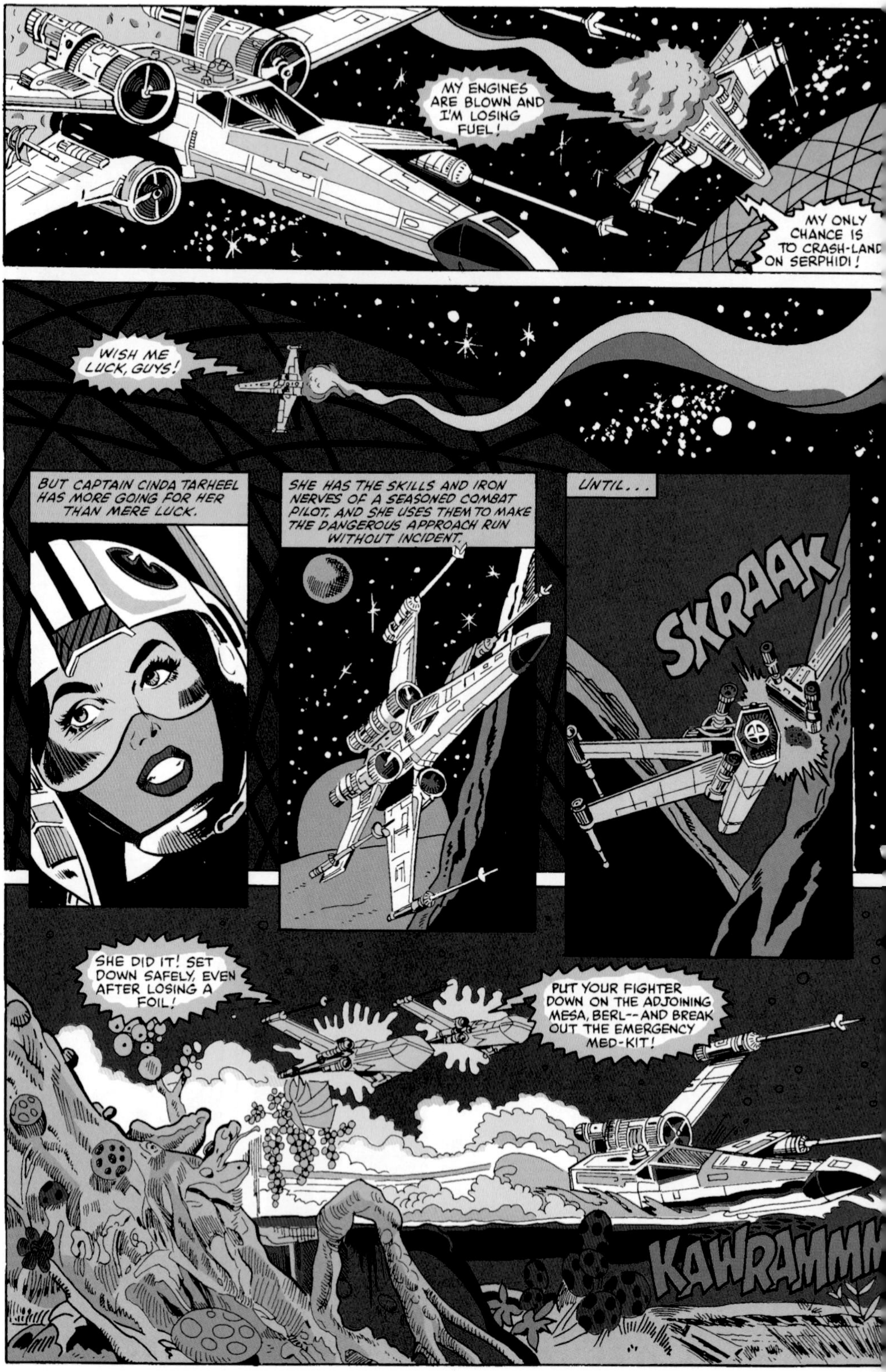
MY ENGINES ARE BLOWN AND I'M LOSING FUEL!
MY ONLY CHANCE IS TO CRASH-LAND ON SERPHIDI!
WISH ME LUCK, GUYS!
BUT CAPTAIN CINDA TARHEEL HAS MORE GOING FOR HER THAN MERE LUCK.
SHE HAS THE SKILLS AND IRON NERVES OF A SEASONED COMBAT PILOT, AND SHE USES THEM TO MAKE THE DANGEROUS APPROACH RUN WITHOUT INCIDENT,
UNTIL...
SKRAAK
SHE DID IT! SET DOWN SAFELY, EVEN AFTER LOSING A FOIL!
PUT YOUR FIGHTER DOWN ON THE ADJOINING MESA, BERL--AND BREAK OUT THE EMERGENCY MED-KIT!
KAWRAMMM

SECONDS LATER...

CINDA! ARE YOU--?

MY SHIP'S SEEN BETTER DAYS, COMMANDER, BUT *I'M* FINE.

THAT IS EXCELLENT! FOR KILLING *WOUNDED* ANIMALS WOULD ADD LITTLE TO THE LEGEND--

EH?

-- OR TO THE GLORY OF... *KING S'SHAH!*

ARMORED SERPS, RIDING IN ON LIZARD MOUNTS! AND THEY'RE --

--ATTACKING! FIRING ENERGY BOLTS FROM THEIR LANCES! LOOK OUT!

BRAAP

BERL!

CINDA!

BRAAP

TSAAK

--OR *MYSELF* -- GET SLAUGHTERED!

ZRAAK!

BRAAAP

I KNOW WE'RE ON A PEACE MISSION, BUT I CAN'T JUST STAND AROUND AND WATCH MY FRIENDS--

ZZZAK!

UNFORTUNATELY THOSE *SERPS* DON'T SEE IT THAT WAY!

THEY'RE CUTTING ME OFF FROM CINDA AND BERL!

AND EVERY TIME I HIT *ONE* OF THEM, *THREE MORE* TAKE HIS PLACE!

I'VE GOT NO CHOICE! HAVE TO MAKE A RUN FOR IT--THEN SNEAK BACK LATER AND TRY TO HELP THE OTHERS ESCAPE!

ONE MALE IS DEAD, SIRE, AND THE OTHER FLEES. SHALL WE PURSUE?

NO, CHAKIS, IT IS LATE.

AND SINCE THE FEMALE IS INTACT, I SHALL CONSOLE MYSELF WITH A *PARTIAL* VICTORY--AND WITH THE ACQUISITION OF...

...A NEW *TOY!*

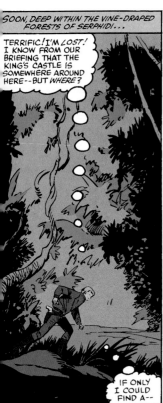

TERRIFIC! I'M *LOST!* I KNOW FROM OUR BRIEFING THAT THE KING'S CASTLE IS SOMEWHERE AROUND HERE--BUT *WHERE?*

IF ONLY I COULD FIND A--

--CLUE...?

QUICKLY, HIS HAND ON THE *BUTT* OF HIS BLASTER, LUKE SPRINTS TOWARD THE SOUND OF THE BLOOD-CHILLING SCREAM. AND THERE DISCOVERS...

GYAAA; AAAA AAAA

HELP! P-PLEASE *HELP* ME!

AN OLD SERP! BEING ATTACKED BY SOME SORT OF CARNIVOROUS PLANT!

HE DOESN'T *LOOK* LIKE PART OF THE GROUP THAT ATTACKED US, BUT I CAN'T BE SURE! I CAN'T...

...AW, HECK, I CAN'T LET THE OLD GUY *DIE!*

ZRAAK!

I AM *ELGLIH*, YOUNG WARRIOR--AND YOU HAVE MY EXTREME GRATITUDE.

DON'T MENTION IT. BUT ISN'T IT KIND OF DANGEROUS FOR SOMEONE OF YOUR, AH, *MATURITY* TO BE OUT HERE ALONE?

PERHAPS, BUT I HAD TO PRACTICE FOR THE DOOM-JOUSTS. I *HAD* TO. THEY ARE THE ONLY HOPE FOR MY PEOPLE...AND FOR MY *WORLD!*

RIGHT. WHAT'S A "DOOM-JOUST"?

FORGIVE ME. YOU SAVE MY LIFE, AND I PRATTLE ON LIKE A TAD FRESH FROM THE EGG.

COME, SHARE MY HUMBLE HOME, AND I WILL EXPLAIN ALL...

AND PRESENTLY, AT A MODEST HOMESTEAD IN A DAPPLED FOREST GLADE...

ARE YOU CERTAIN, YOUNG SIR--

--THAT YOU WON'T HAVE MORE PORRIDGE?

THANKS, MA'AM, BUT I COULDN'T EAT ANOTHER BITE. WHAT I *WOULD* LIKE, THOUGH, IS THE *EXPLANATION* YOUR HUSBAND PROMISED ME.

AND YOU SHALL HAVE IT, WARRIOR, BEGINNING WITH A WORD ABOUT OUR PLANET'S *PAST*...

"YOU SEE, SERPHIDI WAS ONCE A WORLD OF SUPERIOR TECHNOLOGY-- BUT WITH THAT TECHNOLOGY CAME THE URGE TO USE IT FOR ACTS OF DESTRUCTION!

"THUS WAS OUR PLANET TORN FOR CENTURIES BY ENDLESS, SENSELESS WARS.

"UNTIL THAT WONDERFUL DAY WHEN SANITY PREVAILED AND A PACT WAS SIGNED, ONE THAT BANNED TECHNOLOGY--

"--AND UNITED ALL OF SERPHIDI UNDER THE LEADERSHIP OF A SINGLE KING. AGGRESSION WAS THEN SUBLIMATED INTO INTO THE FORM OF HARMLESS, ANNUAL *JOUSTING* CONTESTS.

"BUT WHEN *S'SHAH* CAME TO POWER SEVERAL CYCLES AGO, HE REVIVED SOME OF THE FORBIDDEN *SCIENCE*, APPLIED IT TO THE JOUSTS, AND ALTERED THEM TO *DEATH* GAMES!

"HE THEN PROCLAIMED THAT THE ONLY WAY HE COULD BE DEPOSED AS RULER WAS TO BE *BESTED* IN ONE OF THE DOOM-JOUSTS!"

SINCE THAT TIME, MANY HAVE TRIED--*ALL* HAVE FAILED.

BUT *I* MUST NOT FAIL!

AND YOU, SIR SKYWALKER, WHO PROFESS TO BE FROM A REBELLION THAT WOULD DEPOSE TYRANTS LIKE S'SHAH... YOU SHALL *HELP* ME!

HEY, I DIDN'T VOLUNTEER TO --

--WAIT A MINUTE! THIS COULD BE THE PERFECT WAY TO GET TO S'SHAH'S CASTLE, *AND* TO FIND WHERE CINDA AND BERL ARE BEING HELD!

ALL RIGHT, ELGLIH, YOU'RE ON!

GOOD. THEN I SHALL TRAIN YOU, AND YOU SHALL BECOME MY *SQUIRE.*

"SQUIRE"?!

BUT I'M A *WARRIOR!* I'M STRONGER THAN YOU, I'M *YOUNGER*--!

YES, MY FRIEND, YOU *ARE* YOUNG. *VERY* YOUNG.

AND THAT IS *WHY* YOU SHALL BE MY SQUIRE.

HUH? B-BUT I DIDN'T... I-I MEAN, YOU SHOULDN'T... UH...

...OH.

ELGLIH, YOU DRIVE A HARD BARGAIN.

MEANWHILE...

...AT THE CASTLE OF KING S'SHAH...

MMM, YES, THAT'S MUCH BETTER.

A DELICACY OF YOUR CALIBER SHOULD BE DRESSED PROPERLY FOR THE SATING OF A *KING'S* APPETITES.

LOOK, FROG-MOUTH, I'VE GONE ALONG WITH THIS FARCE SO FAR, BUT IF YOU THINK MAKING A MEMBER OF THE REBEL ALLIANCE YOUR *BRIDE* IS GOING TO BE EASY, YOU'RE--

"BRIDE"? MY DEAR, YOU FLATTER YOURSELF. WHY SHOULD I, A *SERP*, POSSIBLY WISH TO JOIN MYSELF TO ONE OF SUCH PALE, FLIMSY FEATURES?

WHY, I DOUBT YOU'VE EVEN A SINGLE *SCALE* ON YOUR BODY!

NO, WHEN I SPOKE OF SATING MY APPETITE, I MEANT PRECISELY THAT-- THE QUENCHING OF MY EXCEEDINGLY REFINED PALATE. I'M QUITE A *GOURMET*, YOU KNOW.

B-BUT, YOU SAID YOU WANTED ME AS A *TOY*--!

YES, ALAS, YOU'VE DISCOVERED MY SECRET. FOR UNSEEMLY AS IT MAY BE FOR A MEMBER OF ROYALTY--

-- I DO SO ENJOY *PLAYING* WITH MY FOOD!

361

FROM BEHIND THE WALLS OF CASTLE S'SHAH COME THE SOUNDS OF STRUGGLE...

...OF FAILURE...

...AND OF DEEP, FRIGHTFUL SOBS.

WHILE ON THE VAST PLAINS OF THE COUNTRYSIDE BEYOND...

NO, STRIPLING, HOLD YOUR LANCE LOWER! *LOWER!*

OH, YOU'LL NEVER GET IT RI--

THONK

--IIIIIGGHHTT!

ELGLIH?

ELGLIH!

ARE YOU OKAY? I-I DIDN'T MEAN TO--!

WORRY NOT, SIR SKYWALKER, I AM SORE-- BUT I AM WHOLE.

THOUGH I DO BELIEVE YOU'VE SUCCEEDED IN TEACH-ING THE *TEACHER!*

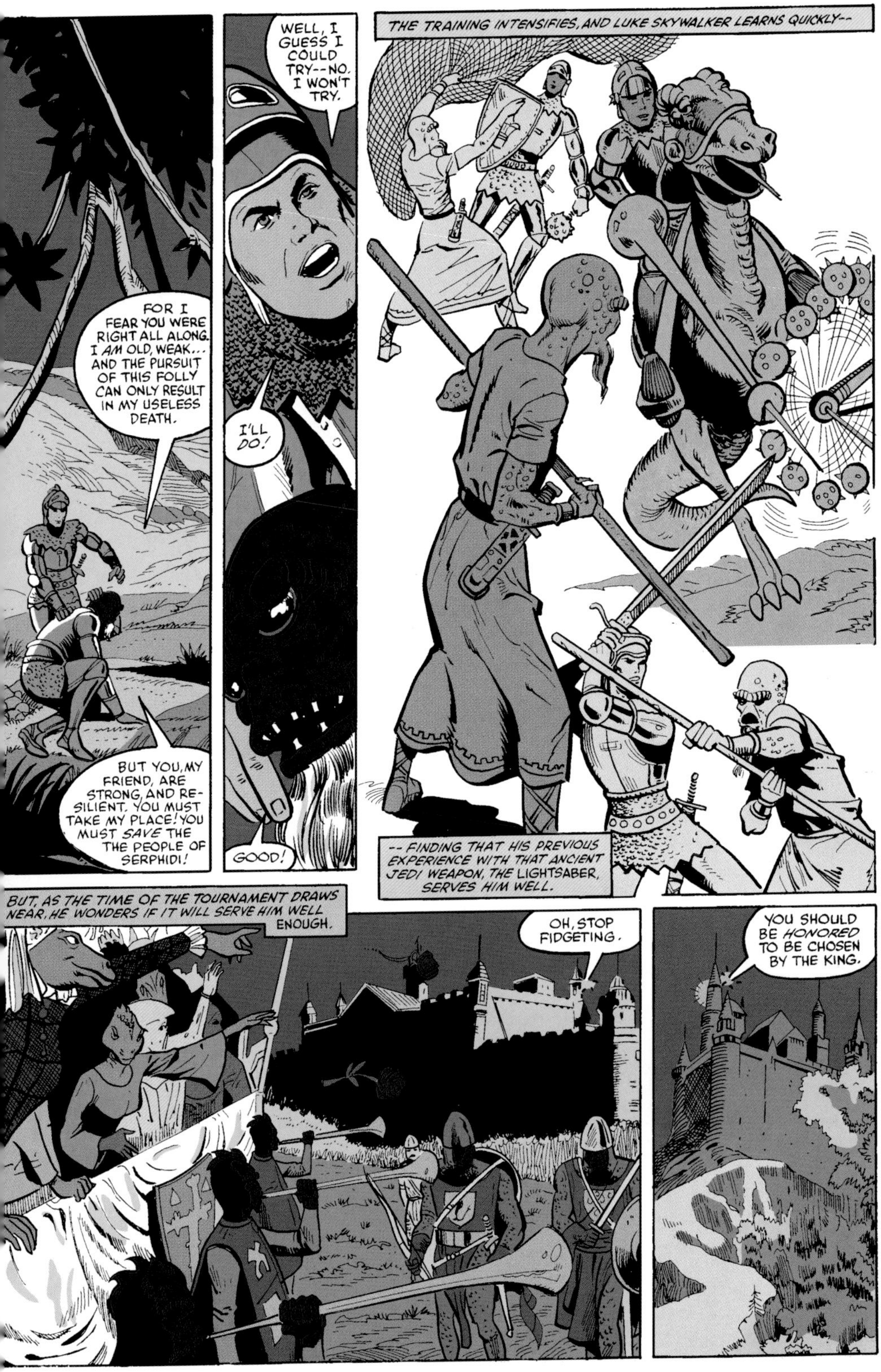
FOR I FEAR YOU WERE RIGHT ALL ALONG. I AM OLD, WEAK... AND THE PURSUIT OF THIS FOLLY CAN ONLY RESULT IN MY USELESS DEATH.
BUT YOU, MY FRIEND, ARE STRONG, AND RESILIENT. YOU MUST TAKE MY PLACE! YOU MUST SAVE THE THE PEOPLE OF SERPHIDI!
WELL, I GUESS I COULD TRY--NO. I WON'T TRY.
I'LL DO!
GOOD!
THE TRAINING INTENSIFIES, AND LUKE SKYWALKER LEARNS QUICKLY--
--FINDING THAT HIS PREVIOUS EXPERIENCE WITH THAT ANCIENT JEDI WEAPON, THE LIGHTSABER, SERVES HIM WELL.
BUT, AS THE TIME OF THE TOURNAMENT DRAWS NEAR, HE WONDERS IF IT WILL SERVE HIM WELL ENOUGH.
OH, STOP FIDGETING.
YOU SHOULD BE HONORED TO BE CHOSEN BY THE KING.

HONOR?! WHERE'S THE HONOR IN BEING STUCK BETWEEN THE SOUP COURSE AND DESSERT!

NOW, MISSY...

HOW GO THE PRE-PARATIONS? THE KING'S *CHEF* IS A PICKY ONE, Y'KNOW.

CH...CHEF? OH, NO!

NO!

LOOK OUT!

NO!

YOU LOOK OUT, YOU COLD-BLOODED SLIMEHOG--

--'CAUSE CINDA TARHEEL'S COMIN' THROUGH!

CHOK

?!

YUNGK--?!

I DIDN'T RISE TO THE RANK OF CAPTAIN IN THE ALLIANCE JUST TO END UP A *SIDE DISH* ON SOME SCALY-TONGUED MANIAC'S TABLE!

WHOCK

THAT TAKES CARE OF THE GUARDS! NOW TO REACH THE OUTER WALLS AND--

WELL DONE, HU-MAN!

EH--?

THERE IS *FIRE* BENEATH YOUR PALLID FLESH! I *LIKE* THAT!

¿UMF!¿

AND ONCE THE TOURNAMENT IS DONE, THAT FIRE SHALL BE MINE! AS WILL BE-- THOUGH PERHAPS WITH A BIT OF SALT--

--THAT *FLESH!*

OOOHHH...

THUNK

AND, SOMETIME LATER, AFTER THE KING AND HIS "GUEST" HAVE BEEN SEATED IN THE ROYAL REVIEWING BOX...

HEAR ALL! THE DOOM-JOUSTS OF SERPHIDI BEGIN! BRING FORTH THE FIRST, AND ONLY, CHALLENGER--

--ELGLIH OF HARMONY GLADE!

ER, D-DUE TO A RECENT INJURY, SIRE, I HUMBLY REQUEST--

--THAT MY CHAMPION BE AL-LOWED TO FIGHT FOR ME.

CHAMPION, EH? THEN LET US SEE THE PEASANT'S FACE!

¿GASP¿ TH-THAT'S NOT EVEN A SERP! IT'S--

LUKE!

CINDA!

SO, THE HUMANS ARE IN LEAGUE! IN THAT CASE--

-- I *ACCEPT* THE CHALLENGE!

AND SOON, ON THE FIELD OF BATTLE...

WARRIORS-- ENGAGE!

THIS GUY'S MORE EXPERIENCED THAN I AM, I'LL HAVE TO HIT HIM FIRST AND FAST, TAKE HIM OUT BE- FORE HE CAN--

BRAAP BRAAAP

--BLAST! HE BLOCKED MY ENERGY BOLT WITH HIS SHIELD! I'LL HAVE TO DO BETTER ON THE NEXT--

CLANGG!

--HUH? LOOKS LIKE THERE WON'T *BE* A NEXT RUN! S'SHAH'S FOLLOWING THROUGH WITH HIS SHIELD, HITTING MY LANCE AND KNOCKING ME OFF--

WHUMPF!

--B-BALA ?!

NOW HE'S MOVING IN FOR THE KILL! I'VE GOT TO SHOOT HIS MOUNT OUT FROM UNDER HIM, PUT US ON EQUAL--

366

--OH, NO! THAT IMPACT BROKE MY LANCE! IT'S NOT WORKING!

TOO BAD I CAN'T SAY THE SAME FOR *S'SHAH'S* WEAPON!

BRRRRAAAPP

BUT MAYBE I CAN STILL USE THE LANCE AS A SPEAR, KNOCK S'SHAH OUT OF THE SADDLE AND--

DIE, HUMAN!

--NO GOOD! HE'S TOO DETERMINED, TOO FIERCE!

UNLESS I WANT TO BECOME ONE WITH THE FORCE *PERMANENTLY*, I'D BETTER DO SOMETHING-- ANYTHING--

THAK!

--AND *FAST!*

S'SHAH WASN'T EXPECTING THAT-- ANY MORE THAN *I* WAS!

HE DROPPED HIS BLAST-STICK!

OKAY, KING, THE CHOICE IS YOURS: DO YOU GIVE UP-- OR DO I DO SOME-THING REAL *NASTY* WITH THIS LANCE?

I... I YIELD.

GOOD. THEN AFTER WE'VE BOTH CLEANED UP, MAYBE WE CAN SIT DOWN AND DISCUSS--

LOOK OUT, STRIPLING! THE CUR'S PULLING A *MICRO-JOLT* FROM HIS TUNIC!

WHA--?

PHHZZT

BRAAP!

IS...IS HE...?

AYE, LAD. THE KING IS DEAD! LONG LIVE--

--*FREEDOM!*

THE REINS OF POWER SHIFT SWIFTLY--AND BEFORE THE DAY IS OUT, THE SOUNDS OF CELEBRATION ECHO THROUGH THE CASTLE OF THE NEW MONARCH OF SERPHIDI...

BY RIGHTS, SIR SKYWALKER, IT SHOULD BE *YOU* WEARING THIS CROWN. AFTER ALL, IT WAS YOU WHO SLEW S'SHAH.

MAYBE, BUT I NEVER COULD'VE DONE IT WITH-OUT YOUR HELP. AND BE-SIDES--

--YOU CAN DO US *BOTH* THE MOST GOOD BY REMAINING KING, BY RULING YOUR PEOPLE WITH COMPASSION, WITH JUSTICE...AND WITH A STRONG BOND TO THE REBEL ALLIANCE!

YOU HAVE MY PLEDGE, SIR SKYWALKER... AND MY GRATITUDE.

PRESENTLY, TWO X-WING FIGHTERS LEAVE SERPHIDI, TAKING WITH THEM A PAIR OF VALIANT REBELS -- AND THE MEMORY OF A THIRD.

I ONLY WISH THAT *BERL* COULD HAVE BEEN AT THE CORONATION...

...THAT HE COULD'VE SEEN THE SMILING FACES, HEARD THE LAUGHTER.

-- I FEEL THE SAME WAY, BUT BERL JOINED THE REBELLION TO BRING FREEDOM TO THE GALAXY, AND I THINK HE'D BE HAPPY KNOWING THAT HE DIED ON A MISSION THAT SUCCEEDED, IN ITS OWN SMALL WAY, IN DOING JUST THAT.

I KNOW, CINDA--

I GUESS YOU'RE RIGHT, COMMANDER, AND I SUPPOSE, AT LEAST UNTIL THIS BLOODY WAR IS OVER--

-- THAT'S ALL *ANY* OF US CAN ASK.

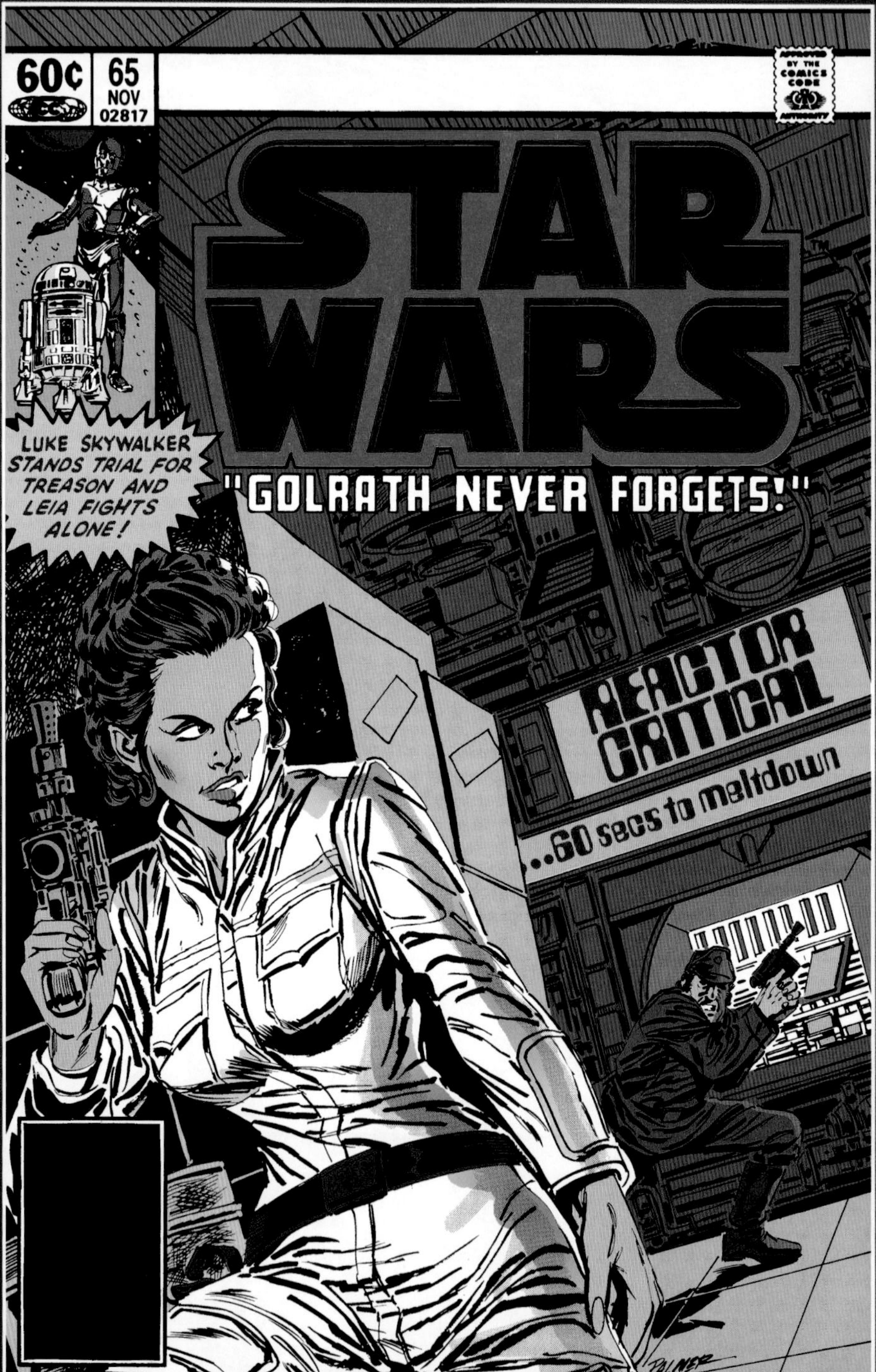
60¢
65
NOV
02817
STAR WARS
LUKE SKYWALKER STANDS TRIAL FOR TREASON AND LEIA FIGHTS ALONE!
"GOLRATH NEVER FORGETS!"
REACTOR CRITICAL
..60 secs to meltdown
PALMER

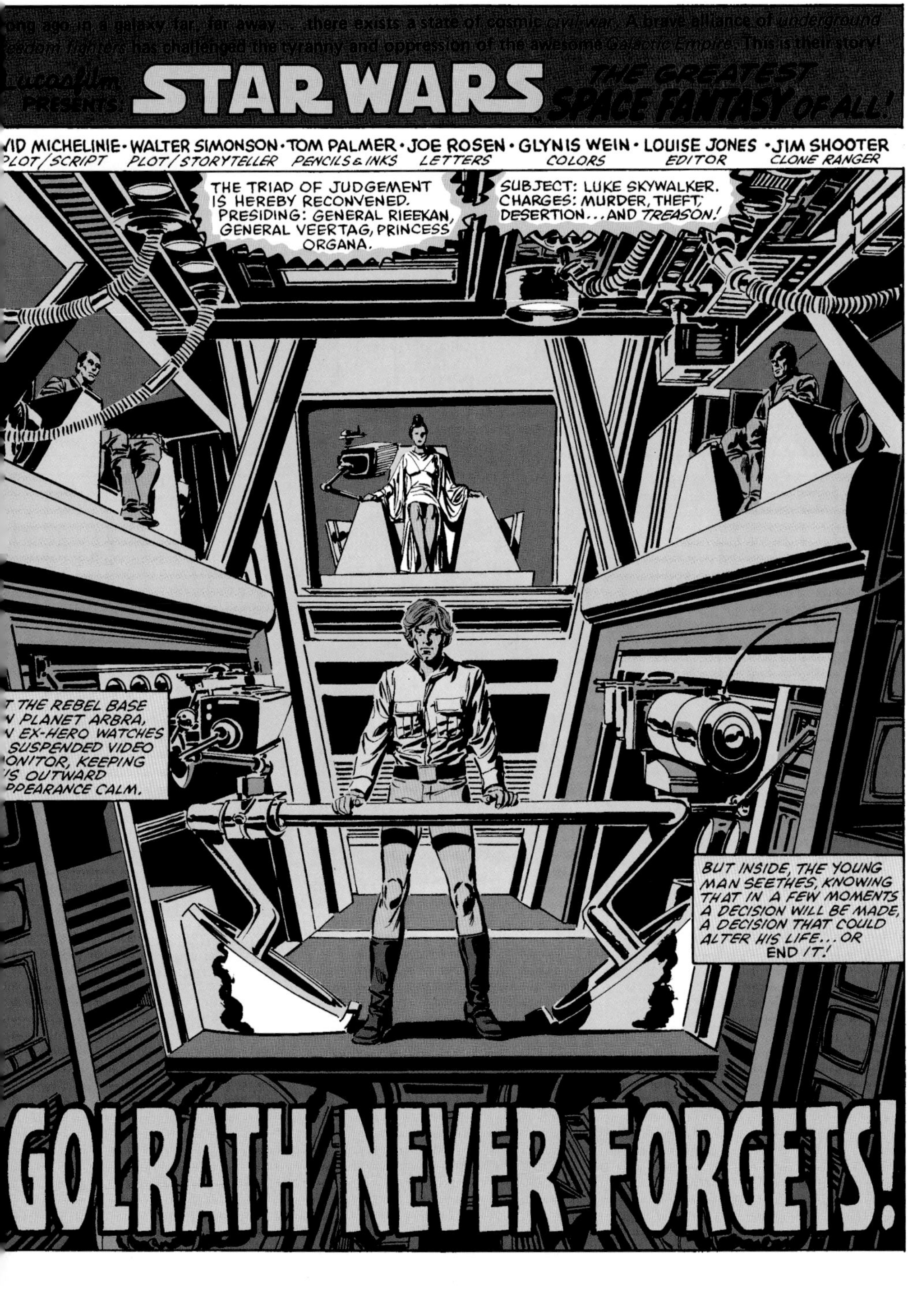
ong ago in a galaxy far, far away... there exists a state of cosmic civil war. A brave alliance of underground
eedom fighters has challenged the tyranny and oppression of the awesome Galactic Empire. This is their story!
PRESENTS: STAR WARS THE GREATEST SPACE FANTASY OF ALL!
VID MICHELINIE · WALTER SIMONSON · TOM PALMER · JOE ROSEN · GLYNIS WEIN · LOUISE JONES · JIM SHOOTER
LOT/SCRIPT PLOT/STORYTELLER PENCILS & INKS LETTERS COLORS EDITOR CLONE RANGER
THE TRIAD OF JUDGEMENT IS HEREBY RECONVENED. PRESIDING: GENERAL RIEEKAN, GENERAL VEERTAG, PRINCESS ORGANA.
SUBJECT: LUKE SKYWALKER. CHARGES: MURDER, THEFT, DESERTION... AND TREASON!
T THE REBEL BASE N PLANET ARBRA, N EX-HERO WATCHES SUSPENDED VIDEO ONITOR, KEEPING IS OUTWARD PPEARANCE CALM.
BUT INSIDE, THE YOUNG MAN SEETHES, KNOWING THAT IN A FEW MOMENTS A DECISION WILL BE MADE, A DECISION THAT COULD ALTER HIS LIFE... OR END IT!
GOLRATH NEVER FORGETS!

THE TRIAD HAS HEARD ALL EVIDENCE, BUT TO INSURE FAIRNESS WE WILL NOW REVIEW THE FACTS AS WE KNOW THEM: SEVERAL DAYS AGO, AS A COMMANDER IN THE REBEL ALLIANCE, MR. SKYWALKER WAS LEADER OF A VITAL MISSION--

--TAKING THREE OTHER PILOTS IN CAPTURED TIE-FIGHTERS ON A RAID AGAINST AN IMPERIAL ARMADA.

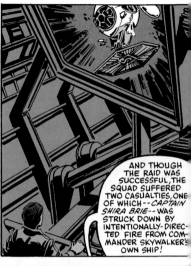

AND THOUGH THE RAID WAS SUCCESSFUL, THE SQUAD SUFFERED TWO CASUALTIES, ONE OF WHICH--*CAPTAIN SHIRA BRIE*--WAS STRUCK DOWN BY INTENTIONALLY-DIRECTED FIRE FROM COMMANDER SKYWALKER'S OWN SHIP!

CLAIMING THAT HE WAS DIRECTED BY THE FORCE TO DESTROY AN ENEMY, MR. SKYWALKER WAS STRIPPED OF RANK AND CONFINED TO THIS BASE PENDING AN INQUIRY.

HOWEVER, HE THEN STOLE A STARSHIP, AND, AS SEEN IN COMPUTER SIMULATION, PROCEEDED TO *SHALYVANE*, CAPTAIN BRIE'S HOMEWORLD--

--WHERE HE CLAIMS TO HAVE DISCOVERED A TRANSMITTER USED BY CAPTAIN BRIE TO PASS RESTRICTED INFORMATION ON TO THE EMPIRE.

MR. SKYWALKER THEN WENT TO THE IMPERIAL DATA VAULT ON KRAKE'S PLANET, TAPPED INTO TOP SECURITY FILE PROGRAMS--

--AND FOUND RECORDS THAT SHIRA BRIE HAD BEEN TRAINED AS AN *AGENT* OF THE EMPIRE FOR YEARS BEFORE JOINING THE REBELLION.

AFTER SUCCESSFULLY DESTROYING THE VAULT COMPLEX, MR. SKYWALKER THEN RETURNED TO ARBRA WITH A RECORDING CHIP BEARING THE FILE DATA HE HAD UNCOVERED. THAT DATA HAS SINCE BEEN VERIFIED.

AND THAT, GENTLEMEN, ENDS THE TESTIMONY GIVEN TO DATE. IF YOU'VE NO FURTHER QUESTIONS--

--PLEASE TENDER YOUR VERDICT.

THE TIME FOR THOUGHT IS OVER AS, SOLEMNLY, THREE JUDGES REACH OUT TO A SERIES OF PRESSURE-SENSITIVE DISCS SET INTO THE ARMRESTS OF THEIR CHAIRS, EACH TOUCHING ONLY ONE. AND THUS IS THIER IRREVOCABLE JUDGEMENT MADE, RECORDED--

--AND ANNOUNCED...

LUKE SKYWALKER, THIS TRIBUNAL FINDS YOU *NOT GUILTY* OF ALL CHARGES! IT FURTHER RECOMMENDS THAT YOU BE REINSTATED IMMEDIATELY TO THE RANK OF COMMANDER!

PRINCESS, GENERALS...

...I ACCEPT!

CONGRATULATIONS, SON. IT'S GOOD TO HAVE YOU BACK.

IT'S GREAT TO BE BACK, GENERAL!

WHOOP-HEY! THIS CALLS FOR A CELEBRATION!

I KNEW SKYWALKER WAS ALL RIGHT!

VA-DOOP!

HMPH! IF YA ASK ME, THE WHOLE HEARING WAS *RIGGED!*

AW, MILO, GO PLAY IN A FUSION REACTOR.

I'M SURE GLAD THE COMMANDER WAS CLEARED. WE NEED MEN LIKE HIM.

YEAH, THORBEN. I ÷YAWN÷ KNOW WHAT YOU MEAN.

'EY, C'MON, GEMMER, THE HEARING WASN'T *THAT* DULL.

SORRY ÷HAWUM÷--

--BUT I DIDN'T GET MUCH SLEEP LAST NIGHT.

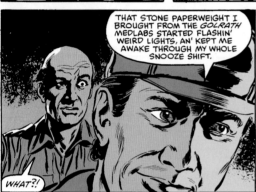

THAT STONE PAPERWEIGHT I BROUGHT FROM THE *GOLRATH* MEDLABS STARTED FLASHIN' WEIRD LIGHTS, AN' KEPT ME AWAKE THROUGH MY WHOLE SNOOZE SHIFT.

WHAT?!

YOU'D BETTER SHOW ME THAT LITTLE "SOUVENIR", MISTER! *NOW!*

UH, S-S-SURE--!

WHILE IN PRINCESS LEIA'S PRIVATE QUARTERS...

IT MUST HAVE BEEN HARD FOR YOU, LUKE-- GOING IT ALONE, BEING AN OUTCAST WHEN SOMEONE YOU CARED ABOUT HAD JUST DIED SO TRAGICALLY.

IT *WAS* HARD, LEIA. AND IT'S STILL HARD LIVING WITH THE TRUTH ABOUT SHIRA. BUT THERE IS SOMETHING THAT MAKES IT A LITTLE EASIER..

FRIENDS. *GOOD* FRIENDS.

CLOSE FRIENDS, LEIA.

LIKE YOU.

PREEEP

HUH?

SORRY TO INTERRUPT, PRINCESS, BUT WE HAVE AN EMERGENCY!

GO AHEAD, THORBEN.

I THINK YOU'D BETTER GET TO THE ANALYTIC LAB FAST! SOMETHING'S COME UP-- SOMETHING THAT COULD ENDANGER THE ENTIRE REBELLION!

WE'LL BE RIGHT THERE!

AND MOMENTS LATER, IN A CAVERN LAB...

SURE THING, DOC, I CAN ALWAYS GET ANOTHER PAPERWEIGHT.

THIS MACHINE WILL ANALYZE THE LIGHT IMPULSES THE STONE'S FACETS ARE GIVING OFF, THEN PROJECT AN IMAGE OF WHAT'S CAUSING THEM. THERE, THAT SHOULD DO IT!

YOU MEAN, THIS *ROCK* IS SUPPOSED TO BE SO DANGEROUS?

THAT'S WHAT DR. WELLA SAYS, PRINCESS.

ALL RIGHT, GEMMER, IF YOU'LL HAND ME THE STONE...?

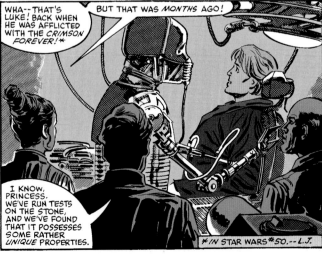

WHA--THAT'S LUKE! BACK WHEN HE WAS AFFLICTED WITH THE *CRIMSON FOREVER!**

BUT THAT WAS *MONTHS* AGO!

I KNOW, PRINCESS. WE'VE RUN TESTS ON THE STONE, AND WE'VE FOUND THAT IT POSSESSES SOME RATHER *UNIQUE* PROPERTIES.

IN STAR WARS #50.--L.J.

WHEN THIS PARTICULAR MINERAL IS HEATED, AS IT WAS ON VOLCANIC GOLRATH, IT ABSORBS LIGHT RAYS FROM AROUND IT.

BUT WHEN IT COOLS, IT RELEASES THOSE RAYS, JUST AS THIS PAPERWEIGHT HAS, PLAYING THEM BACK LIKE A HOLODRAMA!

AND WORSE, THE REASON THE PLANT WAS ABANDONED WAS THAT IT HAD STOPPED TURNING A PROFIT--BECAUSE THE WHOLE PLANET WAS *COOLING!*

THEN IF THE EMPIRE EVER FOUND OUT--!

LUKE! THORBEN! SCRAMBLE BLUE AND RED SQUADRONS AT ONCE! WE'RE HEADING FOR GOLRATH!

BUT THE ABANDONED MAGMA SMELTING PLANT WE TOOK OVER WAS *BUILT* FROM THAT ROCK! ITS WALLS MUST HOLD A LIVING RECORD OF EVERYTHING WE DID THERE--

--FROM VISUALIZATIONS OF CHARTS AND PLANS, TO THE COORDINATES FOR REACHING *ARBRA!*

THE REBEL PILOTS MOVE SWIFTLY, THEIR USUAL EFFICIENCY TINGED WITH AN URGENCY BORDERING ON DESPERATION.

FOR THEY KNOW, AS THEY LEAVE THEIR ARBRAN BASE, THAT THE ONLY HOPE OF AVERTING A MAJOR DISASTER IS FOR THEM TO REACH GOLRATH BEFORE THE EMPIRE.

WHAT THEY DON'T KNOW, HOWEVER, IS THAT THEIR HOPES ARE ALREADY IN VAIN.

FOR AT THAT MOMENT, AT THE DERELICT SMELTING PLANT ON GOLRATH--

--A METICULOUS SEARCH IS BEING CONDUCTED.

A SEARCH CARRIED OUT BY BLAST-ARMORED IMPERIAL STORMTROOPERS--

--AND OVERSEEN BY THE RECENTLY-DEMOTED LEFTENANT MILS GIEL...

I KNOW THIS INSTALLATION WAS ONCE A TEMPORARY REBEL BASE, LEFTENANT, BUT WHY IS IT IMPORTANT NOW?

IT *ISN'T*, SERGEANT MALKA. IT WAS UNIMPORTANT EVEN WHEN REPORTED SOME TIME AGO BY A SPECIAL AGENT PLANTED IN THE REBELLION. BUT *DARTH VADER* DOES NOT FORGIVE EASILY--

--AND EVER SINCE MY ARMADA LOST A SECRET WEAPON TO THE REBELS,* THE DARK LORD HAS SEEN FIT TO ASSIGN ME SUCH PEDESTRIAN DUTIES AS THIS.

*IN ISSUE #61.-- L.J.

BUT INSIGNIFICANT OR NOT, THE JOB SHALL BE DONE PROPERLY. IF THERE'S A SINGLE HINT OF THE REBELS' PLANS TO BE FOUND HERE, IT *WILL* BE FOUND.

BECAUSE, DEAR MALKA, I WANT MY ADMIRALTY BACK. AND SOME DAY, BECAUSE OF LORD VADER OR IN SPITE OF HIM--

--I SHALL *HAVE* IT!

377

TROOPER! WHAT HAVE YOU TO REPORT?

NOT MUCH, SIR. THE FERRET TEAMS HAVE BEEN OVER THIS ENTIRE COMPLEX, AND WE'VE FOUND NOTHING AT ALL TO CONNECT IT TO THE REBELLION.

THEN LOOK AGAIN. THE REBELS ARE ONLY HUMAN, AFTER ALL. THEY MUST HAVE LEFT SOME CLUE..

AND SO THEY HAVE! AS WITNESS, SEVERAL ROOMS AWAY...

YOU SURE IT'S OKAY TO BE GOOFIN' OFF LIKE THIS, CARLI? IF GIEL EVER FOUND OUT...

AW, THE HECK WITH OL' LEADHEAD. WHY SHOULD WE WASTE OUR TIME LOOKIN' FOR SOMETHIN' THAT AIN'T HERE?

WHY, THIS PLACE IS AS DESERTED AS--

--OH, MY GOSH! SCRAPER! LOOK!

WHAT THE--

--REBELS! A WHOLE ARMY OF 'EM!

A-AN' THEY'RE COMIN' STRAIGHT AT US!

BLAST 'EM!

SPRATCH

CHEEOW

FDOW·DOW

≈WHEW≈ GUESS THAT TOOK CARE OF-- HEY! WHERE'RE THE *BODIES?*

I DUNNO, SCRAPER! I-IT DON'T LOOK LIKE THERE *ARE* ANY!

WHAT'S GOING ON HERE? WE HEARD GUNSHOTS!

I-I'M NOT SURE, LEFTENANT! W-WE THOUGHT WE WERE BEIN' ATTACKED, BUT--

SIR! LOOK AT THESE WALL FRAG- MENTS!

HOW EXTRAORDINARY. THIS DEBRIS SEEMS TO HOLD IMAGES OF TRAIN- ING EXERCISES HELD WHEN THIS PLANT WAS A REBEL BASE!

I'VE NO IDEA HOW SUCH A FEAT HAS BEEN ACCOMPLISHED, BUT IF OTHER WALLS HOLD SIMILAR IMPRESSIONS...

MALKA! GET WORD OF OUR FIND TO VADER! AND HAVE OUR TIE FIGHTER ESCORT TAKE TO THE SKY AT ONCE! IF THE REBELS ARE AWARE OF THIS PHENOMENON, THEY'LL TRY TO DESTROY GOLRATH STATION--

-- AND MY CHANCES OF *PROMOTION,* ALONG WITH IT!

YES, SIR! RIGHT AWAY, SIR!

AND, MOMENTS LATER, AS A DOUBLE SQUAD OF X- AND Y-WING FIGHTER CRAFT SKIMS OVER THE BARREN SURFACE OF GOLRATH...

THE JUMP FROM HYPER-SPACE WAS MADE SUCCESSFULLY, PRINCESS. ALL SHIPS AC-COUNTED FOR.

FINE, LUKE. WE'LL MAIN-TAIN A LOW PROFILE ALL THE WAY TO THE SMELTING PLANT --JUST IN CASE.

GOOD IDEA, LEIA. YOU CAN NEVER BE TOO CAREFU--

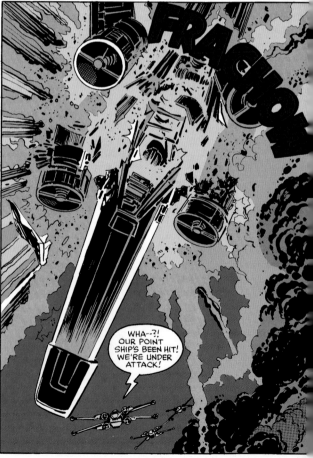

FRACHOW

WHA--?! OUR POINT SHIP'S BEEN HIT! WE'RE UNDER ATTACK!

TAKE EVASIVE ACTION IMMEDIATELY! THEN INSTIGATE ALTERNATE PLAN EPSILON-- MOVE ENEMY CRAFT CLEAR OF THE PLANT!

WHUMPH

--JUST AS SOON AS WE GET THESE JOKERS'--

RIGHT, LEIA--

--ATTENTION!

FOLLOWING A PREPLANNED STRATEGY, THE REBEL WARRIORS LEAD THEIR ATTACKERS NORTHWARD, AWAY FROM THE MAGMA SMELTING PLANT--

--AS ONE Y-WING BREAKS FORMATION, SWOOPING BACK TO THE VOLCANIC CRATER HOUSING THAT SELFSAME INSTALLATION--

--WHERE IT HOVERS JUST LONG ENOUGH FOR ONE CREW MEMBER TO DROP FROM AN ESCAPE PORT, GLIDING GENTLY, USING SHORT BURSTS FROM A ROCKET-POWERED PARABELT--

--TO CARRY HER OVER THE CRATER'S EDGE, TO FLOAT PAST THE LAKE OF BRITTLE, COOLING MAGMA, AND TO LAND SILENTLY ON THE BASE OF GOLRATH STATION, UNSEEN BY HUMAN EYES!

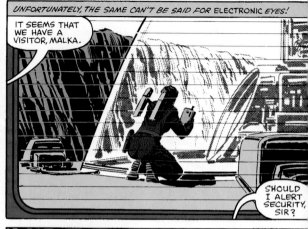

UNFORTUNATELY, THE SAME CAN'T BE SAID FOR ELECTRONIC EYES!

IT SEEMS THAT WE HAVE A VISITOR, MALKA.

SHOULD I ALERT SECURITY, SIR?

NO, THIS GUEST IS A SPECIAL ONE--AND SHOULD BE DEALT WITH IN A SPECIAL MANNER. HER PROBABLE TARGET IS THE REACTOR ROOM, SO STATION TWO GUARDS THERE AND HAVE ALL REMAINING PERSONNEL REMOVED TO THE COMMAND SHIP.

I SHALL HANDLE THIS SITUATION MYSELF!

SO FAR, SO GOOD! EVERYONE'S SO PREOCCUPIED WITH THE FIGHTER ATTACK--

--THAT NO ONE HEARD THE MICROCHARGE I USED TO BLOW A HOLE IN THE DOME!

LUKE? I'M IN! I'LL GIVE YOU ANOTHER BUZZ WHEN I'VE SET THE POWER REACTOR FOR OVERLOAD AND I'M READY TO BE PICKED UP!

OKAY, LEIA! TAKE CARE--

--AND GOOD LUCK!

FOR YOUR INFORMATION: AT THE IMPERIAL ACADEMY, STORMTROOPER BENS FIGG WAS TOP-OF-THE-HEAD-- HIGHEST TEST SCORES, BEST IN SPORTS, ALWAYS GOT THE GIRL.

CONSIDERED OFFICER MATERIAL FROM THE START, IT HAD BEEN GENERALLY ASSUMED THAT, AFTER HIS TOUR OF DUTY AS A ROOKIE TROOPER, HE WOULD BECOME THE YOUNGEST PERSON EVER TO JOIN THE EMPEROR'S PERSONAL STAFF.

IN FACT, IT SEEMED THAT FOR HIS EN- TIRE LIFE, ALL BENS HAD TO DO WAS WAIT, AND EVERYTHING CAME TO HIM. YES, SIR...

THRAK

...EVERYTHING!

ON THE OTHER HAND, BENS' ACADEMY ROOM- MATE, TABBINS VEE, HAD ALWAYS LIVED IN HIS FRIEND'S SHADOW, AS RUNNER-UP, NEXT BEST, A TAG-ALONG. MATTER OF FACT, IT SEEMED THAT WHATEVER CAME TO BENS FIGG ALWAYS CAME TO TABBINS VEE SECOND, WITHOUT FAIL.

CHOK

FUNNY, HOW SOME THINGS NEVER CHANGE...

ONLY TWO GUARDS. GUESS THE REST ARE BUSY WITH THE DOGFIGHTS UP TOPSIDE.

NOT THAT I'M COMPLAINING. NOT WHEN I'VE GOT A CLEAR SHOT AT THE REACTOR ROOM!

WHICH, UNLESS THE EMPIRE'S MADE SOME MAMMOTH CHANGES, SHOULD BE JUST BEYOND THESE BLAST DOORS.

PERFECT! NOW THAT I'VE FOUND THE REACTOR, ALL I HAVE TO DO IS LOCATE THE MASTER CONTROL CONSOLE AND--

--THERE IT IS! THE OVERLOAD DAMPER SHOULD BE THAT PULL-SWITCH JUST BELOW--

WHA-- LASERFIRE!

SHZAK

GOT TO DIVE BEHIND THOSE STORAGE CRATES!

YOU SHOW AN ADMIRABLE AGILITY, MY DEAR--

-- FOR AN EX-SENATOR! OH, YES, I RECOGNIZE YOU. YOU'RE LEIA ORGANA, PRINCESS OF THE ROYAL FAMILY OF ALDERAAN--

--AND *TRAITOR* TO THE EMPIRE! WHILE I, MADAM, AM LEFTENANT GIEL OF THE EMPEROR'S NAVY.

YOU MAY CALL ME "MILS"!

YOU'D BLUSH LIKE A NOVA IF I CALLED YOU WHAT I *WANTED* TO, MISTER! AND IF YOU THINK YOU'RE GOING TO STOP ME FROM BLOWING THIS STATION, YOU'RE CRAZY!

MY DEAR PRINCESS--

-- I'VE NO *INTENTION* OF STOPPING YOU! IN FACT, I'LL EVEN *HELP* YOU!

YOU... *WHAT?!*

THAT'S WHY I ALLOWED YOU TO GET THIS FAR. YOU'RE ONE OF THE PRIMARY LEADERS OF THE REBELLION--AND YOUR *DEATH* IN THE DESTRUCTION OF THIS COMPLEX WOULD DEAL A CRIPPLING BLOW TO YOUR FOLLOWERS' MORALE--

--EVEN MORESO THAN ANY INFORMATION WE COULD EXTRACT FROM THE STATION'S UNUSUAL BUILDING MATERIALS!

BUT IF THE REACTOR GOES CRITICAL, IT CAN'T BE RE-VERSED! YOU'D DIE YOURSELF!

MADAM, I AM AN IMPERIAL.

AND THE EMPIRE WOULD GAIN MUCH MORE FROM YOUR DEATH THAN IT POSSIBLY COULD FROM THE PRESENCE OF ONE MORE OFFICER. BESIDES...

...THERE ARE WORSE WAYS TO DIE THAN AS A *HERO* TO ONE'S CAUSE.

THAT'S SUICIDE!

OBSERVE.

SLAK

HE'S RELEASED THE OVERLOAD DAMPER!

AND NOW HE'S CLOSING THE BLAST DOORS--

WWWWW

--SEALING US *BOTH* INSIDE!

TIK

HE...HE'S *SERIOUS!*

DEAD SERIOUS!

IN THE FEAR-FRAUGHT SECONDS THAT FOLLOW, PRINCESS LEIA THINKS...THINKS HARDER... THEN BENDS AND BEGINS TO LOOSEN THE TIE-DOWN CORD ON HER HIP HOLSTER.

SO THAT, MOMENTS LATER...

ALL RIGHT, GIEL-- YOU'VE WON. THERE'S NO REASON FOR *BOTH* OF US TO DIE.

YOU ARE A NOBLE WOMAN, PRINCESS, AND--

--YOU ARE A *FOOL*!

HIS CONCENTRATION FOCUSED TOTALLY ON THE YOUNG WOMAN BEFORE HIM, LEFTENANT GIEL SLOWLY DRAWS HIS TRIGGER FINGER TIGHTER...

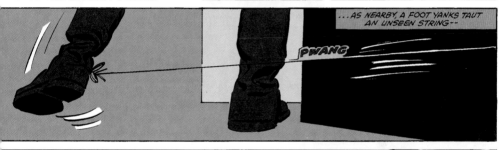

...AS NEARBY, A FOOT YANKS TAUT AN UNSEEN STRING--

PWANG

--ACTIVATING THE THRUST CONTROLS OF A PARABELT THAT HAS BEEN TIED SECURELY TO A CAREFULLY-POSITIONED LOADING DOLLY. AS A RESULT OF WHICH...

CLIK

VRRRRR

KRASH

EH--?!

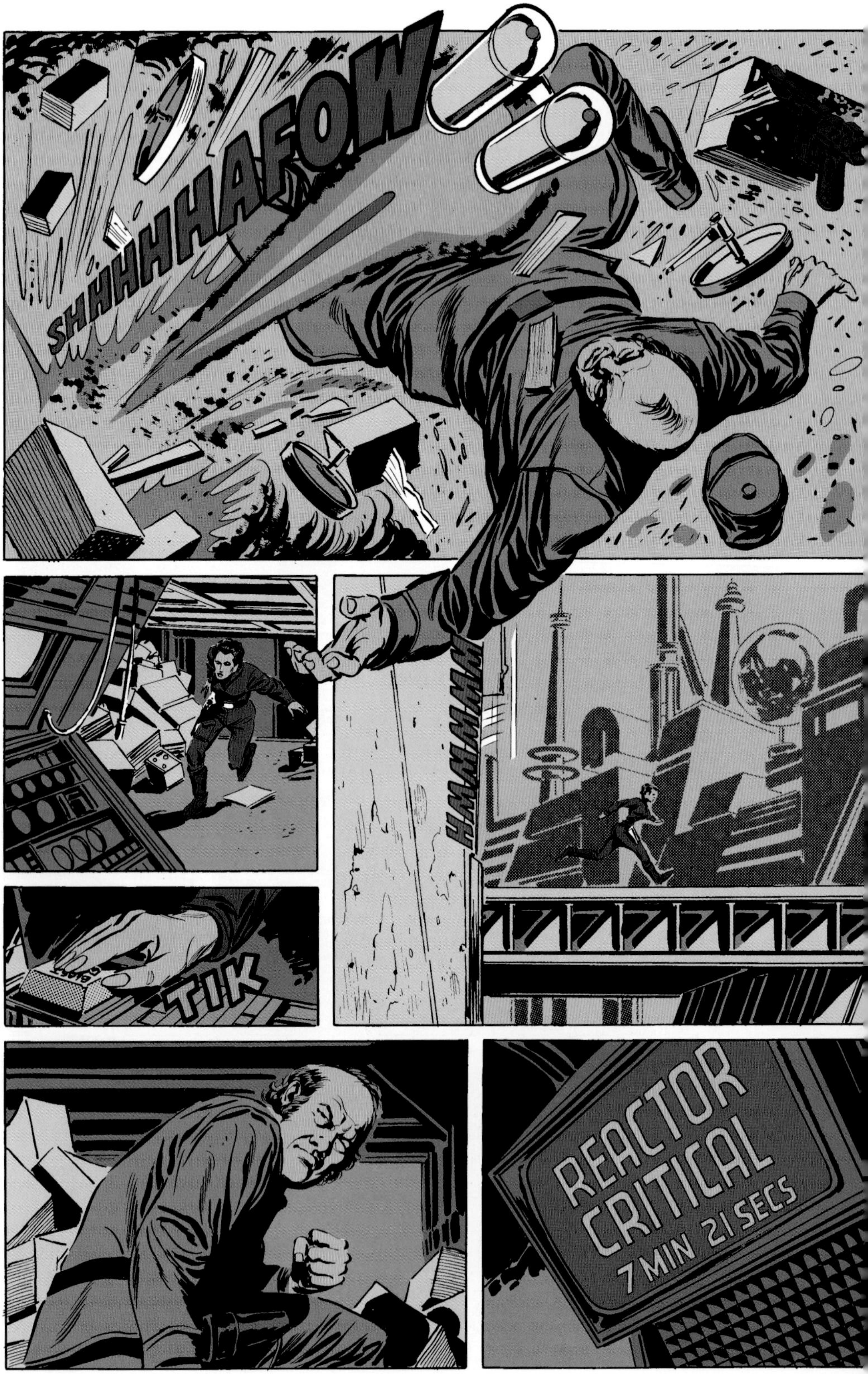
SHHHHHAFOW
HMMMMMM
TIK
REACTOR
CRITICAL
7 MIN 21 SECS

DAMN.

LUKE'S FLYIN' COVER FOR US, PRINCESS, AN' I'M STARTIN' MY APPROACH RUN! KEEP THAT HARNESS HOOK AS HIGH AS POSSIBLE!

OKAY, LANDO! STEADY...

...STEADY...

...CONTACT!

JUST HOLD ON, PRINCESS! THE WINCH'LL PULL YOU INSIDE IN NO TIME!

NICE PICK-UP, GUYS!

ANYONE...

...AT...

HMM. AN IMPOSSIBLE SHOT. THREE HUNDRED METERS AT LEAST.

AND BESIDES, ACTS OF *SPITE* NEVER DO ANYONE ANY GOOD.

SHRAK

...AAAAAHH!

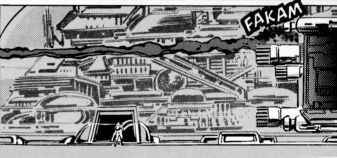

FAKAM

I'M LOATHE TO ADMIT IT, BUT I *DO* FEEL A LITTLE BETTER.

PILOT! PRIME YOUR CONVERTERS!

I ALREADY HAVE, SIR. I TOOK THE LIBERTY WHEN WE RECEIVED A MESSAGE FROM *DARTH VADER* A FEW MINUTES AGO.

HE CONGRATU-LATES YOU ON YOUR WONDERFUL FIND, AND WANTS YOU TO MAKE A PROG-RESS REPORT TO HIM PERSONALLY ABOARD HIS CRUISER.

THEN ORDER OUR FIGHTERS TO CON-TINUE AFTER THE REBELS, AND SET A COURSE FOR THE "EXECUTOR" AT ONCE. TOP SPEED.

AFTER ALL, WE DON'T WANT TO KEEP LORD VADER WAITING. OH, NO--

-- WE WOULDN'T WANT TO MAKE THE GENTLEMAN... *ANGRY.*

DAMAGE REPORT! ANYONE HURT?

I TOOK A SLIGHT HIT FROM A HAND BLASTER, LEIA-- NOTHING TO WORRY ABOUT. DID YOU SET THE REACTOR?

"LET'S JUST SAY *SOMEONE* DID! AND IF COMPUTATIONS ARE CORRECT, THE RE- SULTS SHOULD BECOME EVIDENT RIGHT ABOUT--

"--NOW!"

MISSION ACCOMPLISHED!

OKAY, SQUADS, LET'S HEAD 'EM HOME!

391

ENGINES WHINE, CONVERTERS ROAR, AND WITH A BENDING OF SPACE AND TIME, THE FLEEING REBEL STARCRAFT LURCH INTO THE WELCOME SANCTUARY OF LIGHT SPEED!

ALL, THAT IS, SAVE ONE...

HUH?!

...AN X-WING FIGHTER PILOTED BY A VERY SURPRISED LUKE SKYWALKER!

I...I'M STILL HERE!

MY ROCKET ENGINES ARE STILL FUNCTIONING, BUT THAT PISTOL SHOT MUST HAVE SHORTED OUT MY HYPERDRIVE UNIT! I CAN'T GO TO LIGHTSPEED!

I'M IN A CRIPPLED SHIP RUNNING FROM AN ENTIRE SQUADRON OF TIE-FIGHTERS! ALONE! DARN IT--

--THERE'S NEVER A HAN SOLO AROUND WHEN YOU NEED ONE!

NOTE: IF YOU'D LIKE TO SEE HAN SOLO, CHECK OUT THE 1982 STAR WARS ANNUAL, ON SALE NOW! AND IF YOU WANT TO SEE WHAT HAPPENS TO LUKE, BE HERE IN THIRTY FOR...

"The Water Bandits!"

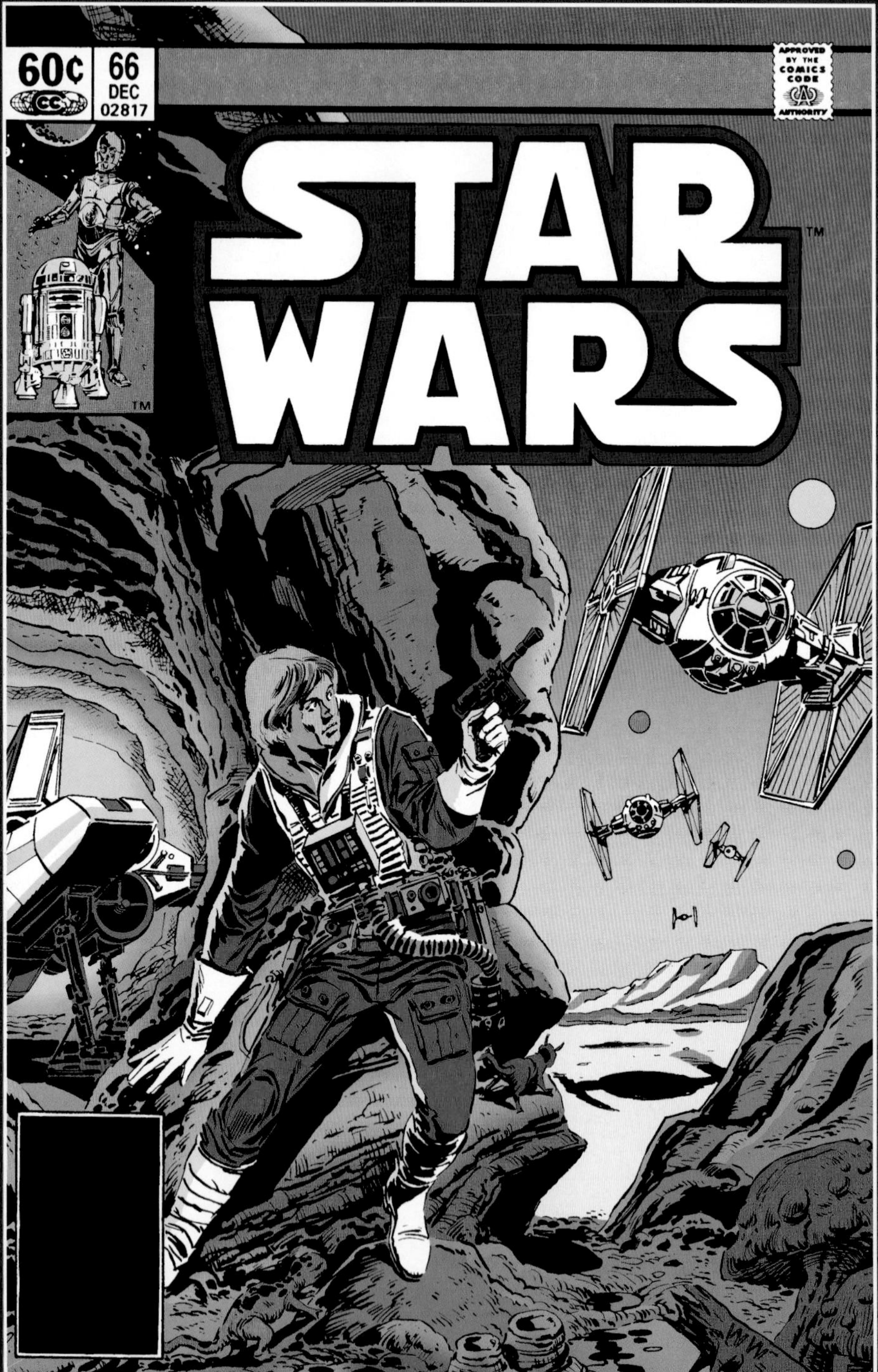
60¢
66
DEC
02817
APPROVED BY THE COMICS CODE AUTHORITY
STAR WARS™
TM

Long ago in a galaxy far, far away... there exists a state of cosmic civil war. A brave alliance of underground freedom fighters has challenged the tyranny and oppression of the awesome Galactic Empire. This is their story!

Lucasfilm PRESENTS: # STAR WARS — *THE GREATEST SPACE FANTASY OF ALL!*

| DAVID MICHELINIE WRITER | WALTER SIMONSON BREAKDOWNS | TOM PALMER FINISHED ART | JANICE CHIANG LETTERS | GLYNIS WEIN COLORS | LOUISE JONES EDITOR | JIM SHOOTER VAPORATOR MAINTENANCE |

THE RAID ON GOLRATH STATION HAD BEEN SUCCESSFUL, BUT RETALIATION HAD BEEN SWIFT. HORDES OF IMPERIAL **TIE-FIGHTERS** HAD CHASED THE REBEL ATTACKERS UNRELENTLESSLY--

--UNTIL MOST OF THE FLEEING SHIPS HAD ESCAPED INTO HYPERSPACE. BUT ONE X-WING, DAMAGED IN THE FIGHTING, HAD BEEN UNABLE TO MAKE THE JUMP.

AND THUS ITS PILOT, **LUKE SKYWALKER**, LEADER OF THE MISSION, HAD GUIDED HIS FIGHTER INTO THE BACKWATER SYSTEM OF **BEHEBOTH**, THINKING TO LOSE HIS PURSUERS ON ONE OF THAT SYSTEM'S INSIGNIFICANT AND ILL-POPULATED WORLDS.

IT HAD SEEMED A GOOD IDEA AT THE TIME...

BLAST!

THE WATER BANDITS!

LOOKS LIKE I'LL BE HERE LONGER THAN I EXPECTED.

THOSE IMPERIAL BLOODHOUNDS DON'T GIVE UP EASILY!

BUT AT LEAST I WAS ABLE TO FIND A HIDEOUT BIG ENOUGH FOR ME *AND* MY X-WING. SO AS LONG AS I KEEP A LOW PROFILE, AND RATION OUT MY EMERGENCY PROVISIONS, I SHOULDN'T HAVE ANY TROUBLE HANGING ON UNTIL THE EMPIRE LOSES INTEREST.

AND SPEAKING OF PROVISIONS, THAT FLY-BY INTERRUPTED MY LUNCH. AND I'M SO HUNGRY I COULD EAT--

--*SAND LICE?!* TH-THEY'VE GOTTEN INTO THE FOOD, THE WATER!

EVERYTHING'S *RUINED!*

GUESS I DON'T HAVE MUCH CHOICE, NOW. EITHER I LOOK UP THE LOCAL TRADING POST AND BARTER FOR GROCERIES--OR I DIE.

SO MUCH FOR PROFILE...

REGRETTING THE ABSENCE OF HIS FREQUENT DROID COMPANION, **ARTOO-DETOO**, COMMANDER SKYWALKER HAS SOME DIFFICULTY LOCATING THE NEAREST POPULATION CENTER.

BUT LOCATE IT, EVENTUALLY, HE DOES. AND SOON, IN THE BUSTLING DESERT OUTPOST OF **GARROTINE**...

MY LUCK'S HOLDING OUT...

BY LEAVING MY FLIGHT SUIT BACK AT THE CAVE, AND BUNDLING MY WEAPONS UP IN THIS SURVIVAL BLANKET--

--I'VE BEEN ABLE TO AVOID UNDUE ATTENTION FROM THE NATIVES.

AND, UNLESS THEY'VE CHANGED THE AROMA OF **BAKED BANTHA** SINCE THE LAST TIME I'VE HAD IT, THAT LOOKS--AND **SMELLS**-- LIKE JUST THE PLACE TO BUILD UP MY LARDER!

INSIDE...

YESSIR, CAN I HELP YA?

I SURE HOPE SO. I'VE COME FROM, UH, THE NORTH, AND I NEED FOOD AND WATER FOR A COUPLE OF DAYS' TRAVEL. DO YOU ACCEPT UNIVERSAL CREDITS?

THAT WE DO, SIR, AND THE FOOD'LL BE NO PROBLEM, BUT I'M AFRAID WE GOT NO **WATER** FOR STRANGERS.

WHAT?!

397

BUT YOU *HAVE* TO HAVE WATER! IT'S BASIC GALACTIC LAW! I COME FROM A DESERT PLANET MYSELF, AND EVEN IN THE HARDEST DROUGHTS WE SHARED WHAT WE HAD!

HEY, DIDN'T THAT FOOTER SAY HE CAME FROM THE NORTH?

YEAH! SO WHAT'S THIS ABOUT BEIN' FROM ANOTHER PLANET?

I'LL BETCHA HE'S ONE O' *THEM*!

GRAB 'IM!

HE'S A *BRIGAND*!

LOOK, THERE'S BEEN A MISTAKE! I'M NOT--

OH, GREAT! WHAT DID I DO NOW?

LIAR! WE'LL STUFF YER GUT FULL O' *SAND*, AN' SEE HOW *YOU* LIKE DYIN' DRY!

OKAY, I TRIED TO TALK THIS OUT! NOW *BACK OFF*--

~ULF!~

--AND I'LL JUST LEAVE WITHOUT ANY TROUBLE!

YOU'VE ALREADY *GOT* TROUBLE, FOOTER!

AN' MORE'N YOU CAN *LIVE* WITH, I'M BETTIN'!

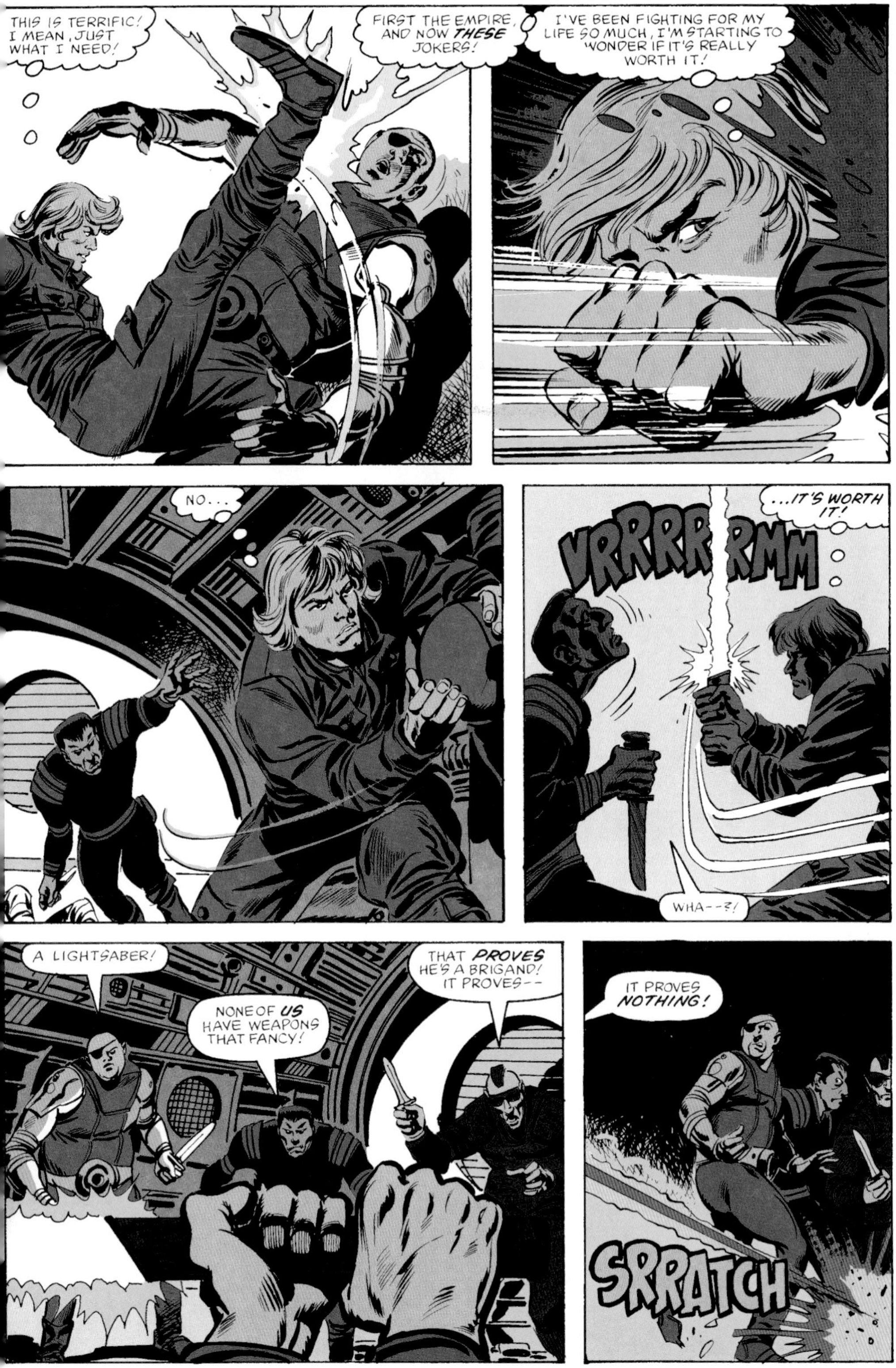
THIS IS TERRIFIC! I MEAN, JUST WHAT I NEED!
FIRST THE EMPIRE, AND NOW *THESE* JOKERS!
I'VE BEEN FIGHTING FOR MY LIFE SO MUCH, I'M STARTING TO WONDER IF IT'S REALLY WORTH IT!
NO...
VRRRRRRMM
...IT'S WORTH IT!
WHA--?!
A LIGHTSABER!
NONE OF *US* HAVE WEAPONS THAT FANCY!
THAT *PROVES* HE'S A BRIGAND! IT PROVES--
IT PROVES *NOTHING!*
SRRATCH

NOW LEAVE HIM ALONE!

B-BUT, *DARIAL!* HE'S--

HE'S A *STRANGER*-- AND THAT'S ALL WE KNOW!

FOR PITY'S SAKE, MAN, THE BRIGANDS HAVE TAKEN EVERYTHING ELSE FROM US-- WATER, COMMERCE, SOMETIMES OUR LIVES...

... LET'S NOT LET THEM STEAL THE COMMON DECENCY THAT'S ALL SOME OF US HAVE LEFT!

HE'S A WANDERER WHO'S DONE US NO HARM. I SAY WE RETURN THE FAVOR.

WELL, I DON'T KNOW...

I DO. DARIAL'S LED OUR FIGHT AGAINST THE BRIGANDS, AND HER FARM SUPPLIES US WITH MOST OF WHAT LITTLE WATER WE STILL HAVE. IF *SHE* TRUSTS THE FOOTER, THAT'S GOOD ENOUGH FOR ME.

AYE, AND ME.

THANKS, NEIGHBORS. I'M PROUD OF YOU.

ALL RIGHT, FRIEND, IF YOU'LL COME WITH ME, I'LL SEE THAT YOU GET OUT OF TOWN SAFELY.

AND OUTSIDE...

LISTEN, I REALLY APPRECIATE YOUR HELP. MY NAME'S LUKE.

UH, "LUKE THE FOOTER."

HI. I'M *DARIAL ANGLETHORN.*

I RUN THE BIGGEST MOISTURE FARM ON THE PLANET. THAT'S WHY I HAD SO MUCH PULL WITH THOSE FOLKS BACK AT THE INN.

THEY'RE MOSTLY FARMERS, TOO. OR AT LEAST THEY WERE BEFORE THE *BRIGANDS* ARRIVED.

JUST WHO ARE THESE "BRIGANDS", ANYWAY?

BANDITS. THEY RAID AT NIGHT, IN SOME WAY WE HAVEN'T FIGURED OUT. WE JUST WAKE UP, AND THE WATER'S GONE.

WORD IS, THEY BLACK MARKET THE STUFF FOR A FORTUNE.

I'VE BEEN LUCKY SO FAR-- MY PLACE HASN'T BEEN HIT. BUT I GUESS IT'S JUST A MATTER OF--

--HMM. NOW THAT I THINK OF IT, LUKE, YOU'RE PRETTY GOOD IN A FIGHT. HOW ABOUT SIGNING ON AS A GUARD? I PAY TOP WAGE.

THANKS, DARIAL, BUT I ALREADY HAVE A JOB. AND I REALLY CAN'T--

--AH, ON THE OTHER HAND, GETTING AWAY TO THE COUNTRY FOR A FEW DAYS MIGHT DO ME A *WORLD* OF GOOD. ¿AHEM¿

401

AND SOON, AS A WELL-WORN SANDSKIMMER SKIMS OVER THE ARID WASTES BEYOND GARROTINE...

Y'KNOW, LUKE, YOU DON'T *LOOK* LIKE A WANDERER. YOU'VE GOT A HARDER, A QUICKER *EDGE* THAN MOST FOOTERS.

WELL, UM...

...LET'S JUST SAY I'VE WANDERED SOME HARD AND QUICK PLACES.

MY, WHAT A POLITE WAY OF SAYING "MIND YOUR OWN BUSINESS!" OKAY, NO MORE QUESTIONS. ANY-WAY, WE'RE ALMOST--

--HOME!

THIS IS A *FARM?* IT LOOKS MORE LIKE A *FORTRESS!*

I KNOW. WE'VE HAD TO TAKE SOME RATHER EXTREME PRECAUTIONS SINCE THE BRI-GANDS SHOWED UP.

I'M IMPRESSED.

NO KIDDING! A FULL SQUAD OF IMPERIAL *STORMTROOPERS* WOULD HAVE TROUBLE GETTING PAST THIS OUTER WALL!

AND THE ONES WHO DID WOULD NEVER SURVIVE THE GUARDS AT THIS SECONDARY BARRACADE!

THIS IS A LOT FANCIER THAN THE MOISTURE FARM I GREW UP ON.

THANKS. I'VE PUT EVERYTHING I HAD INTO THIS SPREAD. THE TECHNOLOGY, THE EQUIPMENT, EVERYTHING IS THE BEST THAT CREDITS CAN BUY.

THESE *VAPORATORS*, FOR INSTANCE -- THEY TAKE MOISTURE DIRECTLY FROM THE ATMOSPHERE, CHEMICALLY INCREASE ITS RATE OF CONDENSATION --

-- THEN CHANNEL THE SOLIDIFIED WATER INTO STORAGE TANKS WHERE IT CAN BE MORE EASILY DISPENSED.

THAT'S THE SAME KIND OF OPERATION MY *UNCLE OWEN* AND *AUNT BARU* USED TO RUN -- BEFORE THE EMPIRE *MURDERED* THEM!

I'M FAMILIAR WITH THE EQUIPMENT, DARIAL --

-- BUT WHY DO YOU WANT *ME* TO PROTECT IT? YOU'VE ALREADY GOT MORE ARMED GUARDS THAN A BANKERS' CONVENTION ON *AARGAU!*

MAYBE. BUT I SENSE SOMETHING *SPECIAL* ABOUT YOU, LUKE. WILL YOU HELP?

I COULDN'T SAVE OWEN AND BARU BACK ON TATOOINE -- BUT MAYBE I CAN MAKE UP FOR IT HERE.

I'LL HELP, DARIAL. ANYWAY I CAN.

THE TOUR OF THE ANGLETHORN MOISTURE FARM CONTINUES, THEN CONCLUDES. AND AS NIGHT FALLS OVER THE VAST, WHISPERING DESERT, IT FINDS LUKE SKYWALKER SITTING, WATCHING... AND THINKING.

ACCORDING TO DARIAL, THE BRIGANDS ALWAYS HIT AT NIGHT, AFTER GUARDS AND WORKERS HAVE BEEN KNOCKED OUT. BUT NO ONE SEEMS TO KNOW HOW--

MIND IF I JOIN YOU, LUKE?

OH, HI, BOSS. SURE, PULL UP A ROCK.

THANKS. THE DESERT CAN BE BITTER AT NIGHT, AND I THOUGHT A MUG OF HOT CHAV MIGHT HELP CUT THE COLD.

SOUNDS GREAT!

TELL ME SOMETHING, PARIAL--FROM WHAT I'VE HEARD, IT SEEMS THE BRIGANDS MIGHT HAVE AGENTS *INSIDE* THE FARMS.

ARE YOU SURE YOU CAN TRUST ALL OF YOUR EMPLOYEES?

COMPLETELY.

EVERYONE WHO WORKS FOR ME WAS BORN ON THIS PLANET, AND THEY KNOW THAT THE ONLY WAY *ANY* OF US IS GOING TO SURVIVE IS IF WE ALL PULL TOGETHER.

WE'RE MORE THAN NEIGHBORS HERE--WE'RE A *COMMUNITY.*

IN FACT, WHEN I STARTED ORGANIZING RAIDS AGAINST THE BRIGANDS, I HAD MORE VOLUNTEERS THAN I HAD THINGS FOR THEM TO DO. AND THOUGH WE HAVEN'T BEEN SUCCESSFUL YET, I... I-I...

DARIAL! WHAT'S WRONG?!

I DON'T KNOW! S-SUDDENLY I FEEL... D-DIZZY! IT...A-A...

...UHHHNNN...

SHE'S COLLAPSED! AND THE GUARDS -- THEY'RE FALLING ALL OVER THE PLACE! BUT WHAT--

DO-NOT-FEAR.

A VOICE! INSIDE MY HEAD! A-AND NOW THINGS ARE...STARTING TO SPIN! WH-WHIRLING AROUND!

WE-DO-WHAT-WE-MUST. WE-WISH-YOU-NO-HARM. DO-NOT-FEAR.

I...I CAN SENSE A PRESENCE! S-SOMETHING... SOMEONE...!

G-GOT TO...FIGHT IT! K-KEEP MY...SENSES! CAN'T...C-CAN'T LET IT...

FTUMP

WHEW-- I FEEL LIKE AN IMPERIAL *WALKER'S* BEEN DOING A TOE DANCE ON MY--

--OH, NO!

WHAT HAPPENED?!

BRIGANDS! THEY HIT WHILE WE WERE UNCONSCIOUS! THEY'VE TAKEN EVERY DROP OF WATER WE HAD STORED!

AND THAT'S NOT THE WORST OF IT!

DARIAL'S GONE! EITHER SHE WOKE UP AND WENT AFTER THOSE THIEVING SCUM, OR... OR WORSE.

BUT WHERE COULD THEY HAVE TAKEN HER?

THEIR BASE IS IN THOSE MOUNTAINS, BUT YOU'LL NEVER GET TO IT!

AYE, WE'VE LOST A LOT OF GOOD MEN TRYING!

THEN I GUESS I'LL HAVE TO TRY HARDER--

BECAUSE I MADE A PROMISE--

--AND I'M GOING TO *KEEP* IT!

AND SO, SOMETIME LATER AFTER A SHORT RIDE AND A LONG CLIMB...

THE FARMERS MADE THEIR ATTACKS WITH VEHICLES, USING TRAILS.

BUT MAYBE BY GOING IN THE BACK WAY, OVER ROUGHER TERRAIN, I CAN SUCCEED WHERE PREVIOUS MISSIONS FAILED.

THAT IS, IF THE *CLIMB* DOESN'T KILL ME FIRST! -; UNGH -;

AT LEAST I'VE GOT THE BULK OF IT BEHIND ME, ACCORDING TO DARIAL'S FOREMAN, THE BRIGANDS' STRONGHOLD SHOULD BE SOMEWHERE AROUND--

--*THERE!*

TERRIFIC. NOW THAT I'VE LOCATED THE PLACE, ALL I NEED TO DO IS FIND A WAY INSIDE!

MAKE ONE MOVE, BOY, AND, YOU'RE FRIED FARMER!

I THINK I'VE FOUND ONE...

OBEDIENTLY--HAVING LITTLE CHOICE IN THE MATTER--LUKE IS LED THROUGH OUTER GATES, PAST TOWERING WATER STORAGE TANKS, AND INTO THE CENTRAL CITADEL...

... WHERE EVENTUALLY HE'S BROUGHT TO THE CRUDELY OPULENT CHAMBERS OF --

GIDEON LONGSPAR, BOY, AT YER SERVICE!

I'M YER HOST--AN' YER MASTER!

THERE'S DARIAL! AND MORE OF THAT SPARKLY STUFF FROM LAST NIGHT!

LUKE! WHAT THE DEVIL ARE YOU DOING HERE?!

CAN'TCHA SEE, SWEETY? THE KID'S COME TO RESCUE YA! HE'S A REG'LAR HERO!

ONLY I'M AFRAID HE'S GONNA BE DISAPPOINTED!

'CAUSE I GOT PLANS FOR YA M'SELF, LI'L LADY. YA BEEN A THORN IN MY SIDE FER TOO LONG--

--AN' YER ABOUT T'BE PLUCKED!

LEAVE HER ALONE, LONGSPAR! IF YOU WANT TO PUNCH ON SOMEBODY, WHY DON'T YOU TRY ME!

-- WHY WORK UP A SWEAT WHEN I GOT A MOUNTAIN FULL O' FOLLOWERS T'DO MY PUNCHIN' *FOR* ME?

SORRY, BOY, BUT YOU AIN'T NEAR AS *CUTE* AS THE LADY! AN' BESIDES--

YES. HE'S -QUITE- GOOD -AT -HAVING -OTHERS -PERFORM -UNPLEASANT -TASKS.

THAT VOICE! IT'S THE SAME ONE I HEARD LAST NIGHT!

AYE, BOY, THAT'D BE THE *TIRRITH*, OR AT LEAST PART OF IT. THE REST I GOT IN THIS VACUUM BOTTLE-- WHICH JUST HAPPENS T'BE CONNECTED TO A PROTON GENERATOR!

LONGSPAR WAS TALKING--OR RATHER, GLOATING--ABOUT THE TIRRITH WHEN YOU ARRIVED, LUKE.

HE SAYS THE CREATURE IS AN *EMPATHIC CULTURE.* THAT IS, WHAT ONE SEGMENT FEELS, THE ENTIRE UNIT FEELS.

--AND NOW GIDEON KEEPS PART OF IT IN HIS GLASS CAGE, THREATENING TO HARM OR KILL IT IF THE OTHER PART DOESN'T DO WHAT HE COMMANDS!

WHEN THE BRIGAND HEARD OF THE CREATURE, THEY CAPTURED IT--

"AND THAT'S HOW THE BRIGANDS GOT INTO OUR FARMS! THE TIRRITH, BEING SOLELY COMPOSED OF ENERGY MIST, ALLOWED ITSELF TO BE DRAWN INTO VAPORATORS ALONG WITH THE MOISTURE IN THE AIR.

"AND ONCE INSIDE, IT REACTED WITH THE CONDENSATION CHEMICALS TO RELEASE A COLORLESS, ODORLESS GAS THAT RENDERS HUMANS UNCONSCIOUS!

"AFTER THAT, ALL THE BRIGANDS HAD TO DO WAS STEP OVER THE SLEEPING GUARDS AND TAKE WHAT THEY WANT!"

PLEASE-FORGIVE-US. WE-HAD-NO-CHOICE-IN-OUR-ACTIONS...

DON'T WORRY, TIRRITH, WE UNDERSTAND. IT'S HARD TO STAY CLEAN--

--WHEN YOU'VE GOT SLIME ON YOUR BACK!

BOY, I SUGGEST YA WATCH YER TONGUE...

...WHILE YA'VE STILL GOT ONE!

ARMS MEN! TAKE 'EM TO THEIR CELL!

OBEYING THE SHARPLY-BARKED ORDERS, ROUGH HANDS LEAD REBEL FIGHTER AND HEADSTRONG FARMER--

--TO A DIRTY, DARK-CORNERED ROOM DEEP WITHIN THE BRIGAND FORTRESS. WHERE SOO.....

I'M SORRY I GOT YOU INTO THIS, LUKE.

THAT'S OKAY, DARIAL--

-- I'VE BEEN IN TOUGHER SPOTS.

I CAN'T *THINK* OF THEM OFFHAND, BUT I'M SURE--

PERHAPS-WE-CAN-HELP?

TIRRITH!

WE-HAVE-NO-SOLID-FORM. WE-CANNOT-DO-BATTLE-BUT-WE-CAN-OFFER-DISTRACTION.

LOOK.

YOU-CAN-BREAK-DOWN-THE-DOOR? ESCAPE-WHILE-YOUR-WATCHERS-ARE-OCCUPIED?

LUKE! PART OF THE TIRRITH IS BUZZING AROUND THE GUARDS, CONFUSING THEM!

NO! THE DOOR'S TOO STRONG! WE'D NEVER GET THROUGH IN TIME! BUT THERE MIGHT BE *ANOTHER* WAY!

STRUGGLING TO CONCENTRATE, LUKE SKYWALKER REACHES OUT WITH HIS WILL,--

--SUMMONING *THE FORCE*, THAT ELEMENTAL ENERGY THAT PERMEATES ALL THINGS.

AND, ALMOST MIRACULOUSLY, THE BOLT ON THE RESTRAINING DOOR BEGINS TO QUIVER...

...TO MOVE...

...TO OPEN!

H-HOW THE DEVIL DID YOU DO *THAT?!*

PRACTICE!

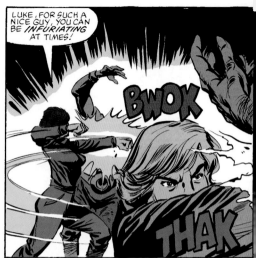

LUKE, FOR SUCH A NICE GUY, YOU CAN BE *INFURIATING* AT TIMES!

BWOK

THAK

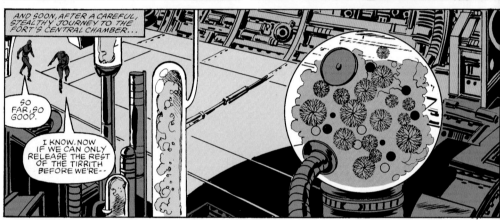

AND SOON, AFTER A CAREFUL, STEALTHY JOURNEY TO THE FORT'S CENTRAL CHAMBER...

SO FAR, SO GOOD.

I KNOW. NOW IF WE CAN ONLY RELEASE THE REST OF THE TIRRITH BEFORE WE'RE--

...SPOTTED?

TOSS THEM WEAPONS AWAY, GRUBBERS, OR I'LL SPLIT YA FROM GULLET TO GIZZARD!

LONGSPAR! WITH MY *LIGHTSABER!*

AYE, WHEN WE FOUND YER GUARDS CLOBBERED, I FIGURED YA'D HEAD THIS WAY. AN' AS FOR YER PIG-STICKER HERE--

--I AIN'T SEEN ONE O' THESE SINCE THE WARS! BUT I'LL JUST BET--

--I CAN FIGURE OUT HOW TO *USE* IT REAL QUICK!

VRRRRAMP

STAY BACK, DARIAL!

NO SENSE IN BOTH OF US GETTING SLICED TO BITS! THOUGH IF I WANT TO STAY IN ONE PIECE MYSELF, I'D BETTER *TRICK* LONGSPAR--

VRRANK

-- BY KEEPING HIM SWINGING WILD, THEN MOVING HIM INTO A POSITION WHERE THAT MEAT CLEAVER HACKING OF HIS WILL DO SOME--

VRRRAKASH

--GOOD!

WE-ARE-UNITED.

WE-ARE-ONE.

WE-ARE-FREE.

WELL, BLESS MY BLOODIED SOUL...

WHADAK

HE FELL FOR IT, LUKE! NICE GOING!

THANKS, BUT IT'S NOT OVER YET! THIS COMMOTION IS BOUND TO LET THE GUARDS KNOW WHERE WE ARE! LET'S GO!

BUT, OUTSIDE...

BLAST! THEY WERE WAITING FOR US! AND WE'RE OUT-NUMBERED TEN-TO-ONE!

WHAT'LL WE DO NOW?

YOU-MUST-SHOOT-THE-WATER-TANKS. FLOOD-YOUR-ENEMIES. THEY-WILL-FALL.

WHAT?! B-BUT, I *CAN'T* DO THAT!

THAT'S *WATER* WE'RE TALKING ABOUT! MY PEOPLE NEED IT, EVEN FROM A BLACK MAR-KET! WITHOUT IT, THEY'LL *DIE!*

WE-ARE-A-CREATURE-OF-LIFE. WE-WILL-NOT-LET-YOUR-FELLOWS-PERISH.

TRUST-US.

TRUST 'IM!

AND THUS IT IS THAT DARIAL ANGLE-THORN MUST REACH TO THE DEPTHS OF HER SPIRIT, SEARCHING FOR COURAGE AMONGST THE FEAR AND UNCER-TAINTY THAT COIL THERE.

SEARCHING FOR SUPPORT FROM HER BELIEF THAT THERE *IS* GOOD IN THE UNIVERSE.

SEARCHING...

...AND AT LAST...

SHAKOW

...FINDING!

CRATCH

KRHHHH SSSSHHHHHH

SHALOOOOOSSHH

LOOK OUT--!

AIIEEEE!

YYAAAAGH!

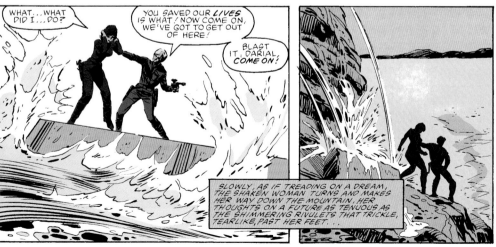

WHAT...WHAT DID I...DO?

YOU SAVED OUR *LIVES* IS WHAT! NOW COME ON, WE'VE GOT TO GET OUT OF HERE!

BLAST IT, DARIAL, COME ON!

SLOWLY, AS IF TREADING ON A DREAM, THE SHAKEN WOMAN TURNS AND MAKES HER WAY DOWN THE MOUNTAIN, HER THOUGHTS ON A FUTURE AS TENUOUS AS THE SHIMMERING RIVULETS THAT TRICKLE, TEARLIKE, PAST HER FEET...

415

EPILOGUE: DAYS LATER, AFTER REPAIRS TO THE ANGLETHORN MOISTURE FARM HAVE BEEN COMPLETED—AND, MORE SIGNIFICANTLY, AFTER IMPERIAL HUNT TEAMS HAVE DEPARTED THE AREA...

EVEN WITH THE VAPORATORS FIXED, THINGS ARE GOING TO BE TOUGH WITH NO WATER STOCKPILED. I... I DON'T KNOW IF WE'LL MAKE IT.

WORRY-NOT.

I HAVE TO LEAVE, DARIAL.

I COULD STILL USE YOUR HELP, LUKE

TIRRITH!

YOUR-TRUST-HAS-NOT-BEEN-BETRAYED. EVEN-NOW-PART-OF-OUR-SUBSTANCE-ENTERS-THE-CLOUDS-OVERHEAD.

IT-WILL-SOON-SPARK-ELECTRICAL-IMPULSES-WITHIN-THOSE-CLOUDS-AND--

RAIN! I-IT'S STARTING TO RAIN! BUT IT HASN'T RAINED HERE IN YEARS!

IT'S THE TIRRITH HE SEEDED THE CLOUDS! FROM NOW ON, DARIAL, YOU HAVE ALL THE WATER YOU WANT

AWED FACES TURN UPWARD, SMILING INTO THE GENTLY FALLING DROPLETS...

...LEAVING AN IMAGE THAT AN EQUALLY-SMILING STAR WARRIOR WILL REMEMBER FOR A LONG, LONG TIME.

THE DUEL BEGINS!

LIGHTSABER CLASH ON THE STEPS OF CLOUD CITY'S CARBON-FREEZING CHAMBER, AS CAPTURED BY *FRANK MILLER*, ARTIST/WRITER OF *DAREDEVIL!*

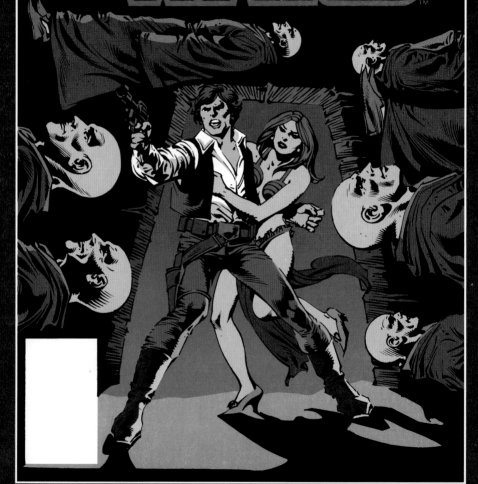

$1.00
2
1982
02551

KING-
SIZE
ANNUAL!

ALL
NEW!

STAR
WARS
™

Lucasfilm
PRESENTS:
STAR WARS

SHADESHINE!

BY
DAVID MICHELINIE
SCRIPTER
CARMINE INFANTINO
PENCILER
RUDI NEBRES
INKER
ROSEN & CHIANG
LETTERERS
GEORGE ROUSSOS
COLORIST
JIM SALICRUP
EDITOR
JIM SHOOTER
WORD SPEEDER

OR LUKE SKYWALKER, *...*ANDO CALRISSIAN *AND* *...*E SHUFFLING TRANS-*...*TOR DROID, C-3PO, *...*L NEWLY-LANDED ON *...*E PRIMITIVE PLANET *...*LLED VENTOOINE--

-- THINGS ARE NOT GOING WELL!

KILL THEM!

HURRY! THOSE IMPERIAL STORM-TROOPERS ARE GETTING CLOSER!

I DO APOLOGIZE, MASTER LUKE, BUT MY MOBILITY CIRCUITS JUST WEREN'T DESIGNED FOR HAIRBREADTH ESCAPES!

THEN MAYBE WE CAN LOSE 'EM BY DUCKING INTO THIS BUILDING!

*...*E'D BETTER! *...*HEN WE SET *...*T TO INVESTI-*...*TE RUMORS *...*F AN INCREDIBLE *...*WER SOURCE *...*N VENTOOINE--

--WE NEVER STOPPED TO THINK THAT THE *EMPIRE* MIGHT BE CHECK-ING OUT THE SAME RUMORS!

SO LET'S JUST HOPE THOSE BLOODHOUNDS GET TIRED OF LOOKING--AND *WE* DON'T RUN INTO ANY MORE SURPRISES!

I- I'M AFRAID, MASTER LUKE--

--THAT WE ALREADY *HAVE!*

THE REBELS TURN, FACING THE INTERIOR OF WHAT WAS ONCE A MAJESTIC TEMPLE, BUT WHICH HAS NOW FALLEN TO RUBBLE AND RUIN.

SAVE, THAT IS, FOR A SINGLE, DUSTLESS MONUMENT, A STATUE IN GLITTERING GOLD THAT JUTS DEFIANTLY FROM THE TEMPLE FLOOR, AN ICON CARVED IN A SEMBLANCE THAT IS AT ONCE HAUNTING... AND IMPOSSIBLY FAMILIAR!

I–IT'S HAN!

HAN SOLO!

I DON'T GET IT! HAN NEVER TOLD *ME* HE'D BEEN TO VENTOOINE!

AND WHY WOULD ANYONE BUILD A STATUE OF A SPICE-SMUGGLER-TURNED-REBEL-HERO?

MIGHT I REMIND YOU, SIR, THAT THOSE STORM-TROOPERS ARE STILL--

PLEASE, GOOD SIRS, YOU WILL TELL ME WHY YOU ARE COME TO THIS PLACE!

HUH?

WHO ARE YOU?

I AM *VETTER PIIN*, A ROV OF THE CHURCH, AND CARETAKER TO THIS SHRINE.

NOW, YOU WILL TELL ME WHY YOU COME, PLEASE.

YOU DO SPEAK GALAXY STANDARD?

SURE, WE'RE SPEAKING IT NOW. AND, UH, WELL, WE'VE COME TO PAY HOMAGE TO YOUR STATUE. ER, *SHRINE!*

HMM, YES, NOW THAT I AM *CLOSER*, I SEE MORE THE LIKENESS. YOU ARE OF THE SAME SPECIES AS OUR SAVIOR.

"SAVIOR"?

HAN?!

YOU'RE KIDDING...

421

NOT AT ALL. THIS SHRINE IS DEDICATED TO HE WHO SAVED OUR PEOPLE FROM THE EVIL REIGN, AND FROM THE DEADLY CURSE OF THE *SHADESHINE!*

"SHADESHINE"? LUKE, THAT'S THE WEAPO--UM, THE ITEM WE CAME LOOKING FOR! CAN YOU TELL US ANY MORE, MR.--; THAT IS, ROV PIIN?

OF COURSE. IT IS MY PLACE AND PRIVILEGE TO RECOUNT THE TALE OF SALVATION TO ALL PILGRIMS WHO DESIRE OF IT.

WELL, *I'D* THINK THAT A WAY OFF THIS UNPLEASANT LITTLE PLANET WOULD BE OF MORE USE TO US THAN SOME PROVINCIAL FAIRY TALE! IF YOU ASK ME--

THREEPIO ...HUSH!

PERHAPS, BEING OF THE SAME SPECIES, YOU WOULD FIND HEARING THE LEGEND IN OUR SAVIOR'S OWN WORDS MORE MOVING, EH?

COME...

WAIT A MINUTE! HAN IS FROZEN IN CARBONITE, A PRISONER OF BOBA FETT! HOW COULD HE POSSIBLY--

SHRRMM

YOU CAN'T IMAGINE HOW SILLY I FEEL TALKIN' INTO A *ROCK!*

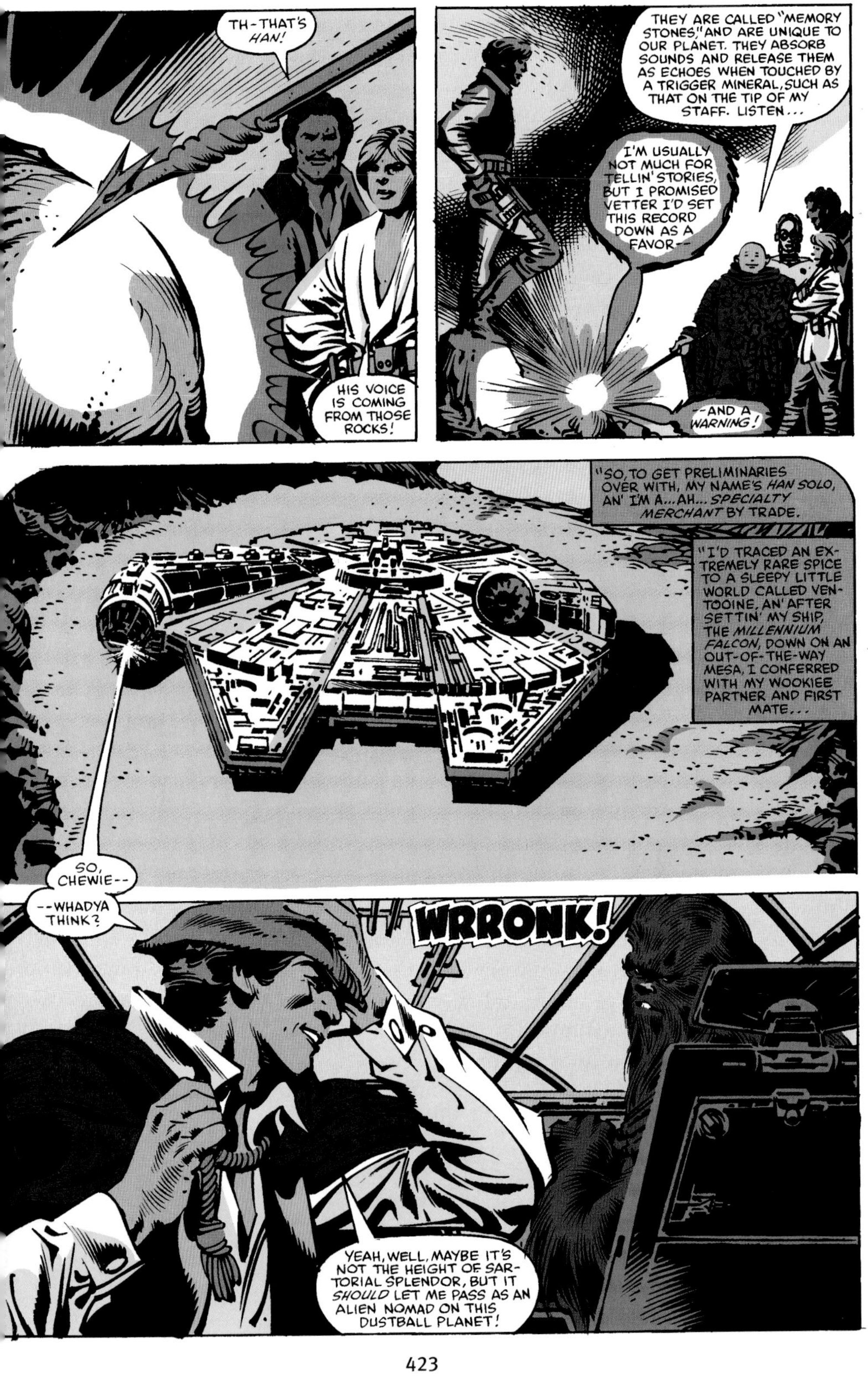
TH-THAT'S HAN!
HIS VOICE IS COMING FROM THOSE ROCKS!
THEY ARE CALLED "MEMORY STONES," AND ARE UNIQUE TO OUR PLANET. THEY ABSORB SOUNDS AND RELEASE THEM AS ECHOES WHEN TOUCHED BY A TRIGGER MINERAL, SUCH AS THAT ON THE TIP OF MY STAFF. LISTEN...
I'M USUALLY NOT MUCH FOR TELLIN' STORIES, BUT I PROMISED VETTER I'D SET THIS RECORD DOWN AS A FAVOR--
--AND A WARNING!
"SO, TO GET PRELIMINARIES OVER WITH, MY NAME'S HAN SOLO, AN' I'M A...AH... SPECIALTY MERCHANT BY TRADE.
"I'D TRACED AN EXTREMELY RARE SPICE TO A SLEEPY LITTLE WORLD CALLED VENTOOINE, AN' AFTER SETTIN' MY SHIP, THE MILLENNIUM FALCON, DOWN ON AN OUT-OF-THE-WAY MESA, I CONFERRED WITH MY WOOKIEE PARTNER AND FIRST MATE...
SO, CHEWIE--
--WHADYA THINK?
WRRONK!
YEAH, WELL, MAYBE IT'S NOT THE HEIGHT OF SARTORIAL SPLENDOR, BUT IT SHOULD LET ME PASS AS AN ALIEN NOMAD ON THIS DUSTBALL PLANET!

AND IF WE CAN DIG UP A GOOD SUPPLY OF *SANSANNA* AROUND HERE, WE'LL BE ABLE TO HIRE THE BEST TAILORS IN THE GALAXY!

THAT STUFF'S SO RARE IT'S BEEN TAXED OUT OF EXISTENCE IN FOUR-TEEN SYSTEMS! NOT THAT A LITTLE THING LIKE *TARIFFS* EVER STOPPED US, EH, BUDDY?

VHRROORP

SORRY, CHEWBACCA, BUT A 7½-FOOT SIDE-KICK MIGHT DRAW UN-WANTED ATTENTION IN THESE PARTS—I'LL HAVE TO GO THIS ONE ALONE.

SEE YA IN A COUPLA DAYS!

"IF I'D KNOWN WHAT I WAS GETTIN' INTO, I'D NEVER HAVE LEFT CHEWIE BEHIND.

"BUT THEN, HIND-SIGHT ONLY COUNT IN MEMOIRS.

"SO, BLISSFULLY IGNORANT, I HEADED FOR THE NEAREST SETTLEMENT.

"TURNS OUT IT WAS A BURG CALLED 'GOYOIKIN', THE CAPITAL OF THE ONLY INHABITED CONTINENT ON VENTOOINE. A PLEASANT ENOUGH PLACE, I SUPPOSE. BUT AS I WAS GETTIN' READY TO ASK DIRECTIONS—

"--I CAUGHT SIGHT O' SOMETHIN' THAT SET THE TONE FOR THE REST O' MY STAY!

OUT OF THE WAY, CHURCH-MAN!

PLEASE, I AM WALKING AS FAST AS I--

NO EXCUSES! WHEN ONE OF THE SATAB'S GUARD SPEAKS--

--YOU OBEY!

WHUUUF--!

HEY, THAT WAS A NASTY FALL, OLD-TIMER! YOU OKAY?

I AM DIRTIED, AND ANGERED... BUT UNHURT.

AND YOU, GOOD SIR, ARE MOST KIND TO HELP A STRANGER.

DON'T MENTION IT. BUT SAY, MAYBE YOU CAN HELP ME. I'M LOOKIN' FOR THE NEAREST WATERIN' HOLE. Y'KNOW, LIKE AN INN, A CANTINA...?

OF COURSE. DOWN THAT PASS-WAY, THIRD PYRAMID, SECOND DOOR.

MUCH OBLIGED.

"VETTER'S DIRECTIONS WERE EASY TO FOLLOW. AND SOON...

WITH THE KIND O' LOWLIFES HANGIN' AROUND THIS JOINT, SOMEONE'S *BOUND* TO HAVE A LINE ON ILLICIT SPICES!

I'LL HAVE A GROG, BARKEEP. AND, UH, MAYBE SOME INFORMATION ON WHERE I COULD LAY MY HANDS ON A LITTLE--

--SANSANNA?

"SILENCE.

"SUDDEN.

"DEADLY.

HEY, WHAT'S THE MATTER? ALL I SAID WAS--

LOUSY SATAB-LOVER!

HNH?!

KLESH

THOK

NICE GOIN', SOLO! LOOKS LIKE YOU'VE STEPPED ON SOME VERY *SORE* TOES!

AN' YOU'D BETTER MATCH THAT WITH SOME SORE *HEADS* IF YOU WANNA GET OUT O' THIS PLACE ALIVE!

PLANKSH

WHICH, CONSIDERIN' THAT THERE'RE *TWENTY* O' THEM AN' *ONE* O' ME--

--IS SOMETHIN' I'D BETTER TAKE CARE OF REAL SOON!

BLAST! THOSE MUSCLE-HEADS FROM THE BAR ARE FOLLOWIN' ME!

GOTTA LOSE MYSELF! MAYBE IN THAT *CROWD* UP AHEAD!

'COURSE, I DIDN'T KNOW WHAT WAS ON THE *OTHER SIDE* O' THAT CROWD...!

SHOW RESPECT, PEASANTS! MAKE WAY FOR *CHRYSALLA*, TIERESS OF VENTOOINE--

--AND CHOSEN WARD OF THE ALL-HIGHEST SATAB!

KEEP BACK, SCRABBLER, OR I'LL SEE THAT YOU FACE JUSTICE FROM THE SATAB HIMSELF!

O-OH, NO! I-I-I'LL MOVE!

THEY'RE GETTING CLOSER, ROV PIIN. SOON I'LL BE ABLE TO DROP THIS BOMB RIGHT INTO THAT SMIRKING SHE-DOG'S LAP!

PLEASE, PHALAF. MUST YOU TAKE SUCH PLEASURE IN YOUR TASK? VIOLENCE IS ABHORRENT IN *ANY* FORM.

IF ONLY WE COULD WAIT FOR THE FUL-FILLMENT OF *THE FORETELLING*--

--THE PROPHECY THAT PROMISES A BEING WITH WAYS AND WEAPONS FAR DIFFERENT FROM OUR OWN, A BEING WHO WILL HELP LIFT THE YOKE OF THE SATAB'S TYRANNY!

BUT...UNTIL THAT TIME...I SUPPOSE WE MUST DO WHAT WE CAN TO HELP OURSELVES-- EVEN IF THAT MEANS *ASSASSINATING* MEMBERS OF THE ROYAL FAMILY!

SO TENDER YOUR MALICE WITH COMPASSION, MY SON--

--AND SEE THAT YOUR AIM IS TRUE!

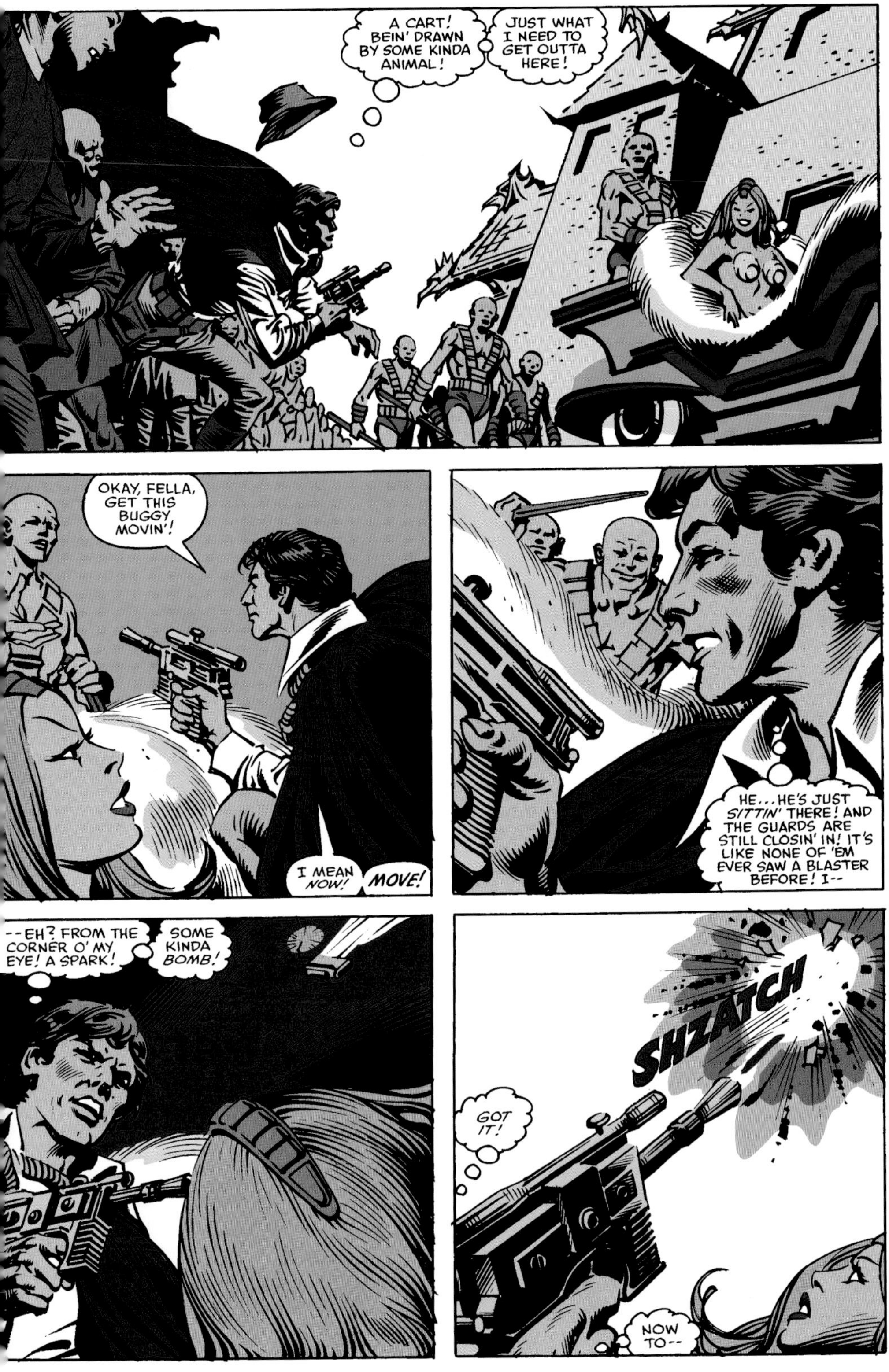
A CART! BEIN' DRAWN BY SOME KINDA ANIMAL!
JUST WHAT I NEED TO GET OUTTA HERE!
OKAY, FELLA, GET THIS BUGGY MOVIN'!
I MEAN NOW!
MOVE!
HE...HE'S JUST SITTIN' THERE! AND THE GUARDS ARE STILL CLOSIN' IN! IT'S LIKE NONE OF 'EM EVER SAW A BLASTER BEFORE! I--
--EH? FROM THE CORNER O' MY EYE! A SPARK!
SOME KINDA BOMB!
SHZATCH
GOT IT!
NOW TO--

WAIT! THIS STRANGER IS A HERO!

I AM?!

YOU MUST HAVE SEEN THOSE INSURGENTS ABOUT TO THROW THEIR EXPLOSIVES, AND SOUGHT TO TAKE MY CART TO A POSITION OF SAFETY!

YOU SAVED MY LIFE!

I DID?

I- I MEAN, I DID! YEAH! THAT'S IT!

YOU HAVE WON MY UNDYING GRATITUDE, AND THE ETERNAL PROTECTION OF THE SATAB'S HAND.

"PROTECTION"? LADY, RIGHT ABOUT NOW THAT SOUNDS REAL GOOD!

THEN, GUARD—SEND A RUNNER AHEAD TO THE PALACE! SEE THAT PREPARATIONS ARE MADE FOR A GRAND CELEBRATION!

IN THE MEANTIME, MY HANDSOME RESCUER AND I WILL GET TO KNOW EACH OTHER BETTER.

A LOT BETTER.

CAPTAIN SOLO, YOU MUST BE LIVIN' RIGHT!

I AM PLEASED YOU WERE ABLE TO ESCAPE, VETTER. BUT I AM SORRY THAT YOUNG PHALAF WAS NOT SO FORTUNATE--HE'S BEEN TAKEN INTO CUSTODY BY THE SATAB'S GUARD!

THAT IS MOST SAD.

AYE, AND WORSE, IT APPEARS THE SATAB HAS GAINED A NEW ALLY--A *POWERFUL* ONE!

SO IT WOULD SEEM. AND YET...

...THE ALIEN WANDERER STRUCK ME AS BEING KIND, IF SOMEWHAT BRASH, AND HE SHOWED NO OUTWARD LOVE FOR THE SATAB. I ALMOST THOUGHT... WELL...

THAT HE WAS THE ONE IN THE FORE-TELLING? PHAW! HE SAVED THE SATAB'S CHOSEN! EVEN NOW HE RIDES IN THE ROYAL CARRIAGE, A GUEST OF THE TIERESS!

THE ALIEN MAY BE A SPY, OR HE MAY BE AN UNWITTING INNOCENT. BUT WHATEVER HE IS, IF HE SHOULD STAND BETWEEN US AND OUR ABSOLUTE GOAL...

YES. I KNOW.

HE MUST *DIE!*

"I'M AFRAID I DIDN'T PAY MUCH ATTENTION TO THE TOWN WE PASSED THROUGH-- I WAS KINDA PREOCCUPIED-- BUT MY EYES PERKED RIGHT UP WHEN WE GOT TO THE PALACE.

"IT WAS QUITE A SIGHT.

"AN' SO WAS THE BANQUET HALL WE WERE USHERED INTO. I'D GUESS THAT EVERY ELITE MUCKY-MUCK ON VENTOOINE'D BEEN GATHERED AROUND A SINGLE TABLE, ONE SET WITH A FEAST FIT FOR A KING. OR, IN THIS CASE, FOR THE UNQUESTIONED RULER OF THE ENTIRE PLANET--

"--THE SATAB!

WELCOME, MY FRIEND! COME, SIT BESIDE ME!

THE RUNNER HAS TOLD ME OF YOUR DARING ACTIONS ON CHRYSALLA'S BE-HALF. HE SAYS YOU SELFLESSLY RISKED YOUR OWN LIFE FOR HERS, SHOWING GREAT COURAGE AND NOBILITY. IS THIS TRUE?

UH... RIGHT!

THEN YOU MUST STAY HERE AS MY GUEST, AND I SHALL SEE THAT YOU HAVE ONLY THE BEST-- IN FOOD, IN DRINK, AND... ENTERTAINMENT!

GUARDS!

"THAT'S WHEN THEY BROUGHT IN VETTER'S FRIEND, *PHALAF*...

DEATH TO TYRANTS! DEATH TO THE SATAB! TORTURE ME AS YOU WILL, BUT I'LL NEVER RENOUNCE MY BELIEFS!

TORTURE YOU? WHY, DEAR BOY, I MERELY WISH--

--TO SHAKE YOUR HAND!

WHA--NO! D-DON'T TOUCH ME! DON'T-- *AAAAGGGHH!*

"THE BOY SCREAMED ONCE.

"THAT'S ALL HE HAD *TIME* FOR.

" 'CAUSE SECONDS LATER HE LAY ON THE FLOOR, MUSCLES SLACK, TEETH YELLOW, SKIN DRAWN AN' CRACKED LIKE CHEAP PARCHMENT.

"A BOY OF MAYBE EIGHTEEN YEARS, DEAD...OF *OLD AGE!*

"AN' THOSE SLUGS SITTIN' 'ROUND THE TABLE JUST CACKLED AN' CLAPPED LIKE SOMEBODY'D TOLD AN OFF-COLOR JOKE..."

BY THE WAY, MY FRIEND, THE MESSENGER SPOKE OF AN ODD WEAPON YOU POSSESS, ONE THAT SPITS FIRE. MIGHT I SEE IT?

"SPITS...? OH, SURE!"

THIS PLANET MUST NOT HAVE A MECHANICAL TECHNOLOGY--THAT'S WHY NO ONE'S EVER HEARD OF A BLASTER!

BUT IF OL' SATAB THINKS I'M GONNA GIVE UP MY ONLY MEANS OF SELF DEFENSE, HE'S--

--ONE SHREWD SONOVAGUN! ⸴GULP⸴

HERE YA GO. TAKE GOOD CARE OF IT, WILLYA? IT WAS A GIFT FROM MY MOM.

OF COURSE. NOW, I BELIEVE WE MAY ENJOY OUR MEAL...

"EVERYBODY STARTED TO DIG IN--

"--AN' THAT'S WHEN I HIT PAYDIRT!

WELL, WELL, WHAT HAVE WE HERE?

IF THAT SPARKLY POWDER THE BIG GUY'S SPRINKLIN' ON HIS FOOD ISN'T *SANSANNA*, THEN I'M A BANTHA'S UNCLE!

SATAB MUST HAVE A CORNER ON THE SANSANNA MARKET--

-- THAT'S WHY HIS "LOVING SUBJECTS" GOT HOSTILE WHEN I ASKED HOW TO GET SOME!

BUT NOW THAT I KNOW WHERE IT IS, I KNOW WHERE IT'S GONNA BE THIS TIME TOMORROW.

WITH ME ON BOARD THE MILLENNIUM FALCON!

"THE SLEEPING QUARTERS I WAS SHOWN TO THAT NIGHT WERE THE FANCIEST I'D SEEN IN SOME TIME. I GOTTA ADMIT, THAT SATAB WAS ONE HECK OF A HOST.

"NOT THAT I *TRUSTED* HIM, THOUGH. UH-UH. NO MORE THAN HE--

"-- TRUSTED ME.

"THERE WAS NO WAY I COULD GET PAST THE GUARDS HE'D POSTED AT MY DOOR.

"SO I DIDN'T USE THE DOOR! NOT WHEN IT WAS SUCH A SIMPLE MATTER TO DROP TO THE BALCONY BELOW--

"--TIPTOE PAST A COUPLE OF SNORING NOBLEPERSONS--

"--AN' SLIP INTO AN ADJOINING CORRIDOR. I FIGURED I'D SNOOP AROUND, FIND WHERE THE SATAB KEPT HIS SANSANNA AN' THEN STEA--ER, OBTAIN, ENOUGH TO MAKE MY TRIP WORTHWHILE!

"THE PLAN WAS JUST HOW I LIKE 'EM --

"--SIMPLE, FOOLPROOF AN' EASY!

"BUT THEN A HAND DROPPED ON MY SHOULDER--

"--AN' MY HEART DECIDED TO TAKE THE REST O' THE DAY OFF!

436

"THAT IS, UNTIL I SAW WHO *OWNED* THE HAND..."

I BELIEVE YOU'VE TAKEN A WRONG TURN, CAPTAIN SOLO.

WHA-- CHRYSALLA! ; WHEW ;

I THOUGHT YOU MIGHT COME TO ME, CAPTAIN, AND I'M MOST FLATTERED.

YOU'RE SO BRAVE TO RISK DISCOVERY BY THE SATAB'S GUARD JUST FOR ME.

YOU MEAN... THE SLEEPING QUARTERS ARE *PATROLLED?*

REALLY, SUCH JESTS! BUT COME, THE SOLDIERS APPROACH -- WE MUST GO TO MY ROOMS!

UH, YEAH, THAT MIGHT NOT BE A BAD IDEA!

BESIDES--

-- I WANT TO SHOW YOU THE SUNRISE FROM MY TERRACE!

"SUNRISE"? BUT THE SUN WON'T BE UP FOR ANOTHER SIX HOURS!

I KNOW...

CAN YOU SEE THEM, MASTER?

OF COURSE I CAN, PLODGETT--

-- THE SHADESHINE IS WORKING PERFECTLY!

NO MATTER HOW MANY WALLS LIE BETWEEN ME AND WHAT I WISH TO SEE--

--I CAN SEE WHATEVER I WISH!

THEN YOU WILL PUNISH THE STRANGER FOR HIS TREACHERY? AND YOUR THANKLESS WARD FOR HER BETRAYAL?

NO, PLODGETT. AS LONG AS CHRYSALLA CONTINUES TO AMUSE ME, SHE CAN BE FORGIVEN HER LITTLE...ESCAPADES. AND AS FOR THE DASHING CAPTAIN SOLO, WELL...

...HE HAS ADMIRABLE RESILIENCY, GREAT STAMINA AND SHALL WE SAY--

--INTERESTING MORALS? I BELIEVE HE MAY JUST BE A PERFECT CANDIDATE--

-- FOR THE NEXT ONE!

"HOURS PASSED--NOT UNPLEASANTLY-- AN' AS THE SUN ROSE OVER VENTOOINE...

SO THE SATAB GETS HIS POWER FROM THAT ROCK HE WEARS AROUND HIS NECK--THE ONE YOU CALL THE "SHADESHINE?"

MM-HM.

SATAB IS THE LATEST OF OUR YEARLY RULERS, AND THEY'VE ALL MADE USE OF THE SHADE-SHINE. AFTER CONTACT, THE STONE HEIGHTENS ONE'S SENSES TO AN INCREDIBLE DEGREE, TURNING SOME--SUCH AS SIGHT AND TOUCH--INTO TRANSMITTERS AS WELL AS RECEIVERS.

THUS, BY MERE TOUCH, THE SATAB WAS ABLE TO SEND THAT INSURGENT'S METABOL-ISM RACING, AGING HIM BY DECADES IN SECONDS!

BUT IF THE SATAB'S SUCH A ROTTEN GUY, WHY DO YOU STAY WITH HIM?

I...WAS JUST ANOTHER PEASANT BEFORE THE SATAB'S REIGN. I LIVED HAND TO MOUTH, DAY TO DAY. BUT NOW, AS A ROYAL WARD, I HAVE EVERY COMFORT IMAGINABLE. AND ALL I GIVE IN RETURN IS... COMPANIONSHIP.

BUT IS IT WORTH IT?

THAT DOESN'T MATTER, I...

...HAVE NO CHOICE.

KNOCK KNOCK

TIERESS? THE MORNING MEAL IS BEING SERVED.

HURRY! YOU MUST RETURN TO YOUR SUITE BEFORE YOU'RE DISCOVERED!

GOTCHA!

"AS I CLIMBED BACK UP TO MY ROOM--

"--I THOUGHT THAT IF I HAD TIME AFTER GRABBIN' THE SANSANNA, I'D SURE LIKE TO DO SOMETHIN' *NASTY* TO THE SATAB.

"JUST FOR THE HECK OF IT...

"AN' THEN, SOMETIME LATER AFTER WE'D EATEN...

GOOD MORNING, CAPTAIN SOLO. I TRUST YOU SLEPT WELL?

AND CHRYSALLA, MY DEAR. I MISSED YOU LAST NIGHT. WHAT A PITY YOU WERE ILL.

UH, YES, W-WASN'T IT?

"SHRUGGIN' OFF THE SATAB'S RE-MARKS, WE MOUNTED UP AN' HEADED OUT FROM GOYOIKIN. THE BIG GUY SAID HE WANTED TO SHOW ME SOME OF THE LOCAL SIGHTS.

AS YOU KNOW, CAPTAIN, OURS IS A MINERAL-BASED CULTURE.

MUCH OF OUR COMMERCE, AND EVEN OUR RELIGION, IS BASED ON WHAT WE CAN EXTRACT FROM OUR MANY EXCAVA-TIONS--SUCH AS THIS ONE.

PERHAPS YOU'D LIKE A CLOSER LOOK?

I THINK YOU MIGHT FIND THE EXPERIENCE MOST EDUCATIONAL!

THE WORKERS USE TOOLS MADE OF A MINERAL THAT *REACTS* WITH THE STONE WALLS, CUTTING THROUGH THE ROCK QUITE EFFICIENTLY.

AND WE *USE EVEN* MORE UNIQUE METHODS UP AHEAD, IF YOU'D CARE TO LOOK?

SURE, WHY NOT?

I'LL JOIN YOU.

NO, CHRYSALLA, I THINK NOT.

BUT--!

PLODGETT! YOU KNOW WHAT TO DO.

AYE, MASTER!

" I NEVER SAW SATAB'S LACKEY THROW THE STONE SWITCH. I NEVER SAW THE HIDDEN CAGE CREAK OPEN.

"BUT SOON, I SAW THOSE ACTIONS"--

"-- RESULTS!

GRRRARR!

HUH--?!

WHAT'S A THING LIKE THAT DOIN' HANGIN' AROUND A WELL-POPULATED MINING OPERATION LIKE THIS?

ON SECOND THOUGHT, I *KNOW* WHAT IT'S DOIN'!

IT'S COMIN' AFTER *ME!*

"BUT FORTUNATELY, IT DIDN'T COME *FAR!*

CHHAK

UURRRRGGH...

EXCELLENT! CAPTAIN SOLO HAS PASSED THE *TEST* MOST ACCEPTABLY-- HIS SURVIVAL INSTINCT IS EVEN HIGHER THAN I'D HOPED!

INDEED, PLODGETT, I BELIEVE WE'VE FOUND THE PERFECT CHOICE--

-- FOR THE *NEXT SATAB!*

WHAT--?!

ROV PIIN MUST HEAR OF THIS!

"AN' HE *DID!* BECAUSE THAT AFTER NOON...

IT IS FACT, O ROV! IT HAPPENED JUST A I SAID--

--THE SATAB HAS CHOSEN THE ALIEN TO BE HIS *SUCCESSOR!*

THIS IS MOST PUZZLING. IF THE WANDERER IS TRULY IN LEAGUE WITH THE SATAB--

--WHY DID HE RISK HIS LIFE TO SAVE COMMON WORK- ERS FROM THAT CAVERN MONSTER?

THERE IS MORE HERE THAN MEETS THE EYE-- BUT I'M AFRAID WE HAVEN'T THE TIME TO FIND OUT *WHAT!* IF WE HOPE TO END THE EVIL REIGN, WE MUST ACT BEFORE THE CHANGE OF POWER--

--TONIGHT!

"THE REST OF THE DAY PASSED PEACEFULLY, GIVIN' ME TIME TO POLISH MY PLANS FOR MAKIN' OFF WITH THE SANSANNA THAT NIGHT."

"BUT AS EVENIN' ROLLED AROUND, I WAS SUMMONED TO A SMALL TEMPLE IN THE PALACE, WHERE THE SATAB AN' A BUNCH OF HOODED WORSHIPPERS WERE WAITIN'..."

AH, CAPTAIN SOLO, I'M SO GLAD YOU COULD JOIN US.

THE RITUAL WE ARE ABOUT TO PERFORM IS A MOST HOLY ONE, AND IS CONDUCTED QUITE RARELY. BUT THE COURAGE YOU SHOWED AT THE CAVERN THIS MORNING PROVED YOU TO BE A WORTHY PARTICIPANT.

THEREFORE, I AM GOING TO ALLOW YOU TO SHARE THE HONOR, AND THE WONDERS, OF... *SHADESHINE!*

WELL, WHADYA KNOW? LOOKS LIKE THE OL' SOLO LUCK IS HOLDIN' OUT!

WITH THE POWERS I CAN GET FROM TOUCHIN' THAT STONE, PICKIN' UP SOME SANSANNA SHOULD BE EASY!

BUT FIRST--

-- I BELIEVE WE HAVE SOME UNINVITED GUESTS TO TEND TO! *GUARDS!*

HUH?!

SATAB! HOW DID YOU KNOW--

-- THAT WE HAD INFILTRATED YOUR CLERGY?

IT'S THAT OLD MONK FROM THE VILLAGE!

VETTER PIIN, YOU SHOULD REALIZE BY NOW THAT WITH MY POWERS I CAN, QUITE LITERALLY, *SMELL* A PEASANT A MILE AWAY!

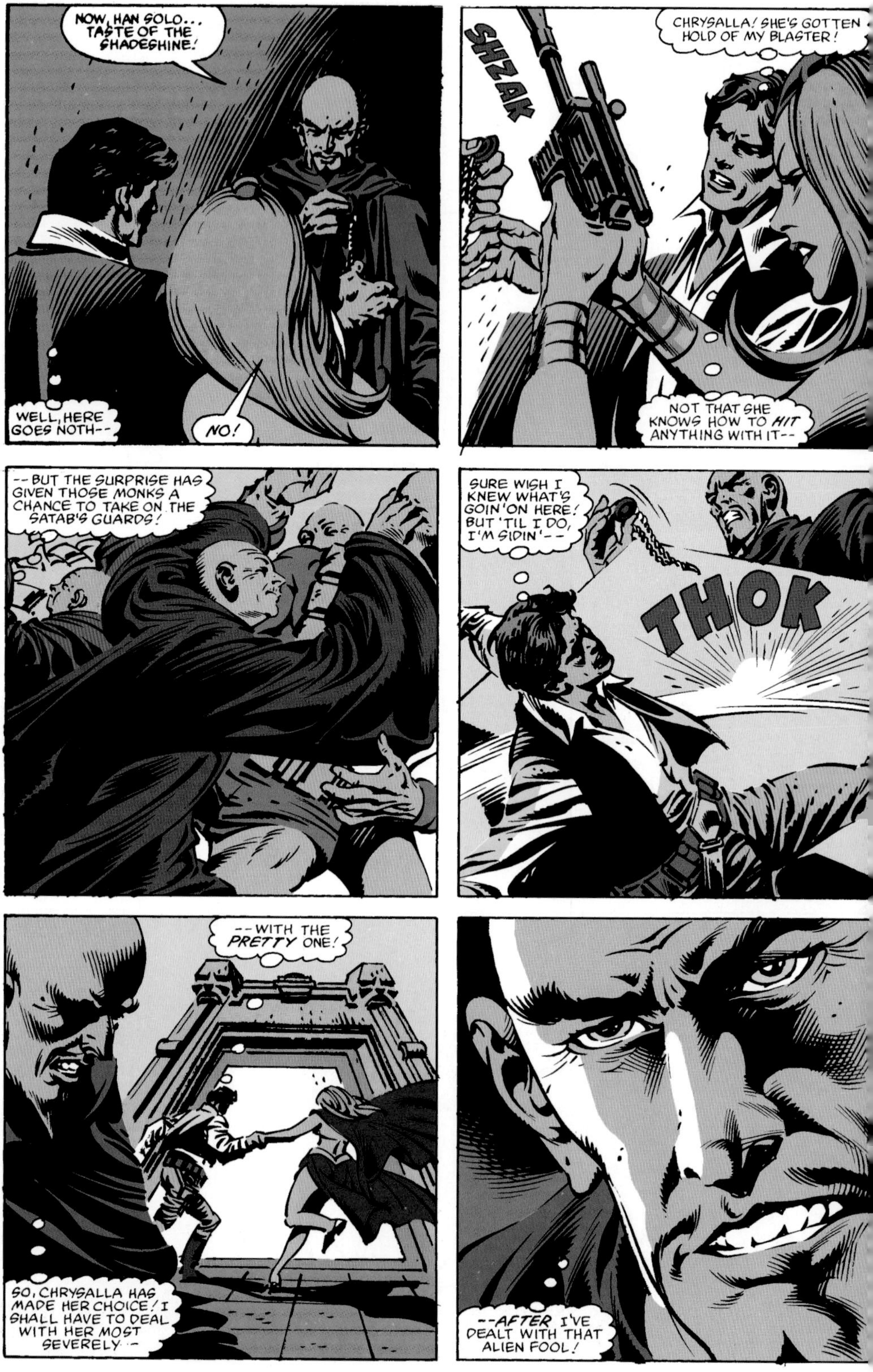
NOW, HAN SOLO... TASTE OF THE SHADESHINE!
WELL, HERE GOES NOTH--
NO!
SHZAK
CHRYSALLA! SHE'S GOTTEN HOLD OF MY BLASTER!
NOT THAT SHE KNOWS HOW TO *HIT* ANYTHING WITH IT--
--BUT THE SURPRISE HAS GIVEN THOSE MONKS A CHANCE TO TAKE ON THE SATAB'S GUARDS!
SURE WISH I KNEW WHAT'S GOIN' ON HERE! BUT 'TIL I DO, I'M SIDIN'--
THOK
--WITH THE *PRETTY* ONE!
SO, CHRYSALLA HAS MADE HER CHOICE! I SHALL HAVE TO DEAL WITH HER MOST SEVERELY--
--*AFTER* I'VE DEALT WITH THAT ALIEN FOOL!

"SECONDS LATER, WHEN WE'D REACHED THE RELATIVE CALM OF THE THRONE ROOM...

GREAT WORK, CHRYSALLA! NOW GIVE ME THE BLASTER-- I'LL NEED IT TO GET THE SHADESHINE!

BUT YOU CAN'T--

SURE I CAN! WITH THE POWER THAT STONE GIVES, IT'LL BRING A HIGHER PRICE THAN ALL THE SANSANNA ON VENTOOINE! I'M GOIN' AFTER IT!

BUT HAN--

--THAT'S JUST WHAT THE SATAB WANTS! THE SHADESHINE DOES GIVE GREAT POWER--

--BUT IT TAKES A TERRIBLE TOLL AS WELL!

HUH?! WHAT'RE YOU TALKIN' ABOUT?

WITHIN A YEAR, THE SENSES OF ANYONE TOUCHING THE SHADESHINE BECOME SO SENSITIVE TO EXTERNAL STIMULI THAT THE PERSON CAN'T STAND IT-- THEY BURN OUT! THUS THE REIGNING SATAB MUST FIND A SUCCESSOR--

-- SOMEONE TO WATCH OVER ALL OF THE PREVIOUS SATABS, WHO HAVE GONE INTO SUSPENDED ANIMATION IN HOPES THAT ONE DAY THE EFFECTS OF THE SHADESHINE CAN BE REVERSED!

AND THE NEW SATAB MUST COMPLY BECAUSE, ONCE AFFECTED, HE FACES THE SAME, INEVITABLE FATE! IT IS A CRUEL FATE, HAN, AND ONE THE SATAB WANTS FOR YOU!

I DON'T KNOW, CHRYS. THAT'S A LOT TO TAKE IN.

THEN PERHAPS THIS WILL CONVINCE YOU!

"SOLEMNLY, THE LADY PASSED HER HAND OVER A NEARBY 'ORNAMENT'--

"--AN' LIKE THE SUNS OF ORD MANTELL, A SECRET DOOR IN ONE WALL BEGAN TO RISE, SLOWLY, SILENTLY...

THIS IS THE *HALL OF SATABS*. IT IS WHERE OUR LEADERS GO WHEN THEY ARE NEAR DEATH.

THE MINERALS THAT COMPOSE THE CHAMBER'S WALLS NULLIFY BOTH GRAVITY AND LIFE FUNCTION. THUS A SATAB MERELY WALKS IN, AND SECONDS LATER IS RENDERED IMMOBILE, FLOATING IN A STATE OF SLEEPLIKE SUSPENSION.

"AGAIN, CHRYSALLA GRAZED A HIDDEN SWITCH. SOFT LIGHT FLOODED ON--

"--AN' I SAW SATABS. *HUNDREDS* OF 'EM! ALL FLOATIN' LIKE UGLY STARS IN A NIGHTMARE SKY.

SO THAT'S WHAT THE SATAB WANTS ME TO PROTECT... AND TO *BECOME*, SOONER OR LATER.

I BELIEVE, CAPTAIN SOLO, THAT THE OPERATIVE WORD IS--

--"SOONER"!

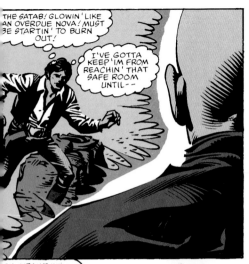

THE SATAB! GLOWIN' LIKE AN OVERDUE NOVA! MUST BE STARTIN' TO BURN OUT!

I'VE GOTTA KEEP 'IM FROM REACHIN' THAT SAFE ROOM UNTIL--

FOR A PRO-SPECTIVE SATAB, CAPTAIN, YOU'RE NOT VERY BRIGHT! ALL I NEED TO DO IS TOUCH THE ATOMS BETWEEN ME AND YOU TO SEND ALONG A VIBRATORY IMPULSE THAT CAN SHATTER YOUR WEAPON!

OH, YEAH? WELL, IMPULSE THIS, YA LUNATIC!

WHA-- I DIDN'T EXPECT A PHYSICAL ATTACK!

BUT NO MATTER! BY THICKENING THE AIR BETWEEN ME AND THAT STONE HEAD--

--I CAN TURN IT INTO A MISSILE--

--OF MY OWN!

KHATASH

TOO MUCH DEBRIS! CAN'T GET OUT OF THE WA--AGH!

NOW, CAPTAIN, I BELIEVE THAT ADDING A FEW DECADES TO YOUR AGE SHOULD MAKE YOU MUCH MORE COOPERA-TIVE! JUST HOLD STILL WHILE I--

--AAIIEEE! M-MY HAND! BURSTING INTO FLAMES!

THAT IS BECAUSE, SATAB, YOU ARE NOT THE *ONLY* ONE WITH THE POWER!

THE SHADESHINE! YOU'VE *TOUCHED* THE STONE!

I HAD HOPED TO SPARE YOU, CHRYSALLA! BUT I AM AFRAID THAT I CAN NO LONGER AFFORD THAT INDULGENCE!

YOU'LL NOT KILL ME, SATAB--

--AND YOU'LL NOT KILL HAN! EVEN AT THIS DISTANCE, I CAN TOUCH THE SPACE AROUND YOU, AND HEAT IT TO A LIVING INFERNO!

IDIOT CHILD! YOU MAY HAVE THE POWER, BUT *I* HAVE THE EXPERIENCE IN WIELDING IT!

SO IF IT'S FLAMES YOU WANT, MY DEAR--

--IT IS FLAMES YOU SHALL *HAVE!*

: UNF! : W-WAS BARELY ABLE TO THICKEN THE AIR... I-IN TIME TO DEFLECT THE FIRESTREAM!

NOW TO...T-TO...NO! I-I CAN'T THINK! MY SENSITIVITY...PEAKING!

I-I CAN FEEL THE VERY AIR ON MY SKIN! CAN HEAR A SPIDER...C-CLIMBING UP THE WALL! M-MY METABOLISM... IS RACING!

A-AND I CAN'T... SHUT IT OFF!

I CAN'T STOP IT!

M-MUST GET TO THE NULLIFICATION CHAMBER! E-EVEN WITHOUT...A SUCCESSOR!

HAVE...H-HAVE TO...

SORRY, SATAB--

--I CAN'T LET YOU DO THAT!

"I ONLY WANTED TO SLOW THE SATAB DOWN, DELAY HIM UNTIL CHRYSALLA AN' ME COULD TAKE 'IM ON TOGETHER.

"BUT I GUESS THE BIG GUY WAS TOO FAR GONE. ONCE HE FELL, HE JUST LAY THERE, TREMBLING...

"...TURNIN' BLACK AS HE BURNED UP FROM INSIDE! AN' THEN, WITH A CLOUD OF STENCH AN' SMOKE LIKE A BACKFIRIN' SANDCRAWLER--

"--HE WAS GONE!

449

YOU HAVE DONE IT! YOU HAVE KILLED THE SATAB!

YOU ARE TRULY THE SAVIOR SPOKEN OF IN THE FORETELLING!

IT WAS MY PLEASURE, YETTER--*BELIEVE* ME!

BUT TO BE HONEST, I NEVER COULDA DONE IT WITHOUT THE LITTLE LADY HERE.

SO, C'MON, CHRYSALLA, HOW ABOUT WE THROW A CELEBRATION THAT'LL KEEP THIS WHOLE PLANET HUNG OVER FOR A WEEK?

I...I CANNOT GO WITH YOU, HAN.

EVER!

HUH?

ONCE THE SHADESHINE IS TOUCHED, ITS EFFECTS ARE *PERMANENT.* THUS IF I DO NOT ENTER THE SUSPENSION CHAMBER, I WILL ULTIMATELY DIE IN AGONY LIKE THE SATAB!

AND THERE SEEMS LITTLE REASON TO PROLONG THE PARTING.

BUT--!

GRIEVE NOT, HAN SOLO-- I DID WHAT I HAD TO DO.

AND BESIDES, SUSPENSION IS NOT TOTALLY UNPLEASANT. IT IS MUCH LIKE A LONG, LONG SLUMBER, AND I PROMISE, HAN...

...I WILL DREAM OF YOU.

"AN' THEN SHE WALKED INTO THE HALL OF SATABS, TALL, WITH A CALM AN' GRACE I DON'T THINK EVEN *I* COULD'VE MATCHED.

"VETTER PASSED HIS HAND OVER THE STONE SWITCH--

"--AN' THE DOOR SLID DOWN, HEAVY, CLOSIN' WITH A CRACK LIKE THE SOUND OF A BREAKIN' HEART...

"THERE WASN'T MUCH LEFT TO DO AFTER THAT. JUST GATHER SOME MEMORY STONES AN' MAKE THIS RECORD.

"VETTER GAVE THE *SHADESHINE* TO ME FOR SAFEKEEPIN'--SAYS I'LL KNOW WHAT TO DO WITH IT. AN' I GUESS I DO.

"FINANCIALLY PAINFUL AS IT MAY BE, THAT HUNK O' ROCK'S GOIN' INTO THE FALCON'S *THRUST TUBES*, TO BE VAPORIZED WHEN WE TAKE OFF--

"--SO NO MORE MICROMINDED MANIACS'LL BE ABLE TO TAKE UP WHERE THE SATABS LEFT OFF!"

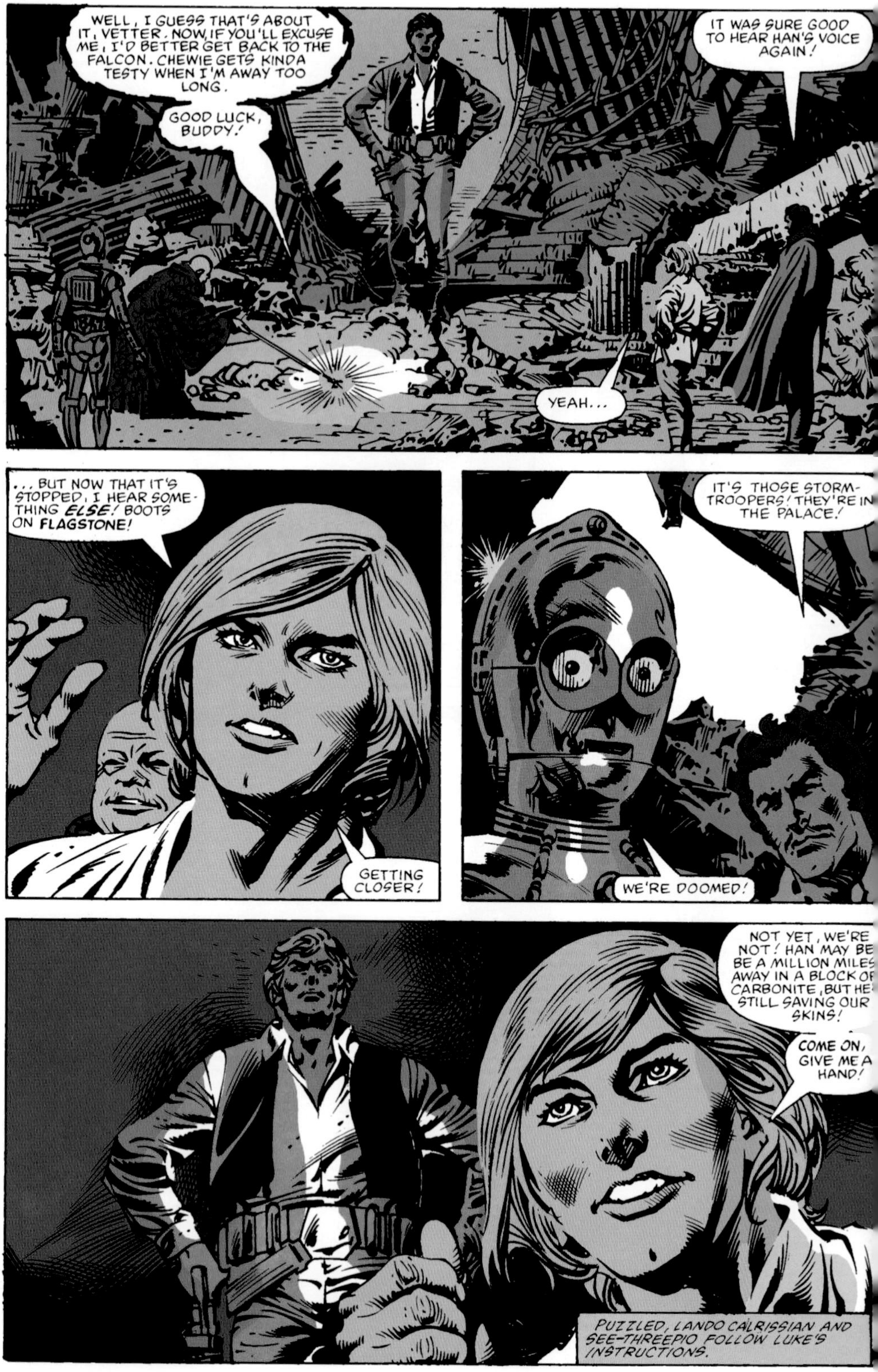

WELL, I GUESS THAT'S ABOUT IT, VETTER. NOW, IF YOU'LL EXCUSE ME, I'D BETTER GET BACK TO THE FALCON. CHEWIE GETS KINDA TESTY WHEN I'M AWAY TOO LONG.
GOOD LUCK, BUDDY!
IT WAS SURE GOOD TO HEAR HAN'S VOICE AGAIN!
YEAH...
...BUT NOW THAT IT'S STOPPED, I HEAR SOMETHING ELSE! BOOTS ON FLAGSTONE!
GETTING CLOSER!
IT'S THOSE STORMTROOPERS! THEY'RE IN THE PALACE!
WE'RE DOOMED!
NOT YET, WE'RE NOT! HAN MAY BE BE A MILLION MILES AWAY IN A BLOCK OF CARBONITE, BUT HE'S STILL SAVING OUR SKINS!
COME ON, GIVE ME A HAND!
PUZZLED, LANDO CALRISSIAN AND SEE-THREEPIO FOLLOW LUKE'S INSTRUCTIONS.

AND, SOON...

THAT'S FUNNY, OUR SCANNERS ARE PICKING UP MULTIPLE LIFE READINGS IN THIS QUAD. BUT NO ONE'S HERE!

THEY'RE HIDIN'! THEY GOTTA BE! THEY--

IF YOU WANT US, BANTHA-BREATH, THEN COME AND GET US!

THEY'RE IN THAT ROOM! LET'S NAIL 'EM!

CAREFUL, NOW...

...THE REBELS MAY BE ILLITERATE SCUM, BUT THEY'RE *TRICKY* ILLITERATE SCUM!

AW, YER GIVIN' 'EM TOO MUCH CREDIT! THE DAY THOSE TRAITORS CAN OUT-SMART AN IMPERIAL STORMTROOPER, I--

--I...F-FEEL DROWSY! G-GETTIN' HARD...TO THINK!

HEY! WHAT'S GOIN' ON, GUYS? GUYS?

HOLY CRUD, I-I AIN'T GOIN' IN *THERE!*

M-ME, TOO! C-CAN'T... STAND... UUUUUP...

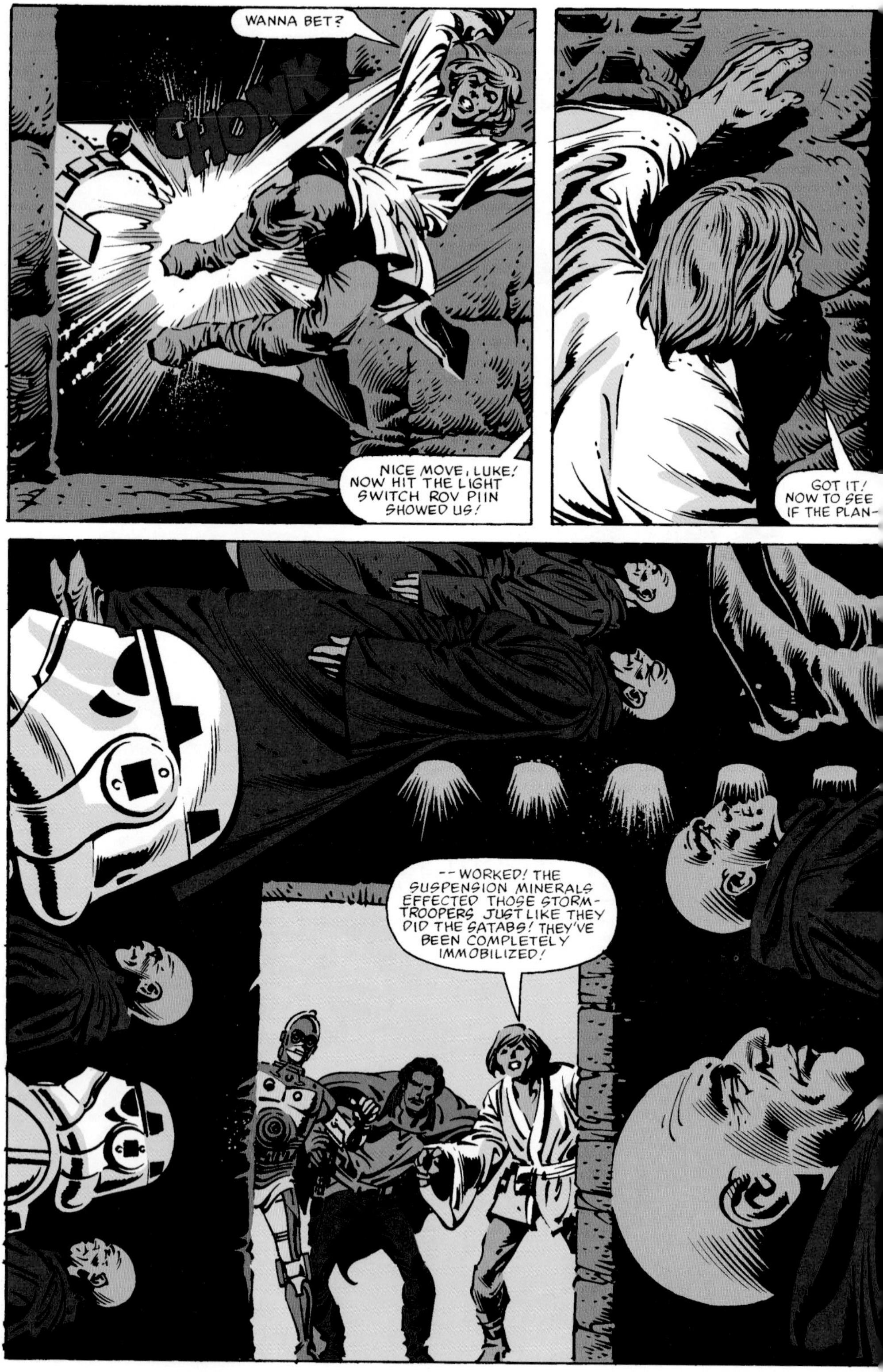
WANNA BET?
CHONK
NICE MOVE, LUKE! NOW HIT THE LIGHT SWITCH ROV PIIN SHOWED US!
GOT IT! NOW TO SEE IF THE PLAN-
--WORKED! THE SUSPENSION MINERALS EFFECTED THOSE STORM-TROOPERS JUST LIKE THEY DID THE SATABS! THEY'VE BEEN COMPLETELY IMMOBILIZED!

WHAT A BRILLIANT IDEA, MASTER LUKE-- RECORDING YOUR TAUNT ON ONE OF THOSE MEMORY STONES, THEN ACTIVATING IT AND TOSSING IT INTO THE NULLIFICATION CHAMBER TO LURE THOSE IMPERIALS INSIDE!

THANKS, THREEPIO, BUT I NEVER WOULD'VE HAD THE IDEA IF IT HADN'T BEEN FOR HAN'S STORY.

AND HAN WOULDN'T HAVE LIVED TO *TELL* THAT STORY IF NOT FOR--

--HER!

CHRYSALLA!

YES, MY CHILDREN, I BELIEVE WE ALL OWE THEM *BOTH* A GREAT DEAL...!

AND SO, SOMETIME LATER, A REBEL STARCRAFT TAKES OFF FROM VENTOOINE, ITS CREW JUGGLING MIXED EMOTIONS. FOR THOUGH THEY HAD NOT OBTAINED THE SECRET WEAPON THEY HAD COME FOR--A WEAPON THAT MAY WELL HAVE *DESTROYED* THEM--THEY DO LEAVE WITH A GENTLER PRIZE...THE SPECIAL FEELING OF HAVING HAD THEIR LIVES TOUCHED ONCE MORE BY AN OLD FRIEND, AND...

...BY A NEW ONE.

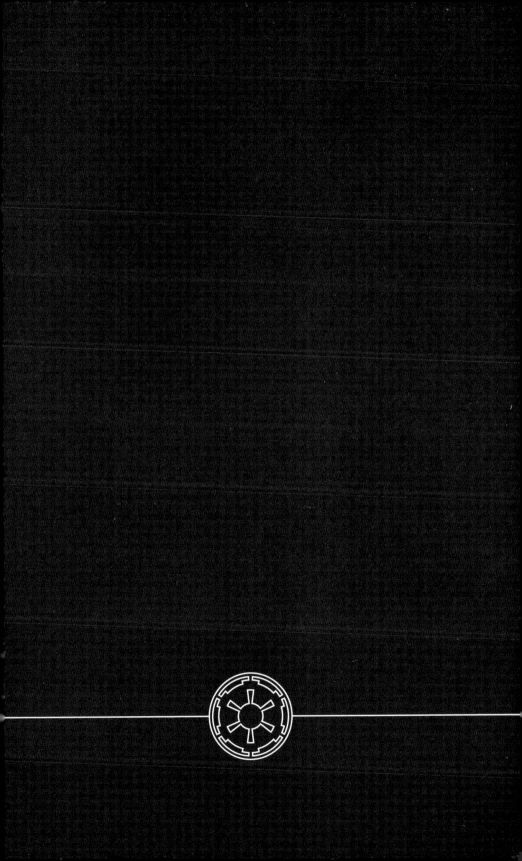

60¢
67
JAN
02817
APPROVED BY THE COMICS CODE AUTHORITY
STAR WARS

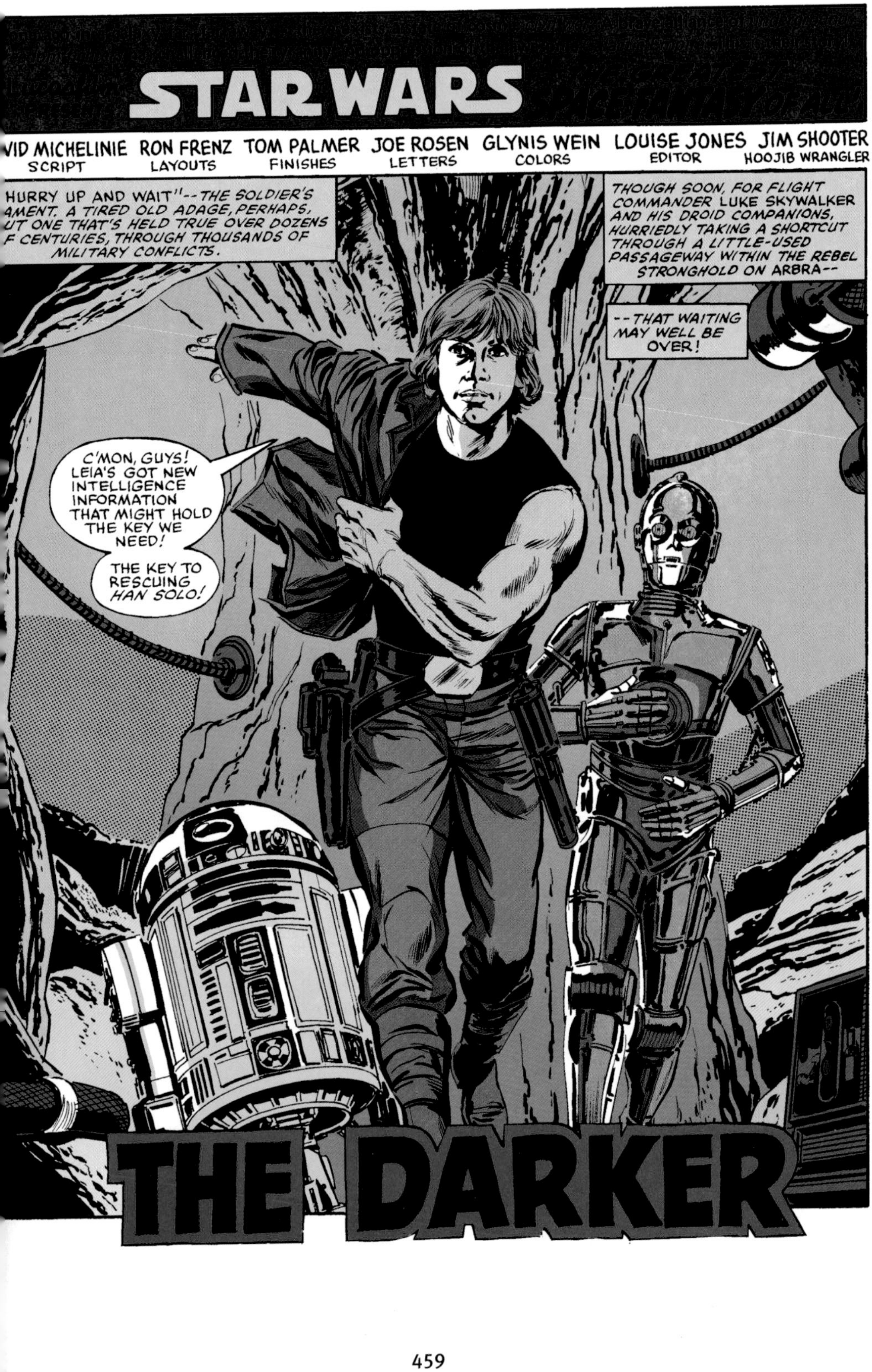
STAR WARS
VID MICHELINIE SCRIPT
RON FRENZ LAYOUTS
TOM PALMER FINISHES
JOE ROSEN LETTERS
GLYNIS WEIN COLORS
LOUISE JONES EDITOR
JIM SHOOTER HOOJIB WRANGLER
HURRY UP AND WAIT"--THE SOLDIER'S AMENT. A TIRED OLD ADAGE, PERHAPS, UT ONE THAT'S HELD TRUE OVER DOZENS F CENTURIES, THROUGH THOUSANDS OF MILITARY CONFLICTS.
THOUGH SOON, FOR FLIGHT COMMANDER LUKE SKYWALKER AND HIS DROID COMPANIONS, HURRIEDLY TAKING A SHORTCUT THROUGH A LITTLE-USED PASSAGEWAY WITHIN THE REBEL STRONGHOLD ON ARBRA--
--THAT WAITING MAY WELL BE OVER!
C'MON, GUYS! LEIA'S GOT NEW INTELLIGENCE INFORMATION THAT MIGHT HOLD THE KEY WE NEED!
THE KEY TO RESCUING HAN SOLO!
THE DARKER

ARE YOU QUITE CERTAIN YOU'RE *UP* TO SUCH AN ADVENTURE, MASTER LUKE? AFTER ALL, YOU JUST NOW RETURNED FROM THAT HARROWING EPISODE ON BEHEBOTH! *

I'LL ADMIT THAT BATTLING THOSE WATER BANDITS WAS TOUGH, THREEPIO--

*LAST ISSUE.

--BUT IT *CAN'T* BE AS BAD AS WHAT HAN'S GOING THROUGH! BEING FROZEN IN A BLOCK OF CARBONITE'S NO PICNIC, AND IF THERE'S ANYTHING AT ALL WE CAN DO--

-- WE'VE GOT TO HELP HIM!

HELP! PLEASE H-HELP... MEEEEE...

PA-DRR1?

INPUT: AUDIO ENTREATY, HUMAN RANGE, DESPERATION NUANCE.

PRESCRIBED ACTION: ALERT COMPANIONS.

PROBABLE OUTCOME: ADMONITION TO STOP "HEARING THINGS!"

PROJECTED ACCURACY OF PEER JUDGEMENT: 94%.

CONCLUSION:

WHAT THE HECK...

AS NEARBY, A NATIVE HOOJIB WATCHES.

A HOOJIB WHOSE LARGE EYES GROW EVEN LARGER; WHOSE SMALL BODY BEGINS, EVER SO SLIGHTLY, TO TREMBLE.

PLIF MUST HEAR OF THIS! OH, YES! H-HE MUST HEAR OF IT--

-- QUICKLY!

MOMENTS LATER, IN A HUSHED BRIEFING ROOM.

...IS HOW WE *GOT* THE INFORMATION. MEMORIAL SERVICES FOR LEFTENANT HAMMERTREE WILL BE HELD TOMORROW.

AND SO, TO SUMMARIZE: WE'VE LEARNED THAT ONE OF THE OTHER BOUNTY HUNTERS INVOLVED IN THE TRAPPING OF HAN SOLO WAS *IN LEAGUE* WITH BOBA FETT, BUT WAS CUT OUT OF THE REWARD WHEN FETT TOOK CAPTAIN SOLO FROM CLOUD CITY.

IT SEEMS REASONABLE, THEN, TO ASSUME THAT THIS HUNTER COULD BE SOMEWHAT BITTER ABOUT THE SITUATION, AND MIGHT BE WILLING-- FOR A PRICE-- TO TELL US WHERE FETT IS HIDING UNTIL HIS RENDEZVOUS WITH JABBA THE HUTT.

WE'VE NARROWED OUR QUARRY LIST DOWN TO THREE--

--THE CYBORG CALLED *DENGAR*--

-- THE PURSUIT DROID DESIGNATED AS *IG-88*--

-- AND *BOSSK*, REPTILIAN MONARCH OF THE QOTILE SYSTEM.

ANY QUESTIONS? GOOD. THEN COLONEL GREYMARK WILL BEGIN HANDING OUT YOUR INDIVIDUAL ASSIGNMENTS.

YOU THINK WE'VE GOT A CHANCE, LANDO?

NOT ONE I'D CARE TO BET MY SPARE CHANGE ON, LUKE-- LET ALONE MY *LIFE*!

BUT I GUESS WE JUST HAVE TO PLAY WHAT WE'RE DEALT.

ISN'T IT WONDERFUL, ARTOO? CAPTAIN SOLO MIGHT BE BACK YELLING AT US VERY SOO--

ARTOO?

WHY, YOU'RE NOT ARTOO-DETOO! YOU'RE--

--PLIF!

GOOD AFTERNOON, DEAR FELLOW. NOW DO STEP ASIDE, WON'T YOU? WE'D LIKE A WORD WITH PRINCESS LEIA.

IT'S RATHER URGENT.

OF ALL THE IMPERTINENCE!

I'LL HAVE YOU KNOW THAT THE PRINCESS IS ENGAGED IN VITAL REBELLION BUSINESS--

--AND CANNOT BE DISTURBED!

BUT ONE OF US SAW YOUR FRIEND--THE ROUND STUBBORN ONE?--GO DOWN AN UNEXPLORED TUNNEL! ALONE!

THAT DOESN'T SURPRISE ME, ARTOO RARELY BEHAVES LIKE A CIVIL MACHINE, AND IF HE INSISTS ON TRUNDLING DOWN SOME FILTHY SUBTERRANEAN MOUSEHOLE, THEN THERE'S NOTHING THAT I--

BUT THAT TUNNEL'S DANGEROUS!

DANGEROUS?

H-HOW DANGEROUS?

I'M AFRAID WE DON'T KNOW EXACTLY. NONE OF US HAS EVER ENTERED IT. BUT WE HAVE SENSED A GREAT EVIL THERE FOR AS LONG AS WE'VE LIVED BENEATH ARBRA.

WE'VE NEVER BOTHERED IT, AND IT'S NOT BOTHERED US. UNTIL NOW.

WELL, I SUPPOSE I *HAD* BETTER GO FETCH THE LITTLE OIL MISER BEFORE HE--

NO!

I APOLOGIZE FOR BE-LABORING A POINT, OLD CHUM, BUT IF YOU TRAVEL THAT CAVERN WITHOUT PROTECTION-- I DARESAY YOU'LL NOT RETURN!

OH, WELL OF COURSE, IF YOU PUT IT *THAT* WAY...!

CHEWBACCA? DO BE A GOOD WOOKIEE AND COME ALONG, WON'T YOU? THERE'S A LITTLE ERRAND I'D LIKE YOU TO HELP ME WI--

MRRAARRGGH

Y-YES, I *REALIZE* HOW EAGER YOU ARE TO START LOOKING FOR CAPTAIN SOLO--

--BUT IT WILL TAKE *HOURS* TO GET THE SHIPS READY, AND YOU'LL ONLY GET NERVOUS AND FIDGETY JUST WAITING AROUND.

FRFF

SPLENDID! I KNEW YOU'D UNDERSTAND! AND I'M SURE THIS WON'T TAKE MORE THAN A FEW MO-MENTS ANYWAY...

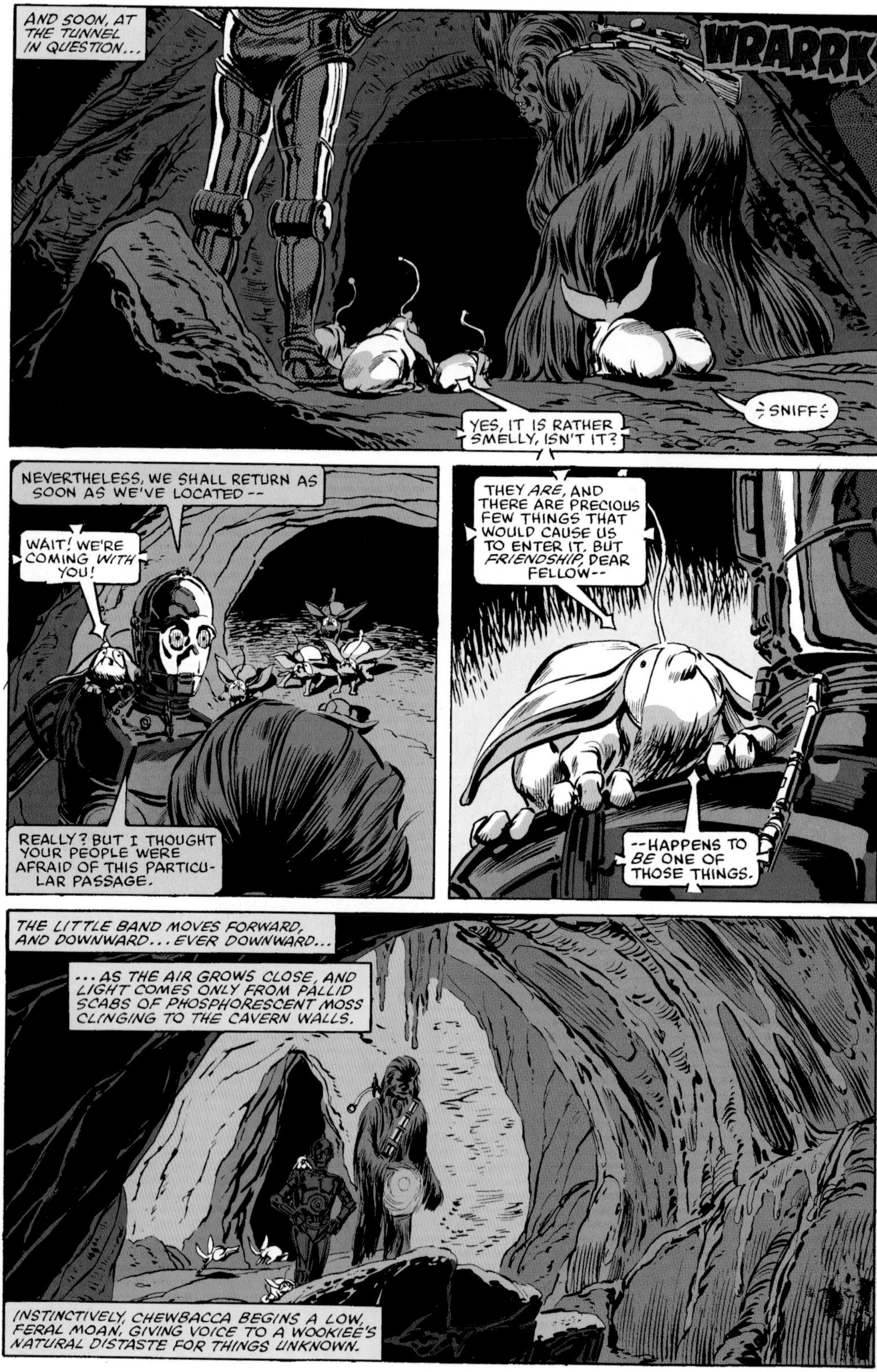

AND SOON, AT THE TUNNEL IN QUESTION...
WRARRK
YES, IT IS RATHER SMELLY, ISN'T IT?
SNIFF
NEVERTHELESS, WE SHALL RETURN AS SOON AS WE'VE LOCATED --
WAIT! WE'RE COMING WITH YOU!
REALLY? BUT I THOUGHT YOUR PEOPLE WERE AFRAID OF THIS PARTICU-LAR PASSAGE.
THEY ARE, AND THERE ARE PRECIOUS FEW THINGS THAT WOULD CAUSE US TO ENTER IT. BUT FRIENDSHIP, DEAR FELLOW--
--HAPPENS TO BE ONE OF THOSE THINGS.
THE LITTLE BAND MOVES FORWARD, AND DOWNWARD... EVER DOWNWARD...
...AS THE AIR GROWS CLOSE, AND LIGHT COMES ONLY FROM PALLID SCABS OF PHOSPHORESCENT MOSS CLINGING TO THE CAVERN WALLS.
INSTINCTIVELY, CHEWBACCA BEGINS A LOW, FERAL MOAN, GIVING VOICE TO A WOOKIEE'S NATURAL DISTASTE FOR THINGS UNKNOWN.

UNTIL...

THAT'S ODD. MY SENSORS DETECT SOME SORT OF *ENERGY FIELD*, UNDOUBTEDLY THE RESULT OF THE GEOTHERMAL POWER RODS THAT PROVIDE HEAT FOR THE LARGER SHAFTWAYS.

IT *SEEMS HARMLESS ENOUGH*, THOUGH. WE SHOULD BE ABLE TO PASS THROUGH WITHOUT HINDRANCE.

AND SO HE DOES.

AS DO THE TENTATIVELY FOLLOWING TELEPATHIC HOOJIBS.

BUT THEN...

SPZZT

HOW UNUSUAL. THE ENERGY APPEARS TO BE THICKENING--

--AS IF IT'S TRYING TO KEEP CHEWIE FROM GETTING THROUGH!

BUT A 7½-FOOT WOOKIEE-- ESPECIALLY A 7½-FOOT TICKED OFF WOOKIEE--IS NOT ONE TO BE DENIED...

VRRROWFF!

...FOR LONG!

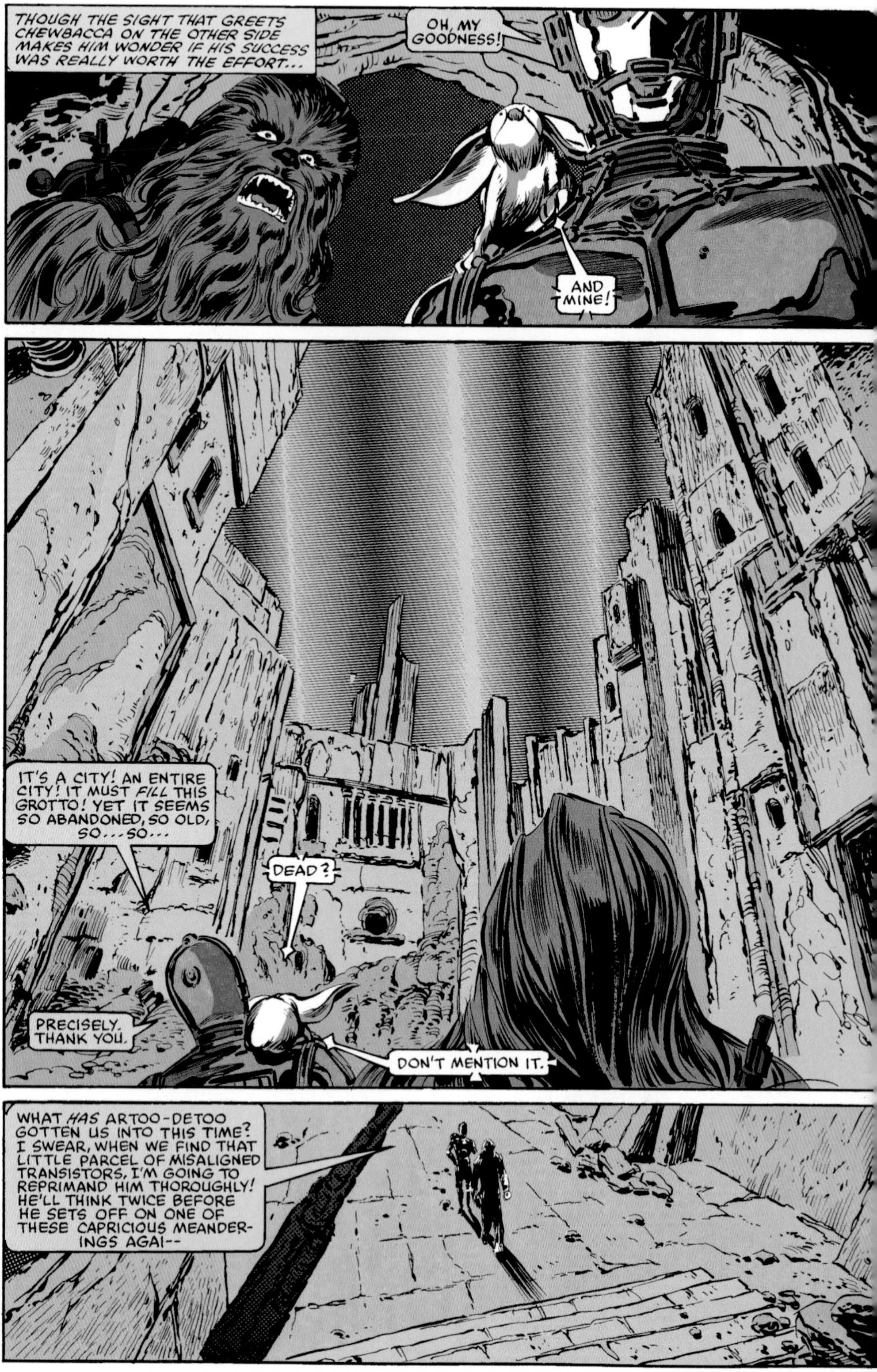
THOUGH THE SIGHT THAT GREETS CHEWBACCA ON THE OTHER SIDE MAKES HIM WONDER IF HIS SUCCESS WAS REALLY WORTH THE EFFORT...
OH, MY GOODNESS!
AND MINE!
IT'S A CITY! AN ENTIRE CITY! IT MUST FILL THIS GROTTO! YET IT SEEMS SO ABANDONED, SO OLD, SO... SO...
DEAD?
PRECISELY. THANK YOU.
DON'T MENTION IT.
WHAT HAS ARTOO-DETOO GOTTEN US INTO THIS TIME? I SWEAR, WHEN WE FIND THAT LITTLE PARCEL OF MISALIGNED TRANSISTORS, I'M GOING TO REPRIMAND HIM THOROUGHLY! HE'LL THINK TWICE BEFORE HE SETS OFF ON ONE OF THESE CAPRICIOUS MEANDERINGS AGAI--

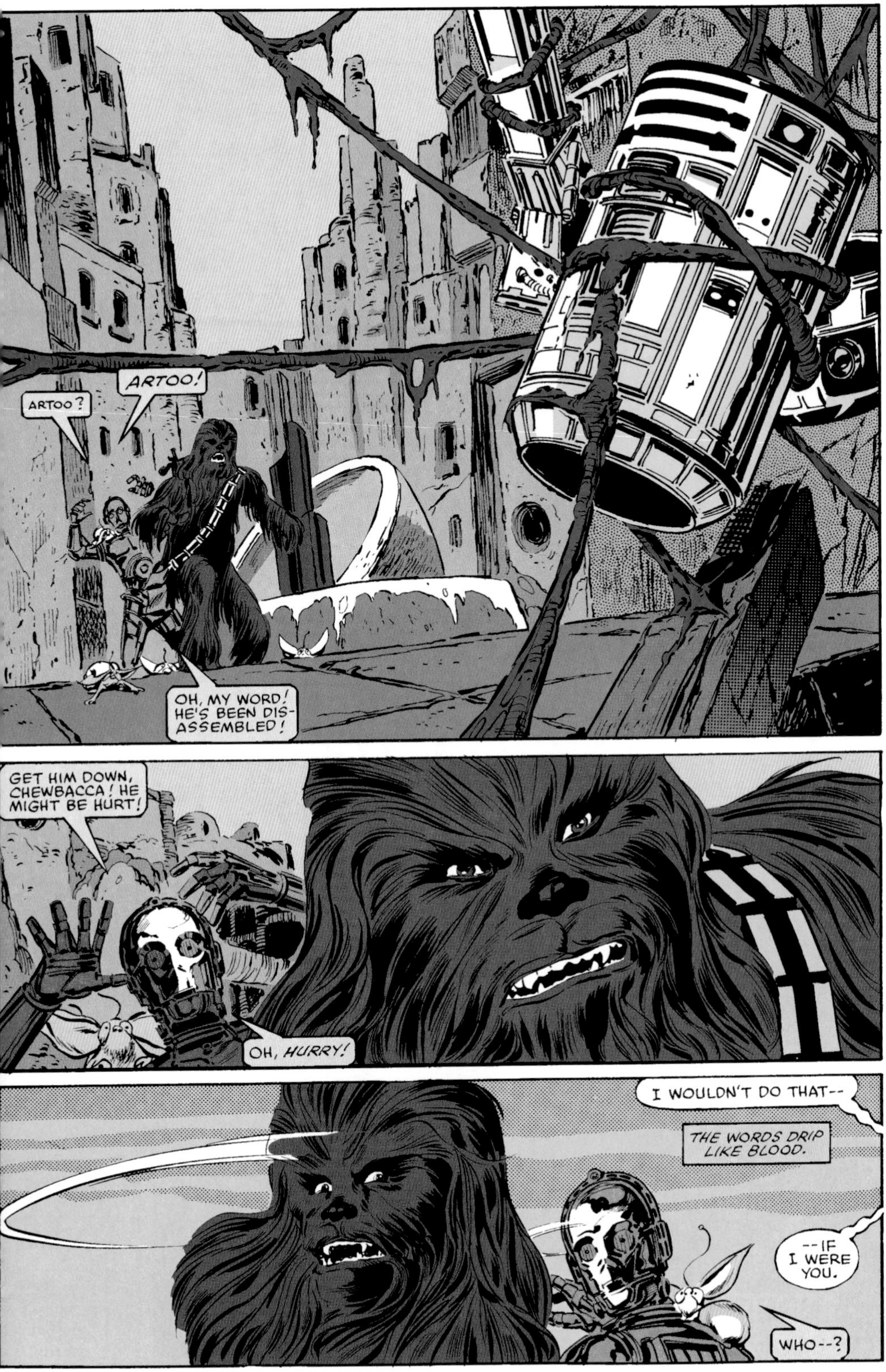
ARTOO?
ARTOO!
OH, MY WORD! HE'S BEEN DIS-ASSEMBLED!
GET HIM DOWN, CHEWBACCA! HE MIGHT BE HURT!
OH, HURRY!
I WOULDN'T DO THAT--
THE WORDS DRIP LIKE BLOOD.
--IF I WERE YOU.
WHO--?

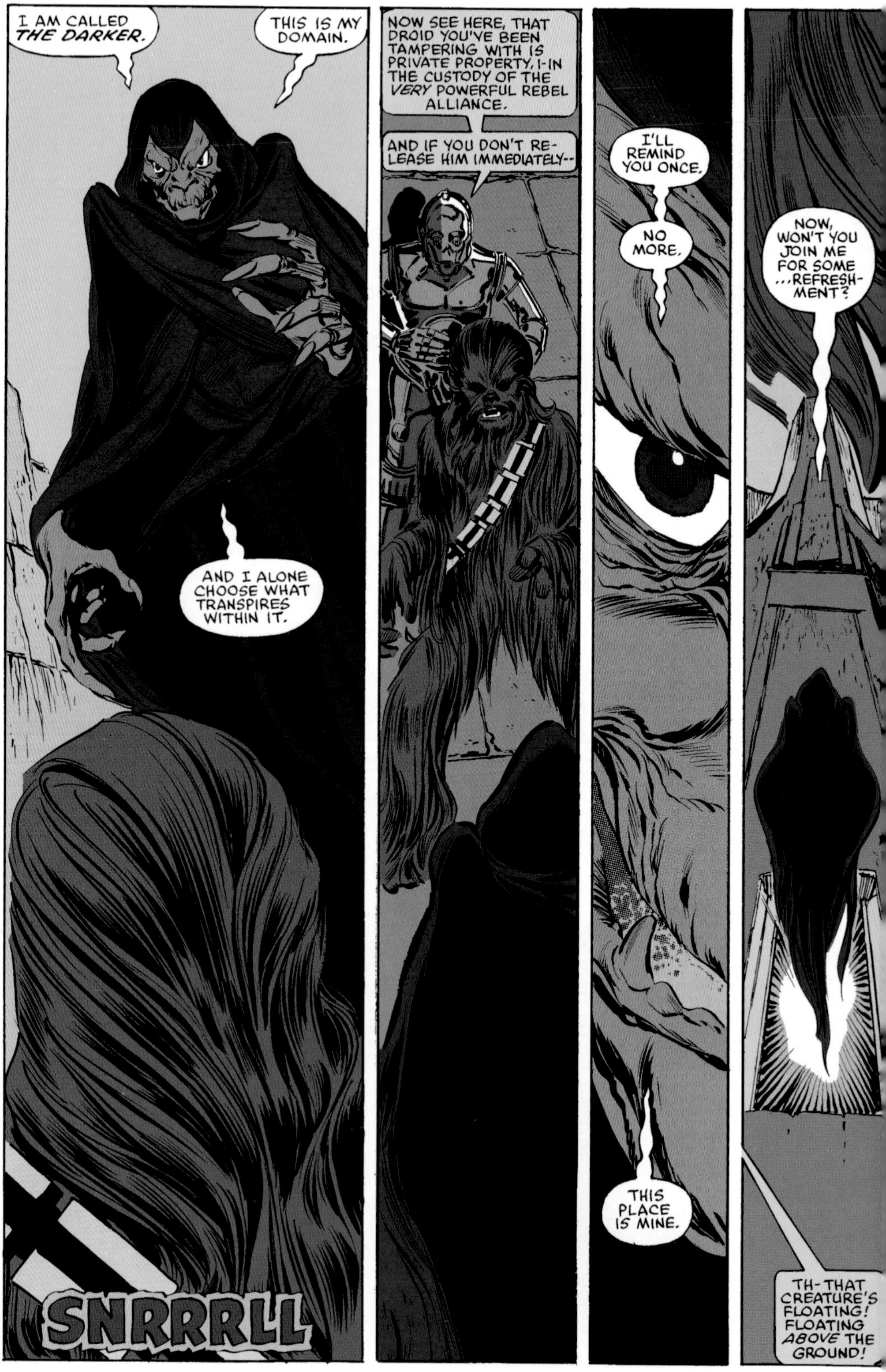
I AM CALLED *THE DARKER*.
THIS IS MY DOMAIN.
AND I ALONE CHOOSE WHAT TRANSPIRES WITHIN IT.
SNRRRLL
NOW SEE HERE, THAT DROID YOU'VE BEEN TAMPERING WITH IS PRIVATE PROPERTY, I-IN THE CUSTODY OF THE *VERY* POWERFUL REBEL ALLIANCE.
AND IF YOU DON'T RE-LEASE HIM IMMEDIATELY--
I'LL REMIND YOU ONCE.
NO MORE.
THIS PLACE IS MINE.
NOW, WON'T YOU JOIN ME FOR SOME ...REFRESH-MENT?
TH-THAT CREATURE'S FLOATING! FLOATING *ABOVE* THE GROUND!

PERHAPS YOU *HAD* BETTER INFORM PRINCESS LEIA OF THIS, PLIF!

I HEARTILY CONCUR!

TO THE BRIEFING ROOM, HOOJIBS!

AND SOON, IN A DUST-LADEN DINING HALL...

PLEASE, HELP YOUR-SELVES. THE CUISINE IS QUITE EX-CELLENT--I CONCOCTED IT MYSELF.

WOULD YOU LIKE A BIT OF *CHEESE*?

WH-WHY, THAT HAS *THINGS* CRAWLING ALL OVER IT!

REALLY, THIS HAS GONE FAR ENOUGH! I *DEMAND* THAT YOU TELL US--

I'LL TELL YOU WHAT I WISH. PERHAPS I SHALL TELL YOU OF THE PEOPLE WHO IN-HABITED THIS PLANET EONS AGO, A PEOPLE WHOSE CIVILIZATION PROGRESSED TO THE POINT--

--WHERE THEY SOUGHT TO *RID* THEMSELVES OF THEIR BASER EMOTIONS: ANGER, HATRED, FEAR AND THE LIKE. EVENTUALLY, THEIR TECHNOLOGY ALLOWED THEM TO SUCCEED!

BUT THEY QUICKLY FOUND THAT THE DARK ENERGY THEY DRAINED OFF COULD NOT BE *DESTROYED*! AND AS YOU MAY HAVE GUESSED... THAT ENERGY WAS ME.

SOON AFTER, THE NOBLE RACE ABANDONED BOTH CITY AND PLANET TO BEGIN ANEW ON ANOTHER WORLD, LEAVING THEIR EVIL ASPECT BEHIND, TRAPPED WITHIN A SELF-PERPETU-ATING FORCE SCREEN--

--A SCREEN PARTICU-LARLY SENSITIVE TO NEGATIVE EMOTIONS, WHICH IS WHY YOUR HIRSUTE AND RATHER TANTRUM-PRONE COMRADE HAD SOME DIFFICULTY GETTING THROUGH.

THEN YOUR ALLIANCE ARRIVED, AND I SENSED THAT THEY POSSESSED A TECHNOLOGY THAT COULD BE USED TO SHORT-CIRCUIT THE FORCE SCREEN.

AND THUS I WORKED FOR MONTHS TO PUSH THROUGH A MENTAL MESSAGE, THE SAME "HELP ME" PLEA THAT BROUGHT YOUR REPAIR DROID RUNNING.

AND NOW HIS ELECTRONIC COMPONENTS--ALONG WITH YOURS, I MIGHT ADD--SHALL ALLOW ME TO ESCAPE MY PRISON, TO SEEK OUT AND... TO REWARD THOSE WHO LEFT ME HERE.

Y-YOU WON'T GET AWAY WITH THIS! I SENT THE HOOJIBS FOR REINFORCEMENTS!

E-EVEN AS WE SPEAK, THOUSANDS OF VERY BRAVE AND WELL-ARMED REBELS ARE STORMING INTO THIS CITY!

YOU THINK SO?

LOOK OUTSIDE.

VERY WELL, BUT I DON'T SEE WHAT--

--OH, DEAR!

WITHIN THE FORCE SCREEN, I HAVE THE ABILITY TO INSTILL NEGATIVE EMOTIONS IN ANY LIVING BEING. THUS WHEN I OVERHEARD YOUR INSTRUCTIONS, I MERELY HEIGHTENED YOUR COMPANIONS' INCLINATION TOWARDS FEAR.

THEY'RE NOT GOING TO WARN ANYONE.

WRROWK!

FRACHOK

VERY IMPRESSIVE, WOOKIEE.

YOU'VE AN ADMIRABLE CAPACITY FOR ANGER.

SHALL WE SEE WHAT OCCURS WHEN THE *LOYALTY* BEHIND THAT ANGER IS CHANGED INTO RAW, UNBRIDLED--

--HATRED?

CH...CHEWBACCA?

RRAARRRGGH!

WE'RE DOOMED!

KACHASH

I-I'M DOOMED!

BUT FORTUNE SMILES ON THE GOLDEN DROID THIS DAY. FOR CHEWIE'S RAGE-INDUCED, MIS-THROWN BLOW BRINGS HALF A WALL DOWN ON THE SNARL-ING WOOKIEE'S HEAD.

A MINOR INCONVENIENCE.

BUT ONE THAT ALLOWS SEE-THREEPIO TO SCAMPER OFF IN AN ESCAPE THAT IS AS WELCOME--

--AS IT IS, INEVITABLY, FOREDOOMED!

I SUPPOSE I SHOULD BE FLATTERED. CHEWIE'S LOYALTY MUST BE GREAT INDEED--

--IF THE LOATHING THE DARKER'S TURNED IT INTO IS ANY INDICATION!

SMALL COMFORT, THOUGH. I'LL SOON BE DISMEMBERED, CANNI-BALIZED BY THAT FLOATING MON-STROSITY! WELL, AT LEAST ARTOO AND I WILL BE TOGETHE--

--WAIT A MOMENT! THIS BUILDING IS A LIBRARY! AND MY PRIMARY FUNCTION--

--IS TRANSLATION! PERHAPS I CAN FIND SOME CLUE IN THESE VOLUMES THAT WILL SAVE US ALL!

OH, BLAST IT ALL! THIS IS A COOKBOOK!

NOW LET ME SEE, THIS LOOKS LIKE...YES... TWO CUPS...BALKA GREENS ...ADD A PINCH OF --

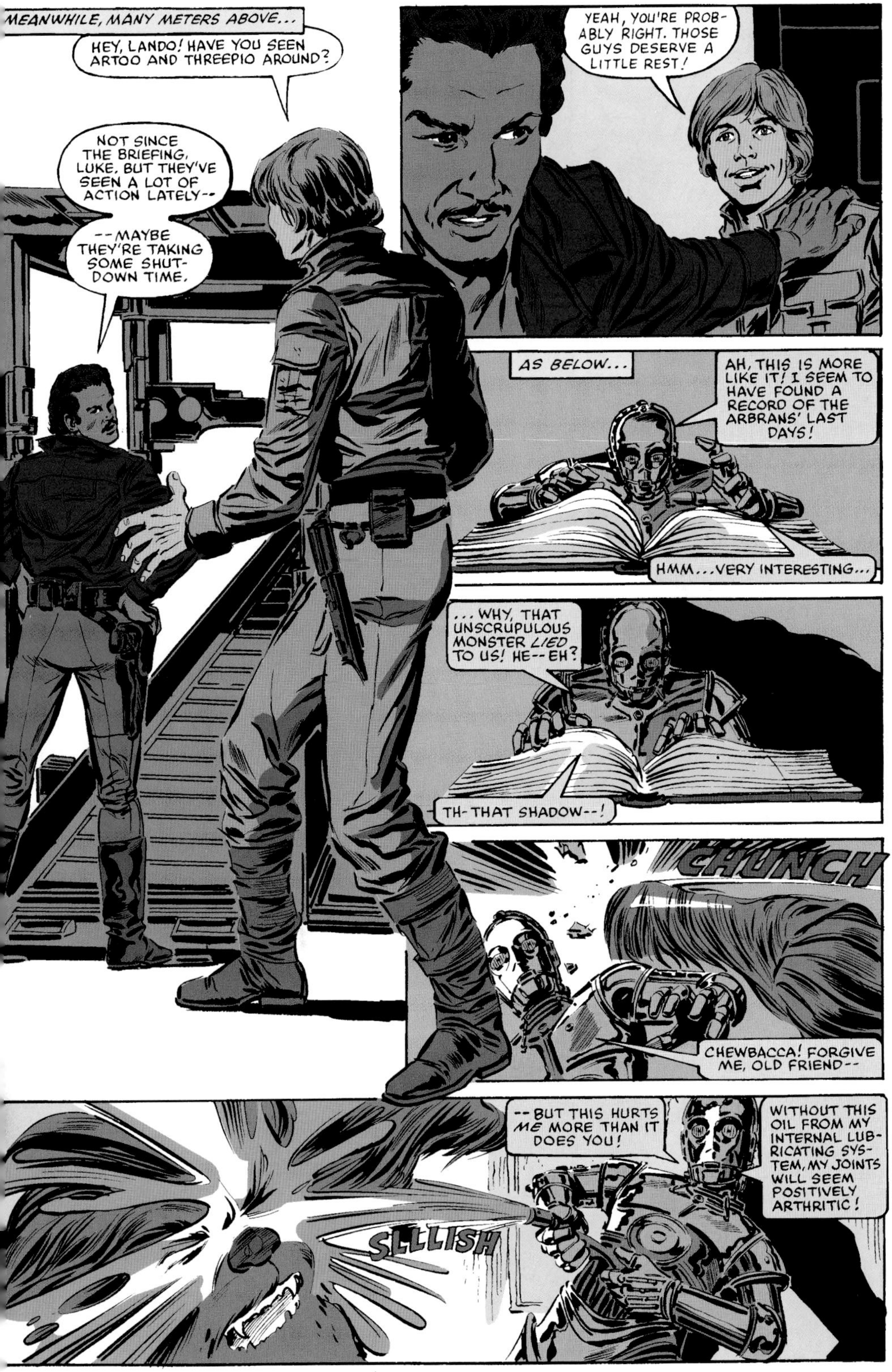
MEANWHILE, MANY METERS ABOVE...
HEY, LANDO! HAVE YOU SEEN ARTOO AND THREEPIO AROUND?
NOT SINCE THE BRIEFING, LUKE, BUT THEY'VE SEEN A LOT OF ACTION LATELY--
--MAYBE THEY'RE TAKING SOME SHUT-DOWN TIME.
YEAH, YOU'RE PROBABLY RIGHT. THOSE GUYS DESERVE A LITTLE REST!
AS BELOW...
AH, THIS IS MORE LIKE IT! I SEEM TO HAVE FOUND A RECORD OF THE ARBRANS' LAST DAYS!
HMM... VERY INTERESTING...
...WHY, THAT UNSCRUPULOUS MONSTER LIED TO US! HE--EH?
TH-THAT SHADOW--!
CHUNCH
CHEWBACCA! FORGIVE ME, OLD FRIEND--
--BUT THIS HURTS ME MORE THAN IT DOES YOU!
WITHOUT THIS OIL FROM MY INTERNAL LUBRICATING SYSTEM, MY JOINTS WILL SEEM POSITIVELY ARTHRITIC!
SLLLISH

AND SOON, IN THE COURTYARD...

OH, I DO HOPE I CAN GET ARTOO BACK TOGETHER. HE COULD BE OUR ONLY HOPE!

ARTOO? JUST KEEP YOUR AUDIO SENSORS FUNCTIONING AND LISTEN CAREFULLY! THIS IS IMPORTANT!

AND SO, AFTER AWKWARD, HURRIED REPAIRS...

THERE, YOU'VE HEARD THE STORY--WHAT DO YOU SUGGEST?

BLA-DIT VOOP!

YOU SUGGEST THAT I BRACE MYSELF?! BUT WHY--OH, NO! CHEWBACCA'S TEARING AT THE WEBBING BASE! W-WE'RE GOING TO--

--FALL!

SHRUMP

KTUNG

CH-CHEWIE! PLEASE! Y-YOU DON'T WANT TO DO THIS! THINK OF ALL WE'VE BEEN THROUGH TOGETHER!

TH-THINK OF THE DEATH STAR! CLOUD CITY! HOTH!

A-AND THINK WHAT WILL HAPPEN IF WE LET THE DARKER WIN! WE'LL NEVER BE ABLE TO RESCUE CAPTAIN SOLO! I-I MEAN, HAN!

HAN, DO YOU HEAR?

HAN!

RRRRRRRRRRRRRRRRRRRRRRRRRMPH?!

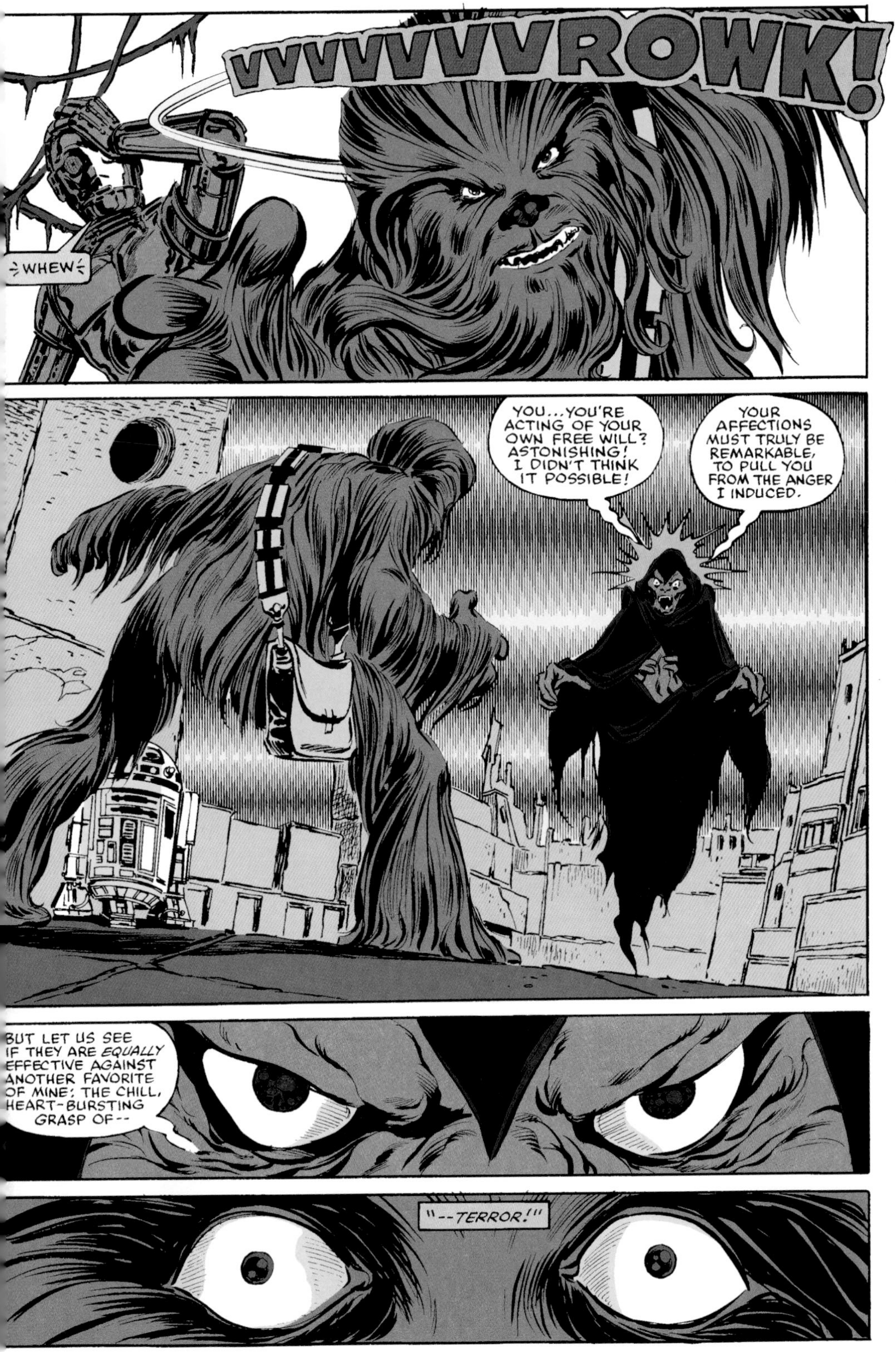
VVVVVVVVROWK!
WHEW
YOU...YOU'RE ACTING OF YOUR OWN FREE WILL? ASTONISHING! I DIDN'T THINK IT POSSIBLE!
YOUR AFFECTIONS MUST TRULY BE REMARKABLE, TO PULL YOU FROM THE ANGER I INDUCED.
BUT LET US SEE IF THEY ARE EQUALLY EFFECTIVE AGAINST ANOTHER FAVORITE OF MINE: THE CHILL, HEART-BURSTING GRASP OF--
"--TERROR!"

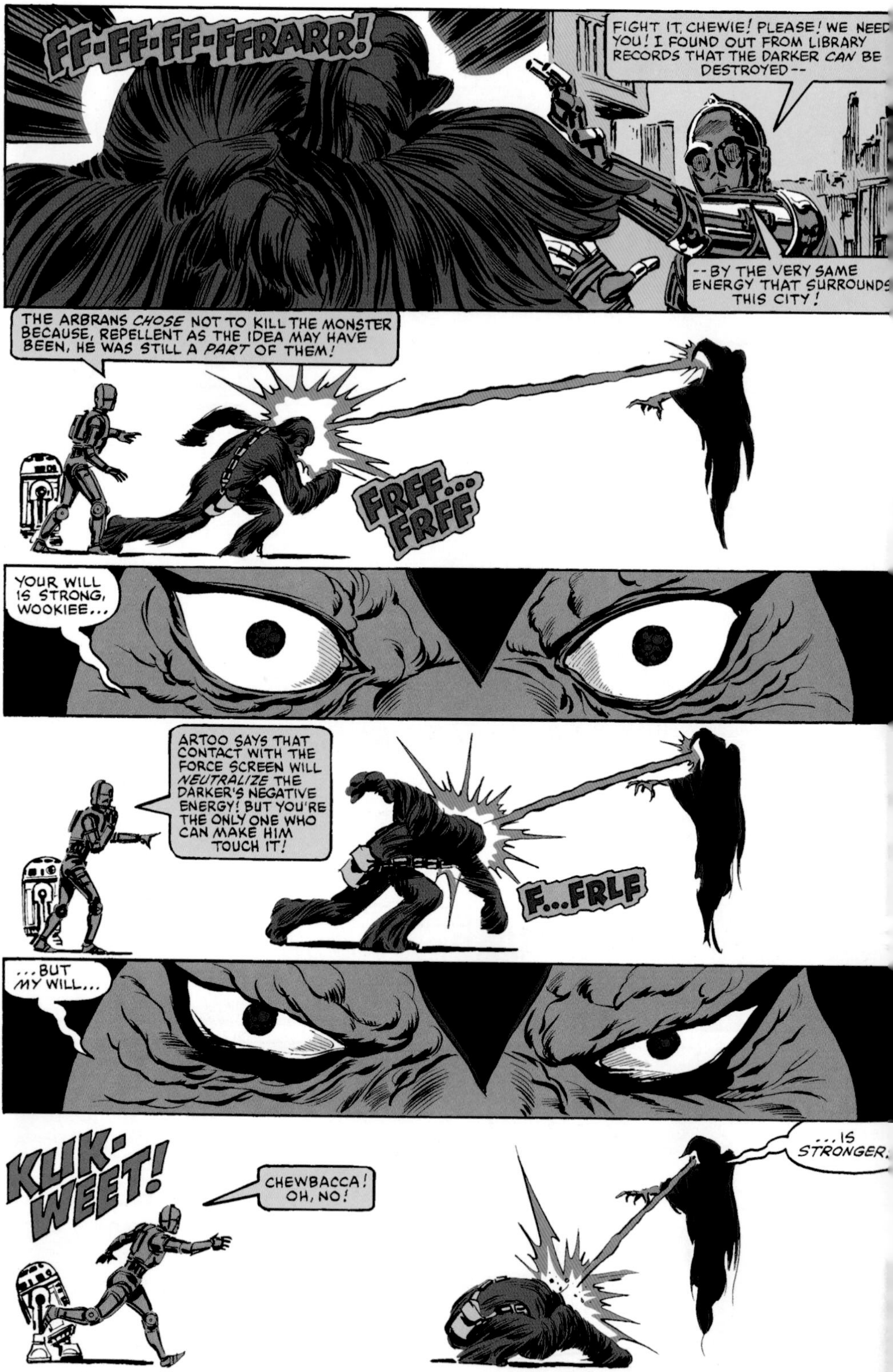
FF-FF-FF-FFRARR!
FIGHT IT, CHEWIE! PLEASE! WE NEED YOU! I FOUND OUT FROM LIBRARY RECORDS THAT THE DARKER CAN BE DESTROYED --
-- BY THE VERY SAME ENERGY THAT SURROUNDS THIS CITY!
THE ARBRANS CHOSE NOT TO KILL THE MONSTER BECAUSE, REPELLENT AS THE IDEA MAY HAVE BEEN, HE WAS STILL A PART OF THEM!
FRFF... FRFF
YOUR WILL IS STRONG, WOOKIEE...
ARTOO SAYS THAT CONTACT WITH THE FORCE SCREEN WILL NEUTRALIZE THE DARKER'S NEGATIVE ENERGY! BUT YOU'RE THE ONLY ONE WHO CAN MAKE HIM TOUCH IT!
F...FRLF
...BUT MY WILL...
KLIK-WEET!
CHEWBACCA! OH, NO!
...IS STRONGER.

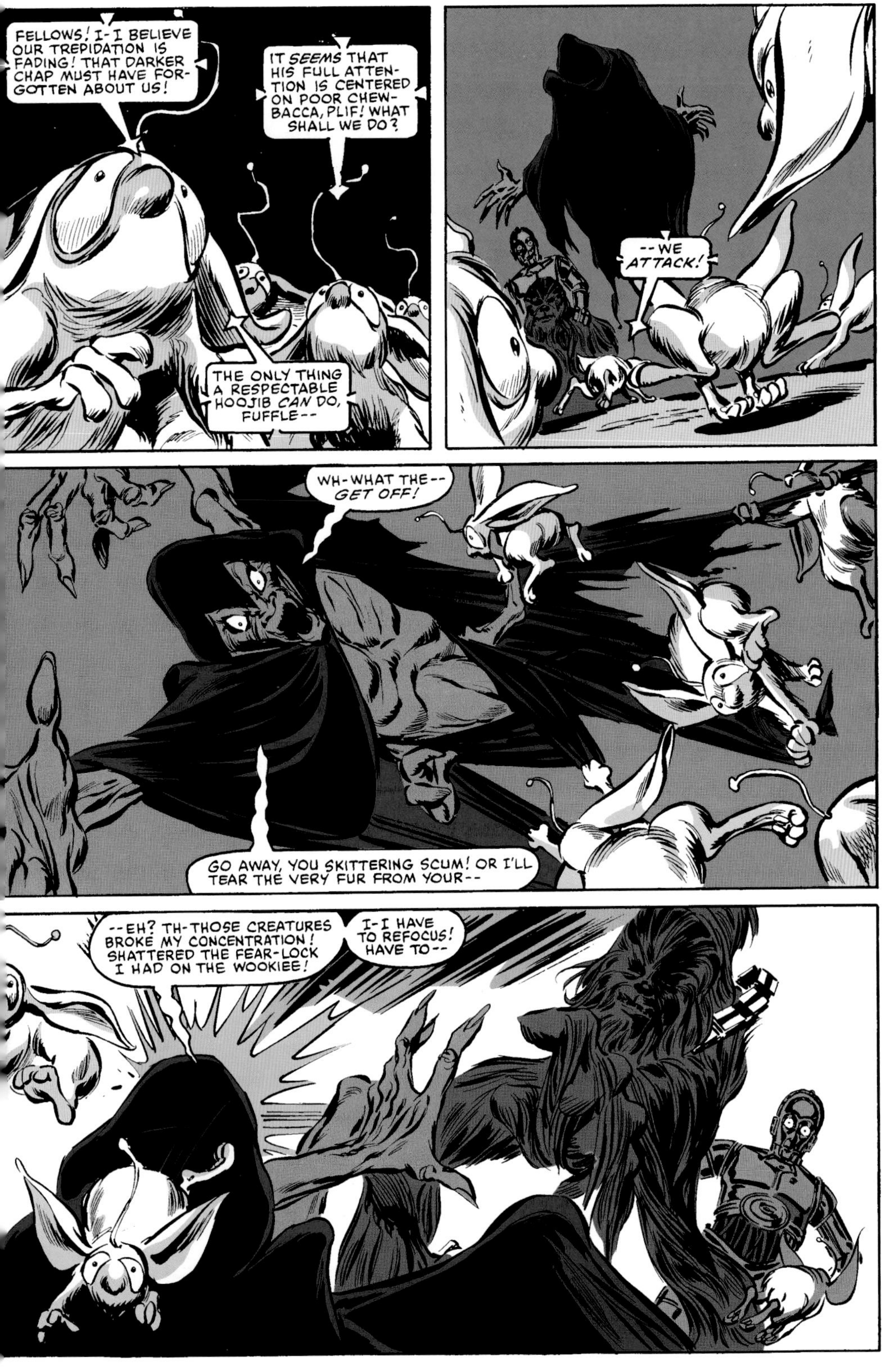
FELLOWS! I-I BELIEVE OUR TREPIDATION IS FADING! THAT DARKER CHAP MUST HAVE FORGOTTEN ABOUT US!
IT SEEMS THAT HIS FULL ATTENTION IS CENTERED ON POOR CHEWBACCA, PLIF! WHAT SHALL WE DO?
THE ONLY THING A RESPECTABLE HOOJIB CAN DO, FUFFLE--
--WE ATTACK!
WH-WHAT THE-- GET OFF!
GO AWAY, YOU SKITTERING SCUM! OR I'LL TEAR THE VERY FUR FROM YOUR--
--EH? TH-THOSE CREATURES BROKE MY CONCENTRATION! SHATTERED THE FEAR-LOCK I HAD ON THE WOOKIEE!
I-I HAVE TO REFOCUS! HAVE TO--

NO! L-LEAVE ME ALONE, CURSE YOU! LEAVE--

GYYAGGH!

SPLUTCH

NOW, CHEWIE! THROW HIM INTO THE FORCE SCREEN--

--NOW!

AAAIIEEEYAAA!

IT WORKED! HE'S DISINTEGRATING!

BUT SO IS THE *FORCE SCREEN!* SO MUCH NEGATIVE ENERGY MUST HAVE DISRUPTED THE SYSTEM'S MATRIX! THE WHOLE *CITY* IS STARTING TO SHAKE!

WE'VE GOT TO GET OUT OF--

--ξULPξ TH-THIS ISN'T EXACTLY WHAT I HAD IN MIND, CHEWIE, BUT I SUPPOSE IT *IS* THE QUICKEST WAY!

DO BE CAREFUL WITH ARTOO!

BUT CHEWBACCA IS LESS CONCERNED WITH PROPRIETY THAN HE IS WITH GETTING HIS COMRADES THROUGH THE WILDLY FLUCTUATING FORCE SCREEN. WHICH HE DOES...

NEXT. ISSUE. SLAVER WARS ON MANDALORE—WITH PRINCESS LEIA CAUGHT IN THE MIDDLE! BE HERE!